Reflections 365

David Z. Ring III

Parson's Porch Books
www.parsonsporchbooks.com

Reflections 365
ISBN: Softcover 978-1-949888-63-8
Copyright © 2019 by David Z. Ring III

All rights reserved. No part of this book may be reproduced or transmitted in any form or by any means, electronic or mechanical, including photocopying, recording, or by any information storage and retrieval system, without permission in writing from the publisher.

Reflections 365

Contents

Introduction 23
On Being There 25
    John 11:20-22
Jumping in the River 26
    II Kings 5:9-14
Lost and Found 27
    Luke 19:9-10
Storytelling 28
    Psalm 107:1-3
A Missing Daughter 29
    Luke 15:11-24
A Smart Fool? 30
    Psalm 14:1-7
Drunk Christians? 31
    Acts 2:5-15
Soul Exercise 32
    Isaiah 55:1-2
Fruit Inspection 33
    Galatians 5:22-23
From Generation to Generation 34
    Genesis 5:1-8
Better to Pray First 35
    Mark 14:32-38
Contemporary Priorities 36
    Matthew 19:4-6
Growing Discipleship 37
    Hebrews 5:11-14
Drownproofing 38
    Romans 3:22-24
Sheltering the Battered 39
    Ephesians 5:25-30
Treading on Dangerous Ground 40
    I John 2:3-5
Word Power 41
    James 3:9-12
Ups and Downs with God 42
    Ezra 3:10-13
A Wilderness Journey 43
    Deuteronomy 2:1-2
A Fiery Ceremony 44
    Matthew 19:4-6

An Answer Already Received 45
    I Thessalonians 5:16-18
A Very Pleasant Surprise 46
    John 20:15-16
The Exciting Challenge of Fishing 47
    Matthew 4:18-22
Learning to Fly 48
    Luke 8:11-15
Never Too Late 49
    Luke 2:25-32
Supportive Leadership 50
    1 Timothy 3:1-7
Hurt and Angry 51
    Psalm 22:1-3
Meeting a Saint 52
    Philemon 4-6
A Fresh Start 53
    Lamentations 3:21-25
Cold Feet? 54
    Revelation 2:2-5
New and Quite Different 55
    II Corinthians 5:17-18
Looking and Also Touching 56
    Romans 8:20-21
Blatant Dishonesty 57
    I John 1:9-10
Enduring Tough Love 58
    Matthew 5:44-47
Godly Risk-taking 59
    Mark 10:28-30
Asking for Money 60
    I Corinthians 16:1-2
Remember Y2K? 61
    Mark 13:32-3561
The Gambler and the Pastor 62
    John 19:23-24
Saying What You Really Mean 63
    Psalm 19:13-14
A Tireless Encourager 64
    II Corinthians 13:11
Perseverance 65
    Joshua 1:7-9
Remembering God's Word 66
    Deuteronomy 11:18-19

Salvation Delayed 67
    Lamentations 2:11
Encouragement in an Unlikely Location 68
    Philippians 4:4-5
Positively Peculiar 69
    I Peter 2:9-10
Differently Born Again.. 70
    Isaiah 66:7-9
Bitten by Sin.. 71
    Jonah 1:11-17
Failure Need Not Be Forever.. 72
    Psalm 51:1-2
Gender-Specific Perception.. 73
    Matthew 19:4-5
Just a Gigolo 74
    Matthew 9:11-12
Strangers and Sojourners.. 75
    Hebrews 11:13-16
A Contagion of Attitude 76
    Ezra 6:22
Unprepared to Preach.. 77
    2 Timothy 4:1-2
The Stellar Panorama.. 78
    Matthew 2:1-2
Addressing Hunger 79
    Luke 9:12-17
Grapevines in the Backyard.. 80
    Jeremiah 17:7-8
Fire on the Altar 81
    I Kings 18:38-39
A Predisposition to Suspicion 82
    Mark 6:1-6
Pool Hopping and Its Consequences.. 83
    Romans 6:21-23
A Uniquely Memorable Baptism 84
    Acts 8:30-39
Creative Thinking in the Church 85
    Deuteronomy 4:6
A Brighter Future.. 86
    Revelation 21:3-5
Invite Them In 87
    Acts 1:8
A Youthful Solution 88
    Psalm 20:5

Love: A Finite Resource?..89
   Matthew 5:43-46
A Cave Adventure...90
   I Samuel 24:3-7
Friendly and Welcoming?..91
   Hebrews 13:1-2
Wrong-Colored Hymnals...92
   Psalm 33:1-3
Wilderness Survival Skills..93
   Exodus 17:1-6
Long Sermons...94
   Acts 20:7
Warning Signs Ignored..95
   Numbers 26:9-10
The Difficult Larger Perspective 96
   Luke 18:15-17
How Many Does It Take?..97
   I Kings 22:12-14
A Link in God's Chain of Love 98
   Acts 19:1-6
The Awesome Freedom of Choice 99
   Romans 6:1-2
Wedding Joys..100
   Song of Solomon 3:1-10
While They're Young...101
   Proverbs 22:6
A Radical Change in Behavior 102
   Colossians 3:20-21
Preachers Far and Pastors Near..103
   Jeremiah 23:16-17
Up and Down, Out and Back In 104
   Romans 11:13-15
God for the Long Run 105
   Joel 2:23-26
Deeply Etched..106
   Deuteronomy 11:18-19
Trustworthy..107
   Exodus 18:20-22
Welcoming the Stranger...108
   Job 29:15-17
A Bad Choice, not to Be Repeated..109
   Mark 1:5-7
Dead Wood..110
   James 2:17-18

Thirsty Christians 111
    Ephesians 5:17-19
A Family Feud 112
    Genesis 25:21-26
Fruitful Competition 113
    I Corinthians 1:10-13
Help in a Time of Personal Need 114
    2 Peter 1:5-7
Keeping Obligations Organized 115
    Psalm 90:11
Taken Seriously 116
    I Timothy 4:11-13
Scarcity and Plenty 117
    John 3:16-17
Word Power 118
    James 3:5-10
Never Off Duty 119
    Exodus 4:10-11
Prayer Includes Listening 120
    1 Kings 19:11-13
Learning to Receive 121
    Acts 4:32-35
Vision for the Future? 122
    1 Timothy 4:12
God's Multi-Generational Family 123
    Matthew 1:1-17
Definitely Not Encouraged 124
    Job 31:32
Focus on Jesus and Only Him 125
    Numbers 27:16-20
Always Be Prepared 126
    Luke 12:16-20
Casual Sex? 127
    2 Samuel 11:1-5
Significance Over Time 128
    Mark 10:42-44
Greater Accomplishments 129
    John 14:12-14
A Very Different Perspective 130
    Psalm 52:8-9
Do You Want to Be Healed? 131
    2 Kings 5:9-12

Scaling Down to Manageable Size 132
    John 14:27
Forgiveness – It's Healthy 133
    Ephesians 4:31-32
Moving Around – a Lot 134
    Ephesians 4:31-32
A Different Sort of Starfish Story 135
    Psalm 50:1-2
Coincidence or Something More? 136
    Revelation 14:13
Trashing a Fifty-Year Relationship 137
    Genesis 2:21-24
Secret Blessing 138
    Ruth 2:15-19
Enemies Can and Do Become Friends 139
    Mark 9:38-40
Aiding and Abetting Irresponsibility 140
    Deuteronomy 21:18-21
Differently Dedicated 141
    1 Corinthians 12:4-6
The Greatest Love 142
    John 3:16-17
A Lenient Judge 143
    Acts 17:30-31
Accentuate the Positive 144
    Luke 23:39-43
In God's Time, Revival 145
    Psalm 85:1-7
Healings -- Natural and Supernatural 146
    Luke 4:38-40
Waiting for God's Timing 147
    Romans 5:5-6
Recharging for the Demands of Ministry 148
    Exodus 18:13-26
Living by Faith 149
    Matthew 23:23-24
Good Old Days? – Not Really 150
    Ecclesiastes 12:1
Tragedy and Triumph 151
    1 Peter 1:3
Code Language in the Church 152
    2 Kings 18:26
Let There Be Enough Light! 153
    Genesis 1:3-4

Flexible at Age 100+ 154
   Deuteronomy 34:7
A Crisis of a Lost Ring 155
   2 Corinthians 12:14-15
Excited about Jesus – But Not for Long 156
   Revelation 2:4-5
Coping with Soreheads 157
   Philippians 2:14-15
An Old Saint Hears Again 158
   1Timothy 5:1-2
Call Ahead Before Visiting? 159
   Luke 19:1-6
Ministry with 'Transients' 160
   Luke 17:12-19
News: Good and Bad 161
   Acts 17:29-31
God in the Details? 162
   Exodus 28:1-5
Exceptions to the Rules 163
   Psalm 25:4-7
Hedging Our Bets 164
   1 Kings 18:21
Just the Right Answer 165
   Jeremiah 33:2-3
Valuing the Peculiar 166
   1 Peter 2:9
Lemons or Lemonade? 167
   1 Kings 3:16-28
No Repeats, Please! 168
   Hebrews 10:1
A Special Glow 169
   Exodus 34:29-35
Christian Faith: Personal but Not Private 170
   Acts 4:18-20
Honoring Our Elders 171
   1 Peter 5:1-4
God-Given Opportunity to Do Good 172
   Hebrews 13:15-16
Life or Death? 173
   Deuteronomy 30:19-20
Lying to the Church 174
   Acts 5:1-11
A Visit from the Christ Family 175
   Galatians 6:9-10

God Loves Bartenders, Too 176
   John 2:1-11
Storytellers, Be Careful 177
   Psalm 107:1-3
A Weird Web of Lies 178
   Psalm 120:1-4
April Fools 179
   Matthew 5:21-23
Not By Logical Argument Alone 180
   Acts 17:22-23
A Global Faith Perspective 181
   Matthew 16:13-19
Conflict in the Middle East 182
   Matthew 15:21-28
Pigeon Problems 183
   Leviticus 20:25-26
Moving Beyond Stereotypes 184
   Matthew 9:9-11
Casting Out the Devil 185
   James 4:7-10
Money Isn't Always the Answer 186
   Matthew 23:23-24
Custom-Tailored Religion 187
   Isaiah 64:1-7
Committed Disciples 188
   John 6:65-68
Are You Joking? 189
   Psalm 126:1-3
Don't Waste Your Time, Nor Mine 190
   2 Thessalonians 3:7-12
Hellfire and Damnation 191
   Exodus 3:1-3
Luck or Skill? 192
   Ezekiel 47:9-10
Hurry Up! 193
   2 Samuel 5:22-25
Two Kinds of Lives, Two Kinds of Endings 194
   Matthew 25:31-46
A Fishing Lesson 195
   Luke 5:1-11
An Unexpected Harvest 196
   Matthew 13:24-30
Gifts: Appropriate and Inappropriate 197
   Revelation 22:16-17

Only One Chance 198
   Matthew 7:1-2
Church Tag 199
   1 Corinthians 1:1-3
Be Prepared 200
   2 Timothy 4:1-2
The Long Run 201
   2 Samuel 18:21-27
Conservative When It's Convenient 202
   Matthew 23:1-4
Ministry Is a Family Affair 203
   1 Timothy 3:1-5
A New Beginning 204
   Luke 1:76-78
A Little Encouragement 205
   Joshua 1:7-9
Be Just What You're Called to Be 206
   Luke 12:13-14
An Unexpected Gift 207
   Acts 3:1-8
With God, Free Really Is Free 208
   Ephesians 2:6-9
Moving On 209
   Philippians 1:20-21
Heeding Good Advice 210
   Ecclesiastes 7:11-12
Giving and Receiving Crosses 211
   Luke 9:23-24
Addicted to Romance 212
   Ephesians 5:21-31
Never Too Old to Learn 213
   Isaiah 43:18-20
Fighting Disease Along with Jesus 214
   Psalm 6:1-4
The Simplicity of Prayer 215
   1 Thessalonians 5:16-18
A Hasty Exit 216
   1 Corinthians 1:10-11
No Strings Attached 217
   Matthew 10:7-8
He Led Three Wives 218
   Deuteronomy 21:15-17

Bearing Fruit That Lasts 219
    John 15:1-7
What's Inside Counts 220
    1Samuel 17:42-47
An Old Reason for New Joy 221
    Matthew 13:52
Harsh Judgment 222
    Matthew 7:1-5
One of Many Valuable Learning Experiences 223
    Galatians 6:1-3
Why Be Afraid? 224
    Exodus 14:10-14
The Value of Blood 225
    Leviticus 17:10-12
Itching Ears 226
    2 Timothy 4:2-4
Seven-Year-Old Faith 227
    I Timothy 4:12
A Good Name 228
    Philippians 2:9-11
Teaching a Memorable Lesson 229
    Job 1:20-22
Fascination with Frogs 230
    2 Chronicles 14:11
Seeking the Wrong Things 231
    James 4:3
Not Afraid of the Dark 232
    Exodus 10:21-23
Get Out There! 233
    Matthew 28:19-20
She Found Her Lost Marbles 234
    Mark 5:15
Speaking and Hearing the Hard Truth 235
    Revelation 21:7-8
Gracefully Taking the Credit 236
    Luke 6:31-33
New Experience for Old Folks 237
    Deuteronomy 34:5-7
Not Much of a Song Leader 238
    Matthew 26:30
Judge Not? 239
    Matthew 7:1
Changing Our Values 240
    Matthew 13:45-46

Lead, Follow, or Get Out of the Way 241
    Daniel 12:3
Climbing to See 242
    Genesis 28:10-12
Teach the Ways of Jesus 243
    Daniel 1:3-4
Wealthy – But Not Independently 244
    Matthew 6:19-21
Sensitivity about Giving 245
    Luke 6:38
Bridging Cultural Barriers 246
    John 4:7-9
Regularly Running 247
    Hebrews 12:1-3
Capable and Effective 248
    Ecclesiastes 11:6
Discernment, Physical and Spiritual 249
    Malachi 3:16-18
Playing Dumb 250
    Acts 6:1-4
Cold Weather in Hell 251
    Matthew 5:22
Change – and Adjustment 252
    Daniel 2:21
Stewardship of the Trees 253
    Genesis 1:11-12
A Very Personal God 254
    John 1:47-51
Canoeing in the Swamp 255
    Ezekiel 47:9-12
Carrying the Bible Around 256
    Psalm 40:11-13
Taking Care of Important Business 257
    Isaiah 30:15
What's in a Name? 258
    Proverbs 22:1
Don't Sweat the Small Stuff 259
    Luke 12:48b
Being Teachable 260
    Mark 10:1
For a Friend 261
    1 Samuel 20:42
Trust in the Lord 262
    Proverbs 3:5-6

Downplay the Wedding 263
   Matthew 22:1-14
Lazy Fishing, Lazy Disciples 264
   John 21:1-14
Effective Service Behind the Scenes 265
   Exodus 4:10
Staying Awake 266
   Proverbs 20:12-13
God's Interest in Genealogy 267
   Matthew 1:1-17
Adult Versus Childish Knowledge 268
   Deuteronomy 11:18-19
God Offers Good Counsel 269
   Job 12:13-14
The Same Man in Two Different Circumstances 270
   Matthew 5:47-48
Long-Distance Relations 271
   Acts 15:3-4
Karma for the Elderly 272
   Leviticus 19:32
Lying for the Lord 273
   Psalm 14:1
The Cost of Divorce 274
   Matthew 19:4-6
Alcohol's – and God's – Power 275
   Proverbs 20:1
In-Womb Baptisms?! 276
   I Corinthians 18:7-8
Sticking to What You're Called to Do 277
   Deuteronomy 22:8
Disaster Recovery 278
   Luke 6:47-49
Clearly Letting Others Know 279
   Joshua 24:15
Not My Sins! 280
   John 2:1-11
Public Prayer 281
   I Timothy 2:1-4
Prayer as Conversation 282
   I King 19:11-13
It's Christ's Church! 283
   I Corinthians 1:11-13
Showing Hospitality 284
   I Chronicles 12:39-40

Enjoying One's Work 285
    Ecclesiastes 3:22
Flowers and Worship 286
    I Kings 6:14-18
Helping the Poor 287
    Leviticus 25:35-36
What Should I Call Him? 288
    John 18:35-37
Christmas Fanatics 289
    Luke 2:4-14
Chronic Speeding 290
    Acts 5:27-29
Talking About the Weather 291
    Ecclesiastes 11:4
Crowd Estimation 292
    Matthew 16:9-10
Is It Really in the Bible? 293
    II Timothy 3:16-17
A Very Long Church Service 294
    Joshua 8:33-35
Remembering Sonya 295
    James 1:27
Accepting God's Will 296
    Romans 9:11-17
Are There Pets in Heaven? 297
    Genesis 1:24-25
Storage Issues 298
    Matthew 6:19-21
A Self-Driving Donkey 299
    Jude 11
Jesus is Gonna Win! 300
    Matthew 16:18-19
When Ancestry Doesn't Count 301
    Jeremiah 31:29-30
Getting to the Core 302
    Mark 12:28-31
Faithfully Showing Up 303
    Psalm 26:2-3
Coincidence -- or Divine Appointment? 304
    John 14:15-17
More Than Suggestions 305
    Deuteronomy 5:1
The Big One That Got Away 306
    John 21:1-7

A Joking Fool for Jesus 307
    Proverbs 17:22
Riding with the Police 308
    Matthew 5:14-16
What It Takes to Be a Winner 309
    Romans 10:9-11
Power Outage 310
    Luke 8:23-25
Honoring Your Parents 311
    Matthew 15:3-6
Firing a Church Member 312
    James 2:8-11
Secrets 313
    Luke 8:9-10
A Wandering Aramean 314
    I John 2:15-17
False Alarms 315
    Matthew 24:5-6
Too Much of Good Things 316
    Mark 6:30-35
A Jokester Preacher? 317
    Proverbs 17:22
Uncle Ralph 318
    Acts 16:14-15
An Unusual Easter Worship 319
    Psalm 28:6-8
God of Many Second Chances 320
    Isaiah 38:1-6
Darkness and Light 321
    Psalm 18:28
Strange – and Strained – Relationships 322
    Mark 14:66-72
Not Taking 'No' for an Answer 323
    Romans 2:7
Don't Go Alone! 324
    Romans 10:14-15
Stars – Earthly and Cosmic 325
    Psalm 8
Calluses on Our Ears 326
    2 Samuel 6:20
Morality Without God? 327
    Matthew 23:23
Blessings 328
    Acts 15:32-33

You Can Go Home Again 329
    James 1:16-18
Behemoths and Leviathans – and God 330
    Isaiah 41:10
Two Kinds of Tithes 331
    Malachi 3:8-10
Superlative God 332
    Revelation 4:8
Accepting Our Dumb Dog 333
    Romans 8:31
Avoiding Worldly Politics 334
    Luke 22:28-30
Valuing Volunteers 335
    1 Chronicles 29:14-18
Credit Scores 336
    Romans 10:9
The Right Size 337
    John 21:20-23
Hidden Second Talents 338
    Matthew 5:14-16
An Abrupt End, But Life Goes On 339
    2 Timothy 4:7
A Creative Solution to Cohabitation 340
    John 4:16-18
Today's Not-So-Exhaustive Concordances 341
    Hebrews 4:12
Is God Calling? 342
    Matthew 9:35-38
Pick Your Battles 343
    Daniel 11:33
Good Trustees 344
    1 Corinthians 12:4-11
Why I Like Peter 345
    John 21:15-19
Brainy Town 346
    Proverbs 1:7
What If We Live a Very Long Time in This World? 347
    James 1:27
Somewhere In-Between 348
    Matthew 22:36-40
The One in the Middle 349
    Acts 10:34-35
Remote Control 350
    2 Kings 5:1-15

A Fishing Story about Children 351
   John 21:1-6
Cutting Corners 352
   Proverbs 12:15
A Long and Ultimately Successful Search 353
   Ecclesiastes 11:1
Spiritual Gifts 354
   Hebrews 2:3-4
Missed Opportunity 355
   John 9:4
Forbidden Fruit 356
   James 1:13-15
Dreams 357
   Daniel 2:1-3
Therapy Pools 358
   John 9:1-12
An Odd Offer 359
   Acts 17:22-34
Where to Start? 360
   Acts 8:26-38
Who Can We Trust? 361
   Proverbs 3:5-6
High-Value Intangibles 362
   Isaiah 44:6-23
I Really Needed Help! 363
   Exodus 18:13-26
Right-Sizing 364
   Psalm 131:1
Hospitality 365
   Hebrews 13:1-3
When You Just Can't Please 366
   Matthew 11:16-19
The Same Core Belief 367
   Mark 9:38-40
First and Second Priorities 368
   Matthew 22:36-40
Inadvertently Starting Something New 369
   Mark 10:13-16
Global Experiences 370
   Mark 16:15
Languages: Spoken and Unspoken 371
   Genesis 11:1-9
It's Christ's Church! 372
   I Corinthians 1:11-13

Life Insurance 373
    John 3:15
Reading Scripture -- Again and Again.................................... 374
    Joshua 1:8
Taking Up the Cross 375
    Matthew 10:38
Turning Negativity Upside Down 376
    Romans 10:15
Nativities – and the Nativity... 377
    John 1:14
Does Prayer Really Make a Difference?................................... 378
    Isaiah 38:5
What's The Worst Sin? 379
    1 John 1:9
Other Sheep?... 380
    Hebrews 11:3
A Second Impression 381
    Acts 9:26-28
Strange Tongues 382
    1 Corinthians 14:9-11
Wishing for More Daylight... 383
    Revelation 21:23-25
Too Much of the Same Old Thing... 384
    Revelation 21:5
Staying Hydrated 385
    Genesis 21:25-31
The Value of a Mentor... 386
    Matthew 10:1
Weather and Sports Prayers... 387
    Matthew 6:9-10
Making It Harder Than It is 388
    Matthew 11:28-30
Fishbowl Living.. 389
    1 Samuel 16:7389
Good Out of Bad 390
    Job 13:15
My Namesake 391
    Psalm 51:1

Introduction

The 365 reflections (plus one extra for leap years) which follow arise from personal experiences with God and life over seven decades on this earth. I share them in hopes that they may bring smiles – or more – to you as you experience God and life for yourself. My recommendation is that you try them one day at a time. Enjoy!

– Dave Ring

March 2019

On Being There
John 11:20-22

It was just after four o'clock on a Monday afternoon. I was sitting in my office at the church I then served, in the remote Big Bend town of Alpine, Texas. The secretary had already left for the day. In tiny Alpine doors were rarely locked, so when I heard the front door open and approaching footsteps, it wasn't all that unusual. There was a tap on the inner door to my office. I said, "Come in." A moment later, a young woman stood before me.

"Are you the pastor?" she asked. I simply replied, "Yes," and she immediately began to cry. I helped her into a chair and held out a box of tissues. For the next 90 minutes, this young woman poured out her story, a long and troubled one, although she was probably no more than 21 years of age.

I listened and, at first, tried to respond to her monologue. But every time I tried to interject even a single word, she only cried harder. So after a few attempts, I simply listened intently. After a full hour and a half, she dried her tears, said, "Thank you for listening," and walked out.

I never learned her name. I never saw her again. All I know is that on one Monday afternoon, now long ago, I was "there" for a young lady who needed someone to hear her. Sometimes, simply "being there" is what is needed. Just listening to a fellow human being may be the best we can do for another precious person. May God bless you as you listen to those you need to hear.

Jumping in the River
II Kings 5:9-14

As a child growing up, at least part of the time, in rural South Mississippi, I hung around with a lot of cousins. In particular, I remember two of my girl cousins, Pat and Marie, who used to go swimming with me. Every time we'd get to the bank of the river where we regularly swam, even on the hottest day, Marie would dip her big toe into the water and jump back, exclaiming, "It's too cold!" But Pat would simply take a running start, dive in, and bob up shouting, "Come on in, the water's fine!" While Marie was still standing on the riverbank complaining, Pat was enjoying a refreshing swim.

I've met many people who've had minimal, negative exposure to the Christian faith. They're not interested in going to church because somewhere, sometime way back, someone offended them -- an usher frowned at them, a preacher said something they didn't like, a well-known church member was seen drunk in a bar -- thus all Christians must be hypocrites.

On the other hand, those who fully immerse themselves in the life-transforming power of the Christian faith find wonderful refreshment therein. Committed Christians discover answers to life's most difficult problems, obtain strength to cope with this world's most stressful challenges, and secure hope for abundant living -- today, tomorrow, and for eternity.

Lost and Found
Luke 19:9-10

Have you ever been lost? I have. I was 19 years of age when a high school friend and I decided to embark on the great American odyssey -- to see the entire country from a Volkswagen Beetle. We headed westward from the east coast city of Baltimore. When we got as far as to Denver, upon seeing the Rocky Mountains for the first time we decided to go climbing. The tallest mountain in nearby Rocky Mountain National Park was Long's Peak. We thought perhaps we could see the Pacific Ocean from its summit -- not realizing that the west coast was yet more than 1200 miles distant.

We pitched a quick tent camp at the base of the mountain and started up the marked trail at about four o'clock in the afternoon. Neither of us had any mountain climbing experience, but we were young and strong and figured we'd reach the summit in a matter of a couple of hours. But at dusk, having no concept of the scale and distance involved in such a trek, we were still many miles from the peak.

Night fell quickly, and we were caught out in the open in short-sleeved shirts, with neither food nor water and not even a flashlight to help get us back down. It was pitch dark, with no moon visible. Every black hole might have been a thousand-foot drop into oblivion; every sound in the night was surely a hungry wolf on the prowl. Despite it being July, it got cold at the altitude we'd reached -- near to freezing. We tried to slowly move downward, losing the trail and becoming hopelessly lost. Finally, we just huddled together, shivering in the night, lamenting our own foolishness.

Just before dawn, we heard voices in the distance. Park rangers, having found our tent unoccupied, had started up the trail during the night, searching for us. When we met them, they were less than friendly. They gave a stern lecture on the folly of what we'd done, ordered us to pack up our tent and get out of their park, and never again to do such a stupid thing. We didn't even protest -- we were just so glad to be found, alive and well.

There are a lot of folk in our world today who embark on all sorts of foolish ventures, behaviors, and practices -- not knowing, not realizing what the potential consequences of their folly might be. There are many who become lost -- lost in sin. But there's good news -- a Savior who is already out searching, looking to find the lost. Jesus is searching for lost people, ready, unlike the park rangers we encountered, to lovingly welcome them as soon as they're found. There's no need for any of us to stay lost -- not when a Savior is already in the world, looking to find us and bless us with eternal life.

Storytelling
Psalm 107:1-3

Today's personal story is about stories. For five years, while serving as senior pastor of the First United Methodist Church of Big Spring, Texas, I provided a daily devotional story for broadcast on that town's best-known radio station. I admit I didn't always come up with completely new ones, but over that lengthy time span I broadcast several hundred different tales. And as those short stories were carried, daily, on the air for years on end, dozens of folks in that small west Texas city would come up to me to ask, "Dave, how do you think up -- where do you get all those stories?"

I would usually respond, truthfully, thus: "Actually, it's not a matter of finding stories to tell. It's just seeing life itself through storyteller eyes. There are stories galore around us all."

Long before, as a seminary student, I recall receiving back from my professor of preaching the first sermon I had submitted in writing for his class. My professor's name was Dr. Gordon Thompson, and he was both a wonderful man and a gifted teacher. So I was more than a bit dismayed when I read, in bold red pen, what he'd written on my paper. My sermon, according to Dr. Thompson, was "Theologically correct, flawlessly presented, and deadly dull."

As I talked it over with him later, Dr. Thompson told me that a well-argued sermon -- without illustrations, is like a well-constructed house – without windows. I hadn't included a single story in my message and therefore, even though it was logically a fine sermon, it was lifeless. It's the illustrations -- the stories -- that let in light and air, that allow a message to really communicate.

Jesus was a master storyteller. We find dozens of his stories in the gospel writings of the Bible's New Testament: They're often called parables. Even if we aren't church goers most of us know the Parable of the Good Samaritan. Its clear point is one that we all understand – in God's sight, everyone is our neighbor.

Jesus could have said exactly that. And people would have nodded their heads in agreement, then quickly lost the lesson. But by making his point via an unforgettable story, Jesus ensured that the principle he wished to teach would live forever. The same is true of the parable of the Prodigal Son, the story of the Lost Sheep, or the Widow's Mite. Stories communicate more clearly than logical ideas. And stories teach better, and are remembered longer, than even well-argued propositions.

I would invite you to look around yourself – and see the many stories of God unfold before your very eyes.

A Missing Daughter
Luke 15:11-24

Back when our three children were all still small, the Ring family decided to visit southern California, with its abundance of child-friendly parks and other attractions. At the San Diego Zoo we were all fascinated to view the Australian koalas. We stood there for several minutes, ooing and aahing at these cute and cuddly creatures. But suddenly my wife, Fran, asked, "Where's Joanna?" I looked down and around me and replied, "She was here just a minute ago." I quickly counted noses -- two sons, but no daughter. Our youngest, then about three years of age, was missing. In a crowd of perhaps 20,000 people at the zoo that day, she had simply vanished into thin air.

The next forty minutes were a frenzied nightmare. We did all the wrong things, I'm sure, running in sixteen different directions shouting, "Joanna! Joanna!" Every imaginable horror story ever conceived about the abduction of a little girl flashed through our minds. Finally, when the adrenaline ran out, we collapsed on a bench, sadly lamenting that we'd probably never see our daughter again.

My wife then voiced the only sane thought of that hour: "We need to notify the zoo police." Just as we looked up to try and identify where to find such, a three-wheeled golf cart driven by a zoo staff member pulled into sight, with Joanna happily perched on the back, licking an ice-cream cone. Our daughter had already been found, safe and sound. Our family, praise God, was whole again!

The joy of that reunion, as well as the despair that preceded it, are both experiences I'll never forget. It all happened in less than an hour, but what an emotional roller-coaster ride!

Can you imagine the feelings that God has for us, his precious children, when one of us wanders away from His care into the perils and dangers of a life of sin? Oh, how it must hurt our Lord to the very depths of His heart to lose one of the children he has so lovingly and carefully made! And can you further imagine the immensity of the joy of our Lord when one of us returns to the family -- rejoining the great circle of the Father's love for all his children?

A Smart Fool?
Psalm 14:1-7

I have a friend from all the way back in high school days with whom I've kept contact for five decades. He's a very intelligent man, quite successful in the world of business. He often travels all over the world and has lived in a number of different countries and cultures. And, one of the most interesting aspects of this man is this: He claims to be an atheist -- he doesn't believe that God exists. Although quite a few folks I've met act as though God doesn't really exist, Elmer (not his real name) is the only person I know well who, up-front, professes atheism.

Some years ago, he stopped in to visit me at the church I was then serving in El Paso, Texas. Like any other person who enjoys his work, I gave him a tour of my place of employment. We walked throughout the church buildings. I showed him classrooms where the Word of God was taught to children; the chapel where, as needed, folks came to pray; the sanctuary where we worshipped God each Sunday. After we'd completed this grand tour, my friend said to me, "Dave, if there's no God, do you realize you'll have wasted most of your life promoting nothing?"

I wish I could say that I had just the right comeback to his remark then and there, but I didn't. I honestly don't remember what my response to him was. I've since thought long and hard about what I ought to have said, and the next time he comes to visit, I'll say, "Elmer, if there is a God, do you realize you'll have wasted eternity?"

I doubt that many who are reading this narrative are professing atheists like this friend of mine. But there are many, many people in our world who live as though God were of no consequence, no significance, to their lives. These may not profess atheism, but from a practical standpoint there's little difference. I sincerely hope you're not one of them.

Drunk Christians?
Acts 2:5-15

Early in my ministry I served as assistant pastor in a large old inner-city church in Nashville, Tennessee. The church building was still beautiful and attractive, but the neighborhood around it had seen much better days. On occasion this meant, among other things, that drunks would disrupt Sunday morning worship services. Our church ushers tried valiantly to keep things under control, but sometimes they failed to sidetrack the local alcoholics.

One Sunday an obviously inebriated man staggered up the aisle just prior to the pastoral prayer. Near the front he stopped, looked up at the senior minister, and shouted, "Preacher, I'm a drunk Christian." Senior Pastor Ted didn't even bat an eye. He just said, "Glad to have you. Sit down. At least you're a Christian, drunk or otherwise."

I'm glad I witnessed Pastor Ted's handling of that situation early in my ministry, because it helped to teach me something important about both the grace of God and the nature of the Church. God loves us, period. He loves us despite who we are and what we do. He simply loves us. A church building is God's house on earth -- a dwelling to which all are welcome to come, and to share in God's unconditional love. Certainly, I much prefer a sober congregation to which to preach on Sunday mornings. But drunks -- and other sinners, including me -- are also always welcome in the house of the Father of love.

Soul Exercise
Isaiah 55:1-2

At the age of 11 I broke my leg in a snow sledding accident. I hit a steel mailbox pole doing what seemed like 60 miles per hour. It was a bad break -- my left femur shattered into twenty-seven different fragments. Back then, today's orthopedic surgeries and rehabilitation procedures were unknown, so my doctor simply put a cast on my leg and hoped the bone would eventually regenerate.

For eighteen months my left leg was completely concealed in a cast, with only the toes sticking out. When the last cast was finally removed, my leg was no bigger around than a garden hose -- all the muscles had completely atrophied from lack of use. It simply dangled from my body -- a useless appendage.

For the next two years thereafter, I struggled to rebuild that leg. It took one full year after the cast was removed before I could walk without crutches. Eventually I could not only walk but run. I began running every day, a practice which I kept up for more than forty years thereafter. I wanted to keep my leg from ever again shriveling up from lack of use.

Just as leg muscles need regular use to maintain their proper functioning, so does the rest of our bodies. And so, do our minds -- something medical science is proving more and more true as it seeks to discover the causes and potential cures for the awful disease called Alzheimer's. And still further, so does the human soul.

God has lovingly provided each of us with a soul -- a wonderful spiritual dimension which is part and parcel of every human being. And exactly like leg muscles, souls must be regularly exercised, lest they shrivel up and become useless. The human soul is best exercised by regularly using it to communicate and interact with its Creator, Almighty God.

Fruit Inspection
Galatians 5:22-23

My wife, Fran, has a habit that I'm sure has raised an eyebrow or two among supermarket produce managers. She's a very demanding shopper when it comes to buying fruits and vegetables for our family. Grapefruits, oranges, lemons and such are always given a good squeeze or two before Fran puts them in her bag. If they aren't pre-packaged, cherries and grapes are hand-selected, one by one, prior to purchase. And watermelons and cantaloupes are always "tapped" sharply a few times as Fran listens to the quality of resonance produced.

Some years back, while we were visiting my parents in Mississippi, we stopped at a local food store looking to buy a watermelon. I simply walked up to what appeared to be the biggest one in the store and hefted it onto my shoulder. But Fran, after "tapping" here and there among the available melons, said, "Put that big thing down. This one here's a better one." And she was right. The melon Fran selected turned out to be one of the sweetest I've ever eaten. My wife's a tough inspector when it comes to selecting fruit, but her grapefruit squeezing, and watermelon thumping pays off.

One of the favorite ways Jesus expressed His desire for Christians to conduct their lives was this: "Bear fruit." In saying this He obviously wasn't talking about growing grapes or picking bananas. Jesus wanted those who would claim to be His followers to live their lives in such ways that others would be attracted to the Christian faith. Having been given God's love, we are to show love to others. Having received forgiveness, we are to forgive those who wrong us. Having been blessed, we are to bless others. And someday, Jesus Himself will return, to inspect our fruit.

From Generation to Generation
Genesis 5:1-8

I was serving a church in Nashville, Tennessee and, as in virtually all churches, had a cadre of elderly, shut-in persons whom I tried to regularly visit. I particularly remember one lady there, Mrs. Keleher (not her real name). She was in her late 80's, wheelchair bound, and in constant pain from both arthritis and osteoporosis. But notwithstanding, she was also a tireless prayer warrior and one whose large-print Bible was virtually worn out from constant use. Every time I visited her, she would say to me, "Pastor, I just don't understand why God keeps me here. I'm old, I'm sick, I hurt. I can't do much of anything anymore and I'm a burden to my family. Why doesn't God take me home right away?"

Even though some think preachers have a direct pipeline to God, I had no wise answers for Mrs. Keleher. In fact, I sort of wondered the same things myself. I would always pray with her that God see fit, in his providence, to take her out of the body and home to Heaven as soon as possible.

In the spring I worked with a group of junior high youth in what are called confirmation classes, training for church membership. On Easter Sunday morning, several of those youth stepped forward to join the church. One of them, a young lady of 13, asked to be allowed to say a word to the congregation. What she said was this: "I'm here today to profess my belief in Jesus because of the example of faith I've seen in my great-grandmother, Mrs. Keleher."

Mrs. Keleher wasn't present to hear her great grand-daughter's witness, but you can bet that I, and several other church members, gave her a full account before the day was over. Even though she didn't know it, nor did I, God was still using her -- old, sick, and in pain though she was -- to witness faith in Christ to a new generation.

Better to Pray First
Mark 14:32-38

I had only recently become pastor of a particular church. A lady from another church in the same city stopped in to visit with me. She had heard about a particular problem that my new church was struggling with, and wanted to know what I, as pastor, was planning to do about it. I responded candidly to her query, "Well, ma'am, first and foremost, I'm praying about it."

The look of puzzlement on this lady's face was obvious. She paused for a long time and then, finally, sort of stammered, "Oh well, of course. But what are you really going to do about it?"

Years before, when I was a much younger disciple of Jesus Christ, my initial response to any problem or issue was to spring into action, immediately marshalling my time, talent, and resources to deal with the situation presented. I also remember once, while I was yet a layman, a lady asking me to sign up for a prayer vigil. My response to her was short and terse. "I'll tell you what, ma'am, you pray, and I'll work." But that was before I began to understand the true value of prayer.

When I pray first, enlisting God's partnership in the enterprise, whatever abilities I may have to deal with issues, tasks, and problems are multiplied. Nowadays I pray first, then do what else is needed. It's an effective model, one that I heartily commend to any and all.

Contemporary Priorities
Matthew 19:4-6

A young woman who sporadically attended the church I pastored called to inquire about being married there. She told me that both she and her fiancé recognized the value of a spiritual bond being established between them, so they definitely wanted to be married in the Church. I was pleased to hear that sort of conviction in her words. I responded, "Certainly, I'd be glad to counsel with you and your fiancé toward being married in the Church of Jesus Christ."

That's when the other shoe started to drop. Well, she told me, she and her intended both worked odd schedules, and it would be difficult for them to come in for any counseling. I responded that I was flexible as to time, and began to suggest various dates and times -- early mornings, evenings, even later at night, on weekends -- all to no avail.

Finally, I suggested, "Why don't you both talk to your employers and arrange to take the same two hours off on one particular day, so we can sit down and discuss your wedding plans?" Her final response is one I can, unfortunately, quote verbatim, "Pastor, we want a Christian marriage, but we certainly wouldn't jeopardize our jobs to have one."

That ended the conversation. I've little doubt that young woman thinks I'm the most unreasonable pastor she has ever met. After all, I asked her to consider putting her job in second place, behind her desire to be married in the Church of Jesus Christ. I'm sure she thinks I have absolutely no understanding of the "real" world: how tough it is to find and keep a job. Silly me, asking someone to consider taking a couple of hours off from work in order to explore the spiritual implications of a lifetime decision like marriage.

Growing Discipleship
Hebrews 5:11-14

Before being called into the ministry by God, I was educated for and practiced a very different occupation. I was an electrical engineer, working for a large U. S. government research facility in Albuquerque, New Mexico, Sandia National Laboratories. There, early on, I was assigned the role of project leader for a particular endeavor, a job which required me to select personnel for my team. After looking over a couple of resumes which, to me, seemed virtually identical, I went to my boss for advice.

"I've been looking over these two men's resumes for possible assignment to my project team," I told him, "and I can't decide between them. They both have 15 years' experience with this kind of work." My boss' response was extremely interesting. He said, "No, they don't both have 15 years' experience. Mike has 15 years' experience. But Fred has one year's experience, repeated 15 times."

In the Christian faith I've discovered the same is often true. Some believers in Christ grow and mature in their faith throughout a lifetime of following Him. But many others simply relive and rehash the same experiences, over and over again, in a repetitive cycle that eventually becomes a rut. Such stuck-in-the-mud believers are pretty much dead weight upon the Body of Christ. But growing Christians make wonderful disciples, to the greater glory of our Lord.

Drownproofing
Romans 3:22-24

When my older son, Dave IV, was barely a toddler, my wife began to take him to special classes at the local YMCA. The "Y" was offering "drownproofing" for infants. The theory was that even tiny babies instinctively know how to swim, so getting an infant to reinforce this instinct at a very early age would allow them to overcome any fear of water and, later on, become better swimmers. One parent, in this case his mother, was needed to take the "class" with the child and help him or her to become "drownproofed."

After three or four sessions of mother and son attending these classes and being given glowing reports of how well Dave was doing, I decided one day to stop in and see this "drownproofing" in action. Wife and son were both glad to see me, and I was again told by my wife how well Dave was advancing in the class. I decided to see for myself. I was dressed in a suit, so I gingerly picked up little Dave, who was already in his wet swimsuit, and dropped him into the deep end of the pool, expecting to see him quickly bob up and start paddling.

He immediately sank to the bottom of the pool and stayed there, totally unmoving. I waited -- 10, 20, 30, 40 seconds. He didn't move. My wife, Fran, was less than supportive. Even though she was in a swimsuit and I in a business suit, she said, "You'd better jump in there fast and retrieve our son." The tone of her voice said I'd best do just that, and quickly. So I rapidly threw off my suit jacket, pitched my wallet out of my back pocket, and dove in -- in dress shirt, shoes, pants, and all.

I grabbed little Dave, who was literally sitting motionless at the bottom of the pool with eyes wide open. When we surfaced, he was just fine -- with not even a tear. I handed him back to his mother, who was less than pleased with me. So much for "drownproofing" our infant son.

My experiences as a pastor tell me that a lot of folks are drowning in sin in this world. And although a substantial number of them are aware that there's a Savior available, they do nothing to reach out for the saving grace of Jesus Christ -- like my infant son who just sat motionless at the bottom of the swimming pool. What a shame that precious souls are lost, for eternity, through such passive inaction!

Sheltering the Battered
Ephesians 5:25-30

I was enjoying a coffee break in the middle of a Monday morning with two of my church's members in the tiny west Texas town of Alpine. One of them happened to be the mayor of that small city, the other the hospital administrator. Somehow, our conversation got around to the subject of visits to the hospital emergency room. The administrator told us that more than half of the Friday and Saturday night visits to that particular ER were women needing to be treated for the effects of having been beaten by their drunk husbands or boyfriends. I was shocked; so was the mayor.

Previously, I had assumed that tiny west Texas town to be free from those sorts of problems; those were the kinds of things you'd expect to hear about in some big, bad city. Battered women in Alpine? It boggled our minds, but the hospital administrator was in a position to know what he was talking about.

Out of that conversation, over the next year, plans evolved for ways to address that problem. Our little coffee fellowship of three expanded to six, then a dozen community leaders, including two pastors from other denominations. Grants were applied for from a variety of foundations and charitable groups. A house was located that could be leased. An administrator was hired. The Big Bend Battered Women's Shelter opened with significant fanfare. And within days after its official opening, it was housing three families in need of its services.

Two decades later, I received a call inviting me to the 20th anniversary of that facility. It had changed names and locations a couple of times in two decades, and it had served a lot of women and children during that time. I wasn't able to go to those festivities, but it was satisfying to know that something I had a part in starting was still meeting human need in that area.

Where does Jesus fit into this story? He was there right from the very beginning. I'm convinced he was the unseen fourth member of that coffee fellowship as we talked that morning. Wherever there's human need, Jesus, via God's Holy Spirit, is present. I believe he got us started -- and I further believe he was pleased with the outcome of his inspiration.

Treading on Dangerous Ground
I John 2:3-5

I was still a layman, just a candidate for the ministry, but I was asked to fill the pulpit of my home church, St. Andrew's United Methodist in Albuquerque, New Mexico for three Sundays in a row while the pastor took an extended vacation. The first of those three Sundays, I announced at the close of worship, "Next week I'll be speaking on the ten commandments. I invite you to read Exodus chapter 20 in the Bible before you come to worship."

The following Sunday, I asked for a show of hands: "How many of you read Exodus 20 before coming to church today?" Two ladies seated near the rear of the sanctuary raised their hands, and I commended them for their good preparation. I began to work through the great ten commandments but had only gotten a little more than halfway through when it was time for worship to be completed. So I concluded by saying, "Next week I'll continue speaking about the remainder of the ten commandments. And in preparation, I'd like everyone to read Matthew, chapter 29, in the Bible."

That third Sunday, as I stepped up to speak, I asked for a show of hands: "How many here read Matthew 29 in the Bible before coming to church today?" Again, the same two ladies at the rear of the sanctuary raised their hands. I responded, "The gospel of Matthew has only 28 chapters. Now, let's begin today's message with the eighth commandment, which is God's prohibition against lying."

I leave the interpretation of that particular personal story to your thinking. However, I can tell you that it was more than 10 years, long after I became an ordained minister, before I was ever again invited to preach in my home church.

Word Power
James 3:9-12

Shortly after I was appointed pastor of Harwood United Methodist Church in Albuquerque, New Mexico, the choir director came to me with a lament. "We don't have enough men in our choir to perform the music properly. Can you come to choir practice Wednesday night and help us out? We're really hurting!" I said I would come.

Wednesday evening arrived and, as promised, I attended choir practice, adding my bass voice to the group. After practice the choir director came over and put his arm around my shoulders. With that, he said, "Dave, we're really hurting, but we're not desperate."

I'm a preacher, and you have to be pretty thick-skinned to stay in my line of work. But I have to admit, that choir director's callous remark really got to me. Fifteen years and four congregations would pass through my life before I again dared to sing in a church choir.

The apostle James, in the Biblical letter which bears his name, sternly warns us to keep our tongues in check, lest we give offense. Hurtful words, like toothpaste once the tube has been squeezed, can't easily be taken back.

Ups and Downs with God
Ezra 3:10-13

While my children were young, I took our family to Busch Gardens in Tampa, Florida to enjoy that particular theme park. At the time Busch Gardens was advertising that their then-new roller coaster, which they called the "Kumba," was the fastest, steepest, and scariest on the planet. I'm quite sure that some other theme park has long-since topped them, but that year the "Kumba" in Tampa was supposed to be the world's toughest roller coaster ride.

I've always been a fan of roller coasters. Thus I excitedly stood in line with my children and hundreds of other teenagers and waited almost an hour until we finally made our way to the front of the queue. As I was being strapped into the car, the young adult attendant, observing my white hair, asked, "You sure you want to do this, gramps?"

I rode the "Kumba" that day. In fact, I rode it twice. And I even bought a t-shirt which says, "I Survived the Kumba at Busch Gardens." Maybe I'll grow old enough to lose my zest for roller coaster rides and other similar adventures later down the line, but not yet.

Jesus said, "I have come that you may have life, and have it abundantly!" Sometimes life itself can seem like a roller coaster ride, but nonetheless, I believe our Lord wants us to live each day to the fullest extent possible!

A Wilderness Journey
Deuteronomy 2:1-2

Decades ago I pastored a two-point circuit in the Big Bend country of west Texas, the two towns being Alpine and Marathon. At Marathon, the smaller of the two, an average Sunday morning attendance might be 15, a really good Sunday 20. There was a total of 45 persons on that church's membership roll, only 30 of whom actually lived in Marathon. Thus I quickly grew to know every local member of that small congregation quite well. Early on, I promised I would visit each resident member in their home during my first year of ministry there which, considering the small number, really wasn't a major task.

One lady who almost never missed church at Marathon, and who was often the first to arrive, was named Patsy Ruth. Strangely enough, she was one of that church's non-resident members. She lived on a ranch far to the south of Marathon, 92 miles distant to be exact. After I'd been serving Marathon for about six months, I told her, "Patsy Ruth, I'm impressed that you're so faithful to drive all this way every week. And I'd really like to visit you. Tell me how to get to where you live."

Patsy Ruth responded by saying, "Preacher, there have been several other pastors who've promised they'd visit me. But none of them has ever actually made it to my house at the ranch." Notwithstanding, I asked her for directions, and she wrote them down for me.

A couple of weeks later I set aside a day to try to find her place. And I came to understand why others had given up. I drove 53 miles on blacktop, then 20 miles on gravel, then 15 miles on what could best be described as a two-path trail – and I still wasn't there. The last four miles were almost impassable. I wished I had a high-clearance, four-wheel drive truck, rather than the little Honda I was driving.

I persevered and finally did make it. Patsy Ruth was delighted to see me. From then on, I was even more impressed with her dedication to God. It was almost a three-hour drive, one way, from her house on the ranch to the church at Marathon. But she faithfully did it virtually every weekend.

On the other hand, there was also a couple on the rolls of that same church who lived directly across the street from the church building -- and who showed up to worship only at Christmas, Easter, and Mother's Day. But that's another story.

In the word of God, specifically the New Testament letter to the Hebrews, tenth chapter and twenty-fifth verse, the apostle Paul admonishes the people of God not to forsake the assembling of themselves together – in order that we may encourage one another.

A Fiery Ceremony
Matthew 19:4-6

It was an elaborate, formal wedding, with pomp and circumstance of every kind. Decorating the sanctuary had involved a team of five working two full days in advance of the ceremony. Flowers, ribbons, and candles were everywhere. The bride wore a beautiful white gown with a long train and lots of lace. As she and the groom knelt to take their wedding vows, he tossed her veil back to uncover her face -- and a corner of the veil touched one of the lit candles.

Instantly, the entire veil ignited in flame. I was wearing my overlarge, tent-like pulpit robe, and I instinctively dove at the bride's head, covering the flaming veil with the folds of my robe. Just as quickly as the fire had ignited, it was out.

Not surprisingly, it took a few minutes for all of us to pull ourselves back together. Fortunately, the only injury to the bride was a few singed hairs. As soon as we had composed ourselves, the wedding continued, and the happy couple were soon walking down the aisle together -- with a wild wedding story to tell for years to come.

I've not kept an actual count, but the number is more than 300 weddings at which I've officiated. Not every one of them has been as memorable to me as that one, but each has been special and significant in its own right. As a pastor, I'd much rather perform weddings than many of the other duties I'm regularly called upon to do. I praise God for the institution of Christian marriage. It's one of the solid pillars of family life which, in turn, makes possible a strong, stable society which, as marriage rates decline, is inevitably becoming less so.

An Answer Already Received
I Thessalonians 5:16-18

One of my endeavors prior to entering full-time ministry was helping to found a volunteer flying missionary society called "St. Jude Express." It began with six of us who, as young men, loved to fly small airplanes -- and also loved God and wanted to serve him. So we began to carry medicine, doctors, and dentists on weekends into remote places, particularly the Sierra Madre mountains of northern Mexico. The Tarahumara Native American people who live there are desperately poor and have little access to health care. So we would go to them, landing on dirt strips in villages accessible only by days of foot travel -- or by air.

One weekend our medical team had seen about 200 patients, rendering what care we could, realizing that even the limited help we had provided was better than nothing. Nonetheless, we were disheartened by the report of our doctor concerning one little boy who had a major heart defect and whose condition required surgery as soon as possible in a hospital. The nearest facility that could do what was needed was over 200 miles away in Chihuahua City, and the cost there would be about $1400. We were forced to leave the boy's situation unresolved, as we had no financial resources in hand. We planned to return to that village two weekends hence.

The following Tuesday evening, back home in Albuquerque, New Mexico, we gathered in our airplane hangar to debrief the weekend, and to pray for the extra $1400 needed to be able to obtain surgery for this Indian boy. After the meeting, someone remembered that we hadn't yet opened the week's mail to our fledgling organization. When we did so, there were two checks therein, one from a soldier stationed overseas and the other from a woman in Wisconsin. Together, they totaled exactly $1400, the amount for which we'd prayed. The answer to our prayers had already been received -- before we even prayed.

Coincidence? Perhaps. Has that ever happened to me again in just that way -- to pray for a specific amount and immediately receive the exact amount asked for? Not exactly. But in that time and circumstance, I have little doubt that God knew the need and answered our prayers before we even offered them. The boy received his operation; his life was saved, and to God be the glory.

A Very Pleasant Surprise
John 20:15-16

The year was 1970. Having just completed two college degrees I was working my first permanent job in Albuquerque, New Mexico. My parents still lived on the U. S. east coast in Baltimore, Maryland, 1800 miles distant. Starting in July that year, my mother began asking me this question every time we'd talk on the phone: "Son, are you coming home for Christmas?" And I'd reply, "Sorry, I don't think I can. It's a long way and I'm pretty involved with my job out here. You'll just have to get along without me at Christmas this year."

Frankly, I was telling a bold-faced lie. But I wanted to pull off a positive surprise on my parents. I already had an airline ticket sitting on my dresser, scheduled to arrive in Baltimore at noon on Christmas Eve, December 24th.

When that day finally came, I flew to Baltimore, had a friend pick me up at the airport and drive me to my parents' house, and sneaked in the back door while they were both still at work. When my mother arrived home at about 4 o'clock that afternoon, I was standing behind the door. As she closed it behind her, I stepped out and said a casual "Hi." You could have heard her scream of pure delight for five miles around! Christmas 1970 was one of the most enjoyable I ever spent with my parents -- and a lot of it had to do with the element of surprise.

Can you imagine the surprise Mary Magdalene experienced when, in the graveyard on Easter morning, Jesus stepped up to her and simply spoke her name, "Mary?" She was looking for a dead body, but instead she found a living Savior. God had a wonderful surprise for Mary that day, and God still has a wealth of pleasant surprises for his people today.

The Exciting Challenge of Fishing
Matthew 4:18-22

I love to fish. Growing up, my dad was both a hunter and a fisherman, and he spent many days trying to teach me both skills. The hunting didn't stick with me, but the fishing did.

Although I've fished in some pretty exotic locations, both salt and fresh water, my favorite kind of fishing continues to be stream fishing for trout. I've spent much of my adult life in the Rocky Mountain region of the U. S. where there are thousands of trout streams, and an abundance of opportunities, to try to catch that wily species.

Trout are one of the very most difficult to catch variety of game fish that exist. They're finicky, they're easily spooked, and -- for fish at least -- they're exceptionally smart and amazingly adept at avoiding the hook. That makes them a challenge, and I enjoy challenges. I even learned the craft of fly fishing to improve my odds at catching the wily trout. Despite all my efforts, on many days my trout fishing expeditions end with an empty creel -- and only stories to tell about the ones that got away. When I actually do catch a trout or two, I always eat what I catch. And the taste is all that much better because of the difficulty involved in securing the catch.

Jesus, the son of God, was partial to fishermen. At least five of his 12 disciples are known to have been fishermen before Jesus met them. As fishermen, they were intrigued by the offer Jesus made to them -- follow me, and I'll teach you how to catch people for the Kingdom of God. It's both exciting and challenging to be a fisherman, either of the finned variety or, for Jesus, the people kind.

Learning to Fly
Luke 8:11-15

As a young man in the process of learning to fly small airplanes, I shared with my half-brother, Robert, that I had begun taking flying lessons. Robert was an experienced, multi-thousand-hour pilot. He said, "Let's go up together and I'll show you a few things." So we climbed into a Cessna and he took us off from the Gulfport, Mississippi field, turning right to fly out over the Gulf of Mexico, climbing to about a mile above sea level.

At that point Robert said, "The controls are yours." I flew for a few minutes, steady and level, getting the feel of the airplane. Robert asked, "Everything OK?" I replied, "Yes." As soon as I'd said that, he reached out, turned off the key to the engine, and pushed the yoke all the way forward, immediately putting the plane into a dead-stick nose dive, heading straight down toward the gulf below.

I could feel my eyes sinking back into my head from the G-force, but I grabbed the yoke, leveled us out, and quickly restarted the engine. In just those few seconds, we'd lost almost 4,000 feet -- and in another handful of seconds would have crashed into the Gulf.

I was about as angry as I'd ever been at my half-brother. "What did you do that for?" I screamed. "You almost killed us both!" Robert calmly replied, "I wanted to see if you had the makings of a pilot in you. You'll do fine."

This is the same brother who, when I was about four years old, tossed me into a river to see if I could swim or not. I survived that test, too.

There are millions of folks in this world who claim to have faith in Jesus Christ. It's a relatively simple profession to make. God has deliberately made it easy to begin a life of faith in His Son. But at some point, in our lives, often when least expected, such easy faith may be tested. May God grant us, each and all, the strength to meet the test, and thereby deepen our faith.

Never Too Late
Luke 2:25-32

Clyde was a mean old man. Everyone who knew him had told me so. Even his wife, Julia, warned me to steer clear of her husband. But I was young and determined, and I had made a pledge to my small congregation that I would visit in every home of a church member during my first six months as their pastor. So I brushed aside Julia's warning and said I would come to visit in her home anyway.

When I arrived at their house, at first it appeared I would be lucky. Clyde was off in a room by himself with his head buried in a book. He barely grunted as I passed by. His wife and I visited for a half-hour or so, then I got ready to leave.

I headed for the back door, going out just the way I'd come in, when I was stopped in my tracks by a single, sharp word, "Preacher!" Clyde was calling out from the room in which he'd been reading. I moved to his doorway, "Yes, sir?" "Preacher!" he boomed out again. He held up a Bible for me to see. "Preacher, if what this book says is true, I need to repent of my sins and accept Christ as my Savior before I die." I couldn't believe my ears. Clyde had just told me exactly what I wanted to tell him -- but didn't have the nerve to say.

I responded, "Yes, Clyde. That's just what you need to do." He said, "Preacher, I'm 82 years old, and I've never been baptized. Am I too old to be baptized?"

The very next Sunday morning Clyde was baptized and publicly professed his faith in Jesus Christ. And for the next 19 months, until Christ called him to leave the earth, he and Julia sat together on the very front row of the church, never missing a Sunday. Clyde was the most attentive listener to my sermons in the whole congregation. He regularly told me he was making up for lost time.

Clyde Hunter received the grace of Jesus Christ at age 82. On the other end of the age scale, I've also baptized two premature infants -- fresh out of their mother's womb. The marvelous grace of Christ is available to all, regardless of age.

Supportive Leadership
1 Timothy 3:1-7

In every church body there are folks who do their best to enable the pastor's life and ministry among them to be successful. There are also those who do their utmost to undermine and ruin a pastor's best efforts. Fortunately, the first category significantly outnumber the second in most churches, otherwise the church would have ceased to exist long ago.

Dr. Clifford Casey was one of the principal leaders, a giant of faith in the congregation I served in the Big Bend town of Alpine, Texas. Although he was 80-plus years of age when I first met him, he had more energy than many 35-year olds. Rock-climbing was one of his favorite sports.

The first time we ever spoke, Dr. Casey told me this, "I've never had a pastor I didn't like, and at my age I'm not about to start disliking anybody. So I'm going to be your friend, and you can feel free to come to me anytime you have a need, about anything." Regarding the overall church body, he also said this, "Our church tries to make every preacher it receives a better pastor. When you leave here, however long you stay, you'll be a better preacher."

Dr. Casey proved to be my friend on more than one occasion during my time in Alpine. He really was there to listen, to encourage, and to assist the pastor in any way he could. And that church body, as a whole, was one of the most supportive groups of people I've ever known. They never tried to drain my enthusiasm for the Lord; rather, they refreshed and replenished me in my ministries for Him.

It's interesting to me that, although my tenure in Alpine was less than three full years, a high percentage of the positive "stories" that I'm able to recall, decades later, came out of that relatively short experience. I've been in other churches for as long as seven years, but none of them has left as lasting an imprint -- for good -- on me as that relatively short time in Alpine. And yes, Dr. Casey was right -- I left there a better preacher than when I arrived.

More church bodies today need to take the attitude that Dr. Casey and the Alpine church exhibited toward me. Instead of "using up" their pastors, then discarding them for fresh ones, they need to empower and enable their preachers to become better -- both for their benefit and for the Kingdom of God.

Hurt and Angry
Psalm 22:1-3

I was attending seminary in Atlanta, Georgia. Although all of my instructors were tough, one of the professors, a middle-aged man with a long, virtually unpronounceable German name, was much more demanding and a lot less friendly than any of the others. He told us students, from the outset, that he was only there to teach us what we needed to learn, no more and no less. He pointedly added that he didn't want to know us, only to get us through the required course material.

Many of my fellow seminarians instantly disliked this brusque, unfriendly prof. But I and a few others wondered why he was so overtly nasty. After some investigating, we discovered that his wife was suffering from a long and painful illness that was slowly taking her life.

One afternoon five of us hung around after class and surrounded this big, burly prof. We told him, "We want to pray for you -- and for your wife." He told us to leave him alone and stormed out of the classroom. So we stayed and prayed there in his classroom without him. We did that after every one of his classes for the next six or seven weeks. He pointedly ignored us, always leaving the classroom immediately upon dismissing the students.

But halfway through the semester, at the end of class one particular day, he didn't make his usual quick exit of the classroom after dismissing us. Rather, he walked over to our little prayer gathering and said, "My wife died yesterday. Your praying accomplished nothing."

One of the others in the group, not me, said in response, "Professor, we've been praying that God would take away your wife's suffering. God has answered that prayer." When he heard that, this big man broke down. "Would you continue to pray for me?" he asked. "I'm so angry at God that I just can't pray." We told him we would pray for him.

He never came to the point of joining our group, but by the end of the semester he would remain in the classroom and listen as we prayed for a few minutes after the close of each class. I hope God's love eventually erased all of the deep hurt and anger he obviously felt.

Meeting a Saint
Philemon 4-6

Many years ago I met a Roman Catholic priest in the U. S.-Mexico border town of Ojinaga, Mexico. His name was Alfonso Payan. The volunteer missionary group of which I was a part had begun flying medicine and other supplies into Ojinaga, and Father Payan met our plane as we landed on a dirt strip at the edge of town. He helped us unload the plane and drove us, and the supplies, into town. The very minute I met him, I thought he seemed a bit different from most folks, but I couldn't immediately put my finger on why.

Later that same day we were walking together around the main plaza in Ojinaga. We were trying to get to know each other utilizing rudimentary communications methods involving my limited Spanish, his broken English, and a lot of hand gestures on both our parts. At that point a beggar approached us. I'd seen hundreds like him and tried to ignore the man. But Father Payan struck up a conversation with him. I couldn't follow their many words, but a minute later they were comparing feet. Then the priest removed his shoes and socks and gave them to the beggar, who donned them and walked off. Father Payan, now barefooted, continued on with me. He resumed our conversation without comment about what had just taken place.

That was just the first of many times I observed this unassuming, diminutive priest do something unexpected and undeniably Christian. I got to know Father Payan well, following his ministry through two additional parishes in Chihuahua City. For more than twenty years he was friend, example, and mentor to me in the Christian faith.

From my Protestant perspective I believe that all followers of Jesus Christ can be termed "saints," but Father Payan was the first of only a handful of persons I've ever met in whom "sainthood" was obvious and overt. That "difference" which I'd noticed in the very first minute I met him was the glow of God's Holy Spirit, which so completely pervaded his life that it literally showed through. I've since learned to recognize that Spirit-filled nature in a few others, and I hope that someday others may see the same in me.

A Fresh Start
Lamentations 3:21-25

Bob and Marian, both active members of a church I pastored, had gotten a divorce. I never did know exactly why, and they never shared the reasons with me. After their divorce Bob had even moved halfway across the country, leaving Marian to raise their teenagers alone. But the kids missed their dad -- and he missed them. After one of them spent the summer with him, he decided to move back to El Paso, Texas so he could see more of them. This, of course, meant that Bob and Marian saw each other quite regularly. In fact, they both sang in the church choir, which meant sitting near one another on Wednesday evenings for choir practice, as well as on Sunday mornings.

One day, a year or so after he had returned to El Paso, Bob asked if he could talk to me. When I said, "Yes," he proceeded to ask me one of the stranger questions I've ever been asked as a preacher, and I've certainly been asked some very strange ones. His query was this: "Do you think God would allow me to have Marian back?" My response was, "Would Marian allow you to have her back?" "Oh, yes!" pastor, was his reply. "She and I have been talking a lot lately, and we'd really like to get back together. But some of our friends tell us we'd be committing an even worse sin than divorce if we re-married each other -- that we'd compound the wrong we've already done."

I didn't follow his logic, but rather than personally arguing the issue, I continued our dialogue by taking Bob through every Biblical text I knew on the subject of divorce -- assuring him that there was no Biblical prohibition against re-marriage to one's former spouse. I further assured him that I believed God would be pleased, not displeased, if he and Marian reunited.

So it was that, four years after their first marriage broke up, Bob and Marian stood before their friends, fellow church members, and God -- and reunited in a fresh covenant of Christian marriage. The two most excited and pleased people present were their teenage son and daughter, who had been instrumental in bringing their parents back together.

Not every story has a happy ending; not every shattered marriage can be restored. But sometimes, praise God, "Humpty Dumpty" can be put back together again.

Cold Feet?
Revelation 2:2-5

My wife, Fran, and I had been married for just a short time when I decided that we should do together what I had often done before solo -- to go tent camping in the mountains. Fran was raised a city girl, and she readily admitted her unfamiliarity with anything wild and untamed. Her words were, "I go where the cement grows." But notwithstanding, to please her husband, she agreed to accompany me on the venture.

We camped near Red River, New Mexico. I put up my little pup tent, we did some hiking together, and I fished in the nearby stream. Fran did a creditable job of making dinner over a small, open fire. But when it came time for sleep, I realized something was amiss. My tiny tent had been fine for just me, but the two of us simply couldn't both fit comfortably into it. Being newlyweds, we were more than willing to snuggle up very close, but that still wasn't enough. About six inches of my legs and feet stuck out no matter how hard we tried to creatively maneuver ourselves into the limited available space.

Shortly after nightfall it began to rain -- a cold, drizzling rain that lasted most of the night. My feet were repeatedly getting soaked, and I was becoming chilled. I finally gave up and climbed into the car to sleep. Fran, on the other hand, slept like a baby, warm and comfortable in the tent. In the morning, she was bright and chipper. "You know, this camping business is better than I expected," was her opening statement to me. I grumbled something back at her which was less than positive. The experienced camper wasn't having any fun, but the novice city girl was truly excited.

One of the many odd things I discovered as a pastor of churches is that, in the Christian faith, long experience is not always a good thing. New Christians are usually excited about and eager to share their faith with others. Those who've spent many years in the faith, and who ought to value their Christianity even more, are more often unwilling to share the joy and excitement of knowing Jesus than novice believers. It doesn't make logical sense, but it's the way things are. Maybe some of these long-term church-goers, like me after camping out at Red River, are suffering from cold feet.

New and Quite Different
II Corinthians 5:17-18

I attended my 35th high school class reunion. That was the first such reunion I'd ever attended, and I approached it with a mixture of both fear and anticipation.

To that point I had never before attended a class reunion -- because thirty-five years previously I was a very different person. I spent my teenage years on the edge of a big, decaying eastern U. S. city, Baltimore. I was a member of a "street gang" long before gang problems caught the attention of the American public at large. Even though I was a very bright student in school I was frequently suspended for misbehavior, some of it pretty serious in nature. Virtually all my teachers, and most of my fellow students, expected that I would grow up to be a "criminal mastermind." In fact, my graduating class voted me "Most Likely to Serve Time in Prison for a Felony." You might think that prior statement a joke. It wasn't.

Fortunately, while I was a sophomore in college, I had a roommate who shared the love of Jesus Christ with me. At first, I resented -- no, I really hated -- this young man's spouting of Bible verses at me. But even solid rocks can be worn down by the dripping of water on them, and my roommate's witnessing eventually served its purpose. In November 1966 I accepted Jesus Christ as my personal Savior and, slowly but surely, my life began to change.

The contemporary version of Dave Ring is a very different man than the high school "criminal wannabee" of teen years. When I finally got up the nerve to attend that 35th class reunion, I found that most of my high school acquaintances were, as probably could be expected, amazed to discover that I'd become a preacher. I'm living proof that Christ really can change a human life, that He can make a completely new man.

If you need to make a fresh start in life, whether you're 18 or 88, Jesus Christ can do for you what He has done for me -- He can re-make you into a new creature. Just ask Him – that's the first step.

Looking and Also Touching
Romans 8:20-21

I've always enjoyed God's great natural creation, including the many wild animals therein. And, unlike most folks who are satisfied to simply look at wild creatures, I like to reach out and touch them. I'm not as crazy as some of the outdoor adventurers who appear on television, but I've had my share of close encounters with wildlife. I've got several scars from beaks, teeth, and claws to show for my fascination with getting up close and personal with wild things who would rather I had left them undisturbed.

One of my earliest memories in this regard is of a ground squirrel that I chased into my great-aunt Lillie's root cellar one day. I closed the door, trapping the squirrel inside, and reached out to grab the little creature as he clung to one of the dirt walls. I caught him -- momentarily. But I let go quickly as he took a hunk out of one of my fingers with his sharp teeth. After that, I willingly opened the door and gladly let the squirrel escape.

The wound wasn't too severe, but I wasn't about to tell my parents what had happened. Even though I was only eight or nine years old at the time, I knew that squirrels sometimes carried the disease of rabies, and I didn't want to have to take those painful rabies shots. A friend of mine had been bitten by a skunk and had had to undergo those shots, so I definitely knew they weren't fun.

On the other hand, by not telling I knew that I risked developing the awful disease of rabies. For weeks afterward, long after the bite had healed, I worried that I would swell up and begin foaming at the mouth -- symptoms I'd heard were associated with rabies. I didn't know if I was infected or not, but I was definitely afraid to do anything about it. I never developed the disease, so I was fortunate -- lucky not to have come down with rabies from that squirrel's bite.

There are millions of people in our world today who are infected with the spiritual disease of sin. Sin is a truly terrible disease, for ultimately it's 100% fatal. But the good news is that the cure for sin is simple and painless. The Word of God, speaking about Jesus, says, "If we confess our sins, He is faithful and just and will forgive our sins and cleanse us from all unrighteousness."

Blatant Dishonesty
I John 1:9-10

While I was in seminary, studying for the ministry, money in our household was pretty slim. So when I saw an ad in the local paper for the U. S. Internal Revenue Service -- they were hiring part-time clerks at what seemed to be a pretty good hourly wage -- I applied. I got the job and began working a couple of shifts weekly at a giant IRS regional center in Chamblee, Georgia, just a few miles northeast of Atlanta.

Although I was only a lowly file clerk, I did get to glance, at least in passing, at a lot of tax papers. And I saw some amazing things. There were single individuals who claimed 99 dependents on their 1040 forms. I guess they stopped at 99 because the check box allowed for only two digits. There were families with $10,000 annual incomes who claimed $25,000 in charitable deductions on Schedule A. There were huge, well-known corporations which, through the judicious use of reams of paper, claimed they hadn't made a dime, despite revenues in the hundreds of millions of dollars. The papers I was pulling were for audits, and, frankly, I wasn't surprised that they were being audited.

My time as an IRS employee was short, and now more than four decades ago. What I learned there made me realize that, while most people I know are pretty solid folks, there are at least some in our society who are blatantly dishonest. And they're not even afraid of the dreaded IRS.

In our world sometimes dishonest people get away with shady dealings. And sometimes honest folks wind up bankrupt. Fortunately, the Word of God promises that He will even the score in the economy of eternity. "Vengeance is mine," says the Lord, "I will repay." God, who knows all things, will work it out. Our task as believers is to indiscriminately share God's love with all, both the good and the bad.

Enduring Tough Love
Matthew 5:44-47

I know that preachers, like Jesus, are supposed to love everybody. But I have to admit that my capacity for loving others has been strained to the max on more than one occasion. In particular, I recall some years back when a newly-retired lady moved into the community and church I was then serving. Her name was Charlotte, and she was a former high school English teacher.

Each Sunday morning from the date of her arrival onward, Charlotte would take copious notes while listening to my sermon message. Then, on Monday morning, she would come into my office and review with me all the things I had done wrong in that sermon -- the grammatical errors I'd made, the times I'd scratched my nose while in front of a couple of hundred people, the unwarranted pauses while trying to get my notes in order for the next point to be made.

It became a routine, one that I dreaded. Every Monday about 10 AM Charlotte would show up with her clipboard and critique my sermon, meticulously highlighting all its flaws. Of course, she had the best of intentions; she always reminded me that her purpose was to make her pastor a better preacher. I believed her, but that didn't make it any easier to be reminded of all my Sunday errors and mistakes every Monday morning.

That weekly exercise lasted for about two years, and the result was this: Charlotte's critiques accomplished their purpose. Gradually my grammar improved, my focus upon the audience was sharpened, my ability to deliver a clear, flowing message was enhanced. When I left that church, Charlotte was one of the many people I thanked for helping me to become a more effective preacher.

On the other hand, I'm genuinely glad not to have had a "Charlotte" in any of my other congregations. I don't know if I could have stood much more of such intense weekly reviews of my preaching, regardless of the positive intent thereof.

In the book of Revelation, chapter 3 and verse 19, God says to the Church, "those whom I love I reprove and chasten." It's always hard to receive censure, but when it's offered in love -- as God's reproof always is -- criticism can help us to grow and improve.

Godly Risk-taking
Mark 10:28-30

I was talking with a successful Christian businessman who belonged to the church I was then serving. In the course of our conversation, he asked about our mutual congregation's financial circumstances, so I told him that, as usual, we were struggling. His response was essentially this, "I'd like to help, but all of my money is tied up in my business. I'm sure God wouldn't expect me to risk my business for the Church." I smiled, bit my tongue, and said no more to him on the subject.

What I really wanted to say to him -- what I should have said -- was this: "Yes, God really does expect you to risk your business for His Church. If you truly believe that Jesus is Lord of this earth, there should be absolutely no doubt in your mind that you can and should make every last resource you have available to God in support of His Kingdom. The Word of God clearly and repeatedly promises that He will reward you many times over for everything you invest in His work."

Yes, I could have said that. I should have said that. But I didn't, because I also believe I know what His reaction would have been. "O Lord, our preacher's gone off the deep end. He's become a fanatic!"

Imagine -- actually believing what God promises in His Holy Word. I suppose that does qualify as fanaticism in today's post-modern, post-Christian world. But God hasn't changed, nor has God's ability to fulfill his promises in trustworthy and tangible ways.

Asking for Money
I Corinthians 16:1-2

Preachers are exposed to a lot of "sentimental" stories over and over again. In today's world, with the ubiquity of the internet, there are literally thousands of cute, sweet tales that make the rounds of cyberspace. I have dozens of friends and fellow church members who routinely "forward" such stories to me, often with comments like, "You simply have to read this!" What they don't realize is that, in most cases, I've already received the same tale ten or twelve times previously. In addition, folks often mail me paper copies they've printed out and want to make sure I see -- more copies of those same stories.

So it is that I had heard this little story maybe a hundred times: One man was complaining about how much money his son at college was costing him -- repeatedly calling and asking for additional funds for clothes, cars, tuition, etc. The second man, who listened to the complaint, replied, "My son hasn't asked me for a dime in over a year. But I sure wish I could spend some money on him." To which the first man responded, "A son who doesn't ask for money? That's a real blessing!" But the second ended the conversation with these words: "No, it's not. My son died last year."

Like so many similar stories, I'd heard that sentimental little tale many times. But then one of my young adult sons, while in college, almost died. For days his life hung in the balance while his mother and I prayed for his recovery. Fortunately, our son survived. And for some years thereafter he continued to ask me for money -- often more money than I thought was reasonable. But I held my tongue and wrote the checks, silently thanking God that I had both means and opportunity to support him.

People often grumble to me, "I resent that the church is always asking for money." My response to that complaint is simple: "Churches that are alive ask for money. Dead churches don't."

Remember Y2K?
Mark 13:32-35

As the end of the year 1999 approached there was a man, attending the church I then served, who predicted doom and gloom and cataclysm of every kind. According to this individual the turnover of the calendar to "Y2K," as it was then called, would mark the start of years of tribulation to come. He stockpiled food, water and fuel for himself and his family, as well as buying a gasoline-powered generator in anticipation of the failure of publicly-distributed power. And he urged everyone he knew to do the same, me included.

This man was well-versed in Biblical knowledge, so he underwrote all of his dire admonitions with Bible references, principally from the Book of Revelation. For months he regularly filled my mailbox with tracts and treatises on the coming Y2K disaster, and became increasingly frustrated with me as I failed to heed his many warnings. As the dreaded date approached, he grew genuinely angry at my repeated refusals to use my position of pastoral leadership to pass on his doom-filled predictions.

When January 1, 2000 dawned a normal day the world over, you might think that this man would have admitted his foolishness. Frankly, I was personally hoping that he would call and apologize, simply and forthrightly stating, "I was wrong." Instead he moved his predictions forward a few months, claiming that the predicted cataclysms would begin on September 9, 2000. When that day, too, passed without notable problems, he then updated his predictions to Jan. 1, 2001. That third date also has long since passed, and this world is still humming along. But as far as I'm aware this man is yet predicting doom and gloom on the near horizon, though his latest prognostications have no specific dates associated therewith.

What is amazing to me is that there are quite a few folks who still believe what this man has to say. I suppose there are some people who so much want to see our world in chaos that they'll believe anyone who predicts bad times upcoming, regardless of how often that person has missed the mark in the past.

Predicting the end of the world is way beyond me. That's God's territory, and I'm careful to leave it to him. Rather, I believe in focusing on what God has given me to face today. And in that regard, I commend to you the words of Psalm 118, verse 24: "This is the day which the Lord has made; we will rejoice and be glad in it."

The Gambler and the Pastor
John 19:23-24

On the way out of the church door one Sunday morning Kitty told me she wouldn't see me the following Sunday. She said, "I'll be out of town; I'm heading to Laughlin, Nevada." I said, "Oh, are you going there to gamble?" She replied, "Yep!" To which I jokingly responded, "You know, you'll need to tithe your winnings."

Two Sundays later, on the way out of church, I again saw Kitty. So I asked, "Did you win in Laughlin?" She said, "Yep, I sure did. I won $10,000." I joked with her again: "Wow! Remember, you need to tithe that." She immediately reached into her purse and handed me a check, already made out to the church, in the amount of $2,000. "I already decided to double-tithe my winnings," she said with a smile.

I'm glad Kitty made that helpful choice for her church. I certainly don't believe that God allowed her to win just because she was prepared to tithe. Gambling is merely taking a chance with one's money, no more and no less.

Kitty was one of the many "characters" I met over the decades I served as a pastor. Despite being a little rough around the edges, Kitty's heart was basically in the right place. Certainly, I'm not an advocate for gambling. But had I jumped on her with both feet about it when she first told me she was headed for Laughlin, we would both have missed an opportunity. God had something for me to learn about Kitty, and for Kitty to learn about giving. I'm glad He gave us both a tale to tell for many years to come.

Saying What You Really Mean
Psalm 19:13-14

Within days after I arrived at the first church which I ever served as senior pastor, Jim, the chairman of the personnel committee, stopped in to see me. He told me that he had been chairman of that particular committee for 12 years in a row, that he was tired of so serving, and that he hoped I would find someone else to take the position as soon as possible. I told him I would try. Within a couple of months, I found another member of the congregation who agreed to take over that important job, thus relieving Jim of the responsibility.

Shortly thereafter, I had three or four different individuals stop me in the church halls to say, "Jim is really upset that you replaced him as chairman of the personnel committee." I was dumbfounded -- I thought he would be pleased that I'd gotten him off the hook.

I talked with these friends of Jim's further, and what I discovered was this: Jim really didn't want me to find someone else to do that job. Rather, he'd brought the subject up hoping that I, as several pastors before me had done, would beg him to please stay on for a little while longer. He wanted to be reminded of how important his position was, to be told how no one else could fill his shoes, etc. When I took his request at face value and actually found someone to replace him, he was caught completely off guard.

That was one of the early lessons I learned in church politics. Even in the house of God, although it ought not to be, people don't always say what they mean nor mean what they say.

From Jesus' longest recorded message in the Bible, the Sermon on the Mount, one of my favorite verses is this: "Let your 'yes' be yes and your 'no' be no. Anything more than this comes from the evil one." In other words, say just what you mean and mean exactly what you say. Don't play games with people; rather tell it like it really is.

A Tireless Encourager
II Corinthians 13:11

Charlotte was East End United Methodist Church's "sunshine person." Although a shut-in herself, she had a list of every member of the church, along with their birthdays, and she made sure to call each one on their special day. She also had a list of all the other shut-ins of the church's extended family, and of the widows, and of others who needed some sort of special support. On the anniversary of the death of a spouse or child, she'd call with an encouraging word to the surviving family members. She checked in with the church office every morning to ask for a list of the sick, so she could call them and cheer them up.

Just to pick up the phone and hear Charlotte's voice on the other end was a day-brightener. She "oozed" good cheer with every word she spoke. From the first day I arrived at that church onward, Charlotte was my instant "phone pal."

I'd been the associate pastor at East End for about three months when, in the midst of one of my almost daily conversations with her, a new thought came to me. "Charlotte," I said, "I've talked to you almost every day since I arrived here, but I've yet to meet you in person. I'd love to drop by and see you." Her response was, "Preacher, you've got a lot of other folks you need to see who are in greater need than I am. You go visit them first. It's not necessary that you come to see me."

A couple more months passed, and I again broached the subject of a visit with Charlotte. "Sure, you can come if you really want to. But I warn you, my house is a mess," she responded. I scheduled the visit, and when I got to her house, sure enough, it really was a mess. Charlotte met me at the door in her wheelchair. She stuck out her bony right hand, and I could readily see the many deformations of the fingers from severe arthritis. She was hunched over in the chair in that painful posture which, in older women especially, is a sure indicator of advanced osteoporosis. Her table was virtually a drugstore in itself -- she must have been taking twelve to fifteen different prescription medications.

Most of the members of that congregation, whom Charlotte regularly called, always bringing good cheer, had no idea of what the "sunshine person" who regularly contacted them was herself facing. The pain and problems in her body never diminished the joy of Charlotte's spirit. To the very day God called her home, she was still spreading good cheer to others via the telephone.

Perseverance
Joshua 1:7-9

More than four decades and nearly 100 excess pounds ago, I used to run cross-country for my high school. I remember when fall practice started -- while it was still hot summer outdoors. The coach set a goal that we should each run six miles in 36 minutes. I thought he was absolutely crazy, and so did all of my teammates. The first day that we tried to run six miles, most of us stopped running after the first mile or two and just walked the rest of the way. But after about two weeks of daily practice I and most of the others were running the full six miles -- in about forty-five minutes.

By the end of the fourth week of practice the day came when I actually clocked in at just a few seconds under 36 minutes for six full miles of running. I was ecstatic; I felt like I'd just won an Olympic gold medal. The coach's response was less approving than I'd expected. He simply said, "Very good, Dave. From now on your goal will be to run it in 32 minutes."

The most amazing part of this story is that I didn't complain about the coach's unreasonable demand, nor quit the team in disgust. Instead, I set my sights on meeting this higher goal -- and before the season was over, six miles in 32 minutes was actually achieved. It wasn't easy, but I was determined to be a winner in that sport.

Several times in the New Testament of the Holy Bible, the apostle Paul reminds those who would claim to be Christians that a life of faith in Jesus can be compared to a long-distance foot race. The goal -- the prize – isn't a gold medal, but life eternal with God. The most important thing, says Paul, is to keep running. Don't tire out, don't drop out, don't give up. Keep your eyes fixed on Jesus, and you'll ultimately be rewarded with that imperishable prize.

Remembering God's Word
Deuteronomy 11:18-19

When my oldest child, named Dave after his dad, was 10 years old, he won a Bible-memory competition called "Bible Bowl" in El Paso, Texas. This qualified him to be invited to the "national finals" of the Bible Bowl in Fort Worth, Texas. I traveled with him to this competition, which was held in a large church in Richland Hills. There were about 150 contestants from all over the United States, including a team of about 20 from a well-known non-denominational church in Atlanta, Georgia who looked, in Christian terms at least, really tough.

The competition consisted of a variety of different Bible knowledge exercises and took all weekend to complete. When it was finished, I was proud that my son placed sixth out of everyone present. Two interesting characteristics of the five children, two boys and three girls, who placed ahead of Dave were this: every one of them was a Korean-American, and every one of them had memorized the entire Bible from cover to cover. Yes, that's right. These children had memorized the entire Bible, from Genesis 1:1 to Revelation 22:21. They knew every word of God's word by heart.

Can you imagine the time, effort, and discipline it must have taken for a child of ten or eleven to memorize the entire Bible? I mean, it's over a thousand pages in most editions, and most of us have trouble remembering even the 23rd Psalm. You probably think it's an impossible task to memorize the whole Bible, and I might have agreed with you -- until I met these Korean-American children. They had done it.

There are numerous times in the Bible when God Himself encourages us to learn His Holy Word -- and to store it up in our hearts. Ever since that Bible Bowl weekend I've tried to be more intentional, and more disciplined, about learning the Bible. I don't yet have it all memorized and probably never will. But I'm trying to learn all I can, and I encourage you to do the same.

Salvation Delayed
Lamentations 2:11

I could tell, from the very first time I met him, that Larry wasn't a happy man. Although he attended church faithfully, virtually every Sunday morning, he always arrived late, with a frown on his face, and more than once departed with tears running down his cheeks. Since I believe that being a part of God's church is supposed to uplift and encourage others, I was concerned by Larry's unrelenting sadness. Frankly, I hoped I wasn't causing any of it.

One Sunday as he was leaving, I asked Larry if he could stay and talk for a few minutes. After the rest of the congregation had dispersed, I said, "Larry, you always seem sadder when you leave church than when you arrive. I hope I'm not depressing you with my sermons." He responded with a half-smile. "No, preacher, it's not you. The reason I'm so sad is because I have to attend church by myself. And I know what the rest of my family is missing."

After a few further prompting remarks from me, Larry poured out the rest of his story: "Preacher," he said, "I didn't come to know the Lord until I was 66 years old. My wife and I raised three sons. They're all grown now, and I'm a widower. All three of my boys, with their wives and families, still live here in this neighborhood. So every Sunday morning, I stop by each of their houses on the way to church. I always invite them to come with me, but they blow me off. They all say, dad, you waited until you were 66 years old to get religion. We've got lots of time left. Maybe someday we'll come to church with you, but not now."

As a pastor, I know that Larry's story is one that could be similarly told by thousands of other older folks. Too many younger people seem to take the attitude that "God can wait till later. I've got too many other priorities in my life right now to worry about Him." But sometimes God comes calling earlier than expected. When I'm asked to conduct a funeral for an unchurched 30-year-old who tragically left this earth in a car crash, I wonder. Did they really know the Lord, or were they just playing the odds, waiting until later in life to seek faith?

Encouragement in an Unlikely Location
Philippians 4:4-5

As a pastor, one of the most frequent tasks I've had to perform and, frankly, one of my least favored, is visiting the sick in hospitals. A hospital is a tough place to visit, it's an even tougher place to be cheerful in, and it's tougher still to try to offer a word of cheer, comfort, or maybe even encouragement, to a hospital patient. Hospital patients are usually confined to bed, drugged and/or nauseous, and often in pain. Almost no one is at their best, or anywhere near thereto, while a hospital patient. Nonetheless, I've made hundreds of hospital visits every year, and I always try to offer an uplift to everyone I visit.

One particular hospital visit that sticks in my mind, even though it occurred decades ago, was when I stepped into the room of a 77-year-old man who was receiving chemotherapy for the dreaded disease of cancer. As I entered, I quickly observed that he was connected up to an array of tubes and wires in arms, nose, bladder and other places -- a nasty sight to put it bluntly. He was sort of half-propped-up in bed, an awkward position that had to be very uncomfortable. So I quickly steeled myself, mentally, for what I expected would be a difficult experience.

But not so. This wasn't at all like most of the hospital calls I've made. Before I could say so much as "hello," this man had his one free arm out, reaching for a firm handshake, smiling broadly. And before I could ask the standard "How are you feeling?" question, he was asking me how I was. Then, he proceeded to ask all kinds of other questions -- about me, my job, my family, our church -- just as casually and cheerfully as though we were meeting somewhere at an outdoor picnic. When I briefly mentioned a personal problem, he spoke words of encouragement.

After a while, though, I couldn't resist stopping him. "Whoa! Wait a minute!" I said. "You're the sick person. I came here to find out how you are, and to try to cheer you up." His reply was worth framing in gold letters. What he said was simply this: "I'm already cheerful. I'm a Christian!"

77 years old, fighting cancer, confined to a hospital bed, receiving chemotherapy, tubes and wires turning him into a pincushion. And yet, "I'm already cheerful! I'm a Christian!"

What a clear, simple testimony to the unsearchable riches of God. "I'm already cheerful! I'm a Christian!"

Positively Peculiar
I Peter 2:9-10

I was in Albuquerque, New Mexico to visit one of my sons for a day, and I stopped into a barbershop for a haircut. I waited my turn, and when a chair opened up, I was invited to sit down. After asking how I wanted my hair to cut the barber, as most do, began to engage me in small talk. Was I from Albuquerque? No, but I used to live there. What did I think of the present dry spell? I was hoping and praying for rain. What was my opinion of the latest sex scandal coming out of Washington? I didn't like it, but it's only what we've come to expect from our politicians. Had I ever been to the balloon fiesta in the fall there? Yes, I'd been to quite a few such. What did I do for a living? I'm a Christian minister -- a pastor.

The conversation abruptly stopped. The barber laid his scissors and comb aside. He said, "I don't like to cut preachers' hair. I don't like preachers." I asked him why but received not a word of reply. For a minute, I thought he wasn't going to finish my haircut. But he finally picked his tools back up and continued his work. The rest of the haircut was endured in stony silence. He didn't even say "thank you" when I paid him -- including a reasonable tip.

That's not, by any means, the only time I've had someone to act strangely upon learning what my vocation is. I can talk with men, or women, about almost any casual subject -- sports, politics, the weather, television, movies, the stock market. The conversation will be normal, natural, easy -- I can hold my own in dialogue with a wide variety of people.

But let them discover that I'm a minister, and the whole situation changes. Conversation is no longer natural. People choose their words more slowly, more carefully. Or they begin to explain their church involvement, or the lack thereof, even though it means changing the subject completely. Often, they apologize for their previous rough language. Slowly but surely, they move away. Many folks just aren't comfortable being around such a peculiar creature as a pastor.

The Word of God states that all Christians, not just pastors, are supposed to be a "peculiar people." And that peculiarity should attract, not repel non-believers. Why? Because, as Jesus taught, believers in Him are supposed to be recognizable by their obvious love -- for one another and for all the precious people whom God has lovingly created.

Differently Born Again
Isaiah 66:7-9

As the father of two natural children and one adopted child, I have twice witnessed the miracle of human birth. Those two experiences were unique and distinct, each from the other.

When Dave, our first, was ready to be born, my wife's labor began in the wee hours of the morning. We headed for the big-city hospital around dawn. Our obstetrician was out-of-town, so his partner, whom we had never before met, was called to oversee the delivery. Many hours later, although Fran was tiring, there was little progress. A drug was administered to strengthen her labors. It didn't help. Then, the baby's umbilical cord became compressed against the walls of her body, and the fetal monitor showed his heart rate dip dangerously. The doctor carefully repositioned the baby, but not without a lot of pain for Fran. There was still no real progress. Finally, the obstetrician decided a Caesarean section should be performed.

Another hour passed -- there was no anesthesiologist available in the hospital to give her the necessary medication so that a C-section could be done. Almost in desperation at this point, the doctor was forced to perform a high risk, high-forceps type of delivery. Fifteen hours after her labor commenced, eleven hours after we arrived at the hospital, a very tired and sore mother, frayed and fatigued father, and a worried doctor welcomed a healthy, completely normal seven pound boy into the world.

Because of this myriad of difficulties with Dave's birth, when the time came, three years later, for our second son Jonathan to be delivered, we were more than a little worried. By then we were living in the tiny, isolated west Texas town of Alpine, with only a small, minimally equipped hospital and a single obstetrician in the entire region. We seriously considered having Fran go to a larger city for the delivery. But our doctor reassured us concerning the hospital's staff and equipment and promised faithfully that he would not leave town anytime close to her due date.

Once again, Fran's labors began in the wee hours of the morning and, once again, we arrived at the hospital just around sunrise. "Here we go again," I thought, beginning to imagine all sorts of negative possibilities. But that was where the similarities ended. The hospital staff was efficient and professional, the labor intense but brief, and in slightly less than five hours total, it was over. The end result was identical -- a healthy, normal, seven- pound boy, a delightful second blessing to his proud parents.

Jesus, when asked about entry into the Kingdom of God, said these words: "You must be born again." Spiritual rebirth, like ordinary human birth, is unique and distinct unto every person who seeks it. Some folks who seek it experience major, overnight change in everything about their lives. Others gradually come into the Kingdom over a long period of slow but steady reformation by God. There's no one pattern, no single prescription. But the wonderful end is always the same: eternal life, by the grace of God.

Bitten by Sin
Jonah 1:11-17

I was out fishing in the Gulf of Mexico. My friend Mike and I had anchored his boat in a spot about six miles offshore near a sunken shrimp boat. The old sunken boat should provide shelter for fish of various kinds and sizes, so we expected it to be a good location to put out our lines. Sure enough, we had good luck. We were soon catching all sorts of fish, mostly those we simply threw back -- but also a few larger speckled trout that we put on ice for later cooking and eating.

Mike had also brought along a heavy-duty pole and line rigged for shark fishing. I'd never before deliberately fished for sharks, but with the increasing numbers of them reported in the Gulf, plus the alarming increase in the incidence of shark bites, I figured it wouldn't hurt to remove a few of them from the water. Maybe we'd catch a really big one -- that should be fun.

We caught four relatively small sharks that day. But the strange thing I discovered about shark fishing is that it really isn't fun at all. Once you catch a shark, you almost wish you hadn't. When a shark is brought out of the water, it instantly becomes a whirling flurry of flashing teeth. Getting the hook out of a shark's mouth is a lost cause. Anything within its flopping, squirming, wriggling reach is going to be bitten -- wood, metal, plastic, fiberglass, flesh. And a shark doesn't cease biting until it's completely dead. The shark fishing fun I had expected to have was transformed into a lot of hard work, punctuated by more than one moment of sheer terror. And those were just smaller sharks.

My shark fishing experience clearly reminded me of the reality of sin, and its consequences, in human life. Considered from the outside, sin often seems exciting, attractive, even fun. But once you're hooked -- caught in the cycle of sin – it's a very different experience. Sins have consequences -- they turn around and bite us. Sin hurts. How often we wish we hadn't gotten involved in sin in the first place! But thank God, there's a ready remedy for sin -- the forgiveness of God expressed in the sacrifice of Jesus Christ for human sin.

Failure Need Not Be Forever
Psalm 51:1-2

It's not often that a preacher is at a loss for words, but I recall one time when I was actually stunned into silence. It happened midway through my career as a pastor. I hadn't been at that particular church very long -- just a few weeks. It was a Wednesday night and chancel choir practice time. I knew that the choir was planning to hold a birthday party for its director after practice that evening. What I didn't know, nor expect, was the six-foot-tall cake that was wheeled into the church's choir room promptly at 8 PM -- and the young woman who jumped out of that cake and began to perform a sexually-explicit dance and strip-tease right then and there, before God and everybody.

I was sitting in the back row of the choir with the other men who sang bass. The man next to me carefully observed my reaction to the unfolding display. Then he asked, "Well, what do you think of us, preacher?" I was simply too shocked to respond. I just sat there dumbfounded. Finally, literally minutes later, I found the words I needed to say, "I think I have a lot of work to do here."

I wish I could say that I succeeded in transforming the attitudes and behaviors of that congregation to something less worldly, more honoring of a holy and righteous God. But I didn't. That short pastorate, just one year in length, was the worst failure of my four decades of ministry for the Lord Jesus Christ.

Everyone fails at one time or another. I've heard that Thomas Edison, who invented the electric light bulb, failed over 5,000 times in the effort before he finally found a successful combination of metals and other elements that could produce a lasting, reliable source of light. Edison also considered every failure a learning experience. Afterwards, Edison said he knew 5,000 ways not to make a good light bulb.

Failure is only final if we allow it to be so. But if we pick ourselves up from our failures and move forward, failure can be a learning experience, something positive. We all fail. But we don't have to stay failures.

From a spiritual standpoint all humans are sinners -- failures at attaining the righteousness of God. But we don't have to stay that way. All we need do is ask, and God will forgive our sins and grant us a fresh, new start.

Gender-Specific Perception
Matthew 19:4-5

In every congregation that I served as pastor, I rapidly got used to women coming up to me at the close of worship to say, "Pastor, it was too hot in the sanctuary today" or, alternatively, "Pastor, it was too cold in the sanctuary today." Sometimes these comments would be genuinely humorous, as when two women who sat next to each other brought the opposite concern: One said it was too hot and the other too cold. I had hundreds of such complaints brought to me over several decades, and I gradually learned that they usually had little or nothing to do with the actual temperature in the sanctuary. Women simply have very sensitive internal thermostats, and no two are set to exactly the same comfort level.

Interestingly, in nine different church buildings and over 35-plus years of time, I never had a single man raise the temperature concern. Men seem to be largely insensitive to temperature – as long as it isn't freezing or boiling, they can live with any given ambience.

On the other hand, men in church have their idiosyncrasies as well. Not in as great of numbers overall, but I've certainly had, over my years of ministry, fifty or more men complain about their inability to hear the sermon. Although I know that I have a strong voice and most of the churches I served have had good sound systems, some men, especially those who choose to sit on the back pew, are unable to adequately hear my preaching. Just as with the women regarding temperature, I've further come to understand that the problem is only rarely related to the actual volume of sound. Men, especially older men, tend to gradually lose their hearing – and are often too vain to admit it.

Just as I never had a man to gripe about temperature, I've not yet ever had a woman to grumble about inability to hear in church. Some issues are clearly sex-specific. All of the foregoing boils down to the simple fact that men and women are different.

In the first chapter of the Holy Bible, Genesis 1, verse 26, God's word says this: "So God created humankind in His image, in the image of God He created them, male and female He created them." All of us, both male and female, are lovingly made in God's own image. We're different in many ways, but we all share this: God has made us, each and all, very much like Him. What a blessing that is!

Just a Gigolo
Matthew 9:11-12

John, when I first met him, was a pretty strange case. He'd been a high school dropout at 15 and, in the twenty years since, had never really held a job. At 35 his three preoccupations, in order, were drums, drinking, and women. He fancied himself becoming a drummer in a standout rock band, although he'd drifted into and out of several groups over the years without making much of an impression on anyone. He spent most of his days drinking, his nights banging on drums in his apartment -- much to his neighbors' chagrin. The amazing part of John's life was that he didn't lack for money – several women kept him well-financed. I'd heard that such men existed, but until John I'd never met one before. He was a bona-fide male gigolo.

Why he drifted into the Sunday night Bible study at the church I then pastored, I never did clearly know. Probably the simplest way to say it is that God sent him. He was a big guy, physically, and he wasn't afraid to speak up. He immediately joined in our Bible discussions although he knew virtually nothing about the Bible. But his right-off-the-street perspective added an interestingly fresh flavor to our discourse. In the first hour that he was there, I heard more honest, down-to-earth sharing about God, and faith, and Jesus than I'd heard from that group in many weeks before.

John continued to attend the Bible study for several weeks thereafter, and when it came time for that group's spring retreat weekend at a camp 12 miles out of town, he was among the first to sign up. As the weekend unfolded and drew toward a close, everyone there knew that God was working on John's heart. We were in the process of closing the Sunday afternoon session when, although there was no formal altar call, John asked, "Could I be baptized -- right here, right now?" Of course, the answer was yes.

I left that church as pastor shortly thereafter, so I lost touch with John. When I last saw him, he was making slow but steady progress, moving from twenty years of sinful habits into a new and more positive lifestyle. John's, like that of most folks I encounter, wasn't an overnight conversion. But he was definitely to the right road, headed toward salvation.

Strangers and Sojourners
Hebrews 11:13-16

As a pastor one of the groups of people with whom I had decades of frequent contact, but which the ordinary person rarely encounters, is transients. Every church that I served, in big cities and small towns -- in Texas, New Mexico, Tennessee, Georgia, even in faraway Guatemala – was petitioned by numerous transients seeking aid. The church I served for five years in Big Spring, Texas was the most frequently tapped of all my pastorates; that church regularly dealt with 25 to 50 transients weekly. (Another commonly-used term for many of these same persons is "the homeless.")

Early in my ministry I tried to learn about transients – who they are and why they are – and to attempt, if possible, to do more than provide them a few dollars or a sack lunch and send them on their way. What I discovered was disheartening. Some transients are mentally ill; a few are temporarily down on their luck. But the majority of them are entrenched in lifestyles which, when I met them, they weren't interested in changing.

When I tried to probe farther, I determined that many transients had embarked upon a series of bad choices early in life – dropping out of school, becoming alcohol and/or drug addicted, engaging in aberrant sexual behaviors, breaking the laws of the land. Thus they were often living out, and suffering, the consequences of those previous choices. Their problems were deep and systemic and, frankly, beyond the capacity of the average local church pastor to interrupt.

Among the blessings that God, our Creator, has provided to humanity is freedom of choice. To some, that freedom truly is a blessing. They make good choices, which lead to better choices, which lead to still better choices. But for others what was intended as a blessing becomes a curse. They make bad choices, which lead to worse choices, which lead to still worse choices.

All human choices have consequences. Good choices produce positive consequences. Bad choices bring about negative outcomes. God gives us true freedom of choice. But if we ask Him, God will provide us helpful advice as to which choices are good, and which are not, before we have to experience the consequences. Reading God's written Word, the Bible, is a good place to start for finding such useful advice.

A Contagion of Attitude
Ezra 6:22

Something uniquely "21st century" happened to me. But it wasn't a good thing. My computer caught a virus. A friend of mine's e-mail, unbeknownst to him, was infected. When I received and read a message from him to me, my computer picked up the virus. I immediately noticed that something was wrong, as my computer's performance slowed down markedly. Fortunately, later that same day my friend found out about what had happened and sent me instructions on how to cure this particular virus. It took three doses of the necessary cyber-medicine, but my computer's speed was ultimately restored. After that incident I bought a high-end virus-protection subscription for my machine.

Isn't it interesting how, over the most recent couple of decades, we've taken the vocabulary from a totally different realm of human experience -- health and medicine – and employed it to explain a new portion of our lives -- the arena of computers and the internet? The strange part of this vocabulary shift is that it fits and fits well. Just as humans can pick up viruses from the air we breathe, the water we drink and the food we eat, computers can pick up viruses from the electrical impulses which power and nourish them. Just as catching a virus slows us down and makes us sick, so a computer's performance can be slowed and degraded by a virus. And just as we need medicine to rid our bodies of viral infections, computers need "cyber pills" – antivirus software -- to help rid themselves of viral infestations.

Viruses are highly contagious to both human bodies and modern-day computers. Something else which is also highly contagious, among humans at least, is attitude. A bad attitude on the part of one person -- in the workplace, for example -- can rapidly infect everyone else they come in contact with, until a whole group's day is ruined. Fortunately, good attitudes are equally infectious. Someone who comes into work with a smile and a good word for those around him or her will lift everyone's day -- until the whole crew is feeling better.

The word of God, on the subject of attitude, says that as a person thinks in his or her heart, so is he/she. I encourage you to spread a positive attitude -- from your heart to that of others around you.

Unprepared to Preach
2 Timothy 4:1-2

During the years that I was a seminary student, studying to become a preacher, my wife and I took a weekend off to visit my parents on the Gulf Coast of Mississippi. While there, on Sunday morning we attended church. On the way out of church after the service, the pastor, an older man named Bill, shook hands with us. He asked who we were. I responded that I was Dave Ring, visiting from Atlanta. "What do you do in that big city?" he further queried. "I'm a seminary student." The pastor got excited. "Great! You can preach our evening worship service tonight." I thanked him for the offer, but said, "Sorry, but no. We're only here for the weekend, leaving tomorrow morning, and I intend to get in some fishing this afternoon. I don't have time to prepare a sermon."

As planned, I went fishing that afternoon. I'd gotten back to my folks' house and was taking a shower. Fran came to the bathroom door and shouted through it, "Dave, that pastor's here. He insists you're going to preach at his church tonight!" Next thing I knew he was talking to me through the door. "You'd better hurry up. It's 6:15, and the service starts at 7." "But I don't want to preach tonight; I'm not prepared." "That's OK. Just be at church in 45 minutes. If you don't come, there won't be any preaching!"

I'd never before run into such a pushy preacher, but I understood that, like it or not, I was on the hook. So I hurriedly dressed, grabbed my Bible, and hurried off with Fran to the evening service. There were about 75 people present and, just as he'd promised, Pastor Bill welcomed me and introduced me to the congregation as guest preacher for the evening. I opened my Bible and brought a message that was totally impromptu. I don't remember anything of what I said, but it must have been reasonably relevant, as everyone complimented me afterward on the message.

As we were leaving that evening, Pastor Bill thanked me, and added: "If God has really called you to be a preacher, you need to always be ready to preach. Don't ever say no." I didn't much appreciate his admonition at the time, but I've since learned that he was on target. A preacher needs to be ever ready and always willing to speak the Word of God. It's both a wonderful privilege and an awesome responsibility to be called by God to preach His Holy Word.

The Stellar Panorama
Matthew 2:1-2

Several times in my life thus far I've had the privilege of traveling across the equator into the southern hemisphere of our earth. I've been to both Australia and New Zealand as well as to several South American nations. And while in those "down under" lands, my "preacher eyes" noted one particular thing that is markedly different from my home in the USA. When I gazed up at the night sky there really wasn't much to see from the southern hemisphere. About the only constellation that's notable is the Southern Cross. But otherwise there are relatively few visible stars.

Later I checked this personal observation with a friend of mine who is an astronomer at the McDonald Observatory in Ft. Davis, Texas, and he confirmed what I'd noticed. There are only about 1/4 as many stars visible to the naked eye from the southern hemisphere of our earth as there are to us who live in the northern half of our planet. The well-known line to the song, "The stars at night are big and bright, deep in the heart of Texas" could probably never have been conceived anywhere south of the equator.

Way back in the first book of the Bible, Genesis, the 15th chapter, there's a wonderfully appealing story of an encounter between Almighty God and Abraham, the patriarch of three of the world's major faiths. God invited Abraham to look up at the stars of the night sky and try to count them. Then He promised Abraham that his descendants – all of whom would be God's special peoples -- would be as many as that stellar panorama.

I looked at a globe to check and, sure enough, wanderer Abraham's several homelands – countries which are today termed Turkey, Iran, Iraq and/or Azerbaijan -- are all in the northern hemisphere of our earth. So the panorama of stars Abraham saw was truly impressive.

Moreover, modern science tells us that the number of stars we can see with the naked eye, either from our own northern half of the earth or much farther to the south, is only a tiny fraction of all the trillions that are there. The number of stars is nearly infinite – and so also is the loving promise of God to the many, many, many descendants of our spiritual father, Abraham.

Addressing Hunger
Luke 9:12-17

The three Ring children, being a pastor's kids, learned early to deal with a minor problem that most church-going children don't face. That problem was Sunday lunch. Although I was always very solicitous of the congregations I served to make sure they got out of worship in time to make the line at Luby's Cafeteria or whatever other eating place they might choose, with all of the loose ends that needed to be tied up before I could leave church I didn't get home until 1:00 or 1:30 PM most Sundays. That meant that my kids got pretty hungry waiting for dad to make it home so the family could enjoy Sunday lunch together.

Once a month, however, these preacher's kids discovered a compensating mechanism that isn't available to most other children. On Communion Sundays, when they were small, my kids would sneak back into the church kitchen of at least two of the churches I served and finish off the leftover communion elements -- bread and grape juice. I'll never forget seeing one of them – I won't say which to protect them from embarrassment – at about age four, with grape juice smeared all over the face, wolfing down a loaf of communion bread while saying, "This Body of Christ sure do taste good!"

Those of you who have a "high church" mindset may not find that story all that amusing, and I certainly can understand if you feel that way. A few of you might even consider children helping themselves to leftover Communion elements as sacrilege.

The story does have a redeeming feature, however. It highlights a very basic issue in our world – that of hunger. Hungry people need to eat in order to live. Hungry children will eat leftover Communion bread; hungry disciples of Jesus, as recorded in the Holy Bible, will pick and eat field corn -- even on the Sabbath.

Relatively few of us in the USA face severe hunger on a daily basis, and for that we can heartily thank God. But there are certainly some in need in our local area, and those of us who have enough obviously need to share our bounty. And there are many beyond this fortunate nation who are chronically malnourished.

Many charities, sacred and secular, already exist to aid hungry people worldwide. I don't often use devotionals to make appeals, but hunger is one issue that overrides etiquette.

So I dare to urge: Find a hunger-fighting agency that suits you and support it.

Grapevines in the Backyard
Jeremiah 17:7-8

A portion of my growing years was spent back east in Baltimore, Maryland. The old Ring family home there had a huge backyard, and in the very middle of that backyard were two long arbors, about 75 feet in length each, of grape vines. Those grape arbors were often a nuisance to me as a growing boy, for had they not been there, that backyard was large enough to make a great softball field. As it was, I and my friends in the neighborhood tried to use it as a softball field anyway and were constantly having to deal with losing the ball among the grape vines.

There was one time each year when I forgot all about the nuisance that those grape vines created. That was when the grapes ripened. For two or three weeks each summer, those grapes were pure pleasure from heaven itself. When the vines produced their fruit, which is what, after all, grape vines are supposed to do, I wouldn't have traded having them for the finest softball field in the world. They were wonderfully tasty and sweet, some of the best eating I've ever experienced.

Several of the stories – stories which we call parables – that Jesus told had to do with grape vines. The point Jesus made in his grape vine stories is identical to what I learned from boyhood experience. Grape vines have a purpose. Their purpose is to bear grapes. If they only take up space, they're a nuisance. But when they bear fruit, they're a blessing.

The same is true of those who would call themselves followers of Jesus Christ -- Christians. When Christians only hang around, doing nothing, they're not serving their purpose. A lot of so-called Christians are, to put it bluntly, no more than a nuisance. But just as grape vines are supposed to bear grapes, Christians are intended to bear fruit. As like begets like, the fruit that Christians are to bear is -- more Christians. Our purpose is to spread the Gospel of Jesus, so that others may come to know and believe in Him. The greatest task any Christian may undertake in this life is the joyous labor of introducing another precious human being to faith in Jesus Christ.

Fire on the Altar
I Kings 18:38-39

One of the most hilarious misadventures I had as a pastor occurred on Ash Wednesday one spring at the church I was then serving in Albuquerque, New Mexico. That particular church had a local tradition of observing the ancient Christian ritual of putting ashes on the foreheads of worshippers on that date.

Of course, to get ashes you have to burn something. So during worship that evening, as the chancel choir sang a slow, mournful song, I put some dried palm leaves from the previous spring's Palm Sunday celebration – another local tradition – in a metal container. Then, I set it on the communion table, doused the container liberally with lighter fluid, lighted a match and dropped it in. Instantly I had to jump back as flames shot up 20 feet in the air. I'd used way, way too much lighter fluid.

To add to the problem, I'd placed the now burning container directly under a smoke detector, whose siren began loudly wailing. The actual flame which triggered the alarm quickly died down, but the alarm's siren continued to pierce everyone's ears. I ran out of the sanctuary to get a ladder to help reach up and turn it off. Just as I retrieved the ladder and got it set, the alarm stopped on its own. Amazingly the church's choir, undaunted by the spectacle, continued singing a sad anthem through it all.

We finished the evening's worship without further incident and that became one of the most memorable occasions in the life of that congregation. Some of the folks who were present have forgotten my name, but they'll yet long recall what I did that Ash Wednesday evening. Now many years later, the friends I've kept up with tell me that people there still ask one another, "Do you remember the night the preacher almost burned the church down?"

It's good to be remembered, even if it's for something strange, like almost causing a disaster. As a Christian minister, one of the things I find in our mass society is that many feel no one really knows them, no one particularly cares, no one would notice nor remember if they dropped off the face of the earth. The good news that I can bring to such folks is this: God knows you and God cares about you. He knows your life, down to the tiniest detail. Why, even the hairs on your head are numbered by God -- the Bible says so. God loves you, personally, and He sent Jesus to earth to prove His love for you.

A Predisposition to Suspicion
Mark 6:1-6

One of the major foci of my calling by God to Christian ministry has always been the realm of missions. While I very much enjoyed my years of being a local church pastor, part of my heart will always be for sharing the Gospel in those places where there has been limited opportunity to hear the good news of salvation in Jesus Christ.

My first ministry assignment, fresh out of seminary, was to the Central American nation of Guatemala. Guatemala is a tiny, impoverished, unstable country located just south of Mexico. During the time we served there my wife and I lived under conditions that, by US standards, would be considered primitive and backward. We were constantly threatened by oppressive dictators, guerilla warfare, and political upheavals. The son of one of our American neighbors was kidnapped and killed while we were there. We ourselves were almost kidnapped one Christmas Eve, barely escaping flying bullets.

When we returned to the US, I got out of my car and literally kissed the ground at Laredo, Texas – it was wonderful to be "back home," to be in a nation where freedom, stability and economic well-being are the rule, rather than the exception. But with that said, I missed – and still miss -- Guatemala and its people.

One reason why I missed the people of Guatemala was because they were so open to the gospel of Jesus Christ, so willing to accept the gift of salvation that God offers to all. Any time I presented the good news of Christ to folks in Guatemala the response was eager and positive.

Here in the contemporary USA the kind of openness to and acceptance of the Gospel that I found in Guatemala, and subsequently in much of the rest of Latin America as well as many other parts of the world -- just doesn't exist. People here are "hard sells" when it comes to God and the Kingdom of Heaven. Many in this nation know just enough about Christian faith to be inoculated against it.

If I simply tell someone here, "God loves you," immediately they want to ask about the "fine print" behind that statement. But Americans, just like Guatemalans and all the rest of the world, need Jesus. Our country may be more advanced in some ways, but our need for salvation is no different from that of any other humans, the world over.

Pool Hopping and Its Consequences
Romans 6:21-23

Some of my growing years were spent down on the Gulf Coast of Mississippi. While that area wasn't as fully developed for tourism then as it is now, there were already quite a few motels up and down coastal US Hwy. 90, all in a row about five miles in length. As a teenager, late one night I squeezed into a car with about seven other friends and we went pool hopping from motel to motel. Our method of operation was to jump into the motel's pool, splash around and make a lot of racket until folks staying there woke up and started complaining, then jump back into the car and drive to the next motel. There, we'd jump into that pool, create commotion, wake everybody up, and do it all over again. It was a typical teenage prank – no major malice intended; just wanting to make some noise.

We were working on about our sixth motel pool disruption that night when a car from the Harrison County Sheriff's Department pulled up with lights flashing. Since I wasn't the driver and that particular motel was only a couple of miles from my house, I quickly figured I could get away undetected by running off into the nearby woods. So I did just that, sprinting as fast as I could into the forest.

About 200 yards in, I ran full tilt in the darkness into a single strand of barbed wire fencing. I was moving so fast that although it caught my leg, I vaulted right on over it. As I did so, the barb tore a long gash in my upper right thigh. It wasn't deep, but it was long. I continued running, successfully escaping and eventually making my way back home. My friends, it turned out, weren't arrested or anything serious – they simply received a stern lecture from the sheriff's deputies who caught them. And I, to this day, have a long scar on my leg to remind me of my foolish behavior that night. I got away, but I still paid a price!

The word of God tells us that all wrongdoing -- wrongdoing for which God uses the term "sin," has consequences. A price has to be paid for sin. Sometimes we pay the price for our sins up front, sometimes the consequences of sin catch us farther along in life. And sometimes, although we may think we've gotten away scot-free, God judges us for our wrongdoing beyond this world – in the afterlife of eternity.

There is one sure way, however, to avoid paying the penalty for our wrongdoings in eternity. Jesus, the Son of the Living God, has already suffered the consequences for the sins of humanity by dying on the Cross. When we call upon Jesus for salvation, God puts the penalty for our wrongdoings on Jesus, and lets us go free. And what a strange but marvelous blessing that is.

A Uniquely Memorable Baptism
Acts 8:30-39

Pam, age 15, wanted to be baptized. Her immediate family were all unchurched people, but she'd started attending my congregation's youth fellowship a year or so before and had gradually learned what it meant to be a follower of Jesus Christ. Now, she was ready for the big step – to receive the Sacrament of Christian Baptism, which included publicly professing her faith in Christ. I checked with her parents and while they didn't really understand their daughter's desire, they weren't opposed to it. So we began to plan Pam's baptism.

In the particular Christian tradition which I follow the person who is to be baptized may decide how much water is used, be it little or much. Pam wanted much. She asked to be baptized by immersion. It was winter, and my church didn't have a baptismal pool. But a nearby community church had a large baptistery, and the pastor there agreed to let us use it on a Sunday afternoon.

All of our youth wanted to witness Pam's baptism, as well as a good number of her school friends and even most of her family members. Thus we had a sizeable crowd assembled, about 60 persons.

The community church had two small dressing rooms for baptisms, so I put on some old clothes, that I didn't mind getting wet, in one of them, while Pam went into the other dressing room. When she emerged, she had donned a white baptismal gown that the community church folks had conveniently left for her to wear.

I climbed up, then down, a u-shaped ladder and waded into the pool, which was constructed from glass all around so that the audience could see what was happening. Next Pam came down the ladder into the pool and, as she entered the water, it seemed as though her baptismal gown just disappeared. The fabric turned absolutely transparent, and Pam had foolishly kept nothing else at all on under it. Everyone present got a clear view of her – all of her. A collective gasp went up from the audience.

That has to be the quickest baptism I've ever performed. I dunked Pam, asked her if she accepted Christ as her Savior, and quickly shooed her out of the pool, where her mother was conveniently waiting with a large towel to cover her as she came down the ladder.

Only after it was all over did Pam learn what had happened. She didn't realize that her baptism had produced such an unexpected show. She'd been focused upon doing only what she knew Jesus wanted her to do. She hadn't even been aware of her outward appearance. And that was as it should have been.

As a Christian pastor I wish more of us were like that 15-year-old girl, Pam. No, not because she put on an unplanned strip show, but because she kept her focus on Jesus Christ in spite of difficult outward circumstances. I advise us all to do likewise.

Creative Thinking in the Church
Deuteronomy 4:6

As we prepared to build a new educational building at the church I was then serving in El Paso, Texas, we needed to demolish a no-longer-used parsonage that was located on the site. Such demolition wasn't included in the winning contractor's bid; we'd somehow overlooked it. So we called a local company, the only one in El Paso offering to demolish houses and had them come and look at the old place. It was a simple frame structure, sitting on blocks with no basement, about 1200 square feet in size. How much to tear it down and haul off the remains? Thirty-five hundred dollars – twenty-six hundred to demolish, plus an extra nine hundred more to haul off the debris.

> The church's Trustees felt that was a rather high bid but were on the verge of accepting it when one of the members of the group spoke up. "I think we can get our own people to help us tear that house down and make enough money in the process to pay for hauling off the remains." We all listened attentively. It was an intriguing plan.
>
> So it was that my church promoted the opportunity to come and swing a sledgehammer at the old house, two Saturdays hence at $10 per person. Nearly two hundred people showed up, many carrying their own sledges. Several dozen of them weren't even church members -- just men and women from the surrounding community who wanted the opportunity to help demolish something.
>
> I never realized the amount of aggression that some folks have pent up in them until I saw that mob begin to tear down that house. Everybody had a great time contributing to its demise. The El Paso newspaper even sent a photographer to take a picture of half a dozen folks gleefully swinging their hammers. In less than two hours the house was reduced to rubble. After paying to have the debris hauled off, the church had nearly $1,000 left to put toward construction of the new building.
>
> One of the attributes of wisdom that the famous King Solomon of the Bible repeatedly demonstrated was an ability to offer creative options for solving seemingly impossible problems. Too often today, I find that the Church of Jesus Christ asks folks to give God their hearts, which is good, but not their heads, which is utter folly. Thus the kind of optional, creative thinking that saved my El Paso church several thousand dollars in unnecessary expenditures is rare in Christian circles.
>
> Remember, people of God, that He has given each of us both our hearts and our brains -- and He desires that we offer all we are back to God and the service of His Kingdom.

A Brighter Future
Revelation 21:3-5

In 1993 I had the opportunity to visit the nation of Russia just as it was emerging from 75 prior years of communist dictatorship. The church I was then serving was supporting a missionary there, and he needed some critically important supplies, including medicines for sick children in the city where he served. At that time, we realized that the odds of anything we might try to ship there actually arriving were slim, so the church decided to send me to personally deliver what was needed.

While the prospect of traveling to Russia may seem, at first thought, an exciting adventure, there were two factors that made this trip somewhat less than a pleasurable boondoggle. First, the missionary I needed to visit was located in the literal middle of Siberia, in a city named Irkutsk, five time zones east of Moscow. And second, the trip had to be made in winter. Can you imagine anyone willingly heading to Siberia in winter?

I made it to Irkutsk, successfully delivering the needed supplies. And while I was there, my missionary friend had arranged for me to speak to several groups. In particular, I had the chance to address a large group of several thousand teenagers in Irkutsk in a meeting hall called the "Pioneer Palace." This hall took its name from the "Young Pioneers" – a communist youth organization that, only a year before, had ceased to exist.

For decades throughout most of the 20th century the youth of Irkutsk had been indoctrinated into the principles of communism in this hall. As I stood up to speak there, huge portraits of Karl Marx and Vladimir Lenin, two great heroes of the communist era, still hung on the walls behind me. But I had the privilege of sharing, from within that former stronghold of communism, the Gospel of Jesus Christ. The youth of Russia were hearing a new and different set of beliefs – including the freedom God provides through the love of His Son, Jesus.

Whenever people tell me how bad the world is getting, and how things were much better back in 1980, or 1960, or 1945, I remember how much better life is, today, for the hundreds of millions of people of Russia, and Poland, and the Czech Republic, and dozens of other similar nations, than it was back in those so-called "good old days." And I have to politely respond, "No, I don't agree with you. The Gospel of Jesus Christ is advancing, and the world is a better place today because of it. And tomorrow it's going to be even better."

Invite Them In
Acts 1:8

One of the aspects of my personal history that I often discover to be unique among the people with whom I regularly associate is that I was not raised in the church. I grew up in a secular home; my parents weren't "for" or "against" church or the Christian faith. Rather, it was simply absent from our lives. Until my mid-teen-years the number of times I was ever in a church could be counted on the fingers of one hand – all those were occasions when my maternal grandmother took me while I was visiting in her home.

As I look back upon those early years, I had plenty of friends who did attend various and sundry churches, but no one ever invited me to go with them. I don't think they intended to ignore nor exclude me; they probably just assumed that I already had a church of my own. And I honestly can't say whether I would have responded positively or negatively to an invitation to attend church back then -- because I was never afforded the opportunity to consider the possibility.

My experience has taught me that many church people are very naive about what the secular world is really like. The majority of Christians in America spend their time associating with other church people; they read Christian books and listen to Christian music on the radio – and they naively assume that everyone else is just like they are. They don't deliberately exclude those who don't know Jesus. No, they just neglect to mention him outside their own circles, circles which consist of already-believing Christians.

The religious reality of virtually any U. S. town today, large or small, is that less than 1/2 of the population has any association, active or inactive, with a local Christian fellowship. Every other person you see at Walmart, or McDonald's, or the gas station, is completely unchurched. These folk may or may not be open to an invitation to accompany you to church next Sunday – but the only way to find out is to ask them. If you claim to be a Christian, that's your responsibility. I didn't set it up that way, but Jesus did.

A Youthful Solution
Psalm 20:5

St. Mark's United Methodist Church in El Paso had a problem. The rope lanyard for its 28-foot-tall flagpole in front of the church had broken. A new rope needed to be threaded over and through the roller at the top of the pole so that flags could again be hung.

We first called the El Paso Fire Department, which in the past had assisted us with reaching the top of the pole, but they apologetically told us that new insurance regulations now forbade them helping out in such a way. So we contacted a couple of local companies that we knew had cherry-picker buckets. The prices quoted seemed truly outrageous; one firm wanted $600 to attach the rope to our pole, the other a full $1,000. We were stymied.

My middle child, son Jonathan, overheard my wife and me talking about the problem. Jonathan loved to climb; he could climb before he could walk. He was just six years old at the time, but he eagerly volunteered himself. "Dad, I can climb that pole and put that rope where you want it!"

Without telling the members of the church's Board of Trustees, who would have been horrified at the prospect, I took Jonathan and the new rope to the pole out in front of the church. He grabbed the rope, shinnied up the pole, and attached the rope through the roller. In less than five minutes he was back on the ground, proudly smiling at his accomplishment.

When I told the Board of Trustees how the problem had been solved, they insisted on giving Jonathan $100 for his labor. I put it into his college fund. At age six, my son had earned his first actual income, employed for the Church of Jesus Christ. And at a pretty substantial hourly rate -- $100 for five minutes' work!

In Luke's gospel, Jesus is recorded as saying, "Let the children come to me, do not hinder them, for of such is the Kingdom of God." Let us take care not to undervalue nor overlook the skills and talents of our children, thereby depriving ourselves of the benefit of their talents – and their fresh outlook on life itself.

Love: A Finite Resource?
Matthew 5:43-46

I was raised as the only son of an only son of an only son. I had a half-brother on my mother's side of the family who was raised by my grandmother and already 17 years old when I was born. And at age 60 I was surprised to discover that I had a deliberately hidden half-brother on my father's side as well. But as far as my childhood rearing was concerned, I was treated as an "only child."

When my wife Fran and I had our first child, a son, after seven years of marriage, my parents were delighted. I had done my proper part to keep the Ring family line going for another generation. But when we announced to them, two-and-a-half years later, that Fran was pregnant with our second child, my parents -- especially my father -- were very concerned. "How can you possibly love and take care of two children?" was their question. "You'll be dividing your love between little Dave and this new baby, so they'll both be getting a bad deal." And when, three years later still, we added daughter Joanna to our family, my parents were convinced we were utterly mad.

My mother and dad are long deceased now. To the very ends of their lives I don't believe they ever really understood that love doesn't divide, like slices taken out of a pie, until it's all used up. Rather, love is more like a muscle in the human body. The more it's exercised, the bigger and stronger it grows.

Jesus, the Son of the Living God, said that Christians should distinguish themselves by their obvious and overt love for one another – and beyond, for the world at large. Certainly, Jesus never worried that love might be a finite, limited resource. Rather, he encouraged those who followed him to indiscriminately spread love far and wide, ultimately touching every human being with the outreaching care of God for them.

In our present world rife with mistrust and even terrorism, Jesus' advice may seem naive to many. But on the other hand, perhaps the time has finally come for Christians to take seriously Jesus' advice to love all persons, including our enemies. What might happen if we really did just that? Would there be enough of Jesus' love to reach them all?

A Cave Adventure
I Samuel 24:3-7

While serving God's church in the Big Bend country of west Texas, I came to know a member of one of my churches there who was the manager of a large fluorite mine owned by the DuPont Corporation. The mine was located south of the U. S. border in Mexico, about 20 miles from a little-known border crossing called La Linda. This mine manager invited me to visit his work site, and I agreed.

On the day agreed to, he picked me up in Alpine and we drove a total of four hours to get to the mine -- the last ten miles on virtually non-existent road, just a trail across the desert. The mine was a huge, open-pit operation. After I'd looked over the site and been introduced to a number of the workers, he asked me if I'd like to explore something unique. While cutting the pit, the miners had unexpectedly opened up an entrance into a small cave.

We put on miner's lamps and, carrying lanterns, made our way into this cavern. We could manage to crawl, mostly on our hands and knees, only about 200 yards into the fissure. But it was truly spectacular -- with all sorts of interesting rock formations -- a Carlsbad Caverns National Park in miniature.

While in there, the mine manager asked me if I saw any formations that particularly impressed me. I pointed out three or four really beautiful ones. As soon as I had done so, he pulled out a hammer and knocked each of them off for me. "Here, take them with you," he said. I was dumbfounded. He'd just destroyed many thousands of years of nature's handiwork, and I was responsible, because I'd foolishly told him I liked what I saw.

Seeing the look on my face, the mine manager explained to me that, as the mine expanded, this cave would eventually be destroyed in the search for more fluorite. Notwithstanding, I felt guilty. I still have those broken-off cave formations somewhere in a shoebox among my possessions, but I've never displayed them. I'm afraid someone might ask me how I got them.

Psalm 24 tells us, "The earth is the Lord's, and the fullness thereof." I'm not a tree-hugger, but I do believe that we are to be responsible stewards of the world with which God has entrusted us. Let's not mindlessly ruin this earth, for both God's sake and the sake of our children, who must also depend upon its resources to sustain their future.

Friendly and Welcoming?
Hebrews 13:1-2

I was a young adult, still at college, working toward my master's degree in engineering. During spring break, I was invited to spend a few days with some Jewish friends in Cincinnati, Ohio. My university's spring break coincided with Passover that year, so I had the pleasure of sharing my first-ever Seder celebration with this family. But on Sunday morning, it being Easter, I wanted to go to church. So I drove to a nearby Methodist church building and walked in.

At that time, I was a pretty-new Christian and, excited to be in a church I'd never been in before, wanted to meet the people of that congregation. Having arrived early I walked around in the sanctuary as folks gathered for worship, shaking hands and introducing myself. Many of the worshipers were obviously surprised by my friendliness. I remember one lady in particular who asked me, with suspicion in her voice, "Why are you doing this?" I don't know what prompted me to say it this way, but I responded with, "Because you aren't."

That was the first of many times when I've visited churches in unfamiliar places and surroundings and, sadly, the first time of many times I've discovered that most church people aren't particularly friendly. A visitor can walk into a congregation of just about any church in America, denominational or independent, and be virtually ignored. But if you ask church goers about their particular congregation, they will invariably say, "Oh, that couldn't happen here. Ours is a friendly church."

Most churches <u>are</u> friendly enough – to those they are familiar with and know well. But the plain truth is that most church goers are clueless when it comes to welcoming new and unfamiliar persons. They assume that someone else – an usher, a lay leader, maybe the pastor – will make the newcomer feel welcome. They're often so involved with catching up on the latest happenings with their friends that they don't even see the visitor. It's not that they intend to snub anyone; rather, it's usually just benign neglect.

The Word of God repeatedly admonishes the people of God to "welcome the stranger in

your midst." If the Christian faith is to have significant effect upon the world at large in the future, those who are already in local churches need to stop treating their premises as private clubs open only to the familiar and the well-initiated. Rather, we need to spread the doors open wide, and overtly seek to welcome newcomers. Then, and only then, will we truly be the Church -- of Jesus Christ!

Wrong-Colored Hymnals
Psalm 33:1-3

In one of my pastoral church assignments we were in the process of acquiring new hymnals. Our denomination had recently printed a new hymnal, and that local church had raised the necessary money to buy enough copies for the entire congregation. All was going well until the time came to decide what color the cover of these song books should be. Most of the congregation wanted red, which would match the color of the carpet in the sanctuary. However, a small but vocal minority wanted blue-colored song books. Though I tried hard to keep them from so doing, the leaders of that church insisted upon resolving the issue by putting it to a vote. The vote was duly taken; a lopsided 91% voted in favor of purchasing red hymnals. And six members immediately quit that church – they'd been on the losing side.

That was one of the first times that I began to realize how deeply the concept of "one issue politics" has influenced even the people of God today. Though those folks believed in the same God, the same Lord Jesus Christ, even the same particular denominational stances as the rest of that church Body, they chose to make a stand on what was, to me, a totally trivial issue. For them the outcome of that one decision became the litmus test by which all else about their church was measured.

Certainly I'm not suggesting that Christians compromise themselves on matters that are truly of significance. The Lordship of Jesus Christ is one such. But more often than not, folks move into and out of churches over much lesser issues. "The new pastor at the Baptist Church preaches too long, so I'll find a new congregation." "The music director doesn't sing all the verses of the hymns I like, so I'm off to another church – at least until they find someone else to direct the music back there." "The head usher frowned at me last Sunday morning, so I'll show them: I'll just quit going to church altogether."

In the Word of God, Ephesians 4, verse 32, Christians are advised to conduct themselves in the following manner: "Be kind to one another, tenderhearted, forgiving one another, as God in Christ has forgiven you." In a world where radicals are increasingly setting the agenda for our lives, this remains very wise, contemporary advice for the people of God.

Wilderness Survival Skills
Exodus 17:1-6

For several decades as a younger adult I had a passion for backpacking. I enjoyed, both then and now, getting out in the woods somewhere up in the mountains of New Mexico, or out in the rugged Big Bend country of far west Texas, exploring places that are accessible only to persons on foot. To those who've never been off the beaten track, you may be surprised to be told that roughly half of our nation's territory is inaccessible by road. The sights in that vast amount of wilderness are among the most impressive I've ever seen. But if you want to see such places you have to walk to get there.

Backpackers, as the name implies, take with them only what they are willing to carry on their backs. This means that while you are out on the trail you have to eat, sleep, and enjoy life sustained by only what you've brought along with you. Unless you're an unusually physically fit person, forty to fifty pounds of "stuff" – whatever it may be, is all you really want to lug around all day on your back. That means a lot of careful choices have to be made.

For a dozen or more summers, I used to take groups of teenagers with me on four to five-day pack trips. Well in advance I'd always send those who were planning to go a carefully thought-out list of what to bring and what not to bring. And inevitably, they'd arrive with overstuffed packs weighing far more than they could possibly carry for more than a few minutes.

Thus one of the first things I'd do, before daring to take one step away from civilization, was to get each teen to spread out absolutely everything in their pack, then tell them what must be left behind. These youth always groused at me for insisting that they leave music players, six packs of Coke, or extra pairs of the latest in fashionable slacks in the cars at the trailhead. But by the end of the first day on the trail most of them were begging me to allow them to further lighten their loads by abandoning items in the forest – something which is never done. When backpacking, if you bring it in, you must pack it out.

Jesus, who traveled from place to place on earth by walking, had some practical advice for backpackers – and for all of us. He said, "Take heed -- a person's life does not consist in the abundance of his possessions." I would paraphrase Jesus by saying "Travel light." Don't burden yourself down by trying to lug too much around on your back. Travel light – through life.

Long Sermons
Acts 20:7

In 1985 I was invited to be one of a group of 17 preachers who traveled to the south Pacific island nation of Fiji to preach Christian revivals throughout that land. Fiji consists of two major islands plus hundreds of smaller ones. Some of the other preachers in that group wound up in some very remote settings, but my assignment was fairly near to civilization, a trio of small towns surrounding the capital city of Suva, a population center of nearly 100,000 people.

I rapidly discovered that "church" in Fiji is radically different from church as I'd previously known it. For starters, many church buildings have only roofs overhead. Walls are largely unnecessary, as the outside temperature is rarely either too hot or too cold to be comfortable. And the worship service itself lasts a long time – much longer than I was used to.

On the first occasion I was to preach to a Fijian congregation, we'd already been assembled for almost two hours when that time came. We'd sung -- a lot, prayed -- much, read many passages of scripture, and heard "short" messages from three other persons, each of which would have qualified as a full sermon in America. So when I was finally introduced, I figured people would be ready to hear a final message and move quickly to the close of the service.

The message I had prepared and preached was actually longer than I usually speak to U. S. congregations -- about 27 minutes in length. But when I came to its end and offered to turn the leadership back to the pastor, he completely surprised me. He said, "Thank you, Dr. Ring, for that wonderful introduction. And now, would you please bring us the message?"

Worship in Fiji is typically a three-to-four-hour experience. And the main sermon is usually an hour to an hour and a half in length. By the time I left Fiji after ten days of preaching, I had presented the equivalent of a year's worth of Sunday sermons to congregations in America.

I'm not saying that longer is better, nor implying that Fijian Christians are more dedicated to God than American believers because they spend more hours in church. Jesus, when queried on the subject of worship, indicated that worship should not be defined by time, place, or circumstance. Rather, He stated that real worship occurs when those present seek God "in spirit and in truth." Short or long, true worship happens when the hearts and souls of those seeking God resonate with his Holy Spirit.

Warning Signs Ignored
Numbers 26:9-10

The church I was serving in El Paso, Texas was expanding. We were breaking ground for a new building. As a preacher I don't normally get directly involved in church construction projects. But before becoming a pastor I used to be an engineer. So I have a little more interest in, and understanding of, such endeavors than perhaps the average pastor. In any case, the day before the contractor was to break ground, the on-site foreman came to me and asked me where the gas line to the church building was located. I showed him. Later that day, I thought further about it, so I went outside and put yellow and black warning tape directly over the route of the gas line, all the way from the meter at the roadside to its entry into the church building.

The following morning, I was in my office, occupied with more typical church business matters, when we were suddenly ordered to evacuate the church premises. That particular church had a day school of over 100 small children, so I got involved in helping get them safely out as well. We also had to ask folks in homes for several blocks around to leave their dwellings.

The construction crew had brought in a backhoe and begun digging, and the backhoe operator -- ignoring the warning tape I'd prominently put over it, had immediately cut the church's large gas supply line.

It took half a day for the gas company to repair the line and allow life to return to normal in that neighborhood. Our church was charged $1,100 for the wasted gas and the repair costs – which bill I promptly passed on to the contractor whose employee had cut the line. He refused to pay it; his workman, of course, claimed he didn't see the tape.

In the Gospel of Luke Jesus tells a rather grim story about a man who, after death, went to hell. In torment there he entreats heaven to send someone back from the dead to warn his family of the terrible dangers ahead for those who ignore God's law. But Abraham, the patriarch of people of faith, tells him that God has already provided more than adequate warnings to those on earth.

Whether it's yellow and black tape over gas line routes or prophetic admonitions from the Bible, humans have a talent for ignoring warnings. And when called to account, we love to claim ignorance as our excuse. That may at times work with other people, but God can't be fooled. The time to heed his warnings and enter into a right relationship with God is now!

The Difficult Larger Perspective
Luke 18:15-17

She was 12 years old, a bright, cute, vivacious little girl teetering on the verge of womanhood. She'd gone to school one morning and, before noon, complained of a headache. So her mother picked her up from school and, once at home, she went to her bedroom to lie down. She never woke up.

There in the hospital bed she looked like a sleeping princess, ready to awaken at any magical moment. But the doctors revealed that she had been stricken with Reyes syndrome, a rare and terrible ailment which, in her case, had destroyed all of her higher brain functions.

For 11 days she lay there, and for those 11 days I spent many of my waking hours in her room with the family. They weren't church people; I'd been asked to help out by a cousin who was, at best, a peripheral participant in my congregation. But they were glad for my presence and constantly entreated me to offer prayers for the little girl's healing. I heard many unsolicited promises made during my visits of faithful church attendance for years to come, of lavish future giving to God's work, even of full-time ministry service by family members.

On the 12th day, in the morning, the little girl died. And the family members immediately turned their backs to God, to me, and to the many faith promises they'd made over the prior week and a half. To them God had failed. They'd called upon God in time of trouble and had not received the only answer they were willing to accept.

Recognizing that grief can cloud people's thinking, I tried to follow-up with this family. A week, a month, six months, a year later -- there was no change. Their brief flirtation with God and faith was ended.

Jesus, the Son of the Living God, came to earth to grant us, among many other important gifts, the gift of perspective on human life. Jesus, although he himself died after but a short 30-plus years on this earth, revealed that here and now is but a tiny fraction of the totality of life – abundant life – that God has in store for those who place their faith in him. Jesus did not say that we would not die, rather, he spoke these words: "He who believes in me, though he die, yet shall he live."

Yes, bad things – even death – can and do happen to good, innocent people on this earth. But thanks be to God that there's more, much more, to life than earthly existence only.

How Many Does It Take?
I Kings 22:12-14

One of the interesting phenomena I've observed among church people when an unchurched friend or loved one falls ill is something I term "piling on the preachers." A member of my church will call me and say, "My friend Sam, who doesn't go to any church, is in the hospital. I'm worried about him. Would you please go and visit him?" Of course, I readily agree to do so.

When I arrive at the hospital room, I often find one, two, or even three other pastors already there. For Sam has additional friends who go to other churches, and they've made exactly the same call to their pastors. On the table beside Sam's bed there may be a stack of business cards from still more preachers who've already been to see Sam. If we all showed up at the same time, why, we could hold an area-wide ministerial alliance meeting, right then and there.

While it's commendable that church people care about their unchurched friends enough to ask their pastors to make hospital calls, the truth is that such calls rarely yield fruit for the Kingdom of God. Despite popular misconceptions, very few are "saved" while they're ill and hospitalized. People respond to Jesus Christ far better when they're healthy and clear-headed, rather than sick, drugged, and in pain.

If you are a Christian believer who has unsaved, unchurched friends or relatives, the time to be concerned about their souls is not when they're faced with serious illness and perhaps imminent death. Rather, the best time to approach them about seeking faith is while they're hale and hearty and able to respond to what you want to tell them. Don't put it off – now is always the best time to share your Christian witness with someone you love.

One other aspect of this story is this one: Sending a preacher to witness to an unchurched person is often counterproductive. I learned long ago that I'm viewed in a different light than a "normal" person. To those outside the church preachers are an eccentric, peculiar group. To many we're a strange, third sex – maybe only partially human. Unchurched people will listen to their friends, relatives, neighbors -- to them, you're a real person. But they're far less likely to pay attention to a preacher, especially one they've only just met for the first time.

Yes, I know that church members will still call me to visit their unchurched friends in the hospital. And I know that I'll go and do just that. But I also know that "piling on the preachers" is a largely futile exercise. Sharing Christ, friend to friend, loved one to loved one, is far more likely to be fruitful.

A Link in God's Chain of Love
Acts 19:1-6

Tom was a hard worker at one of the churches I formerly served as pastor. He was always there when something needed to be done. He did physical labor for the church; he served on committees and ministry groups. He was a tither. He rarely missed Sunday morning worship; he even taught an adult Sunday School class. In short, he was a preacher's dream – the kind of church member every pastor would like to have more of.

One year, when it came near to the time for my church's annual "Laity Sunday" when the preacher sits down and the lay people conduct worship, the lay leader told me he wanted to have an old-fashioned testimony meeting, an opportunity for various lay persons to share their personal faith in Christ. I said that would be fine and told him to be sure to ask Tom to give his personal witness.

A week or so later Tom asked to see me in my office. I welcomed him and he began the conversation thus, "Preacher, you've got me all wrong." "What do you mean, Tom?" I asked. He continued his story. "Preacher, I grew up in this church. I love the church; I love the people here. I'll do almost anything for my church. But I can't get up in front of folks and talk about my faith in Jesus Christ. I'm a churchman, yeah. But I've never understood that business about a personal relationship with Jesus. I can't talk about what I don't have. Give me something else to do, but not that!"

I wish I could say that I came up with some golden words which caused Tom to open his heart to Jesus. I didn't, either then or later.

But this particular story does have a happy ending. Eight years later, five years after I had departed that church, Tom called me up. He was excited. He began the conversation with these words, "Dave, I've got it!" It had been a long time since my last conversation with Tom, so I responded with, "What have you got, Tom?" "I've got a personal relationship with God. I accepted Christ as my Savior last week! And I wanted you to know it, because you tried so hard to help me find Jesus while you were here."

In the New Testament of the Holy Bible the apostle Paul talks about how various Christians serve God's purpose in sharing Christ with non-believers. One plants, another waters, but God is ultimately in charge of the harvest.

In this particular case, I didn't get to see the harvest while I was his pastor, but God was working in Tom's life. And I, praise God, had a part in that all-important work.

The Awesome Freedom of Choice
Romans 6:1-2

I had a cousin in another state who was somewhat older than me, and who died a number of years ago. For this story let's call him "Sam" which, deliberately, wasn't his real name. Sam was an example of just about everything negative in a human being that I can think of. He was a ne'er do-well who sponged off of every friend and relative he could possibly wheedle anything out of. He was a chronic drunk and a frequent womanizer. He beat his kids, cheated on his wife. He used illegal drugs. I really don't remember him ever working an honest day's labor in his life.

But Sam often claimed to be a Christian. If you found him in a sober moment, he could even tell you the time and place when he became a Christian, at the age of 12. Once, I dared to confront Sam about his behavior. "Sam," I asked, "If you really are a Christian, why don't you try acting like one?" Sam had a ready response. He told me, "If God wants me to act right, he'll make me act right."

Despite what Sam used as the excuse for his chronically sinful behavior, God isn't about to <u>make</u> any of us "act right." When God made humanity, he made us in the image and likeness of Almighty God. That includes the ability to make choices on our own. As his highest creation, God both loves and respects humanity too much to force us to do anything.

If God put a hammerlock on any of us to compel us to toe the mark, that certainly wouldn't be love. No, love can only beckon, it can't compel. Which leaves us with the awesome freedom of choice – and the burden of responsibility for the choices, for good or ill, that we make.

God, however, hasn't left us completely in the dark about right and wrong, good and bad, sin and righteousness. God has given us his Holy Word, the Bible, as a guidebook for the conduct of human life. And, for those who believe in Jesus Christ, we further have the indwelling presence of God's Holy Spirit to aid and guide us in our choices.

But again, even these wonderful, powerful influences can only point us toward the right. We can still choose to follow such Godly guidance, or we can go our own way. For better or worse, it's up to us.

Wedding Joys
Song of Solomon 3:1-10

As an ordained minister one of the duties I'm regularly asked to perform is weddings. Most of the weddings I've done are normal and routine, but a handful of them of them have been unusual, especially as regards location. I've performed at least one mountaintop wedding -- after climbing all day to reach the chosen site. And I was asked to do a skydiving wedding, to which I agreed. However, the couple changed their minds beforehand and chose a ceremony on solid ground which, frankly, was a little disappointing to me.

I've also performed two weddings while flying in hot air balloons. Albuquerque, New Mexico, one of the cities where I've twice pastored, is the "hot air balloon capital of the world," and both of them took place there.

Other than being up in the air in a basket suspended from a huge sack of hot gases, one of those weddings was otherwise normal. But the second such became perilous just after the completion of the aerial ceremony, as the balloon's pilot had trouble controlling our descent and it appeared, we were headed for entanglement in some high voltage power lines. In the midst of that moment of crisis the newlywed couple entreated me to throw their marriage license out of the basket, so that if the balloon burned up after crashing into the power lines, it might be found and serve as proof that they had died only after being legally married.

I did so and, as it turned out, the emergency quickly passed. We missed the power lines and landed just beyond, in a farmer's field. But we never did find their license; they had to get a new one issued, which I duly signed some weeks later.

Weddings, for me, are one of the high points of being a Christian minister. Nothing else in human life so closely approximates the unconditional love that God has for us, his children, as the romantic love which a couple expresses for one another at the time of their wedding. At the moment of marriage most couples are so completely focused upon each other that each sees the other as perfect -- without spot, flaw, or blemish.

Although experience teaches us that this unquestioning love between a bride and a groom will inevitably change with time and distance from the wedding ceremony, God's unconditional love for us will never fade. The Bible even says that the Church of Jesus Christ – which is the collective people of God – is the bride of our Lord, to which God has joined his Son for eternity. I guess that's why I enjoy weddings so much; for me they're a preview of what God has in store for his children in the world beyond this one.

While They're Young
Proverbs 22:6

I have three grown children, two boys and one girl. They're pretty closely spaced, so they were all small at more or less the same time. Back when they were little, there was absolutely no doubt as to where we'd wind up whenever I said, "Let's go out to dinner tonight. Where should we go?" All three would respond with a mighty chorus of "McDonald's."

Even today, although they're all grown up, McDonald's remains high on the list of places where my children like to eat out, even when offered the option of much fancier and more expensive restaurants. It's become such a habit for my kids that they'll probably be McDonald's fans for the rest of their lives. My hat is off to the marketing gurus at "Mickey D's."

Habits, both good and bad, develop early in life for human beings. Psychologists tell us that much of who we are and how we'll behave throughout our lives is established in early childhood.

As a pastor, I worry when I talk to parents who profess to be Christians, but who also say to me, "Oh, we don't believe in making our children go to church. We'll just let them make up their own minds when they're older." But by then, the habit of not regularly attending the worship of Almighty God will be so well-established that such is likely to continue for a lifetime.

Parents: Don't let this happen to your precious children. Bring them -- and yourselves -- to the worship of God every possible Sunday.

A Radical Change in Behavior
Colossians 3:20-21

My father, who died at the age of 80, never liked children. He was raised in a strict household where it was taught that "children are to be seen and not heard." That became his byword for relating to youngsters. He didn't enjoy his own childhood and, when he grew up, he didn't like kids, period. Frankly, my father really didn't even like me when I was a child; I was over 30 years of age before we began to develop a genuine relationship with one another. As my dad moved into old age, his dislike for children intensified, becoming almost an active hatred of anyone younger than 21. He wanted as little exposure as possible to children. That was just how he was, and I learned to tolerate his idiosyncrasies.

In January 1997, shortly before declining health forced his confinement to a nursing home, I had the joyous privilege of leading my father to make a first-time profession of faith in Jesus Christ. And, several months after he entered the nursing home, I came to know how real my dad's new-found faith in Christ actually was.

I was visiting him there, sitting in a large lounge area, when I heard that a group of schoolchildren was about to arrive, coming to sing to the nursing home residents. I quickly began wheeling him out of the area, intending to sequester him in his room until the children had safely come and gone. I told him why: "Some kids are coming to sing, so we're going back to your room until they're gone."

While in the nursing home my father talked primarily in short phrases, but this time he formed a complete sentence: "I want to hear them." I couldn't believe my ears. "Are you sure, dad? These are children, and they'll be noisy and rowdy." He repeated, "I want to hear them." So we sat in the commons room and listened to this children's group, some 30 in number, give about a 15-minute concert. And my father smiled, occasionally laughed, and even sang along with them on a couple of songs.

The high point came when, as they finished up, they spread out among the nursing home residents. A little girl of about eight shoved a piece of paper -- a drawing of some sort -- in my father's face. I saw his hands come up; I was momentarily afraid he was going to slap her. But he was reaching out to touch her -- and, almost, to give her a hug. I knew then, for certain, that Jesus Christ had truly come into my father's life. Jesus said, "Let the little children come to me, and do not stop them; for it is to such as these that the Kingdom of God belongs. Truly I tell you, whoever does not receive the Kingdom of God as a little child will never enter it."

Preachers Far and Pastors Near

Jeremiah 23:16-17

I was new as pastor at this particular church and was making my initial round of visits to the members thereof. Among them was Grace, an older lady who was totally inactive as a church member. But Grace readily agreed to my request to visit her and warmly welcomed me into her home. Early in the conversation, however, she made it clear to me that I shouldn't expect to see her on Sunday mornings. She said, "I've never heard you preach, but I know you aren't as good a preacher as ...." She named a nationally-popular television evangelist. "I just love his sermons, and I listen to him on TV every Sunday morning. He's _my_ pastor." I politely heard her out, making no substantive comment in response. Other than that, she and I enjoyed a pretty good initial visit.

Several months later one of the other older ladies of my congregation, a friend of Grace's, called me to say, "Grace is in the hospital." I did some checking by phone and discovered that Grace's hospitalization was for a minor ailment, nothing life-threatening. Then I called her friend back and told her, "Grace's pastor is ...." I named the well-known TV preacher. "She told me so when I visited her. His toll-free telephone number is ...." I gave her the number. "Why don't you call him and ask him to visit her?"

Over the next several days I had six or seven additional calls from Grace's female friends, all asking me why I didn't visit her. I provided each of them the same information I'd given to the first caller. Interestingly, several of them actually called the TV evangelist's number and tried to get through to him. They were all fended off by his staff.

The surprising result of that incident was that ten to twelve previously inactive members of that church began attending worship on a regular basis. When word spread that I wasn't interested in providing pastoral care to those who chose to receive their spiritual nourishment elsewhere, they decided they'd rather rely on a local preacher than a faraway TV evangelist.

Even Grace got the message – she began showing up for worship on a semi-regular basis. By the time I left there she paid me a halfway compliment. She said, "I was right. You don't preach as well as...." She again named her favorite TV preacher. "But you're not bad." I figured that was as high of praise as I could reasonably expect from her.

It's hard to have a genuinely personal relationship with a television signal or, in our contemporary world, with an internet website. Just as we each need a personal relationship with Jesus Christ, we also need a local church fellowship in which to nurture and practice our faith in Him.

Up and Down, Out and Back In
Romans 11:13-15

Quite a few years back, while I was still a layman attending a church in Albuquerque, New Mexico, I was asked to speak at Sunday morning worship about my Christian faith. I remember being rather frightened at the prospect; back then I wasn't used to public speaking. But I reluctantly agreed. I recall nothing of what I said that morning, but when I finished, the pastor in charge closed the worship service with a traditional altar call. A young lady, 19 or 20 years of age, responded. She gave her life to Christ, publicly professing her faith in Him, and joined that church.

Several months passed. The entire incident had faded from my mind when the pastor called to ask if I would follow up on the young lady who had come forward on that occasion. She had been to church just that one time, and not at all since. The pastor felt I was the obvious person to check on her, since she had responded to Christ after hearing my personal witness. I agreed to do so. However, when I reached her by telephone it was like talking to the iceberg that hit the Titanic. She said that her response had been "over-emotional" and, upon later reflection, she'd decided that she had made a serious mistake. She wanted no further contact with me or with the church. She punctuated the conversation with a few well-placed expletives, then hung up. Sadly, I reported her as lost to the pastor.

Seven years later, after entering the ministry and completing seminary training, I was invited back to that church to be the guest speaker on a Sunday morning. After _that_ service, a smiling young woman walked up and asked, "Do you remember me?" "I'm sorry, but I don't," I responded. "I was the girl who gave my life to Christ the last time you spoke at this church," she said. "It took me four years to realize how important that decision was, but I've been back in the church for three years now."

What a difference! As far as I'm aware, that woman is still an active, vital leader in that congregation, and her faith in Christ has drawn her entire family to Jesus by now. But I had mistakenly thought her lost to God a few years before.

All of us have "ups and downs" in our walks of faith. Some days we may feel very close to God; at other times far, far away. And who among us has not "backslidden" in a commitment we made to God or His Church at some period in our lives? When we are experiencing such a time in our lives, those who remain faithful to the Church may, at that moment, regard us as lost. The secular world, which looks at Christians with an eye for inconsistencies, may call us hypocrites. But in God's sight we are still his children.

Wandering, wayward sheep we may be – prodigal sons and daughters indeed. Yet we ever remain subjects of his unfailing love. And God is constantly seeking to restore us to full fellowship in his family, no matter how long or difficult the journey may be.

God for the Long Run
Joel 2:23-26

I attended my 35th high school reunion, the first such I'd yet been able to make. There I was re-introduced to a man who had been a high school friend, but whom I'd not seen at all in the 35 years since graduation. This man, after getting over his amazement at my being a preacher, confessed to me that he also had felt called into the ministry of God years before. But the circumstances of his life at the time -- family, finances, other responsibilities -- had been such that he had felt unable to respond, so he'd ignored God's leading. As we continued to talk, he poured out his many problems and frustrations to me. His family was disintegrating, his job unchallenging and unfulfilling, his entire life a barely-held-together shamble.

In 30 minutes' time in the middle of a crowd of people at a high school reunion, miracles are not easy to come by. I assured him that, although it might not seem so, God was still in control of the many circumstances of his life. I admonished that he should seek God, regularly and diligently, that he might again hear what the Lord's purpose for him really was. Even at more than 50 years of age, it was not too late to turn back to God and serve him. I shared with him that I was currently working with another man who, at more than 60 years of age, was a candidate for full-time, ordained Christian ministry. Perhaps God's long-ignored call was still waiting for him.

As a pastor, I often talk with folks who are frustrated with and/or disappointed in the choices they've made in life. Certainly not all such have been called into Christian ministry, but many are aware that they're not doing what God really wants them to be about. However, they're also fearful that their circumstances are so fragile that, if they dared try to change -- even a little -- the whole fabric of their lives might come crashing down around them.

The good news is that, through it all, God is with us. And when we turn to him, he will help us to get our lives back in place, to find our purpose, to pursue our destiny. We don't have to continue being stuck in a life rut that is frustrating and fruitless. God will begin to set us back on track if we but ask him.

Deeply Etched
Deuteronomy 11:18-19

I knew very little about the lady I was asked to visit in the nursing home that afternoon. Her name was a common one -- Mrs. Smith. I was told that she'd been in that eldercare facility in Alpine, Texas about a year and a half. A lady who said she was her niece had called me from another city in Texas and asked if I would take the sacrament of Holy Communion to her aunt. I said I would.

When I walked into her room Mrs. Smith appeared to be awake – at least her eyes were open. I greeted her but received no verbal response. "Would you like to receive Holy Communion?" I asked. I might have imagined it, but thought she nodded slightly. So I opened my small pastor's portable communion set and began to offer a prayer of consecration. When I got to the Lord's Prayer, "Our Father, who art in Heaven, hallowed be Thy Name…," I noticed that Mrs. Smith was repeating the words along with me, all the way to the end. I placed a small piece of bread in her partially open mouth, and she ate it. Then I poured a tiny, plastic cup of grape juice into her mouth, and she swallowed the liquid. Afterward I offered a closing prayer and I clearly heard her say, "Amen" along with me at the end thereof.

I then turned aside for a moment, tidying up the items in my pastor's communion kit. When I looked back at Mrs. Smith, she was back into the "eyes open but just staring" state in which I'd first found her. I called her name several times, "Mrs. Smith…Mrs. Smith…Mrs. Smith." There was no recognition; no response.

As I left the room one of the nursing home workers asked me what I had been doing in Mrs. Smith's room. I explained that Mrs. Smith and I had just shared in Holy Communion. She told me this, "Mrs. Smith is totally aphasic. She hasn't spoken a single word since she arrived here nine months ago." Yet I had heard her repeat our Lord's Prayer, word perfect. The memory pathway for that special prayer was so deeply etched in her mind that it overrode the effects of the dementia, stroke, or whatever other ailment had robbed her of normal speech.

The Bible, many times over, advises us to diligently study the Word of God -- to learn it so completely that it becomes part of our very being. Obviously, Mrs. Smith had done just that, to the extent that even age, and infirmity could not take it from her.

Trustworthy
Exodus 18:20-22

In a former congregation that I served, one of the members came up to me after church one Sunday and told me she had found a quarter under one of the pews. She asked me to allow her to see the pew registration pads for the section of the congregation which had sat in the area where she'd picked up the coin. Then she spent the better part of two hours that Sunday afternoon calling people.

Finally, she found a man who said, "Yes, that quarter is probably ours. Our seven-year-old daughter lost the quarter we'd given her to put in the Sunday School offering." Only then was this woman satisfied, having worked two hours to locate the owner of a lost twenty-five cent piece.

My first reaction to that lady's insistence on finding the owner of a lost quarter was that she was obsessive. It was only a quarter, after all, not a $100 bill. And since it was found under a pew at the church, there was a high probability that the people who sat there wanted it to go into the church's offering anyway. So why spend so much time and effort over a mere 25 cents?

Then I thought further. Jesus had something to say about this kind of behavior. In Luke 16, verse 10, Jesus said, "Whoever can be trusted with very little can also be trusted with much, and whoever is dishonest with very little will also be dishonest with much." The amount is not the issue, be it 25 cents, 25 dollars, or 25 million.

People run true to form. A lady who will take two hours out of her day to locate the rightful owner of a lost quarter is the kind of person who can be trusted with just about anything. My respect for this member soared and, among other things, I made sure she was placed on the church's finance committee the following year. I knew she'd take very good care of God's money.

Welcoming the Stranger
Job 29:15-17

It was a small congregation in a growing neighborhood of a growing city. But it had remained a small congregation for more than two decades. Despite being ideally located, this church simply would not grow. I was asked to fill its pulpit one particular Sunday morning. I arrived and met the folks -- about fifteen in all, mostly older, each related in some way to one another. They seemed friendly enough, at least to me.

We began the worship. About 15 minutes into the service, a young woman with two small children came in the back door. She sat down near the back with her kids; they were the only children in the church. For the remainder of the service, since I could easily see what was going on from my perspective facing the small group, I noticed that she spent most of her time trying to corral her little ones. They were normal, active preschoolers, so they weren't particularly interested in sitting still for the duration of a worship service.

When the worship time ended, I especially wanted to greet this young lady and welcome her to the congregation. But the lay leader of the church beat me to her. As I walked up, he was, kindly but firmly, explaining to her why she shouldn't come back to that congregation. "Ma'am, we're glad you came today. But as you can see, we don't have many folks your age here, and we don't have any programs for your children. You'd be better off going to First Church downtown; they can provide what you and your kids need."

It was almost five years later when I sat as part of an area-wide denominational committee which was tasked with voting on the formal closure of that particular church. The remaining handful of old members from that congregation lobbied hard for keeping it open. But with a clear conscience I voted with the majority to close it. As far as I was concerned it was already a closed body; that church certainly wasn't open to anyone new.

One tidbit of scripture that is repeated over and over again in the Bible, going all the way back into the book of Genesis and continuing into the New Testament church era, is this: God's people are admonished to "Welcome the stranger in your midst." This is one of God's commands that isn't harsh or burdensome. It's simple, it's obvious, it's easy, but it's something we often ignore.

The next time you're worshipping God in a fellowship gathered in his Name, be sure to make a special effort to welcome someone you don't know. It's easy, and it's important!

A Bad Choice, not to Be Repeated
Mark 1:5-7

One of the aspects of God's great outdoors that I learned early was the delectable edibility of mushrooms. One of my relatives, my great Aunt Bessie, harvested about half of everything she ate from the wild fields and forests around her home, and I lived with her for a portion of my growing years. In particular, she loved mushrooms, and she taught me to recognize well over 100 varieties of such.

Contrary to popular misconception most mushrooms are edible; relatively few are poisonous. And some, like tiny morels and giant portabellas, are among the tastiest foods to be found on this planet.

While my wife and I were in seminary we lived in suburban Atlanta, Georgia near a large public park called Stone Mountain. The climate around Atlanta is such that mushrooms grow in profusion. Many a Saturday morning I would take a basket and drive out to Stone Mountain Park. In less than an hour I could usually harvest eight to ten pounds of delectable mushrooms – free of charge. We were somewhat poor while seminary students, but we often had gourmet mushrooms to go with our otherwise Spartan meals.

Years later, while serving a church in arid El Paso, Texas – where mushrooms are a rarity -- I went out one day to find a lone mushroom growing in the side yard of our parsonage. It had been a long time since and a different area of the country wherein I had learned to recognize various mushroom species. But I was so mushroom-deprived that I quickly picked it and, without really examining other than to brush it off, ate it whole right then and there.

Two hours later I was one very sick man. For the next several days I suffered from a high fever and lots of other, unmentionable digestive ailments. I lost 11 pounds during that ordeal and, although it might normally be beneficial for me to lose weight, that definitely wasn't a healthy way to do it.

Some days later-- after I'd recovered from my folly -- I went outside to find two more mushrooms growing in the same area where I'd picked the first one. I examined them carefully, and, sure enough, they were those rare but deadly species of mushrooms which are severely poisonous. I had picked and eaten an amanita, otherwise known as the "death cap," mushroom. After that incident I had to promise both my wife and my doctor that I would cease picking wild mushrooms. Nowadays I buy any mushrooms I eat from the store.

The Bible says, "There is a way that seems right to a man, but its end is death." That's usually interpreted to have spiritual meaning, but in my case, it proved almost literally true. I thought I knew what I was doing, but I was wrong – and my error almost cost me my life. I praise God that He spared me from the full consequences of my bad choice.

Dead Wood
James 2:17-18

I was new to this particular congregation and just beginning to learn something about each member thereof. One day, just as I was looking over the membership records of a particular family – I'll call them the Joneses – an older man, a member whom I'd already met and begun to like, came into my office. So I asked this gentleman, named Clyde, if he knew anything about the Jones family. Who were they, and how could I get to know them? Without a moment's hesitation Clyde responded, "Dave, you might as well take their membership cards and write 'B. P. O.' on them." "B. P. O.?" I asked. "What's that mean?" To which Clyde replied, "Burial Purposes Only."

At that time, I was also new to the Christian ministry -- and more than a bit naive. I was shocked that Clyde could say such a terrible thing about another member family of our mutual church. So I became determined that this family, the Joneses, would become active members of the church during my pastorate -- if only to prove Clyde wrong about them.

Unfortunately, Clyde was right. It was I who was proven wrong. The Joneses really were on that church's roll "B. P. O." -- for Burial Purposes Only.

Four decades and seven additional churches later, I've learned that "B. P. O." accurately describes the membership commitment of about one of every four church members I've pastored. Many other pastors I know, of a variety of denominational persuasions, would echo my words. About a fourth of all those whose names are on a church roll keep them there for one reason and one alone – so that some pastor will have to take the responsibility for performing their funeral. They'll never attend, never contribute, never communicate in any way with the church body—except to vehemently respond, when asked, that they definitely want to remain on the membership roll. Otherwise they want to be left completely undisturbed by the church until it's time for their funeral.

Jesus once told a story -- a parable about sowing seed under various conditions of soil. His parable was really about people and how they respond to the call of God upon their lives. Some start out eagerly, but quickly lose interest. That's probably how folks wind up on a church roll – then hang around lifeless and limp, weighing down the Body of Christ until it's time to plant them -- under six feet of soil.

"B. P. O." – Burial Purposes Only. I hope none of you reading this, if you belong to a church, is that kind of church member. But praise the Lord -- anyway!

Thirsty Christians
Ephesians 5:17-19

I enjoy visiting liquor stores. That statement might have raised your eyebrows, especially assuming you know I spent most of my life as a preacher. So I would tell you the story of how my interest in liquor stores began.

I wasn't raised in a "churchly" family; thus liquor stores were never forbidden territory as far as I was concerned. While I was serving as pastor of the first church to which I'd ever been assigned, one of my wife's cousins, who lives in the eastern United States, asked me if I could get him some Coors beer, which at that time was not distributed east of the Mississippi River. I said I thought I could, and proceeded, the following Saturday, to stop in at the then-largest liquor store in Albuquerque, New Mexico, a warehouse operation called Kelly's, to find such.

I'd just walked into that store when I spotted the lay leader of my congregation with a shopping cart piled high with six or more cases of beer. So I walked up to him and, smiling, said, "Hi, Ken!" To say the least, Ken was surprised to see me in that liquor store. He looked up at me, looked down at the mountain of beer in his cart, then looked up at me again. To his credit, he thought fast. His response was, "Preacher, what are <u>you</u> doing in a liquor store?" I guess he figured the best defense was a good offense.

For the next two hours I hung around that big liquor warehouse, meeting and greeting a variety of people. At least eight of the folks who came in during that time period were known members of my church. The surprising result of those encounters was this: Every one of the members whom I greeted in the liquor store on Saturday was in church the next day.

Since that time I've made it a point to stop in local liquor stores from time to time. I never know whom I'll see there. And I really do enjoy visiting those liquor stores, because such visits always seem to result in improved church attendance by those I see there.

A Family Feud
Genesis 25:21-26

Identical twin brothers, both middle-aged men, were members of one of my previous churches. For this story I'll call one Bob and the other Bill -- although those weren't their actual names.

They were both faithful church attendees, but Bob and Bill had a long-standing feud between them. You might think I'm exaggerating when I tell you this, but Bob always sat on the left corner of the front pew in the church, while Bill sat on the right corner of the back pew -- diagonally as far from each other as they could possibly get while in the same sanctuary. Bob would enter and leave via the front door, Bill via the back, so they need never encounter each other.

As I got to know that congregation, other folks filled me in on the situation between Bob and Bill. Fifteen years earlier they'd jointly owned a highly successful chain of stores in about 20 area towns. But theirs was a tough, demanding business, and a decade before, one of the two, Bob, had decided he no longer wanted the strain. He cashed out his share of the business, which put Bob in a major cash flow crunch. Bad went to worse, and the 20-store chain rapidly contracted back to just a couple of stores, then only one, which Bill still operated. Bill felt Bob was responsible for the demise of most of the business. He hated Bob, and Bob responded in kind.

After I'd been their pastor for about a year, I decided to see if I could help get them back to at least speaking to one another. After all, they were identical twin brothers. So I visited first with Bill and heard his "side" of the story. After listening for about an hour, I finally said, "Bill, I understand your hurt and your anger. But that all happened ten years ago. Isn't it time to forgive and forget?" To which Bill replied, while shaking his fists in front of himself, "Oh preacher, I've forgiven all right, but I'll never forget!" Obviously, he had done neither.

I wish I could say I found a way to reconcile the differences between those twins, but I didn't. As far as I'm aware, assuming they're still on this earth, Bob and Bill are yet sitting at opposite corners of that church building every Sunday. But at least they're regularly hearing the gospel. And maybe one Sunday, the truth of Jesus' statement in our Lord's Prayer – "Forgive us our trespasses, as we forgive those who trespass against us" – will hit home with these two long-estranged twin brothers.

Fruitful Competition
I Corinthians 1:10-13

Churches really aren't supposed to be competitive with one another, but I once served a congregation which engaged in pretty intense rivalry with two other churches of the same denomination. All three congregations were of about the same size and all were located in the same section of the city. Thus whenever one of those other two churches held a bake sale, my church had to have a bake sale also. And ours had to be bigger and better than theirs. If one of the other churches reported receiving five new members in a given month, then my church's goal became to receive six the next month. If one of them signed up ten youth to go to summer camp, then my church had to sign up eleven. And so it went. These three congregations were perennially competing with each other.

Those other two churches' pastors were good friends with me, and we'd all three get together for coffee each week. Many were the times we laughed at our congregations' competitive spirits. "Well, Dave, our men's club sold $600 worth of stuff at last week's parking lot sale. As soon as your men hear about it, I'm sure they'll organize a sale and try to sell $700 worth, just to top us."

What our congregations' members never figured out was that the three of us could and did conspire to get important things that needed doing in our churches done by utilizing that competitive rivalry. When Pastor Bill's parsonage needed a new roof, we planted a rumor that my church was considering putting a new roof on its parsonage. Sure enough, the folks at Bill's church soon decided to re-roof their parsonage. When my church fell behind on paying its denominational assessments, the other two pastors began publicly bragging on how well their congregations were doing in meeting their assessments. Within just a few weeks, the people of my church had caught up. They weren't about to allow themselves to be eclipsed by those other congregations.

While competition and rivalry aren't usually encouraged in the church of Jesus Christ, there is one notable exception. The apostle Paul, several times in the New Testament, encourages Christians to compete with one another in the arena of love. Paul says that we are to outdo one another in showing love. And if that love takes the tangible form of competing with the congregation across town to raise money to help feed the hungry, that's a good and healthy rivalry -- both to the glory of God and the service of humanity.

Help in a Time of Personal Need
2 Peter 1:5-7

It was early January and my wife and I were traveling a very long distance, by car, back to our then-home in Albuquerque after spending Christmastime with both sets of parents in the eastern United States. The car was filled with Christmas gifts we'd received. We spent our second night on the road in Wichita Falls, Texas. The next morning, when we got up, ice was falling from the sky. But I was determined that we'd make it home that day, so we started out -- driving slowly and carefully.

But not slowly and carefully enough. We'd only made it about 40 miles when I topped a rise and felt the road disappear from under me. The car slid off the road to the right, blew a tire on a culvert and flipped, landing on its top. We wound up hanging upside down, dangling by our seat belts.

A group of National Guardsmen, returning in convoy from weekend maneuvers, had witnessed our accident. They were already heading our way as I attempted to kick open the door of our car and get us out. They were relieved to discover that we weren't injured. With their help we righted the car, changed the blown tire, and, amazingly, were able to drive it back into Wichita Falls. Every window was broken out and the roof was down to the level of the doors, but it ran.

Back in Wichita Falls I met the manager of the body shop at the Mazda dealership. He turned out to be one of the most hospitable auto repairmen I've ever encountered. He made arrangements for Fran and me to spend the night in Wichita Falls, then fly back to Albuquerque via Dallas. He took all of our Christmas gifts out of the damaged car and stored them in his own home. And a month later, when the car was rebuilt, he met me at the airport and invited me to spend the night at his house before driving back to Albuquerque in my restored automobile, despite the fact that he and his family were hosting a major party that night at their home, a party in which I was heartily included.

Before I left him, I asked this man why. "Why did you go out of your way to be so hospitable to me, a stranger fresh off the highway?" He told me this, "I tried to treat you the way I'd want to be treated under the same circumstances. You needed a friend, and I was available."

One of the most often-quoted sayings of Jesus is this: "Do unto others as you would have them do unto you." I don't know whether that body shop manager was a Christian or not, but he certainly knew how to live by this, our Lord's "Golden Rule."

Keeping Obligations Organized
Psalm 90:11

When I first started out in the ministry, I carried a shirt-pocket-sized calendar book around with me. This tiny planner contained an entire year of dates, providing me four lines on which to note the things I needed to do on any particular day. For the first five years of my pastoral career those little organizers served me well. But as time went on I found that I was having to write increasing numbers of appointments and obligations smaller and smaller on those four daily lines until, too often, I could no longer read what I'd written down. I started having to call people to help me interpret my illegible scribbling and, occasionally, I'd even miss appointments because I couldn't decipher my own notes.

Eventually one of my associate pastors introduced me to something bigger and more useful. It's called a Day Timer, and it allows you to write down a whole day's worth of appointments and other obligations. However, Day Timers are only good for one month. Eventually I did get used to Day Timers and they served me well for about a decade. But about ten years along with them, I began noticing that I was again filling up all the available space, writing smaller, making notes in the margins, and so forth. The number and complexity of my appointments and obligations had again gone beyond my capacity to organize them.

What I did then was to go from the "normal" Day Timer system to their "senior" sized, two pages per day organizers. These allowed me to record times and obligations from 6:30 AM to 10:00 PM daily. But even one month's worth of those larger organizers don't fit in a shirt pocket, so I had to learn to carry them along with me, a companion book that, with my Bible, rarely left my side. Yet once again I eventually discovered that my obligations and appointments -- and the notes I needed to make regarding them -- were taxing the available capacity to record. So reluctantly but necessarily I succumbed to learning how to use and employ a "smart" phone -- which electronically holds volumes of information. This device is more than adequate to meeting my scheduling needs. Now that I'm retired, I could probably go back to something less fancy. But having come all this way, moving back to a simpler scheduling system doesn't really appeal to me, at least not at present.

The point of all this is not to impress you that I'm a busy person, but rather to use myself as a tangible example of how modern life, daily, is becoming more and more complex and difficult to cope with. We're all busy people today -- and life itself is getting busier with each new day that dawns.

In the midst of unavoidable complexity and busyness, it's more important than ever before to have a focus, a still point, an anchor upon which to fix ourselves. That focus, that anchor, that still point, is Jesus Christ. He's the same yesterday, today, and forever. No matter how complex life gets, Jesus is always available. You can trust Him.

Taken Seriously
I Timothy 4:11-13

In the first church that I served as pastor it often seemed that I was not taken seriously. Although it was clear that the members of that church loved me, almost all of them were thirty to fifty years older than me. So in their eyes my lack of age usually disqualified me from imparting any shred of wisdom to them, my elders. My wife Fran and I were regularly introduced as "our nice young preacher and his cute little wife." When our first child, Dave, was born, he had more than a hundred instant surrogate grandparents and godparents. He was the only baby to be born among that congregation in over a decade.

One of the things which I strongly believe is that God expects us to put ourselves where our mouths are. Even the scriptures themselves tell us that it's very easy to say, "I love Jesus," but God expects tangible actions -- evidence to back up those words. So, among other topics, I regularly preached on the subject of sacrificial giving – of time, talent, and treasure.

That particular church, being populated with an abundance of senior citizens on limited incomes, always struggled financially. So I was absolutely amazed when, after preaching on sacrifice a month or so previously, one of the retired men brought a check to me for the largest amount I'd ever, at that point in my life, seen -- about $22,000.

As he handed over the check, he explained himself. "Pastor, I heard what you said about sacrificial giving. All my life I've been a good giver, but it was always from what I had left over, after my own needs were met. Yep, I heard what you said, and the Lord convicted me. So I sold my house and moved into a smaller one. And if I ever feel a little cramped, well, that will remind me of what Jesus did in sacrificing Himself for me. Here's the difference. I want it to go to God's work."

From that day on I understood that even a young preacher might, by the Spirit of God, influence his elders. And I also learned, from that old saint, more about the true meaning of godly sacrifice.

Today I have an abundance of gray hair, so I no longer worry about being discounted because of my youth. And I still realize that -- young or old, clergy or lay – all believers can teach one another more – more about living out the truths of the Christian faith.

Scarcity and Plenty
John 3:16-17

At one time we had three cats in our household. Each of them found us; they were all originally strays. Two of them were females – neutered -- which we'd had for a number of years. The third, and more recently acquired, was "Mr. Kitty," a young male.

When Mr. Kitty first arrived our two longer-term cats would try to keep him away from the feeding dish. But he was both larger and a lot feistier than either of them. So after a few losing battles with hisses and snarls, they decided to just station themselves near the food dish and glare at Mr. Kitty while he ate. Whenever Mr. Kitty finished eating those other two cats would rush to the food bowl and eat more themselves – even if they were already full. They wanted to make sure there was still some food left; that this Johnny-come-lately interloper hadn't used it all up.

In a world of seven billion people with more arriving every day, we are only just beginning to seriously address the fact that ours is a finite planet. There's just so much clean air and water, fossil fuel stored beneath the surface, and trees that grow on the face of the land. Natural resources are limited and, unless we soon find effective ways to limit our runaway consumption thereof, we'll use up the earth.

One human response to the finiteness of this world's resources, one that I see more and more of daily, is identical to the reaction of my two older cats to the addition of cat number three. Folks who already have something try to jealously guard, hoard, and keep others away from what they think is rightfully theirs. The attitude is, "I've got mine and, sorry, but there isn't enough to go around for you, too." That's what, right now, is fueling conflicts and wars all over our globe – conflicts between the "have's" and the "have not's."

I don't propose to be able to solve global conflicts and sort out geopolitical dilemmas. But I do have one important bit of good news to share: Unlike limited earthly resources, God's love is not finite. Rather, God's love is unlimited. God's love is in no danger of running out. It can be shared with our neighbors, our friends, our rivals, even our enemies -- and there will still be plenty to go around.

There was enough of God's love to reach all humanity when Jesus walked this earth, and there still is. So feel free to share the love of God, far and wide, with anyone and everyone you meet. There's plenty of divine love available for you -- and for the entire world.

Word Power
James 3:5-10

One of the most interesting of all scriptures for me, personally, is Isaiah 6:5. The setting is this: Isaiah the prophet, in a dream, sees the Lord God Almighty on His throne. Isaiah's personal response is this: "Woe is me, for I am undone. For I am a man of unclean lips, and I dwell among a people of unclean lips, and my eyes have seen the King, the Lord of hosts."

The reason that Isaiah's cry of woe speaks to me so personally is that, for many years, I was very much like Isaiah. I was, to express it biblically, a man of unclean lips. Or, to say it more candidly, I had a dirty mouth.

Being raised in a secular home I grew up with all manner of curses, vulgarisms and epithets as essential portions of my vocabulary. Speaking four letter words – and worse – was as natural to me as saying my own name. No sentence in my household of origin was complete without at least two "cuss words." The F-word and the S-word punctuated virtually every phrase. The scatological language I employed could be described as colorful -- most definitely blue, often purple.

When I became a Christian at age 20, I didn't immediately start speaking with a whole different vocabulary. In fact, the first few times I was called upon to witness, publicly, to my new-found faith in Jesus Christ, I heard numerous "gasps" from the audience. Some of those lifelong church ladies had obviously never heard enthusiasm for one's Lord expressed in such colorful terms.

It took a long time for God's Holy Spirit to cleanse my unclean lips. Even after becoming a pastor there were occasional, embarrassing slips of the tongue that were hard to explain to a group of old saints who had spent most of their lives in the church.

But gradually the Lord replaced my old vocabulary with new words. The four-letter word I most often use these days begins with L. It's love. And the very best word I know is a five-letter one. It starts with a J.

In case there's anyone reading this who hasn't already guessed, that word is Jesus. I use it frequently, and I heartily commend it to you as well.

Never Off Duty
Exodus 4:10-11

Christian ministry can present an opportunity almost anywhere. My wife, Fran, and I had finally found five days to get away from it all – kids, church, responsibilities—and take a once-in-a-lifetime trip to Mazatlán, Mexico. We flew there, took a cab to our hotel, and were in the process of checking in. As we stood there waiting, we observed another couple, about the same age as ourselves, in a heated argument. Fran, who has always been more spiritually sensitive than I, said, "We need to help those folks out."

As soon as we got checked in, we walked over to this other couple, who were still standing there in the lobby arguing, and introduced ourselves. Using the pretext that we were just about the only two American families in the hotel that week, we invited them to share dinner with us. They agreed, and the relationship began from there.

For the entire time we were in Mazatlán we spent much of it with this couple, sometimes all four together, sometimes Fran with the wife and I with the husband. We did a lot of listening and quite a bit of counseling. We shared our faith in Christ with this couple and prayed with them on a number of occasions. When we left Mazatlán we did so with the conviction that we had helped to repair a marriage that had been in severe danger.

Did we cheat ourselves out of a vacation? No, not really. Both of us headed back to the U. S. feeling that we had not only had a good time ourselves but had been able to share our blessings with others. We were both relaxed and satisfied.

Being a Christian isn't an "on and off" kind of relationship. It's part and parcel of one's very identity. And the opportunity to serve Christ is always available, whether you're "on duty" or "on vacation." Christian ministry can happen anywhere, anytime, for any believer. If you'll simply make yourself available to God, you'll be used. It's a 24/7 opportunity.

Prayer Includes Listening
1 Kings 19:11-13

For the entire five years that I lived in Odessa, Texas, I was privileged to be part of a group of pastors who gathered regularly, once a week, for an hour of prayer. By sheer coincidence or, more likely, by God's design, I happened to arrive in that city the very week that a new, city-wide pastor's prayer movement was holding its first meeting. As a newcomer, I wanted to get to know other preachers in town, and that provided an obvious, open opportunity.

Prayer to God was the sole focus and only agenda of that pastor's prayer gathering. For that reason, the group was able to attract and include ministers from a wide-variety of backgrounds, from fundamental Southern Baptist preachers to socially active Roman Catholic priests, from staid Church of Christ pastors to let-it-all-hang-out Charismatic worship leaders. The numbers varied from week to week, sometimes as many as 20, occasionally as few as five, but averaging around 12.

I learned a great deal about prayer from five years of interacting with preachers from such a wide range of backgrounds. One of the most important learnings I gained was the simple fact that prayer includes listening. I'd realized years before that prayer was conversation with God, so I already had no reservations about verbally expressing myself to the Lord, pretty much just the same as I talk with anyone else around me. But that prayer group taught me that conversation with God, just like conversation with anyone else, is two-way. I didn't need to do all the talking. Listening for God's responses was equally important.

In our contemporary society, with the pace of life being both frantic and frenetic for most of us, we aren't used to listening. Listening to God requires us to remain silent, and a time of silence, if longer than a few seconds, can be uncomfortable. But if we're to hear God's response to our prayers, we must be silent, for at least some time, in order to hear them. If you really think about it, almost all prayers should include 50% silence from us humans -- to allow for God's half of the conversation.

People are always asking me, "Does God really answer prayer?" I often respond to such queries with this question in return, "Have you ever really listened to hear His answers?"

Learning to Receive
Acts 4:32-35

It was my very first paid job as a minister, and the very first Sunday morning thereof. While attending seminary I had been hired as part-time youth minister and sort-of associate pastor by a church in suburban Atlanta, Georgia. As the congregation was departing following morning worship, I stood at the rear beside the senior pastor to shake hands with the people. One elderly lady, as she shook my hand, pressed something into it. I opened my hand to find two tightly folded dollar bills. "What's this? I asked her. "It's for you. I thought you might need it," she replied. "I'm sorry, ma'am," I replied, handing the two bills back to her. "But I don't take charity."

The senior pastor, Dr. Reaves, was standing there beside me, and he quickly apologized to the lady on my behalf. "He's new," Dr. Reaves said. "He doesn't understand. Please don't hold it against him."

After the rest of the congregation had filed out, Dr. Reaves pointedly ushered me back to his office for a conversation. He was obviously upset, and I was genuinely puzzled. I had been raised in a home where money wasn't overly plentiful, but we rarely lacked for what we really needed. And I had just left a career in engineering wherein my earnings were more than adequate. I had learned to be a giver. Charity was something I did for others, not something I received. The church was paying me to do the job they'd hired me to do. Why did this lady think I needed an extra two bucks?

Dr. Reaves patiently explained that part of being a servant of God is to graciously receive from others as well as to give. Christian ministry is a two-way street. Whether or not I actually needed the lady's two dollars wasn't the issue. I had offended her by not allowing her to minister to me.

Since that first Sunday's experience I've grown a lot in that category. Long ago I realized that, while I may be the pastor of a church, I'm by no means the only minister thereof. Every believer in Christ is called to be a minister of God's love. Sometimes we are the providers of ministry to others; at other times we are the recipients of ministry from them.

The Word of God, Galatians 6:2, says, "Bear one another's burdens, and thus fulfill the law of Christ." Decades ago, I needed to learn what that meant. Some of you might need to learn it today.

Vision for the Future?
1 Timothy 4:12

My church had just held a major planning conference. Everyone present lamented the fact that youth and children were steadily diminishing in numbers among that congregation. The older they were, the more nostalgic they waxed. "Why, back in the '60's we had a youth choir of 40 voices that sang every Sunday morning -- at the early service." Everyone agreed that the church needed to do more to attract children and youth.

The very next evening one of the circles of that church's women's group was meeting. As pastor, although I'm not a woman, I was invited and urged to attend. So I was present when, halfway through the meeting, two teenage boys walked into the fellowship hall. One of them whispered something to one of the women present, and she subsequently spoke up. "These boys want to play basketball outside on the parking lot. They're asking if we could move our cars away from the hoop so they can play."

Another of the ladies immediately responded with, "Well, I'm not about to move mine. They can just wait until we're finished." All the others nodded in agreement, and the two boys quietly left.

Half an hour later I was asked to close the meeting with a prayer. "O God forgive our blindness!" was my short and succinct prayer. As the group was breaking up, several of the ladies asked me what was meant by my offering of such a strange prayer. I responded, "Well, I suppose it might have something to do with boys, and basketball, and parked cars." There was absolutely no comprehension.

As the Church of Jesus Christ attempts to cope with the 21st century A. D., those of us who profess to be Christians need to remind ourselves that the Christian faith is always just one generation from extinction. If we fail to pass it on to those younger than ourselves, belief in Jesus Christ will die with us.

God's Multi-Generational Family
Matthew 1:1-17

Shortly after I began to serve as pastor of Paradise Hills United Methodist Church in Albuquerque, a strikingly beautiful young woman and her husband joined that church by transfer from another Christian body on the very first Sunday that they visited. That's somewhat unusual -- people typically like to take more time looking over a church before they commit to membership therein. But I certainly didn't complain.

As I spoke to this couple further after others had left that Sunday morning, she asked, "Don't you remember me?" "I'm sorry," I responded, "but I don't. Should I know you?"

She replied, "You ought to. I used to sit on your lap every Sunday back when you were the pastor at Harwood Church. I'm Clyde Crabb's granddaughter."

With that additional information I then remembered. This young lady, about 15 years previously, had been virtually the only child in that congregation back then. Many Sundays, when I began to offer a message for children, she came up and plunked herself down in my lap. She was between four and five years old in those days.

Before I left Paradise Hills, this young woman had borne a child -- a daughter. And just before I moved on to another church her little girl began coming up, with the other kids in the congregation, to sit with me for a children's sermon. Thus I got to serve the child in the same way I'd ministered to her mother two decades before.

That's not the only time I've had the privilege of ministering to a succession of generations of particular families. I've performed a number of baptisms of children of children whom I'd baptized years previously. I've also done several weddings for the children of couples I'd united in marriage long before. After four decades in ministry -- and counting -- such incidents are becoming more and more frequent among my life experiences.

The Holy Scriptures are full of genealogical information that we sometimes regard as tedious: "Abraham begat Isaac and Isaac begat Jacob and Jacob begat Joseph and his brothers..." But how exciting it is to watch the endless line of splendor of God's faithful people unfold, and, even better, to be included in that great, multi-generational family of God which spans human history – and beyond.

Definitely Not Encouraged
Job 31:32

I was an engineer on a business trip to the north coast of Massachusetts in the dead of winter. Having to stay over the weekend, I looked in the yellow pages of the local telephone book for a church of my denomination but found none. So I chose a church of a different but not totally unfamiliar persuasion and proceeded to visit.

The first thing I noticed outside the church was an historic marker, which said that the building had been in existence since about 1760. I was impressed. As I entered, an usher, saying nothing, handed me a bulletin. I sat down; I was early, about 15 minutes before the service was scheduled to begin. As I sat there, I noticed, as others arrived, that they made a large circle around me – no one sat near in any direction, front, back, or on either side.

I scrutinized more carefully the order of worship printed in the bulletin and noticed that the sacrament of Holy Communion was being served that day. I wasn't sure if that particular denomination would allow outsiders to receive the sacrament, so I got up, walked to the back, and asked the same usher who had given me the bulletin if I could, as a visitor, receive communion. He said, "I guess it's all right." I took that for a "yes."

The worship service was reasonably enjoyable, the sermon adequate, and I did receive communion. But no one spoke a single word to me, other than that usher who had briefly responded to my direct question to him. As the congregation was leaving, we formed a line to shake hands with the pastor – a tradition followed by many churches. When I got up to him in the line, the pastor dropped his hand to his side. He fixed me with a stare, asking, "And who are you?" "My name is Dave Ring, and I'm a visitor from New Mexico," I responded. "We don't encourage visitors," was his matter-of-fact reply.

Some of you might think I made that story up, but it really happened to me, just the way I've related it. And while not every church is as overtly unfriendly as that congregation, my personal experience is that very few churches, regardless of denomination or non-denomination, make more than a token effort to welcome the stranger in their midst. Most church attendees are too busy interacting with one another to even notice whether or not there are visitors to their congregation. And then Christians wring their hands over the fact that their numbers are declining in most churches today.

Jesus came to seek and to save the lost – not to spend an extra hour in fellowship with those who already knew the word of God. Wake up, people of God! Pay special attention to those new to your church, not just the old timers.

Focus on Jesus and Only Him
Numbers 27:16-20

I'd recently moved, as pastors do, from one church to another. This particular move had been initiated by me. I had a firm conviction that I'd completed the ministry God wanted me to perform at the prior church and it was, therefore, time to move on. I was open and honest with the leadership of the church I left. We parted on amicable terms.

About two weeks after I arrived at my new church, I received a letter from Gladys, who had been both a faithful member and a good friend at the church I'd just left. She was upset – at her church's leadership, at the denomination, at my former supervisor, even at God – because I had, in her words, been "thrown out" of that pastorate.

As carefully and as lovingly as I could possibly write, I typed a long letter to Gladys explaining to her the truth about my departure from her church. I explained that, although I loved her and many others in that church, it had been my decision to leave. No one had forced me out. I was simply following what I felt to be God's leading for my ministry.

Unfortunately, Gladys never returned to that church. And, although she was a personal friend, I came to understand that she, like many church goers, had missed something vitally important. She had placed too much faith in me -- and too little in Jesus Christ.

As a pastor, I learned long ago that I am not the head of any Church. I'm simply an under-shepherd. Jesus Christ is the real head of the Church. Jesus Christ is the true leader of every Christian congregation that bears his name. He is the only valid reason to join a church. And his will is the only right reason to leave a church. Preachers come and preachers go. But the Lord Jesus Christ remains.

Always Be Prepared
Luke 12:16-20

Her name was Delores, and she was in bad shape. In fact, from the day I met her she wanted me to help plan her funeral. She'd been fighting cancer for a long time, and all her doctors told her she was losing the fight.

Her husband Sam was, by contrast, in the pink of health. He was an outdoors-type who loved to walk and bike and hike all over the area. He tried hard to be a caregiver to his chronically ill wife, but it just wasn't in Sam's nature to sit around the house all day, watching over someone whose life was slowly ebbing away. Fortunately, there was enough money available to them that caregivers could be hired to sit with Delores during the days while Sam was out and about. And he, to his credit, was faithfully there for her every evening and night.

I'd been their pastor about a year, watching Delores continue to deteriorate throughout. Frankly, I was amazed that she was able to hang on to life so long. And then, one morning, a call from the funeral home came: "Sam VanGundy died last night." "No, you mean Delores VanGundy. Sam is her husband," I said. Then the response in return: "No, I really do mean Sam VanGundy. His wife, Delores, is here with me now at the funeral home. Can you do Sam's service on Thursday morning at 10 AM?"

The most amazing part of this strange story is that, from the time of Sam's death onward, Delores began to improve. Her doctors were puzzled but excited by her more or less spontaneous remission from what they had considered to be terminal cancer. Slowly but surely, moving away from the literal brink of death, she regained strength and returned to health. Six months after Sam's death, Delores was back in church on Sunday mornings. A year after that she relocated to another city to live closer to one of her grown children. As far as I'm aware she may still be alive to this day.

Jesus is recorded in the Bible as saying, in reference to the final judgment day, "No one knows the day nor the hour." We all might well take that scripture personally and individually, in reference to our own lives. Delores VanGundy was ready to die – even actively preparing for the event. Her husband Sam, on the other hand, had no idea that he would depart this earth so suddenly – before his gravely ill wife. The point is that we should each be prepared to meet our Maker. The best and most important preparation is to accept Jesus Christ as personal Savior.

Casual Sex?
2 Samuel 11:1-5

I was invited by the youth minister of the church I was then serving to come to the youth fellowship meeting and allow the youth to ply me with questions. He promoted it to the group as "you can ask the pastor anything" evening.

After things got warmed up with a few "softball" queries, those youth began to ask the real questions I expected to hear from them – inquiries about sex. Human nature is pretty constant from generation to generation. Having once been a teenager myself, I had anticipated that this would be the major topic of the evening.

After we had worried the issue up, down, and sideways for a half-hour or more, one of the youth complained, "Pastor, you aren't giving us any answers." To which I responded, "Oh yes, I am giving you answers. You just don't like the answers I'm giving. You want me to say that sex is OK anytime and with anyone, and I'm saying it's not. And in your hearts, you know I'm telling the truth."

One by one, slowly but surely, each of these dozen or so youth began to admit that they not only understood what I was telling them, but that they recognized the truth in it. Deep down, each of their consciences had already convicted them. They knew that casual sex was wrong. But they were trying to find a "loophole" to justify doing what they already knew shouldn't be done.

Conscience, while not a perfect guide, is a good source of moral guidance, a source which Almighty God has deliberately placed within us as humans. The Word of God, specifically Romans 2:15, admonishes us to listen to our consciences. Much of the time they will tell us what is right and what is wrong. We ignore the leadings of conscience at our own peril. And on those occasions when conscience does not clearly speak, we can turn to the Word of God itself, the Bible, to provide true and perfect guidance in every circumstance.

Significance Over Time
Mark 10:42-44

For four years I attended Michigan State University, one of the United States' largest colleges, and one with an up-and-down reputation for American football prowess. I had little to do with it directly, but throughout the years I was a student there, Michigan State was a collegiate football power. One of those years the Spartans were proclaimed the undisputed "national champions" of collegiate football; another of them MSU tied for that honor with Notre Dame University.

I remember the huge pep rallies, the always sold-out stadiums, the wild fervor and deep emotion which gripped the MSU campus on football weekends. I even remember the scores of some of the games, one of which was billed by national television as the "game of the century." It was truly an exciting time to be a Michigan State student; I'm glad I was there.

But the truth of the matter is, that's all-but-forgotten history now. Those collegiate football heydays make for fond personal memories, but little else. What happened with Michigan State football back then had little or no lasting impact on the world of today. The names, the faces, the scores of those oh-so-important championship contests are no longer of interest. Yesteryear's collegiate "game of the century" is today, at best, a minor question in a game of the sports edition of "Trivial Pursuit." That's to be expected -- what I'm recalling happened five decades ago. The world has moved on, as have I.

Two thousand years ago, a man named Jesus walked this earth for a brief thirty years. He didn't win at much of anything; in fact, he was considered a loser by just about everyone who ever met him. He died while still a young man; in truth, he was executed as a convicted criminal.

But who Jesus was and what he did during his short, seemingly unsuccessful sojourn on earth more radically altered the course of human history than any other life ever lived. Two thousand years have passed, and Jesus is still making a difference in the present-day lives of billions of persons the world over.

What seems important to us at a given moment, and what really is important in the long run, can be very different. Thanks be to God that Jesus is of greatest importance -- yesterday, today, and forever.

Greater Accomplishments
John 14:12-14

My daughter, Joanna, is a pretty good tennis player. She currently coaches tennis at the school where she teaches. She was previously on the tennis team at her college, where, one particular year, she was voted "most valuable player." She likewise was previously selected as "most valuable player" back in her high school days. Occasionally she still asks me, her dad, to provide her practice by playing against her, and -- of course -- she regularly beats me all over the court.

It wasn't always that way, though. When Joanna was preparing to enter the seventh grade, she was terrified because she'd been placed in a tennis class -- but she'd never even held a racquet in her hands. So I spent an entire summer teaching her, as best I knew them, the fundamentals of tennis, drawing on knowledge from my own younger days, decades previous.

Throughout her junior high years, whenever we'd play together, I would win. Joanna used to get very frustrated with that. She'd complain, "I'll never get good enough to beat you, dad!" And I'd say, "Yes, you will. In fact, there will come a time when you'll grow so skilled that you'll leave me behind -- and I'll never again be able to win against you."

About midway through Joanna's sophomore year in high school, she started occasionally besting me, and I knew my days as a credible tennis opponent for my daughter were numbered. By the fall of her junior year, I was doing well to simply keep her from blowing me off the court.

I'm glad that my daughter can now regularly whip the socks off me in tennis. I'm proud that she's come so far, maturing in her skills, going beyond anything her dad ever accomplished in that sport.

Because of my experience as an earthly dad, I'm also convinced that our heavenly Father, Almighty God, enjoys growing pride in his children on earth as we mature in our faith. Before he left this earth, Jesus, God-in-the-flesh, promised that those who believed in him would accomplish even greater things than the mighty works he did while here.

A Very Different Perspective
Psalm 52:8-9

Early in our tenure as missionaries to the poverty-ridden Central American nation of Guatemala, my wife and I were determined that we would not be "ugly Americans." We had heard about other American missionaries who went into third world countries and lived as aristocrats, hiring maids and gardeners and chauffeurs and valets, and we weren't about to be like those.

We were assigned a three-room apartment on the second story of a church building in downtown Guatemala City. The senior pastor of that church, shortly after we arrived, offered to help us interview several Guatemalan women as potential maids to cook and clean for us. I was offended and told him so: "We don't want to be like that. We'll do our own cooking and cleaning, thank you."

In response the pastor took me outside the church and introduced me to the 40 or more people who lived beneath an awning just outside our church building. That partially-covered area was literally their home; they had no other. And he began to educate me to the realities of living, as an American missionary, in the third world. My salary – what I considered an anemic $400 U. S. dollars per month – was 20 times the average per capita income back then in Guatemala. Unemployment in Guatemala was, and still remains, a permanent 50 percent.

Most Guatemalans don't beg, and they don't take charity – they'd rather die first. But if I offered gainful employment, at a fair wage by their standards, I would not be acting like an ugly American. Rather, I'd be doing a very positive thing in Guatemala. If I hired a maid, at $30 per month -- or, better still, if I employed a cook and a housekeeper at $30 per month each, I would be enabling two families to survive who might otherwise die from starvation.

I learned much of a very different culture and way of life while I was a missionary. One part of that learning is this: U. S. values and ways may be right and appropriate for us, but they don't always fit the rest of the world.

Praise God, however, there is one thing I know that is equally good the world over: the love of God, expressed in Jesus Christ, for all men and women, boys and girls. From Andorra to Zimbabwe, it's the perfect answer to every human's deepest needs.

Do You Want to Be Healed?
2 Kings 5:9-12

While a seminary student decades ago, one of my earliest experiences with an "official ministry" assignment was as a chaplain. I was given spiritual oversight of a floor of mostly elderly persons in an Atlanta, Georgia nursing home facility. This was a required seminary course, designed to help us students gain practical field experience.

As I got to know the residents of my assigned floor, I began to notice curious patterns of behavior among my charges. One lady who appeared to be in good physical health never got up out of a wheelchair. A man whose arms seemed steady and strong had to be spoon-fed by attendants. A second woman with a weak, but audible, voice would write notes in place of speech 99% of the time. Others on the same assignment noted similar behavior with their patients.

In our student discussion groups, we began to share our observations -- and our frustrations -- with our patients' behaviors. After letting us stew about such matters for several weeks, the head chaplain, who was our course instructor, explained what we had noticed. Yes, Mrs. Jones was capable of walking. But it would cause her some physical discomfort to do so. And besides, she got much more attention as an invalid in a wheelchair. Mr. Smith could feed himself if need be, but how much easier to let someone else do it. And how special and important he could feel as another person occupied themselves totally with his needs, each and every meal. There were dozens of similar stories.

I suppose I had been very naive up to that point, or perhaps only unobservant. But that was the first time I realized that, for more people than I had ever imagined, sickness is preferable to health.

Jesus, as is recorded early in the fifth chapter of John's gospel, once observed a paralyzed man lying nearby. He walked over to the man and posed what might be considered an odd query, "Do you want to be healed?" A silly question? Not necessarily. Jesus, the Great Physician -- the perfect healer—knew exactly what he was asking. "Do you want to be healed?"

The paralyzed man responded in the affirmative and was duly healed by Jesus. What about you? "Do you want to be healed?" Jesus is still the great healer, of bodies, of minds -- and of souls.

Scaling Down to Manageable Size
John 14:27

One of my hobbies upon which I've not been able to spend as much time as I would like in recent years is model railroading. Some of my earliest memories are of being given an "American Flyer" model train set – at age four or five. I've still got that classic old train; it's a valuable collector's item at this point.

Over the years and decades, I've added several other trains, plus a potpourri of buildings, landscaping, even miniature people, to my layout. In order for it all to be properly set up and operational, my "train garden," as I call it, now requires a large room completely to itself. And it also requires about 80 hours' worth of labor to put it all together. Which explains why, at present, it's sitting in large unopened tubs at my house. But I'm firmly resolved to get it out and set it up, just as soon as I find a spare week or two with which to work.

Everything in a model railroad layout, if done properly, is a scaled-down version of reality. My layout is "O" gauge, which means that the scale is 3/16 of an inch to every actual foot. I find a lot of enjoyment in putting the layout together -- arranging the track just so, constructing the surrounding miniature town, landscaping it all very properly with tiny trees and flowers, placing the people in the imaginary park and other places around my little village, setting up the street lights and the crossing gates, and in general creating a microcosm of life.

When it's all finished, I've got a world in miniature to enjoy. Everything is arranged just so, everything functions properly. The trains run smoothly, predictably, around it all. I can watch my train garden for long periods of time, taking satisfaction in how orderly it all looks and functions.

Real life, of course, isn't always so smooth, predictable, perfect. Maybe that's why model railroading is fascinating to me and many others. It's our way of creating an imaginary world where everything is always all right, unlike the real world in which we must live.

If your real world isn't going smoothly, if your present life is far less perfect than you'd like it to be, there is One who can help you to sort it out and get it, to use a railroad term, "back on track." Jesus Christ is the way, the truth and the life. Ask him to help scale your problems down to manageable size. Invite him to be your Savior and Lord.

Forgiveness – It's Healthy
Ephesians 4:31-32

A man called me to apologize for something nasty he had said to me a month or so before. He said it had been weighing on him, daily, ever since he'd said it, and he wanted to get things cleared up between us. By his own account, he'd even been having trouble sleeping.

Frankly, to me it was a barely-remembered issue. Preachers get criticized so often, sometimes fairly and sometimes unfairly, that we learn to shrug off most of the negative remarks that are aimed at us. A preacher wouldn't be able to survive if he or she didn't learn to take lightly both most of the criticism and the praise received.

I gladly accepted this man's apology and, in response to his request, readily forgave him. He was relieved, and I trust he felt better as a result. I even called him up a couple of days later to check on him but managed only to leave him a word of encouragement on his voice mail.

It's interesting to me that this man – the offending party – was more affected by his callous remarks than I – the one who was supposed to be offended by them. That's really, though, what happens often. When we seek through criticism to hurt someone else, we typically wind up hurting ourselves more.

Jesus was, and is, a champion for the cause of forgiveness. Jesus understood, and taught, that forgiveness is a gracious act which helps and heals not only those who are forgiven, but also those who offer the forgiveness.

If you need to forgive someone – just do it. Do it now, do it completely. Call them, write them, e-mail them, text them, and/or talk to them in person. They'll be helped, healed, and encouraged by your forgiveness -- and so will you.

Moving Around – a Lot
Ephesians 4:31-32

It was two days before Christmas. In the parsonage my wife was decorating and wrapping packages – normal pre-Christmas activities. At the church where I was pastor, I was busily preparing for the next day's Christmas Eve worship services. The office phone rang, the church secretary answered, then passed the call on to me.

It was my supervisor in ministry, the United Methodist District Superintendent. He said, "Dave, we want you to move to El Paso." I replied, "When?" He said, "We expect you to be there before January 1st." I responded, "Can I think about it for a while?" His reply, "For thirty seconds, but you can't say 'no'".

So it was that Fran and I said goodbye to our friends and fellow Christians in Alpine, Texas on Christmas Eve, opened our gifts on Christmas Day, then began packing up everything the day after. With our two uncomprehending preschool sons in tow, we arrived in El Paso on December 28th to begin a new life in a new town.

That was the most extreme example of my decades as an "itinerant minister" in the United Methodist Church. Usually we had at least a few weeks' more time to decide, prepare, adjust to a move. But move we did, and often. At this point in our lives we've lived in 17 locations, eight of them specifically occasioned by career-imposed changes.

Frankly, I envy those who have been able to live in a particular house or location for a lengthy period of time. Having "roots" in a specific place is something I've never really experienced.

Early in the Old Testament God chose a man of significant faith named Abram to be the founder of His specially chosen people. And the very first thing that God said to Abram – check it out in Genesis 12 in the Bible – was "Move." At least one other time in Abram's life, God again told him to move. And if you examine the lives of many of the other pillars of faith in the Bible, you'll find that God often disrupted their lives by saying, "Move." The obvious reason is that God desires his faithful to make their home in him and his Kingdom, rather than any particular place on this earth.

A Different Sort of Starfish Story
Psalm 50:1-2

In the year 1985 I had the privilege of preaching a series of revivals in the Pacific Island nation of Fiji. I spent 10 days presenting the gospel to several thousand native Fijians. It was a wonderful experience, producing a lifetime of memories -- and some eternal fruit for the Kingdom of God.

After 10 straight days of worship and preaching, 11 to 12 hours daily, I was totally drained, physically and spiritually. Fortunately, I had been forewarned to schedule myself at least three days of rest and relaxation in Fiji before returning to the states. So I spent the final three days of my stay on that island paradise at an A-frame cabin by a beautiful, deserted beach – just me, God, seagulls and surf.

I love to snorkel, so I spent most of those three days snorkeling in the reefs just 100 yards in front of my cabin. The sea life in that reef was incredibly diverse and colorful. Each time the tide went out, thousands of bright blue starfish were left on the beach. Many of them died between tidal changes and, although I know better than to take live creatures out of the ocean, I decided to take some of these already dead, but still strikingly beautiful, starfish back to show my wife in the U. S. They felt hard as rocks, so after washing the sand out of them and letting them dry on the porch, I simply bagged an assortment of these gorgeous blue stars and threw them into my suitcase.

Four days later, as I was pulling my luggage off an airport conveyor belt, I immediately realized something was wrong. The smell of rotting fish assailed my nostrils. I quickly threw the suitcase into the trunk of my car, not daring to open it until I got home. There, when I did open it -- out in the garage, I discovered absolute ruin. Those seemingly solid starfish had literally dissolved into a gooey, stinking mess -- ruining everything in that suitcase. I had to toss it all -- starfish, clothing, even the suitcase itself -- into a trash bin.

Solomon, the wise king of ancient Israel, wrote in God's word that the beauty of this world is both vain and fleeting. That certainly was underlined for me by my starfish debacle. And Solomon likewise reminds us that the beauty of God is everlasting. These days I no longer pick up dead starfish -- even if they do seem beautiful. But I'm definitely looking forward to seeing the indescribably beautiful face of my eternally risen Savior, Jesus Christ.

Coincidence or Something More?
Revelation 14:13

Another pastor approached me with a request: Was there any way I could help him to obtain a portable personal oxygen supply system for an ailing missionary in the town of Veracruz, Mexico? I said I would ask around, and I did. I talked with several doctor friends and others in the medical profession. And I rapidly discovered that such personal portable oxygen systems are both expensive and in high demand.

Less than a handful of days after I received that request, one of the old saints of my congregation died. She'd been a staunch believer in Christ for many decades, but she'd suffered much from respiratory problems throughout the final year of her life. So her passing from this earth and into the Kingdom of Heaven was, from my point of view, a blessing.

As I was conducting her funeral, the memory struck me. Every time I had seen this lady outside the hospital in the most recent six months, she had been breathing with the assistance of a personal portable oxygen supply.

Immediately after the funeral, I asked her son, her only child – what was he planning to do with his deceased mother's portable oxygen supply system? He said he'd been wondering about that himself; he wanted to give it to someone who needed such. I explained the need of the missionary in Mexico, and he replied that that was exactly the kind of use his mother would have wanted her equipment to go to. Two hours after the funeral, he brought the complete oxygen equipment system to my office. I passed it on to the pastor who'd made the request of me, and he sent it on to the missionary in Mexico who needed it.

I'm often amazed by God's serendipity, and this was one of those amazing, blessed times. I'd never before needed a personal, portable oxygen system until that week -- and God provided one as soon as it was needed. An old saint reached out from beyond the grave to bless someone she'd never met. Praise God for his marvelous, miraculous providence.

Trashing a Fifty-Year Relationship
Genesis 2:21-24

Most of the stories I share are positive; this one isn't. Nevertheless, I share it because it teaches several very important life-lessons.

In one of my churches many years back, a couple were celebrating their golden wedding anniversary. As a pastor I've been part of many similar celebrations. The large church fellowship hall was well-decorated, the guests numbered in the hundreds, and the entire extended family was present -- children, grandchildren, greats, nephews and nieces, cousins galore. It was a truly gala affair.

When the time came for speeches and toasts, the husband of the pair rose up to speak. He began thus: "I've lived with this woman for 50 years. I've hated every day of it, and I don't plan to spend another day with her." From that appalling beginning it got worse. He continued for several minutes longer, berating his wife and cursing her with a multiplicity of terms and phrases that shouldn't be repeated here. Then he stomped out of the room.

Obviously, this man had carefully planned for the opportunity, diabolically plotting to destroy his wife at what should have been their finest moment together in old age – their 50th wedding anniversary. Everyone present was reduced to horrified silence except the wife, who simply sat sobbing at the table. As pastor the only thing I could think was to say, "Let us pray," and lift a prayer to God for healing of the many relationships which this man had just severed from his wife, his family, his friends.

The couple were officially divorced a couple of months later. She died within six months of the anniversary, he within a year. Hate is a terrible thing. It hurts and destroys those who are its objects. It often simultaneously destroys those who foolishly dare to wield it. And the ripples of hate spread, indirectly harming many more with its negative power. The entire congregation of those who witnessed this hateful act was many months recovering from the detonation of that bombshell of malice.

Since that infamous experience in my life, I've regularly counseled those who are married never, never to assume anything about their spouses. Even after 50 years together no marriage partner should ever take the other for granted. Marriage relationships require the regular investment of both love and work -- ever and always.

Secret Blessing
Ruth 2:15-19

My first full-time pastoral assignment was a church full of wonderful old folks in Albuquerque, New Mexico. Some of them were reasonably well-off financially; most were merely OK in that category, but some just barely scraped by.

One particular widow whom I knew was barely surviving financially was Rose. I'd been to her house, and I'd opened her refrigerator while getting a drink of water. To use a pre-refrigeration expression, "the cupboard was bare."

I subsequently spoke privately with a handful of other church members who were substantially better off than she about Rose's empty refrigerator. They all knew Rose and loved her. But they also knew she simply wouldn't agree to let anyone help her. She was stubbornly self-reliant. We tossed around several ideas when, finally, one of the other widow ladies said, "I'll take care of it, and she'll never know."

This particular woman regularly sat next to Rose in the pew each Sunday. And so, every Sunday while Rose was intently listening to my sermon, she would slip a $20 bill into Rose's purse. Rose never caught her doing it, and Rose never figured out what was happening, at least not while I was still the pastor there.

Rose commented to me once or twice about the "magical" way she always seemed to find extra money in her purse that she couldn't remember putting there. I smiled and told her to just enjoy it -- that God loved her and was blessing her. Which was, of course, quite true.

Enemies Can and Do Become Friends
Mark 9:38-40

In the winter of 1993, barely a year after the official demise of the Soviet Union, I had the opportunity to travel to Russia. I journeyed deep into the heart of that huge nation to the Siberian city of Irkutsk, a mind-boggling five time zones east of Moscow.

Going to Russia wasn't, frankly, my first choice of places to travel. All my life thus far I'd been saturated by the idea that the Russians, with their atheistic, communist ideology, were the arch-enemy of all that America stood for. I knew that communism had recently fallen, but I wondered what that really meant. Yes, I welcomed a chance to share my faith in Jesus Christ with virtually anyone, anywhere -- but I could think of a lot of other places where my witness would be better exercised than Siberia -- in winter, no less.

When I actually arrived in Russia, my preconceptions were immediately shattered. There I met some of the friendliest, most hospitable people I'd ever encountered. Most of them looked, dressed and acted like Americans. I had hardly any opportunity to practice the Russian I'd been painstakingly re-learning 25 years after originally studying it in college -- since everyone I met wanted to practice their English with me.

The transparent, excited openness to the gospel of Jesus Christ which I found, was truly amazing. I'd expected to have to debate against staunch defenders of atheism. Instead I found men and women, boys and girls ravenously hungry for spiritual truth. Their old beliefs had proven hollow; they were already searching for new, more solid foundations upon which to base their lives. My Christian witness fell upon highly receptive ears.

Today, while our respective nations' political leaders certainly do not agree on everything, the Russian people have gradually become global friends and sometimes even partners to the American people. Other nations and other belief systems have moved to the fore as current enemies. And perhaps coincidentally, Russia has experienced one of the most rapid revivals of Christianity in the two millennia history of the faith.

Aiding and Abetting Irresponsibility
Deuteronomy 21:18-21

His name was Mickey. He was 52 years of age and weighed well over 400 pounds. He was one of the town drunks – you could find him at the Crystal Bar any time its doors were open. But he drove a shiny new sports car, at least when it wasn't in the body shop being banged out from his latest accident. How he got in and out of it, I don't know – images of a giant shoehorn passed through my mind whenever I thought of that transaction.

Mickey's mother was a member of one of my previous congregations. She was a highly-committed Christian and a genuinely wonderful woman. She could be counted upon to help in the church in almost any way, anytime. She was graciously gentle and quietly soft-spoken -- except when anyone dared to make even the slightest comment about the chronically irresponsible behavior of her son. On those occasions she instantly became a tigress, verbally lashing out at the critic. Many times I can recall her saying, "I don't let anyone criticize my Mickey. He's my baby, you know!"

This 52-year old, 400-pound baby lived at home with his mother. He was an only child. To my knowledge he'd never worked a day in his life. But momma saw to it that he was well-supported....to the mutual detriment of both her son and herself. Everyone could easily see that she was aiding and abetting both his alcoholism and his irresponsibility – except her. Sometimes, love really is blind. Or perhaps, love isn't always what it claims to be.

Proverbs 13:24 in God's Holy Word says this: "Those who spare the rod hate their children, but those who love them are diligent to discipline them." Certainly, I don't recommend literally beating one's kids. But on the other hand, I do believe that consistent, firm discipline is ultimately more loving than simply letting a child run wild. Mickey's bad behavior, at 52, was at least partially a result of momma's laxity – probably back when he was 12.

Differently Dedicated
1 Corinthians 12:4-6

Lucille was a reader. She was a retired schoolteacher and she loved to read -- especially popular Christian literature, both fiction and non-fiction. Lucille also wanted her pastor to read what she read. Every week, sometimes twice weekly, she'd bring a book to me, always with a glowing report. "Pastor, I just read this and you simply have to read it. It will change your life."

My problem was not that I didn't want to read, but I simply didn't have the time available to read -- certainly not at the rate Lucille read. She had little else to do but read; I didn't have that luxury. So the books she brought began stacking up on my desk. And Lucille grew increasingly frustrated with me. I repeatedly tried to explain to her that I didn't have the volume of time available for reading that she had, but she took my excuses as cover-up for lack of interest. After a year or so, she disgustedly stopped bringing me books altogether -- and became a largely inactive member of that church.

In every church I've served, there are ample numbers of folks who are passionate about something which, for them, is singularly important. And some of those same folks insist that their pastor become similarly enthralled with their particular fascination. Golfers want the pastor to play golf with them -- three times or more weekly. Political activists want the preacher to get deeply involved in politics. Runners want the pastor to get up and run with them -- every morning at 6 AM.

Those who are involved in Christian parachurch ministries are often the worst of the lot in this regard. If they are dedicated to a cause, their preacher simply must join them. If they visit prisons, the pastor has to visit prisons, too. If they raise money for world hunger, the pastor better take a significant role there. If they volunteer at the YMCA, the preacher should be highly visible there as well.

In Romans 12, the apostle Paul reminds us that we each have differing gifts from God. And we therefore have differing interests -- and differing roles to play, both in the world and for the church. No one can, nor should, be expected to do it all.

If you are one of those passionate church members who insists that your pastors follow you in your interests and pursuits, consider letting them off the hook. Maybe God has something else for them to do -- like shepherding the flock.

The Greatest Love
John 3:16-17

When my daughter was small, it was usually my job as the father in the family to put her to bed. Or perhaps I should say that my job was to try to put her to bed, for she was an energetic little girl who simply would not go down until she was just about ready to fall down. But I gradually developed a routine with her that included a piggyback ride to the bedroom, reading a story, singing a song, and, finally, helping her with bedtime prayers.

We'd almost always begin her evening prayers with a ritualized review. I'd ask the question, "Who loves Joanna?" And she would reply with a long list: momma, and daddy, and big brothers, and Uncle Tommy, and God-momma Charlene, and fourteen or fifteen other names of family members and friends. Then the listing would continue with our family pets: Sneezer cat, and Benji-barks, even the goldfish. When she finally ran out of other names, I would then ask, "And who loves Joanna most of all?" To which her answer was always an excited, eager exclamation: "Jesus!"

My daughter has now long been an adult, so dad doesn't put her to bed nor go through a nightly review of all the names of those who love her. I trust she knows she is yet loved by many, many people -- plus maybe even a few pets. And most importantly, Joanna still clearly realizes that the greatest love she will ever know is given to her by Jesus Christ, the Son of the Living God.

All normal human beings want to be loved. Failure to seek love is one of the earliest signs of severe abnormality in infants. Some folks find adequate love from others in this world; unfortunately, far too many do not. But above and beyond the love of our fellow human beings, be it much or little, the good news at the heart of the Christian faith is that God loves us all.

If you are fortunate enough to have a loving family and friends, praise God! But even if you are virtually alone in this world, you have a Savior who loves you. His name is Jesus, and his is the best and greatest love you will ever know.

A Lenient Judge
Acts 17:30-31

A faithful member of the church I was then serving called and woke me up in the middle of the night -- about 2:30 AM. His twin sons, juniors in high school and active leaders in our church's youth group, had just been arrested and taken to jail -- forty-five miles away in another state. Could I go with him and help him bail them out? Although I had no idea what good I might or might not be in such a situation, I told him I would go with him. I quickly dressed, he picked me up, and we drove to where the boys were incarcerated.

Because they were juveniles they could be released into the custody of their dad as long as they agreed to appear at a hearing the following week. So we got them out and I heard the story. They'd been gathering firewood for a high school pep rally bonfire, and they'd found what they thought was a bonanza. A huge stack of old railroad ties was just lying there beside the railway, ready for the taking.

They were almost finished loading their pickup truck when the sheriff's car pulled up and they were arrested. They had no idea that old railroad ties weren't fair game for the taking. They belonged to the railroad, and the railway company didn't take kindly to having its ties stolen.

With continuances and other legal delays several months passed before their hearing actually came up. I agreed to go and appear before the judge as a character witness for them. I did appear and stood with them, but I was never actually given opportunity to speak on their behalf.

Their story was simple -- they claimed they didn't know they were breaking the law by taking the railroad's ties. Most of the time ignorance of the law is not considered a valid excuse for breaking it. But this judge must have believed their story, that they really didn't know they were committing a crime. He let them off with a small fine and a few hours of community service each. Their judge decided to grant them grace, when they could have been much more severely punished.

I thank God that he is like that judge. Most of us deserve severe punishment for disobeying his laws. We're all sinners -- some simply through ignorance, others more willfully. But if we throw ourselves upon his mercy, he will always grant us grace. While we still may have to suffer consequences for our actions, such are never as extreme as we likely deserve.

Accentuate the Positive
Luke 23:39-43

In every church which I pastored someone, usually sooner rather than later, asked me to preach a sermon on hell. If memory serves me correctly, I've had far more requests, over my decades of preaching, for sermons on hell than for messages on heaven. I often wonder why that is.

Certainly hell is a real place. Hell is a terrible place. Jesus warns against hell so many times in the Scriptures that even liberal Bible scholars wind up tying themselves in knots when they try to deny its existence.

But the essential truth of the gospel is that Jesus Christ came to save, not to damn people. He even said, on more than one occasion, that it is not God's will that any be lost. Yes, sadly, some will go to hell. But they'll be sending themselves by their rejection of God's Savior. Most certainly, the Almighty is not gleefully anticipating the filling up of the pit of hell.

Why do professing Christians seem so fascinated by hell? Whenever anyone asks me to preach on hell, I first ask them if they're planning to go there. If the answer is no, which it invariably is, then I further ask, "Why, then, do you want me to elaborate on an awful place that you'll never see? That answer is usually, "Well, you need to warn everybody else." To which I respond, "If I have to scare people into heaven to get them there, I'll pass. If I, and you, can't love them into the Kingdom of God, then we certainly won't scare the hell out of them."

More and more often these days, I feel the need to say to fellow-believers, "Lighten up, Christians!" We've good news to share, not bad. The world already has enough doomsayers. It doesn't need additional warnings against hell. Rather it needs to hear more of the hope of salvation -- in Jesus Christ.

In God's Time, Revival
Psalm 85:1-7

While working on my doctorate at Vanderbilt University in Nashville, Tennessee, I also served as associate pastor of a once-great, but at that time declining, congregation located in a changing neighborhood of east Nashville. That church attempted to offer a Tuesday evening outreach ministry to the children of the neighborhood -- 40 to 50 tough street kids whose family situations were indescribably difficult. We provided them a place to gather for about two hours, with food, games, and sports activities. It was my job to offer a short devotional talk to them each Tuesday night.

Attempting to speak to these kids gave me "battlefield" preaching experience. I was constantly booed and hissed at, pelted by thrown food, sometimes even punched while attempting to break up fights between the kids. Late on Tuesday evenings, as we were cleaning up, I would often say to my wife Fran, "I'm not sure this is worth it. We don't seem to be accomplishing anything."

Those experiences all took place long ago. Thirty-five years would pass before I returned to Nashville and had opportunity to once again attend church at East End United Methodist Church. And then I was truly amazed. That congregation had undergone a dramatic resurgence. There were three times as many Sunday morning worshippers as I recalled from my student days. Some of the people whom I met were those very neighborhood kids – by then middle-aged adults with children of their own – whom we had tried to influence on Tuesday evenings so many years before.

In the Holy Bible, Ecclesiastes 11:1 says, "Cast your bread upon the waters, for you will find it after many days." In other words, what you give out won't be wasted -- in the long run. It was extremely satisfying to learn that the seeds we had planted so long ago were later bearing fruit. Praise the Lord -- nothing done in his Name is ever in vain!

Healings -- Natural and Supernatural
Luke 4:38-40

Nearly every day of my four decades in ministry, and without question at least every other day, I was in a hospital to visit a sick person. I ended almost every such visit with prayer, a prayer for the healing of that person. I affirm that God heals via a combination of three methods: human medical science; supernatural, divine grace; and ultimately, through the resurrection of believers in Christ to life eternal.

Medical science today truly performs what would have been termed miracles in past generations, and I praise God that he has chosen to place such wonderful healing power in the hands of men and women. And I further am convinced that God also heals, miraculously, through direct, powerful divine intervention.

I must believe in divine healings because I have personally experienced them. Among the thousands of times that I have prayed for persons to be healed, I know for certain of two occasions during which the supernatural power of God was directly released following my prayer. In those two instances gravely ill patients were immediately and instantaneously healed of their conditions. I knew it -- and they knew it. The power of God was unquestionably, unmistakably manifested.

Some persons have questioned me about that belief. They say, "Dave, if you've witnessed just two divine healings in 40-plus years of praying for the sick, that's not very many. Are you sure God is still performing supernatural healings?"

My answer is an emphatic yes. I don't require constant reminders of God's capability. Two instances, for me, is sufficient evidence -- even if I never personally witness another divine healing in my lifetime. And of course I always pray that God will employ all means, both natural and supernatural, to heal the sick.

Waiting for God's Timing
Romans 5:5-6

The church I was then serving in El Paso, Texas had the kind of problem that most pastors would love to have. We were growing -- growing so much that we were out of room. We needed a larger fellowship hall, more Sunday School classrooms, additional office space, a bigger kitchen.

A Building Committee was appointed to study the situation and, after about a year's work, they developed an expansion plan. Their proposal included several major additions -- with a steep price tag attached. It was controversial; many felt it was too expensive. A congregational meeting was called -- a very well-attended congregational meeting -- and a vote was taken by paper ballot.

For quite a while after the vote, all present waited to hear the result. Finally, one of the counters came out and whispered something to me. I went back to the room where they were counting and was told the result. The vote was tied -- 72 for the proposal, 72 against.

I quickly got on the telephone and called one of my friends -- an older and wiser pastor who had walked with the Lord far longer than I. "What should I do?" I asked him. "I have the deciding vote, and I really believe we need to build as soon as possible." His response was this, "Yes, you do have the deciding vote. But don't you dare cast it. If you do, you'll be asking for trouble. You certainly don't want to start a major building program with half the congregation against it. Just wait -- God will work it out."

So I reported to the congregation that the vote was deadlocked. And we simply referred the issue back to the Building Committee for further study.

The church continued to grow and our cramped quarters became even more so. Eighteen months later the Building Committee brought another proposal before the congregation – really much the same plan as before with a few minor modifications.

By then there was much more agreement regarding the need for additional space -- people had grown tired of sitting in each other's laps. The vote was lopsided to approve the construction plan – 96% in favor. Thus we began to build with virtually unanimous support from the congregation.

The Bible tells us that there is a right time, in God's sight, for every human endeavor. If I'd had my human way, we'd have gone ahead prematurely with a building program that might have failed. But by waiting we allowed God to prepare the way for a much more successful outcome.

Recharging for the Demands of Ministry
Exodus 18:13-26

Pastors today are very probably the last "practicing generalists" in our complex society. One minute he or she may be studying a scholarly work on the life of the apostle Paul, the next trying to help a homeless person avoid starvation for another day. In the morning they may be called upon to counsel a pregnant teen, at midday meet the town's movers and shakers over lunch, in the afternoon sort donated food for the hungry, and in the evening visit prospects who want to learn what the church has to offer them. It's all part and parcel of being a pastor.

The job is almost never boring, for there's sure to be something new and different -- and challenging -- facing a pastor each and every new day. It requires a high energy level and complete disregard for the clock. Pastors are both on-call and on-duty 24/7.

For many years I've been regularly asked, "What keeps you going, Dave? How do you keep from running out of gas?" I recognize that pastors today are leaving the ministry at an unprecedented rate. I'm very aware that many of my colleagues burned out, retired early, or just simply quit because of the unrelenting, often unreasonable demands placed upon them by so many other people. Yet after most of my adult life at it I still love the ministry and can't imagine doing anything else -- at least not for long.

What fueled me as a pastor was simply this: Whenever one precious person came to the Lord Jesus Christ, experiencing that supreme blessing which Christians call salvation, I was energized for another six or more months.

That alone is enough -- it more than outweighs all the protracted committee meetings, the late-night telephone complaints from Aunt Susie about the sanctuary being too cold, the uncertainty over church finances, the screaming children during God's worship.

Nothing else can match being there when a human being is adopted into the family of God for eternity. That, for me, is the bottom line. When one person receives Christ as Savior, I'm like the "energizer bunny" – I'm recharged for the work of the ministry, whatever it may be, for many months to come!

Living by Faith
Matthew 23:23-24

I lived in the small, "Big Bend" town of Alpine, Texas during their year of celebration of 100 years as a city. Among the many interesting endeavors that were undertaken as part of Alpine's centennial was this: Every man in town was supposed to let their facial hair grow during the summer months for a beard-growing contest. If you were seen downtown that summer in Alpine without a beard, you were supposed to pay a $5 fine. It was all good-natured fun, and more than a few Alpine men ignored it. But to show my community spirit I at least tried to grow a beard.

For seven weeks I endured a scraggly, patchy mess of hair on my face. To me, it looked awful -- and it felt worse. Although everyone told me it would stop itching after the first week or two, it never did.

I duly stood on the platform in the Alpine city park on Labor Day weekend to have my beard judged. It didn't win any prizes. And that very evening, as soon as I got home, with great relief I shaved it off.

I've never since tried to grow a beard. Beards are fine for some men -- but I'm not one of them.

Every once in a while Christians ask me about rules and practices from the Old Testament of the Holy Bible. Do Christians today need to observe all the old Jewish laws? My answer is no. Although God's _moral_ law as found in the Old Testament -- such as the Ten Commandments -- is timeless and intended for all humans, much of the ceremonial law of the Jews was meant only for then and there, not for today.

If all of the Old Testament ceremonial laws were still in force, I'd be in constant violation -- because the Jewish men of old were required to always wear long beards. It clearly says so in the Old Testament.

But as Galatians 3:13 in the New Testament relates, Jesus Christ has set us free from such ceremonial laws. We are free today to live by faith -- faith in him.

Good Old Days? – Not Really
Ecclesiastes 12:1

Several years ago, my wife and I visited the beautiful two-island nation of New Zealand. New Zealand, to us, was like going back in time 50 or 60 years in America.

One of the particular aspects of that "back in time" feeling was the availability of television in New Zealand. Everywhere we traveled, whether on the north or south island of that nation, we had a choice in television entertainment. But that choice was quite limited. We could turn on TV channel one -- or TV channel two. That's all.

Older Americans can still remember the days of old when TV channel choices were limited to one, or two, or at most three possibilities. That's most certainly not the case today.

A lot of older folks liked to remind me, as pastor of a church, of how things used to be in the church when they were younger. One comment that I often heard was this: "Why, back when I was a teenager, we had 100 young people coming to church for youth fellowship every Sunday evening. Today's youth just aren't as dedicated to God as we were."

My response was this: "Think back to when you were a teenager. What other choices did you have available to you on Sunday evenings?" Forty or fifty years ago, youth could go to church to be with their friends on Sunday evenings -- or they could sit at home alone and do nothing. Those were about the only two possibilities which existed.

Today there are a rainbow of choices for activities in which to engage outside the home, plus multiple ways to occupy one's self if you choose to remain at home, especially "screen time" on your smart phone or computer.

Thus when a youth comes to church on a Sunday evening today, they've made a significant choice. They've weighed, and sifted out, a multiplicity of other options. To me, that's a far more significant decision than simply joining the crowd at church -- because it's the only option available.

Their numbers may be fewer, but the quality of commitment to Jesus Christ, in my opinion, is far higher today among church youth than it was in 1960. I praise God for the depth of faith that I often find in contemporary Christian youth.

Tragedy and Triumph
1 Peter 1:3

Where were you, and what were you doing, on the morning of Sept. 11, 2001? My guess is that virtually every adult reading this can remember exactly where they were, and what they were doing, when they first heard the tragic news of the terrorist attacks on the World Trade Center in New York City and the Pentagon in Washington, DC. And I suspect that most of us will remember where we were, and what we were doing, on the morning of Sept. 11, 2001 for the rest of our natural lives.

I'm old enough to have had two other tragedies imprint themselves in my memory for a lifetime. The more recent of those two was Jan. 28, 1986, the awful morning when the space shuttle Challenger blew up. I was in the office of the church I was then serving in El Paso, Texas that morning. My secretary called me out to watch a TV monitor. We stood there in shocked silence for the next half hour or more, transfixed by the image of the explosion.

And then, there was the more distant memory chronologically -- but still vivid in my mind -- of November 22, 1963, when U. S. President John F. Kennedy was assassinated. I was a high school student, in a biology lab, when my cousin, Judy, burst into the classroom with the news, "The President's been shot!" Within seconds, the school's intercom began broadcasting the bad news, live from Dallas.

Why does tragedy imprint itself so clearly and so permanently on the human consciousness? I'm sure psychologists and psychiatrists have a biological reason to offer in explanation; I don't know what it is. I just know that tragedy has a way of sticking with us -- for a very long time.

Can you imagine the awful feeling that the disciples of Jesus Christ had, after following Him for years on end, when they saw their friend, teacher, and mentor breathe his last on a cruel cross? That was a tragic memory that would surely weigh them down for the rest of their lives. There was nothing that could erase that tragedy from their consciousness -- except for it to be undone, and that couldn't happen.

Or could it? Three days later, when Jesus rose from the dead, that tragedy turned into a triumph. And they -- and the whole world -- were healed. Yes, Christians still remember the tragedy of the crucifixion, but it's eclipsed by the greater, good news -- of the Resurrection.

Code Language in the Church
2 Kings 18:26

One of the things a pastor learns early is that church people don't always say what they mean nor mean what they say. One of the most frequent examples is this: A member will say to me, "Be sure to add Mrs. Smith to the church's prayer list." That's all that's asked, no more. Early in my ministry, I took such requests at face value, and dutifully added Mrs. Smith to my church's printed prayer list. And then, the very next Sunday, the same person would inquire of me, "Did you check on Mrs. Smith this past week?" "No, but I added her to the church's prayer list, just as you asked. And I prayed for her personally."

I soon discovered that, while I had done precisely what was asked, that wasn't all that was wanted. "Please pray for Mrs. Smith," doesn't only mean "please pray." It also means, "Call her, check on her, visit her if at all possible." "Please pray" is church "code language" between members and their pastor. It really means, "Mrs. Smith requires some personal attention from you."

Another instance in which church folks not only don't say what they mean, but often mean the very opposite of what they say, is this: A faithful old saint will approach me to "Preacher, I've been arranging the flowers, or I've been serving as an usher, or I've been teaching the 3rd grade Sunday School class -- for the past six years in a row. I'm tired. Would you please find someone else to take my place?"

As a young pastor, I regarded such requests as real, and immediately began searching for someone to take over that person's responsibilities. And when I actually found replacements to arrange the flowers, serve as an usher, or teach the 3rd grade Sunday School, I discovered some very disappointed people.

Once in a great while, when someone asks to be relieved of a long-term responsibility in the church, they really mean it. It requires a great deal of spiritual discernment to determine when this is actually the case. But most of the time, this is another form of "coded communication" which has developed in churches between the people and their pastors.

What that person is really asking for is affirmation that they're appreciated for what they're doing. Rather than my finding someone to replace them, what they actually want to hear is, "Sam, you're doing such a fine job as church treasurer I just don't think we could find anyone else to take your place. I'd really appreciate it if you'd continue. Please keep up the good work for another year." Then, nine times out of ten, their response will be, "Well, if you really want me to, I'll continue to serve." And this intricate exercise in church diplomacy has been successfully completed. It's a little strange, but to God be the glory anyway!

Let There Be Enough Light!
Genesis 1:3-4

One of the parts of modern-day church worship in which I enjoy participating is the Children's Sermon. A special portion of Sunday morning worship especially for children, while found in many churches today, is a relatively new phenomenon for the Christian Church, something virtually unknown before 1965. I'm surprised it took the Church so long to develop such. Making the littlest ones among the congregation feel that they are a special, important part of the flock of God is, to me, an obvious implication of Jesus' words in Luke 18:16 – "Let the children come to me, do not hinder them, for of such is the Kingdom of God."

Whenever I have the opportunity to interact with children via a Children's Sermon, I love to ask questions of them. Doing so is somewhat risky, however, because you never know what sorts of responses you'll get. In one particular church, just a few weeks before I was moved to another, I recall asking the children one morning, "What's the first word you think of when you hear the word 'church'?" A little girl of about seven replied with the word "dark." I was puzzled. "Church makes you think of dark? Why?" I asked in response. Her reply was simple and literal: "It's dark in here."

The sanctuary lighting in that church was very inadequate. For five years I'd received a steady barrage of complaints from adults in the congregation who couldn't see well enough to read the pew Bibles or hymnals. But those concerns, while I'd duly passed them on to the Trustees of the congregation, were routinely ignored. Their excuse, the same as I'd heard in many other churches, was this: "We don't have enough money to worry about that."

Several months after moving on I read a newsletter from this former congregation and, praise God, they were getting ready to install new lighting in their sanctuary. The adults of the congregation couldn't get the attention of the Trustees, nor even could the pastor, but that little girl's comment proved to be the catalyst which spurred them to address the problem. Sometimes, as the Bible says, "a little child shall lead them."

Flexible at Age 100+
Deuteronomy 34:7

Adele, a lady in her 70's and a member of my then-congregation in Albuquerque, New Mexico, approached me with a concern. Her mother, Mabel, was soon coming to move in with her. Mabel was 102 years of age and was relocating to Albuquerque from New Jersey. She had lived in the same house in New Jersey all her life -- she had even been born in that house, not a hospital. And now, after 102 years in one and the same place -- even the same house -- Mabel needed to move 2/3 of the way across the country and live with her daughter.

Adele was worried. How would her mother, already a centenarian, adjust to such a complete change in the life she had known since childhood? How could I, and the church, help to ease the trauma of such radical adjustment for a 102-year old lady?

We plotted and planned. A month later, when Mabel stepped off the plane at the Albuquerque airport, not only was her daughter Adele there to greet her, but so were more than twenty other members of our mutual church. I personally presented her a dozen red roses to underscore her welcome to her new community.

Our fears were groundless. Mabel Archer, at age 102, hit the ground running. She joined the garden club, the bridge club, the church women's circle, the senior citizen's center. She and her daughter Adele, together, were two of the most active church members I've ever served. Mabel lived five more years -- to age 107. They were good years for her, for everyone she met, and for the Kingdom of God.

Conventional wisdom says that old folks are resistant to change -- that they become fixated and fossilized. That may be true in some cases, but I've met too many counter-examples, like Mabel Archer, to pre-judge all senior citizens. Many of them are open, flexible, and ready for new challenges, both within and outside the Church of Jesus Christ. Praise the Lord!

A Crisis of a Lost Ring
2 Corinthians 12:14-15

Kim, a young newlywed whose marriage I had performed just two months before, called me in tears. Her gold wedding band had fallen off her finger while she was washing dishes, and she had ground it up in the sink's disposal unit before she realized it was missing. She was terrified. What would her husband say when he got home? And, even more importantly, what she really wanted to ask me was this: Since she no longer had a wedding ring, was her marriage over?

As soon as I could get her to stop crying, I explained to her that no, her marriage definitely was not ended by the loss of her wedding band. I reminded her of the words which had been part of her wedding ceremony itself: "The wedding ring is an outward and visible sign of an inward and spiritual grace…" In other words, the ring was only a symbol of the marriage relationship between her and her husband. A ring, valuable though it might be, could never define a relationship. I assured her that her marriage was still intact and offered her a few suggestions as to how to gently explain the destruction of the ring to her husband when he got home.

I assume the situation worked out OK, as I saw the couple together in church the following Sunday and Kim already had another wedding band on her finger. I deliberately didn't say anything, for I wasn't sure she had told her husband about our conversation. I never heard any more regarding this ring issue.

That incident, however, was a stark reminder to me of how our society tends to overvalue things -- and undervalue relationships. Whether it be cars and boats with men, or diamonds and gold jewelry with women, we all tend to place far too much emphasis on objects – things -- and far too little on people -- our relationships to one another. Materialism with a capital M is a defining characteristic of American life today. And as well-educated as many of us are, we simply ought to know better.

Jesus, in the fifteenth chapter of the Gospel of Luke, said these words, "Take care.... for people's lives do not consist in the abundance of their possessions."

Things – objects, possessions – come and go. But precious people, and our relationships with them, are irreplaceable.

Excited about Jesus – But Not for Long
Revelation 2:4-5

While I was a pastor in the vast Big Bend Country of west Texas, I learned a fair amount concerning "cowboy camp meetings." There are several major cowboy camp meetings held annually in the Big Bend region, most notably Bloys and Paisano. I further discovered that there are a number of other cowboy camp meetings held annually throughout the southwestern United States. Bloys, located near Ft. Davis, is the granddaddy of them all. It has met annually since 1890.

Cowboy camp meetings are combination family reunions and outdoor Christian revivals. Hundreds of people from all over the nation gather and "camp out" for a week or more. They spend those days renewing acquaintance with one another and worshiping God. Daily, from early morning to late night, there are Bible studies, preaching and singing, and much food and fellowship. Some who attend accept Christ as their personal Savior for the first time. Many present rededicate their lives to Him.

A cowboy camp meeting is a high-powered, week-long mountaintop religious experience for those in attendance. I was never able to drop everything else and spend an entire week at one of them, but I could readily sense the power and presence of God during my one and two day visits to several of them each year.

More than a few of the attendees of these camp meetings lived in one of the two Big Bend towns where I then served as pastor: Alpine and Marathon, Texas. So I also knew them outside their camp meeting weeks. And I came to know that quite a few of them really were, just as they willingly described themselves, "camp meeting Christians." They attended no church during the rest of the year; they showed no outward evidence of Christian faith in terms of community involvement or service to their neighbors. Thus I came to understand that a "camp meeting Christian" was often one who got "high on Jesus" one week a year, but who lived like a pagan all the rest of the time.

Of course, that sort of "on" and "off" Christianity isn't confined to those who attend camp meetings. I know plenty of folks who are turned on to Jesus every Sunday morning, but who wouldn't dare speak His name Monday through Saturday. For their sakes, I hope that our Lord returns to gather His followers on a Sunday morning -- maybe even a Sunday morning during camp meeting week.

Coping with Soreheads
Philippians 2:14-15

It was 9:30 PM. I'd just walked in the door after thirteen-and-one-half hours of nonstop driving to reach home. The telephone rang; it was Florence. She was one of my frequent "problem" people. "Pastor, my sister is in the hospital, and you need to go and see her." "OK, Florence, I'll go and check on her in the morning." "No, I want you to go now – right now." "Florence, I'm tired and, besides, it's after visiting hours at the hospital. I promise, I'll see her first thing in the morning." "No, I expect you to go now -- and if you don't, I'll make trouble for you."

I knew Florence well enough to know that making trouble was her specialty. I wasn't particularly afraid of her, but I've also learned that some battles just aren't worth fighting. So I responded, "All right, Florence, if it's that important to you that I go right now, I'll do it. I'll meet you at the front door to the hospital in ten minutes." Florence sputtered, "Why, I don't want to go out at this time of night." I quickly answered with, "Florence, the hospital won't let non-family members in this late, and that includes clergy. So if you really want me to visit your sister tonight, you're going to have to meet me there."

She reluctantly agreed to meet me at the hospital door. We talked our way past the security guard, made our way up to her sister's room -- and found the sister sound asleep. Before leaving the room, I quietly prayed with Florence for her sister's healing. Then we both headed back to our respective homes. And Florence, although she continued to be a problem person, never again made such an unreasonable demand upon me.

In every church -- in all those I've served, at least -- there are many, many wonderful, faithful, supportive, good people. And also, like a highway sign candidly proclaims regarding the population of Stanton, Texas, there are a few old soreheads. Early in my ministry I used to resent such people. Sometimes I'd even let myself be drawn into conflicts with them.

But as I grew in experience and, I trust, in the Christian faith, I gradually realized that there's little point in challenging such folks. Conflict and confrontation only make them worse than they already are. They feed on it.

So instead, I try to do what I believe Jesus would do. I try to empathize with perennially negative people. I pray for them. And I attempt to treat them better than they treat me. Unfortunately, most of them stay the way they are -- soreheads. But every once in a while, praise the Lord, I break through -- and find a precious child of God behind the wall of negativism.

An Old Saint Hears Again
1Timothy 5:1-2

His name was Harry, and he was 90 years old. He was one of the most active members of the church in which I served as associate pastor in Nashville, Tennessee -- and one of the wealthiest. He was also very hard of hearing.

Like many long-time church members Harry always sat in the same spot in the sanctuary, near the back. And almost every Sunday, because of his hearing difficulty, he would yell out at the preacher sometime during the sermon, "I can't hear you!" Clearly, Harry wasn't shy.

At an Administrative Board meeting, the leaders of the church voted to buy some assistive listening devices to put in the pews, since Harry wasn't the only one in that congregation who was going deaf. As we decided to do that, we also realized that older persons with hearing loss can be so vain as to pretend they don't have any need for such hearing aids. Would they be used if we bought them?

I was delegated to go and talk to Harry about the assistive listening project. I explained to him the need and asked if he would agree to be our "guinea pig" for the project. To my relief, he readily agreed. So the next Sunday, I told the congregation what we were going to do. "We're going to put assistive listening devices in every pew, and Mr. Harry Gower has volunteered to be the first one to use them. To which Harry stood up and shouted, "That's right! I want to hear what's going on around here."

If Harry was willing to use a hearing aid in the pew, that was sufficient for all the other hard-of-hearing folks in the congregation. To a person, they all agreed to use them. We got them installed, and at least 15 people who had been unable to clearly listen to the worship for years were able to hear again. The assistive listening devices were a hit, something that the hard-of-hearing members of that congregation wore with pride -- with Harry leading the way.

Because he could now hear the preacher, Harry determined that he also wanted to hear better music in his church. Unsolicited, he decided that the church's massive old pipe organ needed to be rebuilt -- at a cost of $90,000 which, praise the Lord, Harry Gower underwrote in full.

Call Ahead Before Visiting?
Luke 19:1-6

To call ahead or not to call ahead before a pastoral visit? Some pastors, and even a few ordinary church members, feel it's OK for the preacher to just "drop in," unannounced, at any time. But many don't -- and I'm one of them.

Here's why: While I was still a layman, just beginning the process of candidacy for the ministry, the pastor of my church asked me if I would call on a young couple who had visited our mutual congregation the previous Sunday. I said I would, took my wife with me, and showed up at their house one evening during the week.

The couple was at home and they were surprisingly hospitable. After we told them we were from the church they'd visited the previous Sunday, they warmly invited us in.

In their kitchen, around the table, there were two other couples. They were playing cards -- penny-ante poker. They invited us to join them. At first we said, "No thanks," but they insisted. We told them we didn't have even a single penny on us -- which was true. They said, "No problem, we'll stake you. Here's ten pennies for each of you."

Well, we were young and unwise -- and we wanted to establish a friendly relationship. So we joined in the game; after all, how much harm could we do, gambling with only pennies?

For the next hour and a half, between Fran and me, we literally won every single hand that was played. The other three couples completely ran out of pennies -- we accumulated every penny in the game -- a dollar and forty cents in all. Finally, we offered to give them all back their pennies, but they refused. We ended the evening with some lame goodbyes. I'm sure those folks were very glad to see us go.

That couple never again visited our church. And when, two or three weeks later, our pastor asked me for a report on my visit to them, can you imagine how embarrassed I was to tell him what had really happened?

From that day forward, I decided that I would not visit in people's homes on behalf of the church without calling ahead. Even when existing church members tell me, "Oh, just drop in anytime; you don't need to call ahead," I nevertheless <u>do</u> call ahead. The gospels don't record the Lord Jesus Christ ever barging into anyone's home without asking first -- and His is the model I follow.

Ministry with 'Transients'
Luke 17:12-19

The church I served in Big Spring, Texas offered a regular ministry to those we called "transients." Many of them really weren't transient at all; rather they were a permanent part of the population of that community. Some were homeless, some mentally ill. Many were alcohol and/or drug dependent.

They would show up at that church's door virtually every day, asking for all manner of help -- food, clothing, rent, bus tickets, auto repairs, prescription drugs, finding a job, being driven to another city, solving a problem with the police, intervening in a family squabble, whatever. If it's a common human need, that church was asked to fill it on more than one occasion.

To say the least, the stories that those transients brought to the church were colorful. Some of the time I was preoccupied with other church matters, so our church's other staff members heard their stories. But occasionally I did have time to listen; in fact, sometimes I deliberately took the time to hear out a long, wild and woolly tale from a transient.

Most of their stories are made up out of whole cloth -- 90% of transients' tales were "cons." But I already knew and expected that; in fact, my wife told me that I sometimes paid to hear "creative stories" – which was actually true.

There's no way that I, nor my church, nor all the churches of that community, could possibly meet all the demands and solve all the problems that transients presented to us. But we did try to listen, which is at least a start. Most transients desperately needed to find someone who was willing to spend even five minutes paying attention to them. They'd been so marginalized by society that they were invisible to most folks -- and they knew it.

Often we simply tried to hear them out, then send them on their way. And sometimes we were able to provide tangible help as well -- a simple but nutritious lunch, a tankful of gas, a bus ticket to a nearby town, or help with the cost of a medical prescription.

Transients rarely express thanks for being helped. In my experience they usually went away dissatisfied, ranting and raving because their outlandish demands hadn't been met in full. Oh, well....

When Jesus walked this earth, he healed the sick, fed the hungry, even raised the dead. Very few of those Jesus helped thanked Him, so today's Christians shouldn't expect to be treated any differently. We should still go on helping to the extent we're able, trusting that whatever thanks may be due will come later, from Almighty God.

News: Good and Bad
Acts 17:29-31

Once upon a time, upon my arrival at home for lunch, I recall that my wife, Fran, said to me, "I've got two things I need to tell you. One is good news and the other is bad news." I honestly don't recall, now, the content of either of the items, but I do remember my response to Fran. I said, "Tell me the bad news first. I want to get it out of the way so I can enjoy the good news."

Perhaps I'm a bit strange in this regard, for as I read and study how to effectively present Jesus Christ to persons in the 21st century A. D., I'm regularly informed that one is supposed to present the good news first, and the bad news, if at all, last.

According to what church "polling" specialists tell us preachers, people today don't want to hear bad news from the Christian church. They're already inundated with such from the world-at-large. All they really want to hear from preachers are uplifting, positive, pleasant words.

Frankly, I'd like to be able to always and ever bring positive and pleasant messages to others. I'm not a hellfire and brimstone sort of preacher -- I enjoy offering cheer and comfort to others.

But if I did only that I'd be less than faithful to the Word of God. For while there's ample good news to be found in the Bible -- God loves us and has wonderful plans for our future; there's also much sad, bad news to be found therein. Every human being is separated from God by sin, and until we repent of our sins and turn to Jesus for salvation, God's good news doesn't fully apply to us.

I always want to hear good news and I really want to offer good news to others. But first, I have to deal with the bad news of sin in my life. I have to repent of my sin, inviting Jesus Christ to enter my life and make me into a new, wonderful, positive person. Then and only then can I receive the really good news, the wonderful news of eternal salvation that God wants to offer to me.

The same is true for you. You must deal with the bad news of sin first -- then you'll be able to receive God's lasting good news of eternal salvation.

God in the Details?
Exodus 28:1-5

I was asked to bring a message to a class of eighth graders in a private Christian school. I began by asking them a question: "Do you think God understands how to operate a smart phone?" To a person, every one of these 25 of so fourteen-year-olds responded, "No, God doesn't know anything about how smart phones work."

In a world where knowledge is expanding at an exponential rate, it's no longer possible for a single human being to possess more than a surface knowledge of most subjects. A diesel mechanic may be amazingly competent in his field of endeavor, but he'd be lost if you asked him to discuss horticulture. A heart surgeon is a life saver in the hospital but might have trouble balancing his or her own checking account. A clerk in a law office may know everything there is to know about preparing a subpoena, but she hasn't a clue concerning how to repair her washing machine.

And what about God today? We automatically assume that God is specialized, too. God knows about.... well, churchly things. God understands baptism. And God can tell you what's sinful and what isn't. And God can take you to heaven, maybe. But growing cotton? Or fixing a broken pipe? Or trading securities? Or operating a smart phone? No, God wouldn't know about those things.

Why not? When we say that God is all-knowing and all-powerful – which is automatically expected of the title of "god," that doesn't imply just abstract, generalized knowledge. It means down-to-earth, specialized, relevant wisdom as well.

The only reason God is not of more practical value in most of our daily lives is that most of us have never asked Him to be. If we are willing to move beyond narrow preconceptions, falsely exiling God to only churchly, theological matters, we may be amazed at the powers and potentialities of our Creator. If we invite God to permeate our lives, to have real meaning on Tuesday afternoons at work as well as Sunday mornings at church, we may discover that God is a lot smarter than we previously thought.

If we ask God's help in figuring out how, for example, to repair a car, who knows? He might just offer something of value. I invite you to try it – if you dare!

Exceptions to the Rules
Psalm 25:4-7

It was an all-too-typical urban middle school incident in our contemporary world. A bully was working his way up the aisle of the school bus, demanding lunch money from the other children. When he got to my son Jonathan, Jonathan said, "No." The larger boy threatened; Jonathan again repeated, "No!" The bully then pulled out a pocketknife, opened it and brandished the blade. In a flash Jonathan disarmed him and left him nursing a sore arm on the floor of the bus' aisle. Then he calmly walked up the aisle and handed the knife to the bus driver. Six years of twice-weekly karate lessons had paid off.

This should have been the end of this story, but it wasn't. Later that day I learned of all this when I was called to the school office. The principal explained that, while he had interviewed all the students on the bus plus the driver, and virtually every one of them had affirmed Jonathan's version of the encounter, he had no choice but to suspend my son for three days for fighting.

School district policy was clear -- zero tolerance for fighting, regardless of the circumstances. Jonathan would also receive "zero" grades in all of his classes for those missed days. A rule had been broken and the consequences were unavoidable.

The Bible tells the story of a man with a paralyzed hand who came to Jesus for healing. Jesus healed him, restoring the hand to full functionality. Unfortunately for Jesus, the day that the man came to him happened to be the Jewish Sabbath. Jewish law said that no work could be done on the Sabbath. Healing was work. Jesus had broken the law. That He had done good was not a consideration. The law had been broken, and the consequences were clear -- and severe. In the eyes of the Jewish authorities, Jesus deserved to die.

Sometimes -- most of the time -- laws and rules are good and right and beneficial to us. They help us live orderly lives in what would otherwise be a chaotic world.

But as a Christian I'm also very glad that I will not be judged by God in relation to cold, inflexible laws. Sometimes, I need grace and mercy more than justice. We all do. And thanks be to God, those precious benefits are readily available through God's Son, Jesus Christ.

Hedging Our Bets
1 Kings 18:21

I was asked to conduct the funeral of a lady whom I didn't know well. She was a largely inactive member of my congregation in Nashville, Tennessee. Being unable to reach any family members by telephone, I showed up at the funeral home during the scheduled visiting hours the night prior to this lady's planned service, hoping there I could meet family or friends and learn more about this woman and her life, the more so since I had been asked by the funeral director to enact her parting rituals the next day.

While at the funeral home I didn't find any family members, but I did meet a number of her friends. In talking with them I discovered something very interesting. The deceased had not only been on the membership roll of my church, but she'd also been, simultaneously, a member of at least three other local churches in the same neighborhood.

Her friends didn't think that was particularly strange. In fact, several of them also proudly bragged to me of being members of Baptist, Presbyterian, Methodist, Lutheran, Catholic and other community congregations -- all at one and the same time. Between four ladies I mentally tallied seventeen church memberships.

I never did find out exactly why these women maintained multiple church memberships in a variety of denominations and congregations, but from pastoral experience I can hazard a guess or two. Many folks I meet like to hedge their bets when it comes to religious affiliation. Just in case the Catholics aren't right, I'll also be a Baptist -- and split my allegiance between them. If, perchance, the Assembly of God isn't teaching all about the true way, I'll join the Lutherans too. Surely God will be pleased to see how hard I tried to cover all the possible bases.

I'm not sure how God will sort out, nor whether God even cares, regarding the various and sundry multiple church affiliations of Christians, whether simultaneous or successive. But from the Holy Word of God I do know this: the God of Abraham, Isaac and Jacob -- the Father of Jesus the Christ -- is a jealous God. God is most definitely not pleased by those who claim to believe in Jesus, and in Mohammed, and in Buddha, and in scientology – and in maybe six or eight other persuasions. The vaguely-spiritual "buffet" to which an alarming number of folks today subscribe is clearly wrong in the eyes of the Lord. It's just a new name for old-fashioned syncretism. God desires that we pledge our allegiance to His Son Jesus -- and Him only.

Just the Right Answer
Jeremiah 33:2-3

It happened again at the end of the year 2001 while I was serving as pastor in Big Spring, Texas. With just days to go in the calendar year my church needed a large sum of money in order to meet all its financial obligations in full at year's end. I shared the need with my congregation, specifying the figure needed. And I prayed, repeatedly, that God would help us to meet that specific need. It always takes a few days after the close of a year to get the "books" of a church in order, but when all was said and done, my church had received, almost to the exact dollar, the amount needed. We didn't receive more; we didn't receive less. We got exactly what was asked.

That's not, by any means, the first time that has happened to me in my years of Christian ministry. I've faced dozens of similar situations where a specific amount of money has been needed for a specific ministry purpose. I present the need to the people, pray fervently for God to meet it, and God -- through His faithful people -- provides the amount needed. In particular situations, I've prayed for as little as $100 and for as much as $1.3 million. And when God answers, it's the right amount in response -- neither more nor less.

Finances, because they're so tangible and measurable, are the most obvious sphere in which I can identify specific answers to prayer, but there are countless other custom-tailored responses that I've experienced when praying over the years. God's grace has been on time -- neither early nor late, right-sized -- neither too much nor too little, and accurately targeted -- neither to left nor right, but right on the mark. Even with an engineering-trained mind from my first career, I long ago abandoned any thought that such could be mere coincidence. For me it's undeniable: God answers prayer.

Most certainly I'm far from being the only person in the world for whom God repeatedly and consistently answers prayer. The scriptures are clear: Our Lord wants to respond to the prayers of His people; He fervently desires to give good gifts to His children. My personal experience is also that of thousands, even millions of believers the world over.

Does God answer prayer for you? If your answer is not a resounding "yes" then perhaps you need to pray, asking God "why." He will tell you, provided you're willing to listen.

Valuing the Peculiar
1 Peter 2:9

Decades ago now, when my oldest son Dave turned 12 years of age, he joined our Albuquerque, New Mexico church's youth group. A few months later, that youth group went on a winter excursion into the nearby mountains. Their leaders having obtained the necessary permits, they were going to cut Christmas trees from the national forest. Each child could pick out and cut a tree to take home.

Dave was excited; he was going to supply the family Christmas tree that year. They took off in a variety of vehicles, including one large flatbed truck.

When the group arrived back that evening, the man driving the flatbed brought Dave directly to our house. And there, lying on the truck, was a huge evergreen tree, at least 22 feet in length and 10 feet in diameter at its base. Our son, who has always believed that bigger is better, was both proud and pleased with himself. Of course, it never occurred to him that our house's ceilings were only nine feet high. There was no way that tree was going to fit into our living room.

But in order not to squelch our son's pride in his accomplishment, dad – that's me -- got out a saw and began trimming. Actually, it went well beyond trimming. I discarded far more of the tree than I kept. But finally, I was able to bring a substantial portion of the mid-section of that tree into our living room. It looked much more like an overgrown donut than a classic Christmas tree. But we duly lighted and decorated it.

It was the strangest Christmas tree we'd ever seen, but we gradually adjusted to its uniqueness. Over the next several weeks we actually grew to appreciate it. "Normal" trees come and go each year in our household, but that very unusual Christmas tree will always be a treasured Ring family memory.

While it's very clear to me that God loves all of the precious people that he has created, there are numerous times in the Bible when Jesus paid special attention to those who were different -- who didn't easily fit in to the rest of society. Normal folks are relatively easy to love, but those who are strange and different require some getting used to. Maybe that's why they're extra-special in the sight of God, like that peculiar Christmas tree was for my family.

Lemons or Lemonade?
1 Kings 3:16-28

One of the things which my very first full-time church did regularly each week was to record the Sunday morning worship on cassette tapes. Then copies were made – and it was one of my jobs, during the week, to distribute those copies to the shut-ins of the congregation. That church being relatively small, their shut-in list was short, never more than eight and usually about five in number.

Thus, each week I would drop off a cassette tape of the prior Sunday's worship service to each of these shut-in's and, of course, stay for a few minutes of visiting with each. There were two ladies among that group whom I recall well -- I usually visited them back-to-back. (I've changed their names for this story, of course.)

I would visit Mrs. Kimbrough first. She was a lady in her sixties, wheelchair bound, otherwise in seemingly good health. She was also reasonably well off financially. But she was a perennial complainer about anything and everything, including her church and her pastor, me. Nobody paid enough attention to her, nobody helped her enough, nobody cared enough for her. Frankly, I dreaded that visit – but I endured it, listening to Mrs. Kimbrough's weekly litany of criticism for about two years on end.

Immediately after that visit I would usually hurry over to visit Mrs. Williams. Mrs. Williams was also wheelchair bound, and about a decade older than Mrs. Kimbrough. She had numerous other health problems – I eventually wound up conducting her funeral. She was also barely scraping by financially. But Mrs. Williams was a sunshine person. Whenever I'd arrive, she would tell me a story or two about good things that had happened to her in the week since I'd last seen her. She'd fix tea, and we would talk for quite some time.

Mrs. Williams always had busy hands, knitting something – items which would later be donated to the women's bazaar at the church. When she listened to the cassette tape of the worship service, she'd always invite one or two neighbors to listen with her.

Mrs. Williams was a joy to visit; I always left her house refreshed and replenished. Her positivity more than made up for the first lady's negativity.

Two women, both coping with significant physical illnesses. One allowed her situation to turn her sour. The other found joy and purpose in life despite her difficult circumstances. I leave it to you to discern, for yourself, the obvious moral of this story.

No Repeats, Please!
Hebrews 10:1

One of my personal pet peeves is repetition. When I experience something for the first time, I usually enjoy it. Twice is simply acceptable. The third time is boring. And by the fourth repetition, it drives me up the wall.

Thus when I view a movie, although I may love it, I don't particularly desire to see that film again. When I hear a well-known speaker talk on a particular subject, I may be enthralled with that person's wisdom to the extent that I tell my friends – "You really need to hear this person." But on the other hand, I don't personally care to hear that particular presentation a second time. I've been to Walt Disney World and to the Grand Canyon, and I had a truly marvelous time at both those world-class attractions. But I don't have a burning desire to go again to either -- "been there, done that."

Small children love repetition. It's part of the learning process for them. When my three children were little, their constant repetitive banter was a strain I valiantly tried to endure. But my kids saw through me to the extent that, when one of them began to repeat something over and over again, the others would often warn, "Shh! Daddy doesn't like repeats!" Frankly, I'm very glad to be long past that stage in my children's development.

In the Church of Jesus Christ there's a lot of repetition. Some repetition in the Church is to good and useful purposes, but much of it, for me at least, is of questionable value.

Some Sunday School classes sing the same hymn to open their session every Sunday and have been so doing for as long as anyone can remember. That may be meaningful to them, but it's not to me. Some church groups have a standard prayer, or a creed, that they recite every time they gather. Again, this may be helpful to them, but it does nothing for me.

My particular nemeses in the church are so-called "praise choruses" that are sung over and over and over again. Admittedly, many people find worshipful value in these. But to me they are "7-11" religion -- seven words sung eleven times over.

On this particular subject Jesus is recorded in Matthew 6:7 as saying, "...when ye pray, use not vain repetitions as the heathen do, for they think that they shall be heard for their much speaking." You may or may not agree, but personally I'm convinced that Jesus was right on the mark with that statement.

A Special Glow
Exodus 34:29-35

I once had a great saint to spend a couple of nights in my home. His name was Harry Lee, and he was a Chinese Christian. He had spent 25 years of his life in communist Chinese prisons for his faith in Jesus Christ. But he was finally free, living in Canada, and traveling as an evangelist for World Gospel Missions. I'd read his testimony in his autobiographical book, <u>From the Claws of the Dragon</u>. My church had invited him to speak on world missions, so I had the privilege of hosting him under my roof.

I've never been much of a sleeper, and during those five or six hours when I am in bed, I get up three or four times during the course of most nights -- to find a drink of water, to go to the bathroom, to look out a window, whatever.

So it was that while Harry Lee was my guest, I passed by the open door to his bedroom several times during the night. Each time I noticed that he was on his knees beside the bed, praying. One AM, three AM, five AM -- Harry was quietly in prayer.

As far as I'm aware, in the two nights he spent in my home he never slept at all. Yet he was one of the most energetic people I've ever met.

After noticing his second night of all prayer and no sleep, at breakfast I asked Harry about his habits. He simply responded that God gave him the energy he needed -- to pray and not to need sleep.

Frankly, even though I'm a preacher, I have a hard time finding a few minutes a day to spend in prayer with God. Harry Lee spent eight to ten hours daily in prayer to God -- and it showed. He had that unmistakable "glow" that I've observed in maybe half a dozen Christians I've met in my entire life thus far. That glow was the pervasive presence of God's Holy Spirit -- so completely filling him that it visibly showed through.

I'm certainly not there yet, but by God's grace, I hope that someday others will be able to observe that same visible "glow" -- the pervasive presence of the Holy Spirit, in me. I pray the same for you and for all God's faithful children.

Christian Faith: Personal but Not Private
Acts 4:18-20

A high school friend called me from Baltimore, Maryland. He had been contacted by someone else who knew that he was a long-time friend of mine. That person had been asked by a lady who had been diagnosed with terminal cancer in a Baltimore hospital to try and locate me. So he was passing on the word, asking me to please try and contact this lady.

The lady who wanted to talk to me was someone that I had dated, one time, when I was about 17 or 18 years old. I barely remembered her -- the occasion was more than 35 years previous. But according to the message that I received, she knew that I had gone on to become a pastor, and I was the only pastor she knew. So in a time of crisis she was trying to locate me.

Though I made at least a dozen different calls, I was not able to make contact with this woman. She had already been discharged from the hospital by the time I received the message, and hospital confidentiality rules forbade that institution from giving me any personal information about her. I called a number of other friends and acquaintances from long ago but came up blank.

Although I was never able to make personal contact with this woman, I added her to my daily prayers for some months thereafter. What concerned me most about this incident is that this woman, in a lifetime, had had no significant contact with the Church of Jesus Christ. Thirty-five years after making my passing acquaintance, she reached out to me in a crisis -- because I was the only person, she knew who represents the Christian faith.

This all seems a bit strange -- and yet I believe it. So many Christians today keep their faith strictly private that it can be genuinely hard for someone outside the faith to find a believer.

People of God, this simply ought not to be. Jesus called upon us all, not just preachers, to let others know the hope that we profess.

Honoring Our Elders
1 Peter 5:1-4

One of the many duties that I've often had as a pastor is that of visiting folks in nursing homes. Actually that's no longer the correct terminology, as there exist today a multiplicity of residential living arrangements for older persons which span a broad spectrum from virtually independent living through total and complete 24-hour care. But, although it's now politically incorrect to call them such, I've been doing this for so long that the old vocabulary is etched in my brain; I still think of most such facilities as nursing homes.

In my experience of thousands of nursing home visits over several decades in nearly a dozen different cities, I'm convinced that, by and large, those persons in such facilities are well-taken-care-of. I placed my own father in a senior residential facility -- a nursing home -- for the last 20 months of his life, and I'm confident that he enjoyed a better quality of life there than he would have had if I'd been continuously struggling to meet his needs in my home.

What about the many stories we hear of frail, elderly residents who are neglected and abused in nursing facilities? With millions residing in such, I'm sure it happens -- and even one such instance is one too many. But for the most part, such facilities provide a wealth of human contact and care which is missing from the life of a frail senior who insists on either remaining in their own home or moving in with a relative.

It took my dad about one month to get over sulking at "losing his independence" after entering the nursing home. After that he realized he was getting far more personal attention than he'd gotten at almost any other time in his life -- and he began to actually enjoy nursing home life.

Jesus, several times in the gospels, reminded the people of his day of the importance of honoring one's father and mother. I know many adult children today who are laboring under heavy burdens of guilt because they have had to place an elderly parent or other relative, whose health was failing, in an eldercare facility. Some many disagree with me, but I believe, in our day and age, that may well be a positive way of truly honoring our frail, aging forebears. Every family situation is, of course, unique, but I thank God that such facilities are now widely available throughout our land.

God-Given Opportunity to Do Good
Hebrews 13:15-16

One of our sons brought home a friend from high school one day for lunch. His name was Jose. As we talked over a quick midday meal, we learned a little about him. He was a 16-year old junior, bright overall, but with very little plan for his future -- no goals to speak of, not a lot of self-definition.

Jose probably would have been a one-time acquaintance for us except that, as he and our son were leaving that day to return to school for the afternoon, a God-appointed moment happened. Someone had taped a sign to the telephone pole at the corner of our lot, and, as the two boys were walking off, my wife called out, "What does that sign somebody's stuck up there say?" From 35 feet away, our son instantly read the sign. Jose commented that he didn't even know there was a sign on the pole from that far away. "My distance vision isn't so good," he noted.

Later on we asked our son more about Jose's vision problem. "Jose sits up front in every class, so he can see the blackboard. He needs glasses, but his parents can't afford them," our son told us. I knew an optician who was a member of our church, he in turn knew an ophthalmologist who was willing to provide a low-priced eye exam for Jose. Jose got the eye exam, and within just a few days, at very little cost to anyone, Jose had glasses.

As our family's relationship with Jose developed he became, for the next year and a half, our "fourth child," with a key to the house and full refrigerator privileges. Because he could now see, he was getting better grades in school. He developed a desire to attend college. We helped him get a driver's license; then an old but serviceable car. I aided him with the college admissions process and, with a little further push, in obtaining the financial aid needed to pay for attending. With his mother's full endorsement, he eventually went off with great fanfare.

I'm often amazed at the providence of God. In Jose's case one tiny, seemingly trivial remark led to many major changes in his life. We happened to be the agents God put in his path at just the right place and time. I'm very glad we were blessed with such a God-given opportunity.

Life or Death?
Deuteronomy 30:19-20

One of my earliest childhood memories concerns an aunt who was dying. My Aunt Vera chronically suffered from a number of ailments which were life-threatening, and she wanted to be sure everyone else knew all about them. Every time we visited her, after going over all her maladies in great detail, she always ended the visit with the same parting shot: "This is probably the last time you'll ever see me. I'm dying, you know!"

Aunt Vera was always dying. She was what the local ambulance drivers called a "frequent flyer." Half her life was spent in hospitals, most of the other half in bed at home -- with my uncle waiting on her hand and foot. In truth, she really was seriously ill.

Shortly after my wife and I got married, I took Fran to see Aunt Vera. I warned her beforehand, "Aunt Vera is dying. She's been dying ever since I was a child. Our conversation will center upon her and her health problems. That's the only thing she ever talks about." Sure enough, after an hour or so of listening to her litany of ailments, when we rose to leave, Aunt Vera offered her traditional parting shot, but with a bit of a twist for Fran's sake, "Well, I'm glad to have met you. But you'll probably never see me again. I'm dying, you know."

Aunt Vera actually did die some years ago, somewhere around my fiftieth birthday. I recall that Fran and I had, just before her death, celebrated our twenty-fifth wedding anniversary. Aunt Vera lived to be 85 years of age. But everyone who ever knew her remembers her for one and the same reason: She was always dying.

Jesus said, "I have come that you may have life, and have it abundantly." Certainly, my aunt was faced with grave health challenges throughout her years on this earth. I praise God that I didn't have to walk in her shoes. But I often wonder how her life might have been different -- had she chosen to major in actually living life, rather than in continual preoccupation with death.

Lying to the Church
Acts 5:1-11

I'd been hoping for quite a while that my church in El Paso could start some sort of singles' ministry for, although we had quite a few single young adults in the congregation, we had no specific ministry to them. So when a young man, about 35 years of age, joined the church and shortly thereafter actually asked me if he could be allowed to try and start a singles' ministry, I jumped at the opportunity. The church board voted some funds for his efforts and provided him access to our church's membership records. Thus he could develop a contact list of single young adults who, like him, were associated with our congregation.

Three or four weeks later, I was confronted by three young women, all single nurses, who were part of the congregation. This young man, it seemed, was using the information we'd provided him for somewhat different purposes than what he'd represented. He was employing the church's data as a source for prospective dates. I then did some checking, and found he'd contacted at least 20 young women -- and not even one young man -- about his so-called "singles ministry."

I did yet further checking – information verification which I should have done earlier but hadn't. Sure enough, the church from which he'd transferred his membership had experienced much the same problem with him.

I confronted this young man about his misrepresentation and he angrily left the church. Months later, another pastor on the other side of El Paso called me to ask about this same man and his background. I warned that pastor not to give that young man any ministry responsibility.

That's not the first time, nor the last, that I've had folks who have tried to "use" the church for their own personal agendas. Eventually, I learned not to give any new member of a congregation which I pastored significant leadership responsibility until they'd been associated with that church for at least one year.

Frankly, I've lost a few new folks with that policy, as some are really eager to get involved in ministry from day one. I truly wish I could immediately employ their enthusiasm but, in today's world of questionable security, I'd rather be safe than sorry.

The Bible, in Ephesians 5:25, says, "Jesus loved the church, and gave his life for her." I love the church, too -- enough to want to protect its precious people from those who would pervert it for their own private purposes.

A Visit from the Christ Family
Galatians 6:9-10

I was in my office at the church I was then serving in Albuquerque, New Mexico. I glanced out the window as a Volkswagen minivan painted with multi-colored floral patterns pulled up. Out of the van emerged nine young adults, all clad in white robes. They were barefooted and had garlands of flowers in their long hair. Some were males and some females, although it was hard to distinguish. They trooped in the office door, breezed past the secretary, and arrayed themselves in a semi-circle around me in my office.

"Hello," one of them said. "We're the Christ family!" "The Christ family?" I asked, puzzled. "Yeah, the Christ family," one of them responded back. "I'm Joe Christ and this is my brother Mark Christ, and she's our sister Sue Christ." In similar fashion all nine of them introduced themselves to me. "Well, I certainly know one of your cousins, Jesus Christ," I responded, getting into the spirit of things with them.

"Yeah, Jesus is the one who sent us here. We're on a mission from him – to you." "Oh really?" I rejoined, puzzled. "What mission is that?" "Our mission is to give you a chance to practice charity. We need money, and Jesus told us to tell you to give us some."

I must admit, their direct approach was one of the more unique I'd encountered to that point in my life. But I was ready for them. I responded with scripture, from the Book of Acts: "Silver and gold have I none, but such as I have, give I thee."

With that, I picked up a stack of paperback copies of the Good News New Testament and handed them out, one to each of them. "You need to learn more about your family's namesake, Jesus Christ," I said. "Now it's time for you to go."

Interestingly, they didn't have a comeback. Rather they simply trooped back out of my office and disappeared as quickly as they'd arrived.

This so-called "Christ family" is just one example of many, many colorful characters I've met as a result of being a preacher. And I certainly hope they all know Jesus Christ -- not just as a name to borrow, but as eternal Lord of their lives and Savior of their souls.

God Loves Bartenders, Too
John 2:1-11

Paul and his wife began attending the church I was then pastoring. After their second Sunday at my church, I offered to visit them in their home. They put me off for a couple of weeks, but eventually we found a mutually agreeable time to get together.

I arrived at their home at the appointed time, we sat down, and when we'd gotten past the preliminaries of casual conversation, I told them how glad I was that they were attending my church, and that I hoped they'd consider formally joining as members.

Paul responded by saying, "Pastor, be careful what you offer. You might not want us as members after I tell you what I do for a living." At that point, of course I couldn't resist asking, "Tell me, Paul, what is it that you do for a living? Are you an international drug lord, or a contract killer for the mob?" He laughed. "No, I'm just a bartender."

I might have paused for a single second, but no longer than that. I said, "Paul, my Bible doesn't say that bartenders are unacceptable in the Kingdom of God. Do you believe in Jesus Christ as your personal Savior?" He answered, "Yes, I do." "Well, then you're welcome to join any church I pastor. How about this coming Sunday morning?"

In response he and his wife both began to cry. As we talked further, I learned that this mild-mannered, middle-aged couple had been made to feel unwelcome by half-a-dozen churches over the course of their lives thus far – simply because Paul was a career bartender.

Paul Poulin and his wife became members of my congregation and strong supporters thereof. And in the providence of God's grace, within six months Paul met a man in that congregation who offered him a better job at higher pay. He gave up bartending -- not because a church judged him for it, but because a congregation accepted him as he was and, moreover, provided him a better alternative for the future.

The Jesus I know majors in love and acceptance of people, not in judgment. And because they find love and acceptance in Jesus, people often change for the better -- willingly.

Storytellers, Be Careful
Psalm 107:1-3

I began to offer "Tales I Like to Tell" on radio shortly after I arrived in the town of Big Spring, Texas. During my five years as pastor there I recorded more than 260 separate short stories. I recorded them twelve at a time. Then they were subsequently aired by the radio station – but in no particular order. Many times I was able to listen when they were aired, but sometimes I wasn't.

Hardly a day passed in Big Spring that someone didn't come up to me to say, "I listened to you on the radio this morning." That was always gratifying to me; I was glad to know that folks actually heard what I had to say. But sometimes I got a little embarrassed, as when someone asked, "Tell me a little more about what happened to John, the man you talked about in your story today." Listeners automatically assumed that I'd done that day's story live; thus it should be fresh in my memory. But if I didn't listen to it myself that day, I could be hard pressed to recall it – among 260 others. I sometimes had to ask, "Tell me what I said, to refresh my memory." Then the person asking began to wonder if I really was telling the truth about it being a personal story. Truthfully, every tale I told on radio actually came from personal experience.

Only about six months after I began telling those tales on radio, I discovered that I had to be extremely careful about what I said. For example, the local hospital administrator from Alpine, Texas called me, upset by something I'd said in one of my stories about the quality of care at Alpine's small hospital. With Alpine being more than 200 miles distant from Big Spring, he hadn't directly heard the story himself, but someone who had heard it related it to him secondhand. What didn't get passed on to him from the original airing was the stated fact that the tale was from an experience I'd had two decades previously and bore no particular relation to the then-current situation at Alpine's hospital.

The early apostle of Jesus named James, in the third chapter of his Biblical letter, carefully warns all followers of our Lord concerning the power of the tongue. Words, once spoken, can't be taken back. Especially when they're broadcast over the airwaves for all to hear, one's words become very permanent. So I try to do my best to always speak words I won't be embarrassed by, rather than ones I might later have to apologize for saying. That's good advice for all of us, whether or not you're telling tales on the radio.

A Weird Web of Lies
Psalm 120:1-4

My wife and I for many years owned a house in another state, one that we rented out while we lived in various church-owned parsonages. Being the owner of a rent-house made me a landlord, and sometimes that's not the most enjoyable position in the world.

Once I rented our house to a couple who, almost from the day they moved in, were perennially late with their rent. Every month they grew later and later; every month there was a new excuse. Those excuses gradually increased in both complexity and intensity -- husband laid off, wife lost her job, wife hospitalized, husband's mother in hospital and needing help with bills, wife's father faced with bankruptcy, etcetera and etcetera.

Finally, with the rent four months in arrears, I reluctantly but necessarily began the legal process of eviction. A few weeks later I got a default judgment from the court, a judgment which would allow me to have the sheriff physically evict them. After ignoring my attempts at communication for quite a while, the woman of the couple called me. She'd just found out that she was dying of cancer, and they were looking for a smaller place to which to move for her final few months on earth. Could I please back off and grant them just a few more days' grace?

Well, under those awful circumstances I certainly couldn't toss them out into the streets, so I reluctantly agreed. Eventually, weeks later, they moved out, owing me more than $4,000 in back rent -- rent which was never paid.

All that transpired quite a number of years ago. And then, two-plus years thereafter, that same woman called and left a message on my home telephone recorder. She'd driven by our rent-house, thought it appeared vacant, and wondered if I'd be interested in renting to her and her husband again?

There's a special word from the Yiddish language that applies here -- that word is "chutzpah." That woman left me believing that, by now, she was long dead. Out of compassion I never even tried to collect the significant monetary debt she and her husband left me holding. Can you imagine the gall of this lady -- the depth of presumption on her part?

Psalm 37:1 in the Bible says, "Fret not yourself because of the wicked; be not envious of wrongdoers." I'm very glad that verse is there; it helps me to let go and let God handle things that are beyond my human capacity to fathom.

April Fools
Matthew 5:21-23

I was born on April 1st. Although I obviously had no control over that being my birth date, throughout my life it has made me the butt of many jokes. One of the earliest I remember was when, as a junior in high school, I went home with a friend after school on my birthday. We headed down into his basement to shoot some pool. As I got halfway down the stairs, someone flipped on a light, and there were about 50 of my friends. They all yelled, "Surprise!" and immediately left.

Over the years I've been given hollow birthday cakes that collapsed when I tried to cut them, returned important calls from "Mr. Lyon" at the local zoo, even endured, with great pomp and circumstance, the early observance of my own funeral -- that was for my 40th birthday. Most of the jokes played on me for my April 1st birthday have been good natured enough, and I've tried to forget the ones that were less so.

Being an April fool has had its side benefits. I've developed a pretty good sense of humor. And I've certainly learned not to take myself too seriously. I know full well that, as a preacher, I'm neither as good as my admirers think me, nor as bad as my critics claim.

In the Biblical apostle Paul's first letter to the Corinthian church, chapter one, he repeatedly refers to himself as a fool for Jesus. Paul says he is a fool because he preaches that a dead man, Jesus, has risen from the dead. He is a fool because he believes that love is stronger than hate. He is a fool because he claims that issues concerning the Kingdom of Heaven are ultimately far more significant than matters related to this earth. He is a fool because he is convinced that to lose one's life in the service of Jesus is better than to save one's life for a few brief years of self-indulgence.

Maybe because I'm an April fool, I understand where Paul is coming from when he calls himself a "fool" for Jesus Christ. In fact, I agree completely with him.

From back when I was growing up, I recall a pop song entitled "Everybody's Somebody's Fool." There have been some who have thought me a fool all my life, so I might as well, like Paul, be a fool for the King of Kings and Lord of Lords, Jesus Christ. Whose fool are you?

Not by Logical Argument Alone
Acts 17:22-23

While I was in seminary, training for service in Christian ministry, my wife was simultaneously enrolled in a master's program in library science. In her college she met a personable young man from India whose first name was Prakash and whose middle and last names were virtually unpronounceable to us. She introduced me to Prakash, and we jointly invited him to dinner at our apartment.

Early in our dinner conversation I discovered that Prakash was a Hindu, so I immediately began to witness the Gospel of Jesus Christ to him. Prakash was a highly intelligent individual, skilled in logic and debate. We argued for hours; he didn't leave our apartment until well after midnight. Notwithstanding, I didn't succeed in getting him to profess faith in Jesus Christ.

As a young seminarian I henceforth regarded Prakash as a challenge, so I encouraged my wife to invite him over for dinner again. Again he came; again we debated religious faiths until the wee hours of the morning. Again, another stalemate. Over the next several months, we had Prakash as our dinner guest perhaps a total of six times. Each time he and I argued long into the night. Never was I able to convince him to change his faith from Hindu to Christian. Finally, after about half a dozen such encounters, we more or less mutually agreed to give up. The fun of debating one another had worn off; our arguments were becoming repetitive. Prakash ceased accepting our dinner invitations; we more or less drifted apart.

I don't know if he ever accepted Christ as His Savior or not, but from my present perspective of many years of pastoral experience, I know that I went about sharing Christ with him all wrong. I approached Prakash as a challenge to overcome, rather than a precious human being to get to know. I tried to argue him into Christian faith, rather than to love him into the Kingdom of God. I didn't pray, I didn't ask for the Holy Spirit's help and guidance. I simply tried, by my own mental strength, to overpower him. And I failed.

The task assigned Christians, by Jesus, is to share Him with non-believers. But we can't do it without His help. And we certainly can't argue folks into the Kingdom. But with God's help, we can love them into faith.

A Global Faith Perspective
Matthew 16:13-19

In 2002 I made a nine-day mission trip to the Central American nation of El Salvador. With me I took a team of 14 persons, and together we helped to construct additional facilities for a church in a medium-sized town in the northwest highlands of that nation, a place called Ahuachapan.

On Sunday morning, our team was present for a worship service. What was most unique, most distinct from the worship services I experience in churches in the U. S. A. today had nothing to do with language, or music, or preaching style -- although those were all very different from the ways I usually worship God. What was really different was the congregation. It was made up of a handful of adult men, ten or fifteen adult women, and at least 100 children.

I've been involved in short-term missions to other parts of our world for more than four decades now, and that church's congregation was actually more "normal" among what I've encountered in other lands than what I experience at home in the United States. In Russia, I've worshiped in a five-hundred-year-old Orthodox Christian temple -- chock full of young people. In Fiji hundreds of children sat on the ground, greatly outnumbering their parents, as I preached outdoor revival services in those islands. In Latin America, from Guatemala to Chile, Brazil to Panama, I've been in churches filled with eager young faces, excitedly soaking up the gospel of Jesus Christ. In Africa, ditto.

When people in the U. S. say to me that the Christian faith is in decline, or that the church is dying, my personal experience says the opposite. Yes, churches in the U. S. are, more often than not, declining in numbers. And congregations here are ageing at an alarming rate. I wish that weren't the case, and, with God's help, I've done everything I possibly could to reverse those trends in the churches I was called upon to serve. But the reality is that the Christian faith, worldwide, is presently doing very well.

All over our globe, Christian churches are growing -- except in those places where Christians have become complacent and self-satisfied, notably north America and western Europe. Those of us who profess to be Christians in America today need to wake up, and soon, before we lose what remains of the legacy of faith which both God and our forefathers have entrusted to us.

Conflict in the Middle East
Matthew 15:21-28

With violence in the Middle East continuing to make almost daily news headlines in our contemporary world, much of the Holy Bible seems more like current events than ancient history. I traveled to the Holy Land in 1993 and again in 2008; it was virtually the same both those times as today. These ancient conflicts have continuously been a fact of life in that region for 3,000 years now.

From my perspective, and that of many other Americans, I used to ask why -- why can't these factions sit down and talk with one another, people to people, and work things out? Unfortunately, my trips to the Middle East provided me with a bizarre answer to that question.

While I was in Israel the first time, I asked our guide, a well-educated young Orthodox Jew, "Why don't you Israeli's sit down with the Palestinians and work things out?" His answer: "You can't talk to animals. Palestinians aren't human; they're dogs!" Later, while in a shop in Bethlehem operated by Palestinians, I asked the shop owner: "Why won't you Palestinians sit down and talk things out with the Israeli's?" His answer was almost word for word the same as that of our Jewish guide: "You can't talk to Jews. They're not even human; they're dogs!"

When conflicting parties can't acknowledge the basic humanity of each other, it's almost impossible to find common ground. It reminded me of the tragic situation in Australia in the 19th century, when the aboriginal peoples of that continent were almost wiped out by the white settlers. Aborigines were routinely hunted and shot, and even eaten, by the whites -- because they were considered to be animals, not human beings. O God, forgive our blindness!

I don't have a smart answer to resolve 3,000 years of conflict and suffering in the Holy Land, but I do have a recommendation: Pray. Psalm 122, verse 6 in the Holy Bible says, "Pray for the peace of Jerusalem." Perhaps God can provide a way to open the eyes of the parties involved to the basic fact that they are, one and all, fellow human beings.

Pigeon Problems
Leviticus 20:25-26

One of the perennial problems that plagues church buildings is that of pigeons. Church structures typically extend higher up than the other edifices immediately around them, so pigeons love to roost on such high perches. While some folks may think that pigeons are cute and loveable creatures, I know from personal experience that a flock of pigeons regularly roosting on a church building can, over a period of time, cause tens of thousands of dollars' worth of damage. All of the US churches I've served, from Nashville to Albuquerque and several points between, have struggled with pigeon problems.

I remember well the many battles I helped fight, for three long years, against hundreds of pigeons which regularly roosted on the roof of the gymnasium building of the first church I served in Albuquerque. We tried everything we could think of to shoo them. We purchased ultrasonic devices that were supposed to emit high frequency sounds to drive the pigeons away. The pigeons built nests around them. We tried painting the eaves with a special, expensive coating that was supposed to be too slippery for the pigeons to roost upon. It wasn't. We bought plastic owls and hung them at various locations along the roof line. Those actually worked -- for about two weeks. After that, the pigeons began to perch on the artificial owls. They were no longer fooled.

As I was doing research, preparing to write the thirty-fifth anniversary booklet of that church, I chanced upon a copy of a report written by the Rev. J. F. Hamilton, the church's founding pastor 35 years before. In it he reported upon his futile efforts to dislodge the pigeons from the then brand-new roof of the church's gym. Some problems never go away.

Many of you are probably aware that, in the bird kingdom, pigeons are close cousins to doves. Doves are highly regarded throughout the Bible. Noah sent out a dove from the ark following the flood, to determine if the waters had begun to subside. When Jesus was baptized, the Holy Spirit descended upon Him in the form of a dove. Moreover, Jesus admonished his followers, in Matthew 10:16, to be "wise as serpents and harmless as doves." I'm glad that, in God's sight, doves are harmless. I just wish pigeons were equally so. Praise the Lord -- anyway!

Moving Beyond Stereotypes
Matthew 9:9-11

All my adult life I've registered to vote in whatever location I'm currently living. Being a registered voter means at least one thing for sure: Sooner or later you're going to be notified to report for jury duty. It's one of the obligations of responsible citizenship in the United State of America.

Over the years, I've been summoned for jury duty numerous times. But although I did serve once, in Big Spring, Texas, on a grand jury, I've never yet been picked to actually serve on a petit jury. As soon as my occupation is made known, that of pastor or preacher, I'm excused -- usually by the judge, but if not, then by one or another of the attorneys involved. And I've never been told why I'm being excused.

Frankly, I wonder why being a preacher more or less automatically disqualifies me from serving on a jury. More than a few people who are picked for jury duty complain and try to invent excuses to avoid serving. On the other hand, I'm willing -- but my occupation appears to exclude me.

Throughout our society today, preachers are treated strangely. Some folks automatically love all preachers, others hate them. I find both responses frustrating, because they both involve stereotyping. I much prefer to be evaluated for who I am personally, rather than be discriminated by my occupational category. I suspect, whomever you are and whatever you may do for a living, you prefer the same. None of us wants to be prejudged by those who don't even know us personally.

One of the occupational groups that Jesus encountered in his day which was, and probably still is, universally prejudged, was tax collectors. Then and now, it's pretty much automatic: Nobody likes those whose job it is to see that taxes are properly paid to the government. But Jesus looked beyond those stereotypes, and found some interesting individuals: notably Matthew, who became a disciple, and Zacchaeus, a short little man who climbed a sycamore tree to see the Savior. When you dare to move beyond bias and prejudice, and get to know people as individuals, you may find some very good men and women.

That's how Jesus operated. We need to do the same.

Casting Out the Devil
James 4:7-10

Back when I was a seminary student, I had a friend named Ken who was constantly troubled by Satan, demons, and other dark spiritual forces. Whenever Ken would enter a church building, he'd look around the sanctuary and say, "I see a demon in that corner. In the name of Jesus, I bind you and cast you out." Only then did Ken feel free to minister the gospel in that environment.

Ken and I had many discussions regarding the dark side of spirituality. For his part, he sincerely felt I was too naive about the powers and principalities of the adversary, the archenemy of God. Ken wanted to teach me as much as he possibly could regarding "spiritual warfare," because he believed that Satan was constantly attacking all those who attempted to preach and teach in the name of the Lord Jesus Christ. I, on the other hand, didn't often sense the power and presence of the enemy, at least not in the ways Ken regularly experienced it.

In response to his constant preoccupation with the forces of darkness, I would say to him, "Ken, when I walk into a church building, I always say, 'Praise the Lord.' And if there ever were any demons lurking there, they immediately leave before I'm even aware of them."

I'm not much on hellfire and brimstone, and never have been. However, that doesn't mean I'm not fully aware of the reality of the dark side of spiritual power in our world. I often warn Christians, especially new believers, that the devil specially targets such for woe and misfortune.

When someone first becomes a Christian, or when a believer does something significant to advance the Kingdom of God, that enrages the devil. He loves to blindside believers, trying, if possible, to derail their faith and dilute their effectiveness. Jesus was honest with those who would follow him -- in this life, expect troubles and persecutions. The adversary of God does his job, regularly and relentlessly.

Often in our present world, it appears that unbelievers enjoy better lives than those who have faith in Christ. The reason for this is simple: Satan doesn't need to harass unbelievers – they're his already. All he has to do is stand by, waiting a few years until their physical bodies stop functioning.

Hang in there, people of God. The devil's a tough foe, but the Lord is ultimately far stronger. Stick with the winner: Jesus Christ -- for eternity!

Money Isn't Always the Answer
Matthew 23:23-24

One of the odder stories of my ministry in El Paso, Texas arose from visiting one of the women's circles in the church I was then serving. A group of eight middle-aged ladies had invited me to present a program to them and, afterward, to share lunch with them one weekday. I honestly don't remember what I spoke about to them, but after I presented the program, they asked me if there was any particularly pressing need in the church at that present time. "Just name it," they said, "and we'll try to help."

Being thus invited, I responded, "Yes, there is something we really need right now. This coming weekend our church has nine youth who need to get to camp, and I need someone to drive them there." The particular camp was about a two and a half-hour drive from El Paso in the mountains of south-central New Mexico.

Without saying much of anything in response, this group of women then began to serve and eat their lunch. I ate with them. And after the lunch, just before I left them, I was handed eight checks, checks which totaled several hundred dollars.

"What's this for?" I asked. "To help those youth get to camp," was their reply.

I didn't really know how to respond to these ladies' gift. You see, their hearts were in the right place, but their heads weren't exactly thinking straight. Money wasn't the need. We needed someone to give themselves -- their time, not their money. Unless they had some odd idea that I should hire a driver, their gift of money wasn't going to help get those youth to camp.

I know that churches are often accused of always asking for money, and sometimes that charge is justified. But my personal ministry experience is that money is often easier to find in the church than anything else. More often than not, the church needs people to give of themselves, rather than only of their money. An extra fifty dollars doesn't provide a teacher for the fourth grade Sunday School class. A ten-dollar bill can't visit a sick person in the hospital. Eight checks won't drive youth to a weekend camp.

When God seeks commitment from His people, He asks, first and foremost, that we give ourselves. Sometimes, giving money can be a cop out. Far more significantly than our dollars, God wants us.

Custom-Tailored Religion
Isaiah 64:1-7

One of the more or less inactive female members of one of my former churches called me up. "Pastor, I have a question," she said. "I've left my husband and I'm currently living with another man. But I'm not sure whether or not I'm doing right. I've been praying to God every day for several weeks now, asking Him to tell me whether to stay with this man or go back to my husband, but I haven't received an answer. Why won't God give me the personal guidance I keep asking Him to give?"

My response to her was direct: "God doesn't need to give you personal guidance, because He's already clearly spoken on that subject. The seventh commandment in the Holy Bible says, 'Thou shalt not commit adultery.' Therefore, you need to go back to your husband." She didn't like my answer. "It's not that simple!" she responded. "I need more than just a verse from the Bible. I need God to tell me personally what to do!"

That woman personified one of the major problems that I find among Americans today in relation to the Christian faith. We have been so completely immersed in individualism that each one of us desires to invent his or her own customized religion. That God has clearly revealed Himself and His will for humanity in the Holy Bible isn't enough. Like Job in ancient times, every one of us wants a personal audience with the Almighty.

Ethical relativism and spiritual anarchy are the inevitable results of the contemporary American obsession with individualized religion. Today, millions of Americans possess no moral compass whatever. They simply claim to possess a vague sense of "spirituality," whatever that may mean.

In the Holy Bible, God has provided complete and clear guidance for human life -- for all times, cultures, peoples and nations. The Bible is the "operating manual" for life itself. Read it, learn it, obey it. You'll live better as a result.

Committed Disciples
John 6:65-68

As a college freshman at a large state university, I recall stepping into a big lecture hall for one of my first classes. It was a calculus class. There were between 500 and 600 students in that oversize classroom. The professor, barely visible on the platform far below, began thus: "I want every student to look at the person on your right." We all duly turned our heads and did so. "Now," he said, "I want everyone to look at the person on your left." We likewise complied with this second instruction. The professor continued, "Before this semester is over, one of them won't be there." He was right; it was a tough class. Within just a few weeks, between one third and one half of those enrolled had withdrawn or dropped out.

I was always tempted to try that little exercise with the crowds of "celebration Christians" who show up on festival weekends in the church: Christmas, Easter, and/or Mother's Day. As a pastor, I knew that between a third and half of those to be found in such oversize congregations wouldn't be around very long.

Celebration Christians enjoy, as the terminology implies, celebrating good news. At Christmas, "Rejoice, the Savior is born." On Easter, "Christ the Lord is risen today." And on Mother's Day they'll simply show up to please dear old mom.

But celebration Christians won't be present to hear Jesus say, "Deny yourself, take up your cross, and follow me." They couldn't possibly stomach our Lord's stating, "Blessed are you when men revile and persecute you."

The Church will always welcome celebration Christians. In point of fact the Church of Jesus Christ will always welcome all persons, because that's part of our Lord's commission to His Church. But as a pastor, although I was always pleased to see the celebration Christians come when they chose to do so, I knew better than to count on them.

Rather I was far more impressed by the fewer, but more committed, believers who regularly attended on "normal" Sundays. My hat was – and still is -- off to them, because they're the folks who ensure that the Church will yet be around -- the next time the celebration Christians decide to show up.

Are You Joking?
Psalm 126:1-3

The shortest verse in the Bible is John 11:35. It's only two words in length: "Jesus wept." Upon learning of the death of his close friend, Lazarus, Jesus wept.

But Jesus didn't weep for long over Lazarus. Instead, he raised his friend from the dead, proving his power over even death itself.

There's not a contrasting verse in the scripture which says, "Jesus laughed." But personally, I believe that soon after Lazarus walked out of that tomb at Jesus' command, our Lord hugged him and enjoyed a hearty laugh with his old friend.

For several decades I belonged to an informal group of believers in Christ called, "The Fellowship of Merry Christians." This group used to publish a monthly newsletter called, "The Joyful Noiseletter." I got a lot of jokes and other humorous anecdotes out of that publication, some of which produced groans when I shared them with my congregations. More than once I was told, "Don't quit your day job, Dave!" after telling a Christian joke.

Realistically I know that I'm not cut out to be a comedian. But nonetheless, I remain a firm believer in positive, upbeat Christianity.

Strangely enough, though, my happy approach to the Christian faith often raises suspicion among fellow believers in the Lord. Somehow or other, they've been taught that if you're really dedicated to Jesus, you shouldn't be found smiling very often, and certainly not laughing -- not ever. And a preacher who cuts up and tells jokes? I've been asked more than once, "Are you sure you're really an ordained minister?"

If I served a God who had lost his battle with sin and evil, wickedness and corruption, I suppose I might be long-faced and somber most of the time. But my Lord and Savior, Jesus Christ, is the victor over all those negatives. And even more, He's conquered death itself.

Yes, the Lord Jesus once wept. The Bible says so. But I believe He laughed a lot more – and I surmise He's still laughing. To me, it's no accident that "Jesus wept" is the shortest verse in all the Bible.

Christians, get with the Lord's program. You have good news to share with the world. Smile, giggle, enjoy life. Don't repel others from Jesus by your long face; rather, attract them to Him by your laughter.

Don't Waste Your Time, Nor Mine
2 Thessalonians 3:7-12

One of my pet "preacher peeves" used to be those persons who, as they passed by my office door, glanced in, saw that I was there, then proceeded to ask, "Pastor, have you got a minute?" Early in my ministry career I used to naively say, "Sure!" Nine times out of ten, such folks would then plunk themselves down in a chair and take up my entire morning or afternoon -- with a rambling barrage of talk about anything and everything. On the vast majority of such occasions, there was no particular reason for their coming to see me. They merely had time on their hands, and found the pastor a convenient target of opportunity, a captive audience to listen to their many words.

I love people, and I love to share in genuine, two-way conversation with others. But I was also usually busy; the necessary duties of my pastoral positions required a significant number of weekly hours of diligent, focused labor on my part. To some who passed by my door and observed me seemingly idle, it may not overtly have appeared that I was already occupied. But mental labor -- such as sermon preparation -- requires thought, disciplined thought that doesn't proceed very far nor very smoothly when frequently interrupted.

I could have adopted a "closed door" policy, but such makes a pastor appear standoffish. Instead, later in my ministry I developed a reasoned, forthright response to these drop-in interruptees. When someone poked their head in my doorway to ask, "Hey preacher, got a minute?" my response was usually, "No, sorry, but I haven't got even one minute to spare right now. But I do have an hour tomorrow afternoon. Can we schedule an appointment, and I'll be glad to listen to whatever you have to say then?"

I thereby discovered that, if the person really needed to talk with me for a reason, they would gladly set the appointment. But if it was just a desire for idle chit-chat, they instead would say, "No, it's not that important," and move on.

Time is one of God's most precious gifts to each of us. Even though those who believe in Jesus Christ have eternity to enjoy with Him, while on this earth time is a limited resource for every human being. The Holy Word of God, specifically Ephesians 5:16, advises us all to "make the most of the time." That's good advice, and I try hard to follow it. I commend it to you as well.

Hellfire and Damnation
Exodus 3:1-3

I awoke in the middle of the night and headed to the bathroom. As I stood in the bathroom, gazing out the window, I noticed that it wasn't black outside -- as I expected it to be at 3 AM. Looking westward, everything was illuminated by an eerie orange glow. It took me a couple of seconds to gather my wits. Suddenly, I realized what was happening. It appeared that the church I was serving, half a block over to the west, was on fire. I quickly donned clothing and rushed out into the night.

As I got closer, I realized that it wasn't my church that was on fire, but the restaurant and bar building which was located directly in front of it. The local fire department, a small volunteer brigade, was just arriving.

For the next three hours the firemen fought that blaze. It was so far along by the time they arrived that there was no hope of saving the restaurant and bar structure. That building burned completely to the ground. All the firemen really could do was keep lots of water on the adjacent buildings, so that they, too, didn't go up in flames. That included my church.

I stood out there with a garden hose, adding my small contribution to keeping the church's roof wet. It was such a hot blaze that the water sprayed on the church roof immediately turned into clouds of steam. But without that water, the heat from the adjacent burning building would almost certainly have spontaneously combusted the church roof.

By about 6 AM, the fire had died down to the point that it no longer presented a danger to other buildings. The firemen continued to douse the lost structure until its remains were completely soaked.

Upon investigation the fire was determined to be arson, and the owner of the restaurant and bar was charged with the crime. It seemed he had wanted to cash in on the insurance, as the business was failing. All this happened in the tiny west Texas town of Alpine, now four decades ago.

A few years later in my life I was involved in another fire of a very different nature -- a huge forest fire in the mountains of southern New Mexico. Having seen the destructive impact of fire on two occasions, I've personally experienced more than enough burning for one lifetime.

That's probably one of many reasons why I never preached much on hellfire and damnation. I much prefer the soothing water of life that Jesus offers, quenching the fires of hell and providing eternal salvation to all who desire to receive it.

Luck or Skill?
Ezekiel 47:9-10

My father was a fisherman. No, fishing wasn't how he made his living, but fishing was definitely one of the two great loves of his life, the other being hunting. He fished virtually every day of his life -- after work, on weekends, throughout every vacation he ever took. Lakes, streams, bays, oceans -- fresh water or salt -- if there were fish to be found therein, my dad caught them.

When you're out fishing, folks who see you so doing will commonly ask, "Are you having any luck?" From my dad, I learned that fishing really wasn't so much a matter of luck as of skill.

To become an expert fisherman takes practice and experience. My father was highly skilled at fishing. He put a lifetime of patient, persistent effort into becoming such. Thus, when those around him were catching some fish, he was catching many. And even if no one else was catching anything, he'd at least catch a few.

It's recorded in the Gospels of the New Testament that Jesus drew a significant number of his followers from the ranks of fishermen. At least five of his inner circle of 12 disciples were fishermen, possibly more.

But He wasn't specifically interested in these men's skills at catching fish. Rather, Jesus said to them, "Follow me, and I'll teach you how to catch people for the Kingdom of God."

Over the next three years, Jesus slowly but surely taught his disciples how to do exactly that. It took time and effort on both his part and theirs. And after those years of training and practice for them, the ultimate results were excellent. The Bible records that one former fisherman, Peter, convinced 3,000 people to follow Jesus after just a single, well-focused sermon.

Expert fishermen understand that a consistently good catch takes time and effort, patience and persistence on their part. And skilled disciples of Jesus likewise comprehend that there are no shallow shortcuts, no cookie-cutter methods for winning persons to Jesus Christ. Perhaps that's part of why Jesus chose fishermen to be his first disciples: the same sort of dedicated determination is required to successfully catch fish from the sea -- and people for God's Kingdom.

Hurry Up!
2 Samuel 5:22-25

I'd been away from my then-home in Alpine, Texas for a four-day trip, first driving to Midland, then flying out of Midland's airport and returning thereto. I'd retrieved my car from the airport parking lot and was heading back toward Alpine. As I cruised past Ft. Stockton, I switched the car's radio to Alpine's one and only local station, the signal for which could be picked up for about 60 miles in any direction out of town. Local announcements were being aired -- and I heard my name. "Pastor Dave Ring will be conducting a graveside service for Horace Smith this afternoon at 2 PM at the Alpine Cemetery."

I could barely believe my ears. I knew absolutely nothing about that funeral -- no one had contacted me about it. I looked at my watch -- it was ten minutes past one. That meant I had 57 miles to cover in 50 minutes. All this was happening in the days before cellular telephones, so I had no other option but to continue driving, as fast as possible, directly to the Alpine cemetery.

I actually made it to the cemetery with two minutes to spare. A small group of about 20 persons had gathered. The funeral director handed me the obituary card, I briefly met a couple of family members of the deceased, then immediately conducted the graveside rites.

After exchanging greetings with everyone present and expressing condolences to them, I took the funeral director aside. "What on earth were you thinking?" I asked him. "I've been out of town for the past four days; I knew absolutely nothing about this; it was only by luck that I tuned in the radio and heard I was supposed to be here. As it is, I barely made it in time. What if I hadn't shown up?" The funeral director -- one of Alpine's one-of-a-kind local characters -- was unabashed. "Oh, I knew you'd make it," was his only significant response.

Romans 8:28 in the Bible says, "We know that all things work together for good for those who love God, who are called according to his purpose." I'd deliberately embraced that scripture many times previously, but I never really expected it to come true in my life without my even being aware of it. Luck? Coincidence? Maybe. Or -- perhaps it was the sovereign purpose of God, working itself out in my life, just as his Word promises.

Two Kinds of Lives, Two Kinds of Endings
Matthew 25:31-46

Although it's a somewhat "heavy" subject, I want to describe to you two funerals at which I officiated some years ago. The first such was that of Faye Thomas. That wasn't her actual name; I've changed it for obvious reasons. Faye was a completely self-centered, blatantly negative person for as long as anyone who knew her could remember. Many had tried to befriend her over the years, but she eventually drove them all away. She had a grown daughter and a son and a couple of grandkids; none of them maintained more than tenuous contact with her. When she died, alone in her small home, three days passed before anyone realized it. The funeral director called me because a neighbor suggested my name; he was struggling to put together a low-cost funeral, since neither of her children wanted to pay much to plant the old woman.

At the graveside service, there were maybe 12 people. Her son and daughter both showed up. It was a deeply depressing situation; to use a Biblical phrase, there was "weeping and gnashing of teeth." I tried to offer at least some hope, because, after all, funerals are for the living. But no one present was fooled; they all realized that this woman had died -- for eternity.

The second funeral was that of Mel Dickinson. Mel was the kind of man who was always doing something for someone else. He helped out dozens of folks who got into financial binds, although he himself lived on relatively modest means. He was a wonderful grandfather to his six grandkids and a loving husband to his wife, Millie. He was an active leader in the church. When he was diagnosed with cancer eight months before his death, his faith in Jesus Christ, which had long been a quiet part of his character, rose to the fore. As he neared death, despite the constant pain and suffering he faced, he waxed excited about moving beyond this life to meet his Savior in person.

At the funeral itself, over 300 persons gathered to celebrate Mel's passing from this earth. There were a few tears, of course, but a lot more laughter. The stories shared, the fond memories, the loving remembrances of Mel could have filled half a dozen books. All present rejoiced that he had entered the Kingdom of Heaven.

Someday, sooner for some, later for others, each of us will move beyond this life. When that happens, which kind of funeral will yours be?

A Fishing Lesson
Luke 5:1-11

I was out deep-sea fishing, six miles offshore in the Gulf of Mexico. And I was getting plenty of good action -- the speckled trout were hitting my line almost as soon as I cast. But catching them was frustrating, because every fish I pulled in was just barely undersize. The legal limit to keep a trout was 14 inches. But mine, every one of them, were measuring 13 1/2 to 13 3/4 inches long. After throwing back about the tenth such in a row, I told my fishing buddy, Mike, that I was going to keep the next one I caught, even if it was half an inch too short.

Mike, a good friend and a more experienced fisherman than I, warned me against such. He said, "What if the game warden shows up?" I looked around at miles of empty ocean. "Come on, Mike, there isn't another boat in sight. We've never seen a game warden way out here." Still, Mike stuck by his guns. "If it's not full legal size, Dave, don't keep it." Since he was the captain of the boat, I grudgingly complied. Out of perhaps 25 trout I caught that day, I was able to keep only two.

At day's end, as we were at the dock and preparing to pull the boat out of the water, a young man passing by asked us how we'd done that day. "We had a pretty good day; caught quite a few speckled trout. But we were only able to keep a few," we responded. With that, the young man we were talking with pulled out a badge; he was an undercover game warden. Before then, I never knew that such existed. He asked to examine our catch. We, of course, allowed him to do so. Every one of the handful of fish we'd kept was strictly legal size. He thanked us and went on his way.

The fine for keeping an illegal-sized trout where I was fishing is $500 per fish. And, if the game warden wants to be hard-nosed, he can arrest the perpetrators and seize the boat involved as well.

Proverbs 19:20 in the Holy Bible says this: "Listen to advice and accept instruction, that you may gain wisdom for the future." I wasn't too keen on my friend's advice when he gave it to me, but a few hours later I was very glad I'd listened to him.

An Unexpected Harvest
Matthew 13:24-30

After seven years of apartment living my wife and I finally moved into a house -- with an actual backyard. And that backyard had a section that obviously was intended for a vegetable garden. So we decided to become farmers -- at least on a small scale. We dug, prepared and fertilized the soil, and planted seeds -- tomatoes, carrots, peppers, squash, watermelon. In just a few months, we were going to enjoy a great harvest.

Throughout the next several weeks, we watered and waited. Finally, directly in the center of our garden plot, a small leaf broke through the soil. In a few days, it had grown to several leaves. As it spread further, it was obvious that this was a vine of some sort. We assumed it must be either a squash or a watermelon plant. Then vines began to spread in several directions at once, with big leaves. In just a couple of weeks after the plant had first appeared, its vines filled the entire garden plot, spreading twelve to fifteen feet in every direction. Nothing else germinated in that plot. But, oh well, at least we had a singular gardening success.

At last yellow blossoms appeared -- many such. And after the blossoms, tiny fruits became visible. They were round, and they bore stripes -- we were pretty sure they were baby watermelons. We called a friend to come over and look at our garden and brag about it to him. When he saw the huge vine, he started laughing. What had sprung up in our garden, what we had so carefully nurtured and been so proud to have cultivated – wasn't a watermelon vine, nor a squash. It was a wild gourd plant. All we had successfully grown were dozens of hard, yellow, baseball-sized gourds.

While he walked this earth, Jesus related a story about sowing seed. Some of that seed was eaten by birds, and never got to germinate at all. Some of it fell in rocky soil, and wasn't able to last under such poor conditions. Some of it tried hard to grow, but was choked to death by weeds. Only a fraction of what was planted actually bore fruit. I never really appreciated the full truth of that parable -- how hard it really is to grow something of value -- until our family's little debacle with backyard gardening. Since then, I better understand why it's often hard to grow crops -- and to grow effective disciples for the Lord Jesus Christ.

Gifts: Appropriate and Inappropriate
Revelation 22:16-17

Some years ago while on a mission trip to South America I had opportunity to walk along the famous Copacabana Beach in Rio de Janeiro, Brazil. Although I'm a preacher, I'm also a reasonably normal adult human male, so I was admiring the many pretty women who passed by me, most of them clad in revealing bathing suits.

The local Brazilian women's bathing suit at Copacabana is known as a "fio dental." That's Portuguese for "dental floss," and it very aptly describes those suits. There's not a whole lot of fabric used up by their construction. I was so impressed with the beauty of the Brazilian women in these skimpy bathing suits that I bought two "fio dentales" to take home as gifts -- one for my wife and one for my daughter.

When I got home and my wife, Fran, took a look at her gift from Brazil, she was not at all impressed. In fact, I believe her words were to the effect of "There's no way I'd ever wear something like that." She was even less pleased with my buying one for my daughter, who was only seven years old at the time. I said, "She can grow into it," but my wife said, "Over my dead body!" I think those gifts were about the least well-received I've ever given to anyone. They were neither needed by, nor appropriate to, the women in my family.

There is one gift that is always needed -- and always appropriate -- to any person, female or male, young or old, the world over. That gift is eternal life. The giver is Jesus Christ. He holds this gift out freely, to all who will accept it. Many do, praise God, accept Jesus' wonderful gift to them. But many have not yet accepted it, because they've not yet understood the gracious simplicity of Jesus' free gift.

Christians bear responsibility to tell others about this matchless gift. If you are reading this and claim to be a Christian, I challenge you: Tell someone about Jesus' free gift of eternal life -- today. Offer them the opportunity to accept his marvelous grace.

Only One Chance
Matthew 7:1-2

I first met "one shot Sam" at the first congregation to which I was assigned as pastor, now more than four decades ago. I was going over the membership roll of the church and Sam was on the inactive list. I called him and asked if he'd like me to visit. He said, "Sure, why not?" so I scheduled a time to visit his home.

Sam was a decent enough fellow, but he warned me, up front, that he had a problem with preachers. "Every preacher I've ever known has disappointed me," said Sam. At the time, I was young, naive, and idealistic. I responded, "Well, Sam, I won't disappoint you. Why don't you come on back to church?"

I was pleased to see Sam in church the following Sunday. In fact, he became a regular in worship every Sunday, for about six months. Then I noticed his absence one Sunday, then a second. So I called him on the phone. "I've been missing you in worship, Sam. Are you OK?" His response, "You disappointed me, preacher, just like I said you would. I won't be coming back." "How did I disappoint you, Sam?" With that invitation, he pointed out a single sentence in a sermon I'd preached several weeks previous -- a statement with which he disagreed. It didn't fit his personal theology. Though I tried to talk him past it, he wouldn't budge.

I followed up with letters, calls, and a couple of personal visits over the next year or so -- it made no difference. To Sam, I'd made a mistake -- and that was one mistake too many for him.

Quite a few of the long-term members of that church told me that I'd done very well, indeed, with Sam. "You lasted six months with him. That's a record," they told me. "Every new pastor tries to get Sam active, but he only lasts about three months with most of them."

With time and years of experience as a pastor, I learned that there are a number of "one shot Sam's" and "one shot Sally's" in every congregation. They'll give you a chance -- one chance. But that's all. As soon as they find something that doesn't fit their personal preconceptions, they're gone.

I praise God that he's not a "one shot Sam." Jesus was once asked, "If my brother sins against me, how many times must I give him another chance? As many as seven?" And Jesus responded, "No. You need to give him seventy times seven chances."

That's how God is -- and that's how we need to be, too!

Church Tag
1 Corinthians 1:1-3

In virtually every Christian congregation in this nation, regardless of denomination or non-denomination, "tag" is a game that is regularly played by a cadre of inactive church members with their pastor. It's a fairly simple game; I've personally played it many times. A pastor visits with an inactive member of the church, encouraging them to return to attending worship. That member agrees to do so, and actually shows up -- on one Sunday morning. They've thereby completed the "tag." Now it's the pastor's turn again. He or she must again visit with that same inactive member and invite them to church. Once again, they'll come -- one time. And the game goes on.

The main problem with this little game is that it's not played on a level field. In most local churches there is one pastor. However, there are probably several hundred lay members, a substantial percentage of them inactive. If it were a simple one-on-one contest, the pastor might have a chance of winning. But not only must he or she play "tag" with one inactive member, they're also involved in an identical game with a different inactive member -- and another, and yet another, etcetera and etcetera. After two or three rounds of "tag" with a couple of hundred separate inactives, the pastor is exhausted. And the inactives pretend not to understand why the preacher gave up -- after all, it was their turn when the pastor quit playing.

There's also a variant form of the church "tag" game that's played by long-term inactive members with extended families. The preacher visits, they thank him, then proceed to present him with a long list of their aunts, uncles, parents, nieces, nephews and cousins -- plus a few of their best friends -- who also need to be visited. Only when all 26 such additional visits have been completed will they consider returning to church -- maybe once or twice.

I don't know how God will judge our game-playing with the church of Jesus Christ, but I do know that, according to Matthew's Gospel in the Holy Bible, Jesus Himself started the church. And further, in Paul's letter to the Ephesians, God's Word states that Jesus gave His life for the church. Still further, in the letter to the Hebrews, Christians are reminded not to give up regular, faithful attendance at church. If Jesus held the church in such high esteem, shouldn't the people of God do the same?

Be Prepared
2 Timothy 4:1-2

I had been asked to serve as a chaplain on the "disaster response team" for an area hospital. I and the other team members subsequently attended several daylong workshops in which we were provided extensive training regarding our responsibilities should a disaster occur. Then a number of months passed quietly.

One night about 10:30 PM, just as I was thinking about retiring for the evening, the telephone rang. It was the hospital. "Chaplain Ring, there's been a major disaster. A plane crashed at the airport, and they're just beginning to bring the casualties in. Get here as fast as you can." I jumped in my car, sped the five miles to the hospital -- running at least three red lights along the route -- and parked in the chaplain's spot. I rushed in the hospital's back door. There stood a woman with a stopwatch, which she clicked as she saw me. "Eleven minutes. Not bad," she said as she did so. "You can go home now. This was only a drill."

I understand the need for disaster drills, and I also understand the need to make them as real as possible. Had I known it was just a drill, I might have responded more slowly than I did. But I don't think I fell asleep that night until well after 3 AM, when all the adrenaline I'd churned up finally subsided.

On the other hand, I'm most certainly glad there was no disaster. And I'm pretty sure that, as a result of the drill, I and others on the response team were better prepared to handle the real thing, should it ever have occurred.

Jesus often admonished his followers to be prepared. Be especially well-prepared to give account of your faith in him, before God, when you are called before the throne of Heaven to do so. When that time comes there will no longer be opportunity for drills or practice sessions to help you get ready. You'll have only one chance.

But you can become better prepared now for that singular occasion by conducting your own practice sessions while still on earth. That, for a Christian believer, simply means sharing your faith with someone else. Each time you share your faith in Jesus with another precious human being, such sharing aids and strengthens your personal testimony. Christians -- share Christ with your neighbors on earth; it will prepare you to meet God in Heaven above. And it might also help them with just the same preparation.

The Long Run
2 Samuel 18:21-27

I was a runner for almost 50 years. No, I'm not now, nor ever was, a world-class athlete. But from 1962 to 2009, I got up and ran virtually every morning.

I never ran long distances – normally it was just a single mile daily. But I was very consistent and faithful in my running, even when in unfamiliar locations on business trips or vacations. I did some calculating and thus figure I ran about 18,000 miles during my many running years -- which is some two-thirds of the way around the world -- at the rate of one mile per day.

Some years back I was asked to preach a revival in the small west Texas town of Iraan. The first evening I was there, at a snack supper after the worship service, I casually mentioned that I would be out running the next morning. One of the women present asked me if she could run with me. She said she'd meet me at the pastor's house, where I was staying, at 6 AM. Wanting to be friendly, I said, "OK."

That next morning this lady showed up promptly at 6, and I immediately knew I was in trouble. She was wearing a running suit that had so many award patches sewn on it there was barely an inch uncovered. She had run in dozens of marathons, plus having competed in a bunch of triathlons and even in the Iron Man competition in Hawaii. Having recently moved to tiny Iraan, she hadn't yet found anyone there to regularly run with her.

She asked me how far I wanted to run, and when I said, "Well, I usually run just one mile," she practically laughed at me. She said, "Why, I don't even get warmed up in one mile. Let's at least run two miles." Reluctantly, I said, "OK."

It was only as we were running that I discovered her reckoning of two miles meant two miles in one direction, then two miles back to the starting point, for a total of four miles. I was just about dead when we completed the run.

I was in Iraan for four mornings. This woman showed up each of those mornings at 6 AM for a four-mile run.

The apostle Paul in the New Testament of the Holy Bible must have been a runner. In several of his letters to Christians, he likens the Christian life to running. And he urges Christians to keep on running, never to give up, never to stop. For in Paul's words, if Christians keep the faith -- if we keep on running, and don't sit down and rest on our laurels, we will be fit to claim the prize when we leave this earth -- the reward of eternal life in Heaven with the Savior, Jesus Christ.

Conservative When It's Convenient
Matthew 23:1-4

George claimed to be a literal, fundamental believer in the King James Version of the Holy Bible. With great regularity he showed up at my office on Monday mornings to castigate me for something I'd said in the sermon the day before, something which didn't properly align with his personal theology. He would brandish his large black King James Bible in front of me and say, "Every page, every word, every letter of this book is God's Holy Word. If it was good enough for the apostle Paul, why isn't it good enough for you?"

Of course, I had explained long before to George that the King James Version of the Bible was written in 1611 A. D., so the apostle Paul couldn't possibly have had one. And, just as obviously, since the New Testament was originally written in Greek, any English language version of the Bible, be it King James or other, is merely a translation. But George regarded that information as "liberal logic," something designed only to try and confuse a true believer like himself.

One Sunday I preached a message on tithing. Tithing is the Biblical concept by which God commands that 10% of His people's gross incomes be contributed to his temple and the support thereof. Tithing is taught throughout the Old Testament and repeatedly referenced by Jesus and the apostles in the New.

The following day George showed up for his Monday morning critique of my message. But his approach that day was totally different from his normal routine. "Preacher, you shouldn't try to teach tithing to people today. It's an Old Testament concept, so it doesn't apply to Christians. And besides, the Church today isn't the equivalent of the temple back then. And furthermore, the 10% standard only made sense back when we didn't have to pay such high taxes to support governmental social welfare programs." On and on he went, deconstructing the Biblical standard of tithing so completely that he could have qualified for a professorship at the most liberal seminary in our land. From that day forward, I understood that George was only a fundamentalist literalist when it suited his purposes.

The Bible tells us that God, who has best revealed himself to us in Jesus Christ, is the same yesterday, today, and forever. You can count on God – He's always consistent, even if his people aren't.

Ministry Is a Family Affair
1 Timothy 3:1-5

As a young seminary student returning to my home area during the summer for a conference meeting, my wife and I were invited by a middle-aged pastor to stay in his home the week after the meeting. While I appreciated the invitation, I tried to turn it down, for I knew that this pastor was scheduled to move from one church to another. He was inviting Fran and me to visit during the very week that he and his family would be packing up to leave.

However, this pastor insisted that we visit then -- for that very reason. He wanted us to see what it was like for a pastoral family to be in transition from one church to another. He knew that we would experience the same circumstances a number of times in our years of ministry ahead, so he wanted us to be better informed, better prepared.

We went and we learned. We watched as this man and his wife said tearful goodbyes to dozens of church members who came by with gifts to bid them farewell. We took also note of the handful of other church members who stopped by and who, without saying it directly, wished only to gloat at this preacher's impending departure.

At the time we didn't yet have children, so we observed in shocked silence as their teenagers periodically erupted in fits of rage and/or crying binges at being uprooted from their friends. It was a strange and eye-opening week for us. It helped clarify and strengthen our "call" into the ministry. I've always appreciated and admired that pastor for his willingness to allow us to be present during this very intimate chapter of his family's drama.

Most Christian pastors that I know, of whatever persuasion or denomination, are deeply and sincerely dedicated to the ministry of God. They wouldn't stay in the ministry long if they weren't. But the vast majority of those same clergy freely admit that their being in the pastorate has been difficult for and, far too often, harmful to their families. No other profession bears such a dubious distinction.

Christians often tout "family values" as highly important. Those of us who profess to be Christians could make a significant start at living out such values by treating our pastoral families with greater care and respect.

A New Beginning
Luke 1:76-78

Jim and Ann, along with their teenagers, were among the most active families in the congregation of which I was then pastor in Albuquerque. They'd joined only about two years before, but had rapidly gotten involved in a variety of ministries. Their four teens were very closely spaced in age -- 16, 15, 14, and 13. In that particular church those four constituted almost half the active youth group.

One Sunday, on the way out of church, Jim stopped me. "Can Ann and I visit with you this week, pastor? We have a marital issue we need to work out." Of course I said yes, and an appointment time was set. I prayed several times, early in that week, that God would help work out their marital dilemma, whatever it was, before they even came to see me.

When they arrived to talk to me, I was totally surprised by the nature of the marital problem they brought. Jim explained, "Pastor, we began living together when Ann became pregnant with our oldest daughter. That was 17 years ago. Since then, we've just continued to live together. We never bothered to get married. All our kids, and all our friends, assume we're married. But we aren't. As we've grown closer to God over the past couple of years, we've realized that we need to make things right before him. We want you to marry us."

After I picked myself up off the floor from the shock, I said, "Of course. You get a license, and I'll marry you -- quietly in my office, just as soon as you want." Again they surprised me. "No, we don't want to be sneaky about this. We've been living a lie for too long already. We want to come clean, and we want everyone to know. We're going to start by telling our kids about this, and about our plans to get married, tonight."

So it was that we scheduled a wedding for Jim and Ann at the church, with the whole congregation invited. There wasn't a dry eye in the house as they explained to all assembled that they wanted to repent of the error of living together without being married, and to start their relationship over again with God at the center of their marriage. When they took their vows everyone rose in a spontaneous standing ovation.

I thank God that, through Jesus Christ, we always have the opportunity of a fresh start in life, no matter what the past has been.

A Little Encouragement
Joshua 1:7-9

Everyone has a bad day from time to time. Some years back, I remember one such that started out as an all-time record-setting loser. I woke up with a headache, stubbed my toe on the way to the bathroom, found my five-year-old son in a crabby mood and my infant son throwing a crying fit, and had three minor arguments with my wife -- and that was all just before breakfast.

Then, I went over to the church office just in time to get chewed out over the phone by one of the other preachers in town. After I got off the phone, the church treasurer informed me that we had more bills than we could pay, and five different people stopped by to tell me that the roof over the educational wing of our church buildings had leaked during the rainstorm the night before -- and I had better do something about it. Right after lunch, a member called to criticize something I had said the previous Sunday, and the mail arrived with three more bills in it. Next, I tried to visit three patients in three different hospitals, only to find two missing from their rooms and the other sound asleep.

When I got home in the late afternoon, still feeling poorly with that same headache, I tried to lie down for a quick nap before dinner, only to receive three junk phone calls in the space of twenty minutes. During dinner, when the phone rang again, I was just about ready to yank it out of the wall.

But this time the call was different. It was another member of my church, and she was calling to tell me how much she appreciated my visits to her home during a recent family crisis. In closing the brief conversation, she said, "Just thought you might appreciate a little encouragement this evening, pastor. Keep up the good work!"

Well, that lady's call changed my whole perspective on that day. The headache went away, the evening mellowed, and what had seemed destined to be a horrible day went into the record books as not so bad after all. And all it took was a little encouragement.

In Hebrews 10:25 in the Holy Bible, the Word of God says: "Let us encourage one another." From my perspective that's one of the most important pieces of advice in all the Bible. We all need a little encouragement. Try it -- encourage someone you know -- today!

Be Just What You're Called to Be
Luke 12:13-14

Pastors can get themselves into some really strange dilemmas. One particularly odd situation for me developed from a visit with an older church member while I was pastor in the tiny Big Bend town of Alpine, Texas. During the course of my visit, the lady I was visiting mentioned that her TV set wasn't working properly. Wanting to be helpful, I said, "Would you like me to take a look at it?" It turned out that her set needed only a couple of minor adjustments, and within ten minutes I had it working fine.

Older persons in small towns talk to one another, so the word rapidly spread throughout Alpine that Pastor Ring could fix TV's. There was only one television repair shop in Alpine, and it was so completely backlogged that the wait for repairs was two months or more. Within days after my visit to that lady, I had received more than 30 telephone calls asking for my help with malfunctioning TV's. In fact, it turned out that, once he heard I was apparently available to do such, the single TV repair shop owner in town was even telling folks to call me, since he was so completely bogged down in the work. Several of the callers were desperate enough to have their TV's worked on that I was offered $100 just to "take a look" at their sets.

It took me months to explain to all of Alpine that I really wasn't interested in taking on a second job as a TV repairman, either voluntarily or for pay. Some of them, especially those who were members of my church, were genuinely offended when I refused to work on their sets. But eventually I convinced everyone that I already had more than full-time employment as a pastor, and wasn't seeking any sideline work.

In Acts 6 in the Holy Bible, the early church preachers realized that they were foolishly diluting their effectiveness by doing things other than the tasks to which God had specifically called them. So they explained to the laity, "It is not right that we should give up preaching the Word of God to serve tables." And the people understood -- and took some of the load off their preachers. Today's laity should understand the same, and do likewise for their pastors.

An Unexpected Gift
Acts 3:1-8

A month or so prior to Christmas a few years back, my wife, Fran, asked me to give her a "hint" as to something I'd like for Christmas. For several years, I had been wanting to acquire a chain saw to allow me to cut some dead limbs from the trees around our house. I'd seen a small electric chain saw advertised for just under a hundred dollars in a mail-order catalog recently, and it seemed like just what I wanted. So I told Fran, "Look on page 44 of the Damark catalog that we got in the mail last week. There's something there I'd really like to have."

A couple of weeks later, a package was delivered to our house by UPS, and I noticed that it came from the Damark company. It was a long, skinny box, just about the size and shape to hold a chainsaw. Fran made a point of grabbing it away from me before I could shake it, but I felt sure it was what I'd asked for.

That package later showed up, wrapped, under our Christmas tree. I could barely wait to open it. When Christmas morning finally arrived it was the first package I began to undo. The surprised look on my face as I encountered a telescope must have been very apparent. "That's what you wanted, isn't it?" asked my wife. I quickly covered up as best I could. "It's wonderful! I've always wanted a telescope. With this I'll be able to count the craters on the moon and find the planets and identify the stars. Thanks a bunch, honey!"

Later that day, I carefully examined that Damark catalog, page 44. There, exactly where I'd seen it, was the chainsaw. And on the same page, just above it, was something I hadn't previously noticed: the telescope my wife had purchased, more or less where I'd told her to look.

I still have that telescope, and I've spent quite a few evenings of stargazing with it, becoming something of an amateur astronomer as a result. I really enjoy my telescope, unexpected though it may have originally been. I also went ahead and bought myself the chainsaw. After using it once or twice and discovering how dangerous it could be, it's since spent most of its time in the box it came in.

Sometimes when we ask our Heavenly Father to give us something we think we need or want, we may not receive exactly what we asked. But God, who enjoys giving good gifts to his children, always provides that which is best for us in the long run.

With God, Free Really Is Free
Ephesians 2:6-9

At the first church where I served as full-time pastor, I decided to offer a Tuesday evening Bible study. Because many from that congregation were elderly and didn't like to come out in the evenings, I was duly warned that it might not work out. Sure enough, although I tried valiantly to advertise and promote a ten-week study of the Gospel of John, only one person signed up. After over a month of trying without success to enlist others, I apologized to the lone individual who had been willing to attend, and gave up on the idea.

Six months later I decided to try it again. But this time, having remembered my background from outside the church, I advertised the very same course, a ten-week study of the Gospel of John, with a $15 registration fee attached. Sixteen persons signed up, each gladly paying the registration fee and excitedly looking forward to the class. Fifteen of the sixteen who started out completed all ten sessions. It was a solid success.

The secular world in which we are all unavoidably immersed teaches a basic principle that most of us, consciously or unconsciously, use to measure the value of all that we encounter, be it tangible or intangible. It's quite simple: "You get what you pay for." Thus, if something is offered free of charge, it probably isn't worth much. But if you must invest something in order to receive it, its value increases.

This is why, for example, counselors almost never provide free therapy. Rarely does anyone get better from free therapy. But if clients have to invest something in their therapy, the likelihood of their recovery increases.

I personally believe that part of the reason many persons are resistant to the Gospel of Jesus Christ today is that salvation is offered by God as a free gift. In our society, we're automatically suspicious of that which is "free." If it's free, it either must not be worth much, or there's a "catch" -- some hidden, fine print.

There's no fine print in God's offer to us. Salvation really is freely offered to any human who desires to receive it. But remember that it wasn't free to God's Son, Jesus. On the cross, Jesus paid an unimaginably high price for our redemption. And thanks be to God that he did!

Moving On
Philippians 1:20-21

It was December 15th, 1982. I was in my office at the church I was then serving in Alpine, Texas. A call came in; the secretary passed it through to me. It was the bishop -- my boss in churchly affairs. "Dave, I want you to go to El Paso, to St. Mark's Church." I was stunned; I was very much enjoying my church and ministry in Alpine. So I asked, "Bishop, how long do I have to think this over?" His reply: "About 30 seconds, and don't say, 'No.'" Well, that obviously made my choice, or the lack thereof, crystal clear.

At that time my wife and I had two children, both sons, one five years old and the other two. We were further instructed by the bishop to be in El Paso as soon as possible, and definitely before New Year's Day 1983. So we immediately began packing. Christmas Day was especially tough on our small boys. We opened presents that morning, then immediately packed them all back up, along with our Christmas decorations. And we arrived in El Paso, as ordered, on Dec. 28, 1982.

People often ask me, as an itinerant preacher for nearly 40 years, how I coped with the prospect of always being ready to move, never really able to settle down in any particular place. While I readily admit that, from a human perspective, such transience could be tough, not only on myself but on my family as well, I've learned that it has at least a few advantages.

For example, I now have good friends scattered throughout the southern half of the USA. If I want to spend a night in any of nearly a dozen towns, from California to Georgia, I don't have to worry about motel costs. So in this world, moving on average once every four or five years was sometimes a good thing -- and sometimes not so good.

But spiritually, the fact that I might have to "move" at any given time was clearly a very positive reality. Since I had no opportunity to grow "roots" in this world, I grew to understand that my ultimate, heavenly home was really my only long-term dwelling place.

Abraham, the father of God's faithful people of old, was repeatedly told by God that he and his descendants would ever be strangers and sojourners on this earth. In fact, the first time that God ever spoke to Abraham, as recorded in the Holy Bible in Genesis 12:1, he said this, "Go from your country and your kindred and your father's house to the land that I will show you." In other words, "Abraham, get up and move!"

Christians, especially evangelical Christians, frequently sing songs about their desires to move beyond this life into the Kingdom of Heaven. "This world is not my home; I'm just a passin' through" is a line I readily recall from an old gospel hymn. I trust that we, God's people of today, really mean it.

Heeding Good Advice
Ecclesiastes 7:11-12

One of the biggest mistakes I made when assigned as a missionary to the central American nation of Guatemala was taking a car. The church to which I was going was willing to fly me and my wife to Guatemala, but I said, "No, we'll drive. I want the adventure of seeing the countryside, and I want to have transportation readily available once I'm there." After again, several times, advising me not to do so, the experienced missionaries I would be meeting in Guatemala said, "OK, if you insist. But don't say we didn't warn you."

Driving all the way through Mexico to Guatemala surely was an adventure, taking four full days from the U. S. southern border at Brownsville, Texas. And sure enough, as soon as we arrived in Guatemala I rapidly began to learn how much of a liability, rather than an asset, an automobile could be.

For starters, insurance rates were sky high, more than double what you'd expect in the USA. But a foreigner in Guatemala with a car and no auto insurance would be an absolute fool, for Guatemalan traffic regulations are very clear. If a Guatemalan and a foreign national are involved in an accident it is, by law, the foreigner's fault. Circumstances have nothing to do with it. Their rationale for this law is simple: a foreigner doesn't have to be in Guatemala, a citizen does.

Worse than that, however, were the dangers that USA license plates posed for an American in Guatemala. The local police were always looking for bribes from Americans -- and would stop you for no reason whatever, claiming you've violated a traffic law even if you haven't.

But the strongest reason for not bringing a US car into Guatemala is this one: If you ever fail to lock it, and sometimes even when you do, theft is not the biggest risk. Rather a Guatemalan woman may, upon seeing USA license plates, deposit her baby in the back seat. Because life is so hard for the people there, many of the poorer women reason that by giving their child to an American, they will thereby be giving it a better life. It's sad but true -- that exact scenario happened to half a dozen Americans I knew while I was there.

Proverbs 4:1 in the Holy Bible says this, "Hear, O sons, a father's instruction, and be attentive, that you may gain insight." To paraphrase that, it's smart to listen to those with experience. I was young and naive when I went to Guatemala, ignoring the advice of older, more experienced missionaries. So I learned much the hard way while there. But the good news is that, as a result, I grew smarter. Nowadays, at least most of the time, I actually heed the advice of those more experienced than I.

Giving and Receiving Crosses
Luke 9:23-24

As I've served God's people over the years, I've discovered that many of them are generous and loving to their pastors. I've received countless small, personal gifts intended to express love to me and, I trust, love to God through me. Undoubtedly the most frequent gift that I receive as a Christian minister is a cross. I've been given hundreds of crosses -- crosses of many sizes and materials -- some plain, some fancy.

Some pastors I know have tired of receiving crosses, and I can easily understand why. Being given yet another cross, or an additional Bible when you already have dozens of the same, is obviously redundant. But I honestly still enjoy receiving crosses. Each such, to me, is unique; each is deeply appreciated.

Almost all of the crosses I've been given are "pretty." Some are far more than that: they're strikingly beautiful. Every time I receive a beautiful cross I pause to wonder -- does the person who's presenting this to me really understand what they're giving?

Crosses are so popular in our culture that they've become jewelry around our necks, decorative decals on our cars and t-shirts, even advertising logos for commercial ventures that want to promote themselves as "Christian" businesses. Crosses are visible just about everywhere. But does that imply we know the meaning of the cross?

The original cross upon which our Savior was executed was not, by any stretch of the imagination, a pretty thing. It was a rough-hewn, wooden instrument of torture -- a simple but brutally efficient machine of death. In the time and culture of Jesus, no one in their right mind would have imagined that a cross could ever become a gift -- a gift presented in love.

But because Jesus was God's gift of love to us, the cross was radically altered. Intended to signify a degrading, cruel form of capital punishment, Jesus' sacrifice thereon changed the cross into a thing of beauty and glory -- a symbol of abundant, eternal life. Thus transformed, the cross really can be a gift of love, from one Christian to another.

Therefore, this preacher can honestly say, "Bring on the crosses! Yes, I've already got a lot of them, but there's always room for one more!"

Addicted to Romance
Ephesians 5:21-31

Bill and Sherry joined my congregation in Albuquerque. They were an engaged couple, each in their mid-40's in age. Clearly they were romantically drawn to one another. Four months after they joined, they asked if I would perform their wedding. They completed several basic sessions of pre-marital counsel with me. Since they'd both been married previously they didn't want a fancy wedding, just a simple ceremony in the sanctuary with a few friends present.

A few months after the wedding, Sherry called me with a sad report. The marriage wasn't working out to either of their satisfaction, and she was filing for divorce. I suggested counseling, but she said, "No." Shortly thereafter they both disappeared from the church community.

About a year later, Bill called me up. He and Sherry were back together; they'd worked out their differences and they wanted to re-marry. Would I perform their wedding again? I agreed to do so. This time they were married in my office, with just two close friends present as witnesses.

You might think I'm making this up from here on, but reality is sometimes even stranger than human imagination. It wasn't six weeks after the second wedding that Sherry again called me up. Again, the marriage wasn't working out, and again she was filing for divorce. I again suggested counseling; there was no interest. And again, she and Bill both disappeared from the faith community.

Another year passed, and yet another call came from Bill. He and Sherry were dating again; they wanted to re-marry. Could I please perform their third wedding? I said, "No, not without significant counseling. You need to get to the bottom of what's going on between you before you re-marry again." They refused and I saw no more of them. They probably found another pastor who would marry them without asking tough questions.

In our society romance has become the gateway through which couples, should they choose to marry, enter into marriage. When romance fades, as it inevitably does, there is too often little else undergirding the marriage. I believe that's what happened, repeatedly, to Bill and Sherry. When they were romancing one another, everything was fine. But once they married the romance faded -- and they had no other foundation to keep them together.

Love is a far deeper, far more significant commitment than romance. I Corinthians 13 in the Holy Bible describes love as well as any human words can. Read it -- it will aid you in all your relationships, especially marriage.

Never Too Old to Learn
Isaiah 43:18-20

Weldon Bigony was a member of one of my former congregations who resided, for a year, in Waco, Texas, 300 miles from that church. How and why that happened is at the heart of this particular story.

Weldon was an outgoing, gregarious, turned-on follower of Jesus Christ. He loved to greet folks with a big, almost smothering bear hug. At the time I met him, Weldon Bigony was already 81 years of age.

Fifty-nine years before, when the second World War was at its height, Weldon was scheduled to begin his senior year of college at Baylor University in Waco. An outstanding athlete, he'd been attending Baylor on a football scholarship. But just before he returned to Baylor to complete his final year, he felt God, or the pull of patriotism, or possibly both, leading him to join the U. S. military in our nation's fight against its enemies. So he dropped out of school, enlisted, and fought for his country.

After the war, he utilized the skills he'd been taught in the military by becoming a commercial airline pilot. For the next 30-plus years, he flew all over the globe for a number of carriers.

After seeing the entire world many times over, Weldon eventually retired back to Big Spring, Texas, his boyhood home. He often mused about returning to college and completing his unfinished degree. More years passed, but the desire to finish his interrupted schooling stayed with him. Friends in his Sunday School class encouraged him. So did his pastor -- that was me. Finally, nearly six decades after leaving Baylor, he wrote to the president of that college. It took a few months of negotiating, but things were eventually worked out.

Weldon returned to Waco to complete his senior year at Baylor University. To their credit, Baylor honored the remaining year of Weldon's football scholarship -- although they mercifully didn't ask him to suit out. In the spring of 2003, sixty years after his original missed graduation date and at the age of 83, Weldon Bigony received his degree.

It's amazing to me what God does with willing people, of all ages. Young or old, God can empower you – if you allow him. Praise the Lord!

Fighting Disease Along with Jesus
Psalm 6:1-4

For more than a decade and in three different cities, I was pleased to participate in the American Cancer Society's annual "Relay for Life," raising funds to help defeat this horrible array of diseases which plague human beings. Having lost three from my family to cancer: my half-brother, my mother-in-law and my father-in-law, as well as having had my wife successfully struggle through an entire year's fight with breast cancer, I am one who does not need to be prodded to join the fight against these awful maladies. When I was still able to run, I was always excited for the opportunity to jog a few laps to show my support toward finding cures for cancer.

The first time I joined a Relay for Life team, I was presented a t-shirt when I arrived. The shirt I received was an off-white, sort of grayish one. And I noticed others around me wearing white Relay shirts that, to me, seemed much more attractive. So I said to one of the leaders of the Relay, "If you don't mind, I'd like to exchange this shirt for one of the white ones. They're prettier." She responded, "Dave, you don't know what you're asking. You really don't want a white Relay for Life shirt." I answered back, "Oh, but I do! I like that color better." To which the reply came, "Dave, those wearing white shirts are those who have either had cancer or who are currently struggling with it. You really don't want a white shirt." Finally, I understood. "You're right. I certainly don't want a white t-shirt!"

As an ordained minister, people often present me with difficult questions concerning life and death issues. The most frequent such regard diseases which produce extreme suffering and heartache, such as cancer. "Why?" is the basic question. Why do such dreadful sicknesses exist in the first place? Why does God allow such terrible afflictions to plague humanity? Obviously, I have no simple, smart answers. Along with everyone else, I'll have to wait until I leave this earth to ask God those questions.

What I do know, however, is that when God walked our planet in human form, he regularly opposed, and successfully conquered, such ailments and diseases. Jesus Christ cured everyone who came to him for healing. Matthew 8:16 in the Holy Bible says so. So while I don't know why cancer exists, I do know, for certain, that Jesus is against it. And I further know that Jesus can cure it. If Jesus were here today, I imagine that he'd gladly join the fight against cancer. He might even enjoy running in a Relay for Life!

The Simplicity of Prayer
1 Thessalonians 5:16-18

Because I'm a clergyman people often ask, "Would you pray for me?" Or, "Would you pray for my sister who is sick?" To such requests I almost always respond, "Certainly! Let's pray right now!"

What continues to baffle me is the number of those same persons who, when I respond to their request with an offer of immediate prayer, back off. "Oh, I didn't mean right now." Some of them even seem embarrassed. "You mean, actually pray right here, right now?"

I'm always a bit surprised at folks who ask for prayer, then don't seem to really want what they've requested. Perhaps the root of this dilemma is that many people conceive of prayer as formal and ritualized, something done only behind stained glass windows while kneeling on pew cushions.

Long ago I learned that prayer is simply conversing with God. And since God is available at all times and in all situations, initiating a conversation with God is as simple as addressing Him.

One of the simplest and at once greatest examples of prayer to be found in holy scripture is David, the writer of many of the Psalms. While not every psalm begins in this fashion, there are at least a handful of them which start out thus: "Help, Lord!" If David, whom the Bible calls "a man after God's own heart," could pray that spontaneously and that simply, why should we make prayer any more difficult?

People also often say to me, "Pastor, I don't know how to pray." I always ask in response, "Do you know how to talk? If you know how to talk, you know how to pray. Just talk to God, the same as you're talking to me."

Prayer: It's both easier and more significant than you might think.

A Hasty Exit
1 Corinthians 1:10-11

While serving the Lord in El Paso, Texas a middle-aged couple, after visiting for a few weeks, joined the church which I then pastored. For this story I'll simply call them the Joneses. They stepped forward at the end of the Sunday morning worship service and took the vows of church membership before the congregation, pledging their faith in Jesus Christ and their intention to always be loyal members of that church.

Only eight days later, first thing on a Monday morning, the Joneses showed up at the church office and asked the secretary to withdraw their memberships. Although Christians in the modern-day have become notoriously casual about joining and leaving churches, this was somewhat more unusual than I'd previously experienced. So as soon as I became aware of what they'd done, I called and asked them why, after only a week, they were quitting the church they'd just barely joined.

Their answer was straight to the point: While at church the day before, they'd spotted another couple in the congregation whom they'd not previously seen there. They and this couple were long-time, bitter enemies. "If those people are part of that church, we want no part of it," was their response.

They went on to regale me with tales of this other couple's sins and wickedness, and suggested that, if I was really a smart pastor, I'd throw them out of my congregation. They weren't pleased with me when, once they let me get a word in edgewise, I responded to the effect that, if that other couple were as sinful as they described, they obviously needed to be in church so that they might better hear the Gospel of Jesus Christ.

Jesus is recorded in the Gospel of John, chapter 15, verse 17, as saying: "This I command you: Love one another." He further said this, "By this shall all know that you are my disciples, if you show love to one another." When Christians show love for each other, they prove that they really do believe in Jesus. But when those who call themselves Christians hate and exclude one another, they're working for the devil, not for Jesus.

No Strings Attached
Matthew 10:7-8

In one of my former churches, a particular family presented a substantial check to the church, $5,000, earmarked for the purchase of a new organ. We gladly accepted it. However, shortly thereafter we learned that this family had already picked out the particular new organ which they desired that the church purchase. It cost ten times the amount of their donation: $50,000. And, having accepted their contribution, they insisted that we were now committed to their goal. Sure enough, despite several more pressing priorities before that church at that time, the church's leadership was more or less coerced into spearheading a financial drive, for the next 18 months, to purchase a $50,000 organ. Eventually we got the organ, but many other important ministries were neglected in the process.

This is just one of many examples that I experienced in my decades as a pastor of what I call "gifts with strings." Far too often, unusual contributions to the church come with unusual ancillary requirements, sometimes stated, sometimes tacitly assumed. Often, these "strings" can be just plain silly. In one church that I know about, a new van was purchased from memorial donations in honor of a particular deceased member. Eight years afterward, when that van had worn out and needed to be replaced, the family of the deceased refused to allow the church to trade it in on a new one. As far as I know, twenty years later, the old van was still sitting in that church's parking lot -- inoperative and rusting.

While the church obviously has an obligation to use all contributions made in a responsible manner, putting strings on one's giving is contrary to the spirit of the Christian faith. In Matthew 10:8, the Lord Jesus Himself says, "Freely you have received; freely give." God put no strings on his grace to humanity. We have no need to put strings on our response to His grace.

Some time ago I gave $10 to a transient who conned me with a sad story about needing to pay for a prescription medicine. Later that same day I observed him on the street, opening up a brand-new fifth of vodka. Momentarily I was angry. Then I thought further. I had given that money on behalf of the Lord Jesus Christ. From that moment on, it became Christ's money. How it was used was God's issue, not mine. I relaxed, and ceased to fret over that trivial incident.

He Led Three Wives
Deuteronomy 21:15-17

As a pastor, one of the oddest funerals I ever had to do involved a man of about 60 years of age who had joined the church I was then serving some two years before. He'd come forward in response to the invitation following a regular Sunday morning service and made a personal profession of faith in Jesus Christ. Thereafter I saw him in church about 50% of the time. He was almost always solo when at church, although I do recall meeting a grown daughter with him once or twice. His job involved oil well drilling, sometimes stateside and sometimes in foreign places. Typically, he'd be at home for a couple of months, then away for several months, then home again.

Word reached me that this man, whom I'll call George for this story, had died while involved in a drilling operation in a foreign nation. It took nearly a week to get his body released by that country and returned to the U. S. During the interim I asked the director of the funeral home which would be handling the arrangements how I could contact a family member and learn what sort of service was desired. That's when things got very strange. He said, "Dave, George had three families. He had a wife and children here, a wife and children in Mexico, and a wife and children in Venezuela."

I was stunned, but I then asked the funeral director an obvious question: "Do they know about each other?" Again, I was flabbergasted by his answer. "Yes, and all three wives and all three sets of children and grandchildren plan to be here for the service."

So it was that I met and got acquainted with this man's three families. They all spoke highly of him. All three wives said he was a very good husband. All the various children, eleven total with most of them grown, claimed he was a good father and a wonderful provider. I conducted the funeral service bilingually, saying everything first in English, then repeating it in Spanish. The three families got along, and everyone seemed well-pleased.

I relate this story not to imply approval of George's lifestyle, for he was clearly in violation of God's seventh great commandment against adultery. Rather, I was genuinely impressed with the members of his various families. They managed to make the best of what could easily have been a very negative situation. Even so, I hope I don't run into George's like anytime soon again.

Bearing Fruit That Lasts
John 15:1-7

The first time I was actually paid for doing the Lord's work was while a seminary student in Atlanta, Georgia. Like many seminarians, I found a part-time job as a youth minister, in my case at a fairly large church in Decatur, a suburb of Atlanta.

The first Sunday evening I met with the youth, ten teens showed up -- out of a church which had more than 1,000 members. The next week, while at the church's Administrative Board meeting, I reported what I'd experienced thus far; I'd met just 10 active youth at the church's youth fellowship. One of the men present asked me, "What would it take for you to be able to create a dynamic youth ministry at this church? What kind of budget would be needed?" I thought fast, and quoted a number which, in 1973, was a substantial figure. "I think I could develop a significant youth program if 5,000 additional dollars were allocated for the youth ministry." "Fine," he said. "You've got it. Now do whatever it takes to bring our youth program to life." I discovered later that this individual was an extremely wealthy man and an equally generous giver, so his personal commitment was all that was needed for that church to add this money to its budget. Actually, he was willing to provide even more than that amount.

Over the next 17 months, I saw to it that that church offered some of the most exciting youth events I've ever been involved in. We brought in Christian rock bands at least once monthly on Sunday evenings. We provided a full meal every Sunday night, usually featuring pizza as the main entree. We took more than fifty youth on two major mission trips -- one to the mountains of North Carolina to distribute food to the poor of Appalachia, and one to build a Native American church parsonage in southwestern Oklahoma. I led 26 youth on a canoeing venture for a week into the Okefenokee swamp of southeast Georgia -- one of the wildest journeys I've ever made. We went to Six Flags over Georgia more times than I can count. That church's youth program was a constant beehive of activity, and it attracted youth galore. The last Sunday evening I was there, 120 excited youth bid me a fond farewell.

Not quite a year after I'd left that church, I went back to Atlanta for a visit and attended the Sunday evening youth fellowship meeting there, just to renew old acquaintances. There were exactly ten youth present. That's when I realized how little I'd really accomplished for the Kingdom of God. I hadn't focused them upon Jesus Christ; all I'd done was provide "bread and circuses" for those kids.

It was a humbling, important lesson for me, one that I've never forgotten. My work for God since then has never been as flashy and exciting as that first youth ministry, but I believe it's been a lot more significant to Christ -- for the long term.

What's Inside Counts
1Samuel 17:42-47

I was a late-middle aged, gray haired, short and chunky preacher. But the coach of my church's basketball team insisted that I attend and even suit out for the games. One evening, midway through the first half, he said, "Dave, you're going in." So there I was, hustling up and down the court, twenty-five years older than the next oldest person on either team.

Being short, fat, and the oldest player in a basketball game, however, meant that no one paid any attention to me. Whenever my team was on offense, I was able to place myself in the corner of the forecourt. Nobody bothered to cover me. Finally, I caught the attention of one of my team's players when he had the ball. He passed it to me, and I immediately threw up a prayer. It went "swish" through the net, a three-pointer. Everyone stared at me in amazement.

From that moment onward I was tightly covered by the opposition team. I heard them comment to one another, "Stay on that old guy. He can shoot!" I didn't get another open shot opportunity the entire time I was on the court.

The Bible records many times how God can use, for significant purposes, those that everyone else ignores. One particularly interesting story to me is that of the selection of my namesake to be king of Israel. God told the prophet Samuel to find a man among the Israelite people to serve as king. Thousands of men paraded themselves before Samuel, but God kept saying to him, "No, he's not the right one."

Finally, the sons of a man named Jesse were presented before Samuel. God said, in effect, "Close, but no cigar." So Samuel asked Jesse if he had any more sons. Jesse replied, "Yes, but the last one is just a child, too young to be of any use except for tending sheep. And besides, he's a harp player. You need a warrior to lead Israel."

But Samuel further asked, "At least let me see him." And when David was brought before Samuel, God said, "He's the right one." David proved to be the greatest king Israel ever had.

Be careful, people of God, in making assumptions based on outward appearance. God looks at the heart -- and so should we.

An Old Reason for New Joy
Matthew 13:52

One of the most heartwarming moments of my years in ministry occurred as the result of discovering an old Bible in a dusty, long-unused church classroom. A group of members of that church had decided it was time to "clean up and clear out" some of the junk which had accumulated in several such rooms on the second floor of one of that church's classroom buildings. In the process, they found a number of old Bibles, about 12 in all, and brought them to me. Most of them were simply old and worn out, but three of them had names and dates in them. Two of the three were persons whom we couldn't identify, but one was inscribed to a man in his mid-80's who was an old saint in that church.

I've changed his name, just in case he's still alive and might be embarrassed by my using him in this story, but the inscription on the inside front page of the Bible read, "To our son, Randy Williams, from Dad and Mom, April 12, 1930."

I deliberately waited until the middle of the next Sunday's early worship service, which this man regularly attended, to say, "Randy, I have something here you might want." Looking puzzled, he got up, came forward, and I handed him the Bible. He glanced at it, opened the flyleaf, then immediately began jumping up and down, shouting with joy, "Praise the Lord!"

Having an 84-year-old man jump up and down in the aisle in the middle of the early worship service wasn't a frequent occurrence in the churches I served, especially that one. Honestly, there were a few times when I was tempted to get out of the pulpit and go out to take the pulses of all those present at that early service, just to make sure they were still alive.

Randy's excited reaction was, without exception, the liveliest response I ever saw from the early service congregation during the entire five years I served as pastor there. Later, Randy explained to me that his parents had presented him that Bible, 71 years before, on the occasion of his confirmation as a member of the church -- back when he was 13 years old.

He'd lost it, so he remembered, within only a month or two after he received it. And now, almost 3/4 of a century later, it had been returned to him. What wonderful memories it brought back for this faithful octogenarian!

Harsh Judgment
Matthew 7:1-5

I was a single young adult, age 22, living alone in what was then for me a strange, new, big city: Albuquerque, New Mexico. I'd become an actual believer in Jesus Christ less than three years earlier, while in college. A few weeks after moving to Albuquerque, I began searching for a church in which to exercise my still infant faith.

One particular Sunday morning I visited a church whose worship service, as I recall, I much enjoyed. Immediately following that worship, I returned to my apartment, fried a hamburger, opened a can of beer, and sat down to eat lunch. The doorbell rang. I answered it to find the pastor of the church I'd just visited standing there. I was impressed that he'd followed up on my visit so quickly -- why, it was only 30 minutes since worship had concluded.

He introduced himself and I invited him in. He was just beginning to tell me a few things about himself and his church when, as I beckoned him to sit down, he spotted the open can of beer on the table next to my half-eaten hamburger. He frowned, literally stopped speaking in mid-sentence, and without another word turned and walked out the door. I never saw him again.

As I think back on that incident, more than four decades ago, even now I'm still hurt by the heavy judgmentalism that pastor exhibited. By no means am I claiming that beer drinking is exemplary conduct for a Christian. But there are much better ways to respond to a Christian brother or sister who is less than perfect. It's often been said, in jest but with a ring of truth, "The army of God is the only one that executes its wounded."

Galatians 6:1 in the Holy Bible says this, "Brethren, if a man is overtaken in any trespass, you who are spiritual should restore him in a spirit of gentleness." That's excellent advice, not just for ancient believers 2,000 years ago, but for those who would claim to be Christians today.

One of Many Valuable Learning Experiences
Galatians 6:1-3

In my very first pastorate, I learned many lessons that have stood me in good stead ever since. This tale is one of them: Clark, the lay leader of the congregation, had failed me. He was at least 40 years my senior, as were most of the members of that congregation. That church observed an annual Laity Sunday, when the laity of the church were supposed to conduct the worship service. I'd worked with Clark in carefully planning the Laity Sunday; he'd repeatedly assured me that everything would be taken care of. So I scheduled myself to take a holiday that Sunday.

But when Laity Sunday arrived, Clark was nowhere to be found. It was a chaotic Sunday for the congregation, with the preacher off on vacation and the Lay Leader, who was supposed to conduct worship, also missing. A handful of others, praise God, stepped in to fill gaps, but things did not go smoothly. When I returned home and was informed of what had happened, I asked Clark why he'd been absent. All he said was that he'd gotten his schedule mixed up, and inadvertently left town that weekend. Of course, since I was the pastor, the congregation placed the lion's share of the blame for the mix-up not on Clark, but on me.

So it was that when, just a few weeks after that debacle, Clark approached me, asking to be allowed to begin a new Bible study on Tuesday evenings, I was less than 100% thrilled. I knew that what he was proposing required significant time and effort on the part of the instructor, and I wasn't sure I could trust him to follow through. One of the lessons I'd already learned was that it's often better not to start something new in a church than to begin a ministry, thereby raising people's level of expectation, then abandon it after folks have begun to invest themselves in it.

I was brutally frank with Clark. In truth, I used the opportunity to unleash a mini-tirade at him. I told him I wasn't comfortable with his lack of leadership, and certainly wasn't ready to give him yet another opportunity to fail. In response, he picked up a Bible and began to read aloud Matthew 18:21: "Lord, how often shall my brother sin against me and I forgive him. As many as seven times?" Jesus said to him, "I do not say to you seven times, but seventy times seven."

I got the point. I was appropriately chastened. I apologized to Clark. And I gave him full and complete endorsement to begin his proposed Bible study. He did so, and it proved a success. He never missed a session, and a dozen members of that church were advanced in their faith by taking part in that Bible study.

Sometimes -- more often than some of us are willing to admit -- the laity can, and do, teach the preacher.

Why Be Afraid?
Exodus 14:10-14

I attended an event where some of the participants played a not-very-nice trick on the man-in-charge. They placed a large, hairy tarantula in a Styrofoam cup. Then they set the cup, top down, on the table in front of the place where that man was to sit. When he sat down, he immediately noticed the cup, turned it over, and out popped the tarantula.

Most everyone at the table scattered in fright. I didn't. I was seated immediately to the head man's right, and I knew that tarantulas aren't anywhere near as dangerous as most folks think. In my younger days I used to let tarantulas crawl up my arms just to watch the strange reactions from other people.

The tarantulas which are found in the American southwest aren't really poisonous. They rarely bite unless severely provoked. Should one actually bite you, you'll probably just need to make sure your tetanus shot is up to date, as tarantulas, being scavengers, carry many germs.

The majority of all human beings, worldwide, irrationally fear spiders -- especially large spiders like tarantulas. But the truth is that most spiders aren't harmful to us. And, on the positive side of the ledger, they eat a lot of other creatures which are harmful to humans.

On a much larger scale, it's a scary world out there today. Violence, mayhem, and terrorism dominate the news. Actually I'm not sure things are worse today than ever before, but I do know that modern communications grant us instantaneous awareness of everything that goes wrong in our world. And that, in and of itself, is scary.

Far too many of us live with far too many fears these days, most of them unfounded and irrational. A few generations back, one of our U. S. Presidents, Franklin Roosevelt, assured us that "The only thing we have to fear is fear itself." I like that.

For his part God, our Creator, doesn't intend for us to live lives dominated by fear. In fact, when he sent His Son, Jesus, to our world, his announcement of that great gift included these important words of encouragement: "Be not afraid, for behold, I bring you good tidings of great joy, which shall be to all people." In another verse of holy scripture, we are promised that the perfect love of God casts out all fear.

Why be afraid? Nothing -- not even a big, hairy tarantula -- can separate you from the love of God that is personified in Christ Jesus the Lord.

The Value of Blood
Leviticus 17:10-12

One of the simple things that I regularly did for some years for others was serving as a blood donor. I first began giving blood in my 30's when the church I was serving decided to host a blood drive. I'd never really thought about donating blood before that; I just assumed that blood was always around. But when I did begin to consider the concept, it didn't take a lot of pondering to realize that blood given to others in need had to come from a donor.

As pastor of my congregation I was expected to set an example. I approached the donation process with a bit of fear and trepidation as, like most normal people, I wasn't enamored of being stuck in the arm with a rather large needle -- and even less interested in bleeding into a bag for 20 minutes. But I put up a brave front for my church and dutifully endured the procedure.

Surprisingly, aside from the momentary prick of the needle stick, the entire experience was rather ordinary. I didn't feel pain, nor dizziness, nor anything strange. Afterward my arm still worked OK, and so did my mind. Although I walked around for the next several days on hyper alert that something might go wrong with me, it didn't. After a while, I forgot all about it.

Eight weeks later, the local blood bank called me up and asked if I'd like to donate again. Their office wasn't far from where I worked, so I said I would come.

The second time was easier than the first. I wasn't afraid. And so began a more or less regular routine.

Fast forward twenty years and I had given at least five gallons of blood, although because I'd moved around several times the various blood banks hadn't kept up with my records very well. But I had the personal satisfaction of knowing I'd helped countless numbers of others through this simple, yet very personal, way of giving myself to them.

Once I began regularly travelling to other countries, many of them in the third world on mission trips, eventually my blood no longer fit the guidelines for donation that are required to assure the supply of donated blood stays clean. Having been in Africa I'm now disqualified from future donations for life. That's OK; I understand.

When I consider the Savior, Jesus Christ, who gave his body and blood -- all of it -- for the benefit of humanity, I'm still confident I could spare an occasional pint for the good of others. Maybe you can, too.

Itching Ears
2 Timothy 4:2-4

While serving as pastor of a church in a small city I and my wife became friends with the pastoral family of the church which was located, literally, next door to ours. We were similar in age, both couples with small children at the time and, as parsonage families, we had many shared interests -- interests which transcended the relatively insignificant denominational differences between our respective church bodies. We shared our mutual "ups and downs" and prayed for one another on a regular basis.

One of the difficulties which our friends regularly faced in coping with their church was the "board of elders" which governed it. This group -- consisting of nine men --was totally sovereign over every matter concerning that church and its ministry. The group met every single Sunday immediately following morning worship services. There, they would decide if the pastor's message which he had delivered that day was acceptable or not so, and take a vote thereon. If that vote was ever in the negative, my pastoral friend would then be asked to leave the church. During the three years that I knew him, my friend barely escaped that fate on more than one occasion, surviving 5 to 4 votes by this group of nine elders.

There were many important issues which needed to be faced by that congregation, but which my friend could not address -- knowing that to raise such would result in his being terminated by the board of elders. They very deliberately kept him on a short leash, one week at a time. They wished to hear only messages which pleased them, never anything that would disturb their spiritual complacency.

I thank God that in my own ministry I never had to face that kind of churchly blackmail. But in every congregation I've served, and probably in every congregation that exists on earth, there are some persons who only want to hear that which "tickles" their ears, affirming that which they already believe. Should the preacher dare to speak that which challenges their preconceptions, they rise up in anger.

All this is certainly not a new phenomenon. Jesus Himself faced it when He brought good news to the poor, healing to the sick, salvation to the lost. The Pharisees and Sadducees hated every word He uttered. But He spoke the truth, and let the chips fall.

I lost track of my pastoral friend a few years after both of us moved to different towns. I hope he found a church where the people were willing to hear all they needed to hear from their pastor, both that which affirmed them and that which confronted them with fresh spiritual challenges.

Seven-Year-Old Faith
I Timothy 4:12

I was just getting started in formal, paid ministry, serving as minister to youth for a large congregation in suburban Atlanta, Georgia. One weekend just a few weeks into my tenure there, the senior pastor went on vacation -- and I was asked to preach.

The preaching went OK, and when it came time for the invitation to Christian discipleship, I asked if anyone would like to step forward and profess their faith in Jesus Christ. A little boy named Neal, seven years of age, ran down the aisle. For a moment I thought he was just being rowdy. But he ran right up to me and said, "I want to accept Jesus as my Savior."

Even though I'd only been there a few weeks, I knew who little Neal was, as his older brother was in the church's youth group. Neal was always trying to tag along with him, even though he was far too young. Frankly I, at least momentarily, thought exactly the same thing about his expressed desire to profess his faith in Jesus. But he had come forward in response to the invitation, so I gave him the microphone. He offered a short and sincere testimony, repenting of his sins and accepting Christ as his personal Savior. The entire congregation clapped as he scampered back down the aisle to rejoin his parents in their pew.

Over the decades of pastoral experience I've accumulated since that early occasion, I've learned that there are more than a few children who are ready, willing, and able to express their faith in Jesus at an early age. Many churches, of various denominations, insist that a child wait until he or she is 12 or 13 before they are allowed to affirm their faith in Christ. Some church bodies don't recognize youth as "real" members of the church until they achieve legal age in the secular world, that is, 18. But my experience says that chronological age has little bearing on Christian maturity. Some children can be mature believers at age 11; some adults are yet babes in Christ at 55.

Jesus in Luke 18:16 is recorded as saying, "Let the little children come to me, do not hinder them, for of such is the Kingdom of God." Jesus always spoke the truth, and he was certainly right on the spot with this comment. By the way, little Neal, decades later, became a close advisor to one of our U. S. presidents. I was pleased to know that a man of sincere Christian faith, from early childhood onward, was helping steer the course of our great nation.

A Good Name
Philippians 2:9-11

On the very day that I arrived in Odessa, Texas to begin pastoral ministry there, I opened the local newspaper to find a full page ad, taken out by one of the large, independent congregations of that city, inviting folks to "Hear Evangelist David Ring" at that church the following Wednesday evening. As a result, throughout my first Sunday in my then new church in Odessa, I was deluged with questions. "How did you get invited to preach at Temple Church so quickly?" Some in my brand-new congregation were, frankly, more than a little peeved at me. What right did I have to go off and preach for another church the very first week I was in town?

I wound up having to explain, forty or fifty times over, that the "Evangelist David Ring" who was going to speak at Temple Church wasn't me. I knew who he was. That David Ring was, at the time, a well-known national evangelist who did a wonderful job of witnessing the gospel of Jesus Christ despite suffering from severe cerebral palsy.

Our paths have crossed more than once over the past several decades; I've even spoken with him by telephone a couple of times, although we've never, at least not yet, sat down and talked face-to-face. We almost had lunch together once, in Albuquerque, but he had another engagement to pop up that caused him to have to cancel. For years, probably once a month, I would receive a telephone call or an e-mail intended for him that I had to refer to the "proper" David Ring. I don't know for sure, but I suspect he probably experienced some of the same in regard to me.

Because of the coincidence in the time of my arrival and his appearance there, some folks in Odessa never did figure out that I wasn't that "other" David Ring. But I really didn't mind, for he was doing a great work for the Lord Jesus Christ. I was honored to be confused with him.

Proverbs 22:1 in the Holy Bible says, "A good name is to be chosen rather than great riches." I'm trying to keep the name given to me a good one, and I trust that "Evangelist David Ring" is doing the same. But our shared name is ultimately of minor importance in relation to one and only truly great name that is above every other name: Jesus Christ.

Teaching a Memorable Lesson
Job 1:20-22

Every church has a "nosey Rosie" who painstakingly watches and attempts to learn everything she possibly can about the pastoral family -- so she can then share juicy tidbits of gossip about them with her friends. I'm not being sexist with this story; invariably, at least in my personal experience, such individuals have been female. In my first full-time pastoral charge, the local "nosey Rosie" was named Lela. Lela was a lady in her mid-60's who, when I arrived, was chairperson of the parsonage committee. I'm reasonably sure she had carefully maneuvered to obtain that role, as it meant she had more or less rightful reasons to watch over the pastor's home and the condition thereof.

Lela had a key to the parsonage. She used it with impunity, letting herself in and wandering through our house without prior notice -- always, of course, on the pretext of legitimate business. Someone -- never anyone with a name -- had reported to her that a toilet was leaking, so she decided to check it. The drapes in the living room needed to be looked at -- from the outside it appeared that the sun was fading them.

She made it a point to always leave a bowl of fresh-cut flowers on the kitchen table -- both as a statement to my wife and me that she had been there and to blunt any potential criticism of her invading the privacy of our home.

I tried hard to be as nice as possible to Lela, as did my wife, but also to be forthright in telling her that her frequent, unannounced entries into my home were not appreciated. She didn't pay a bit of attention, despite our gentle warnings -- repeated as many as 20 times over.

One particular day it happened that she entered the house while I was in the shower. As I dried off, I heard someone moving around in the house, and I knew my wife had gone out shopping. We had no children as yet, so no one should have been afoot. I suspected it was Lela, although I wasn't sure -- it might even have been a burglar.

I walked out of the bathroom stark naked and began quietly strolling through my house. Sure enough, there was Lela. When she saw me, she received, as they say, the "full monty." She screamed, ran out the door, and never again entered our home unannounced. When I saw her in church a few days later, she said not one word about the encounter. She simply handed me the parsonage key, which I gladly accepted.

It's not often heeded in modern times, but the Bible clearly says that Christians are to respect those who have spiritual oversight over them -- which means pastors. That includes respect for the privacy of the pastor's home, whether or not the church is the landlord.

Fascination with Frogs
2 Chronicles 14:11

For as long as I can remember I have been fascinated by frogs. When I was a boy of seven or eight, I used to regularly go "frog hunting" in streams and ponds near my boyhood homes. I'd usually catch half a dozen frogs and bring them back, alive, to show my mom. Invariably my mother would cast a wary glance at them, make a half-hearted remark such as "Oh, how nice," then order me to return them to the pond or creek from whence they'd come. I always did; I wanted them to be there for me to catch again when I came back the next time.

As an adult, my frog fascination has continued. But nowadays I collect small carved stone or wooden frogs. I've amassed quite a collection of such -- 100 or more. I discovered long ago that I could purchase a small carved frog in just about any state or country in the world, so they've become my trademark souvenir from wherever I travel. Almost every one of my tiny frogs has a small story behind it -- where it came from and what it's made of. I have display cases in which I proudly show them off at home.

Frogs figure prominently in the story of the Exodus of God's people from Egypt, but not in a flattering role. They're one of the ten plagues with which God harassed the Egyptians in order to force them to release his people from slavery.

Apparently, perhaps as one of the side-effects of global climate change, frogs and other amphibians are becoming less and less plentiful in the world today. That makes me a bit sad, for I would hope that tomorrow's little boys could have the same opportunity I had – the fun of frog catching that I so enjoyed during my boyhood.

Not long ago, however, I discovered a positive way to utilize frogs in the service of God. The word "frog" can be employed as an acronym for a great statement of faith: "Fully Rely on God." So today, whenever I see a frog, I'm reminded of that affirmation: F. R. O. G. "Fully Rely on God." It's a lifestyle affirmation that puts frogs in a whole new perspective.

Seeking the Wrong Things
James 4:3

I was part of a group of about 30 men who were meeting, all day, on a Saturday in the Youth Hall of the First United Methodist Church of Big Spring, Texas. Lunch had been brought in to us by a gracious group of ladies. We'd just served ourselves, buffet style, and were sitting down to eat. A man appeared in the front doorway; a couple of the other men who were nearer to that entrance talked to him. Then one of them came over and whispered in my ear, "You need to help this guy." When you're a church pastor, you hear that a lot. So I got up and walked over to listen to his need.

He immediately began to regale me with a long and intricate story of his many woes and misfortunes. It was a more or less typical transient tale; I listened to several thousand such in my four decades of ministry. About five minutes into the narrative, when he momentarily paused to breathe, I asked him to cut it short. "I'm not able to stand here all day and listen, so please tell me exactly what it is that you want from us," I said. "I'm hungry. I need you to give me $5 so I can buy lunch" was his reply.

I pointed to the large amount of food spread out on the buffet tables in the room in which we were standing. "Just walk over there, pick up a plate, and fill it as full as you like," I advised. "And if you want to take some out after you've finished that, I'll provide you a sack to put it in." He frowned at me in disgust, turned around, and walked out the door he'd come in.

That man's response is all too typical of the dealings which I, and the churches I've served, have had with transients, the homeless, and others who come to the church's doors asking for "help." Help, in their vocabulary, is spelled "c..a..s..h." They don't really want food, they don't really want gasoline, they don't really want prescription medicines. Their real agenda is to obtain cash money with which they can buy cigarettes, beer, liquor and/or illegal drugs. And because I -- and most churches -- rarely pass out cash, they usually go away saying, "That church wouldn't help me."

I often wonder how Jesus would have responded to today's hordes of transients, con artists, and other career panhandlers who make a vocation out of trying to separate churches and other charitable organizations from as much cash as possible. In the Gospels of the Holy Bible, Jesus never turned away a needy person who sought his help. But on the other hand, those who approached Jesus for help had up-front, visibly legitimate needs.

I'm sure there were some, even in Jesus' day, who -- like today's transients -- had hidden agendas. But apparently they didn't try to con Jesus, probably because they knew his reputation. He would've seen right through them, and, just like the man who didn't accept the food I offered him, they wouldn't have appreciated being unmasked.

Not Afraid of the Dark
Exodus 10:21-23

As a child growing up in the southeastern United States, I used to go "coon hunting" with my dad. My father always had a coon hound, either a redbone or a blue tick, and he and his friends loved to hunt. It was one of his two great passions, the other being fishing.

I was about eight or nine years old when my dad began regularly taking me on hunts for the wily raccoon. Such hunting is done at night, which meant that my dad always provided me with a flashlight. The forests in which we hunted were pretty thick, and it wasn't easy getting through them. But I never felt the need to turn on my flashlight; I could navigate just fine without it.

Whenever my father noticed that I wasn't using my flashlight, he'd always tell me to turn it on, which I dutifully did. But finally, after many nighttime trips through the woods, he asked me why I didn't ever turn on my flashlight without being told to. Was there something wrong with my eyes?

Actually, it turned out that there was not anything wrong with my vision; rather, eye testing eventually determined that my night vision was considerably better than that of the average person. My eyes were sensitive to light wavelengths somewhat farther down into the infrared part of the spectrum than most people's. I've continued to have better vision than most throughout my life; even in late middle age I didn't have to wear corrective lenses of any kind. But I have to admit that my unusual night vision is now less acute than it used to be, so I occasionally do stumble over things when walking around in the darkness.

Because I was blessed with such unusually good night vision, even as a child I never experienced being "afraid of the dark." And, in truth, there's really no reason for any human being to ever be afraid of the dark. Physical darkness is benign, and spiritual darkness can be overcome. John's gospel says it best: "The light shines in the darkness, and the darkness will never overcome it." This great spiritual light, to which John refers in the very first chapter of his gospel, is Jesus Christ. When Jesus comes into anyone's life, he banishes spiritual darkness -- now and forever.

Get Out There!
Matthew 28:19-20

I particularly enjoyed working summer Vacation Bible Schools with the children of the churches I served -- for a somewhat unusual reason. Unlike most "church people," I wasn't raised in the church, and therefore I didn't have multiple childhood memories of every week Sunday School, and Vacation Bible School, and church potlucks and picnics and the like. So, for me, working with Vacation Bible School wasn't a repeat of childhood memories – it was largely a brand-new experience. The other adults present may have already known all the verses to "Jesus Loves Me," but I was learning them as I worked.

Churches and the members thereof make a lot of false assumptions about people in general, mainly because they think everyone else's experience is just like theirs. When a new person enters a church for the first time, they don't realize that they're not supposed to sit in that particular spot -- because that's where saintly old Mr. Jones always sits and has sat every Sunday for the past 37 years. When the music director says, "Turn in your hymnal to page 335 and let's sing," they might not even be aware of what a hymnal is. Realistically, no one ever uses the word "hymnal" outside a church, do they? When a Sunday School teacher advises, "Open the Bible to 1 Corinthians 11:15," a person without a church background is probably not aware of how to find 1 Corinthians in the Bible nor, further, that the Bible is divided into both chapters and verses. Most books aren't organized that way.

If the Christians of the 21st century A. D. are to help win the world to Jesus Christ, a lot of us need to stop making false assumptions about what the secular world is like. Christians need to cease limiting their associations to Christian friends, their television viewing to Christian programming, and their music listening to Christian songs.

Certainly it's more comfortable to spend time with that which is familiar to us, and we're not likely to be offended by that which is in harmony with our moral and social norms. But Christians who deal only with other Christians simply don't reproduce. Christians are supposed to be out in the world, sharing their beliefs with an, as yet, un-Christian world. God deliberately sent Jesus out into the unbelieving world. That's exactly where Jesus wants his followers to go, too.

Even though I'm retired, I'm yet a preacher. I love the Church. That being said, I'm not about to spend my entire life there, and neither should any Christian who desires to effectively serve his or her Lord in today's world.

She Found Her Lost Marbles
Mark 5:15

I received notice that Mabel had died. She was 93 years of age, and had spent the final three-plus years of her life in a nursing home. The last time I'd seen her, perhaps two months before her death, she weighed no more than 70 pounds. I knew that she knew the Lord Jesus Christ as her personal Savior, so I said a hearty, "Praise the Lord!" when I heard of her passing.

Hearing of her death caused me to recall the first time I met Mabel. Only a few weeks before I met her, she'd been released from seven years of confinement in a state mental hospital. Early in that first conversation, I freely admitted to her that I was unsure of how to approach her, how to speak with her. She allayed my fears with a laugh. She said, jokingly, "Yeah, a lot of folks are afraid to really talk to me. Don't worry. I lost my marbles a while back. It took some doing, but I've found most of them by now."

Mabel turned out to be a delightful person with a wonderful sense of humor. She was well-educated, one of a tiny percentage of women to complete college way back when she was a young adult. She could hold her own in conversation on any of a wide variety of subjects. And she most definitely didn't take herself too seriously; she was always cracking jokes at her own expense.

Getting to know Mabel helped me get over some of my personal anxieties about those who have been mentally ill. I suppose, like a great number of people, I'd assumed that all mental illness was more or less incurable; that those who had suffered mental breakdowns were permanently incapacitated. Mabel taught me that mental illnesses can be little different from physical illnesses. Some are curable, some are not. Folks who've beaten mental illness don't need to be handled with kid gloves; they're no different from folks who've survived cancer or heart disease. They're just plain people.

When Jesus walked this earth, the Gospels record that he healed both physical and mental illnesses. He made no distinction between them. I'm glad Mabel showed me how me to do the same.

Speaking and Hearing the Hard Truth
Revelation 21:7-8

When I was 13 or 14 years of age my parents, after much persuading, bought me a guitar. Like a lot of teenagers with a guitar, I soon learned three chords and, with the use of a capo to transpose unfamiliar songs into my one and only key, was able to play -- at least minimally. I enjoyed jamming with my friends and even made a foray or two into starting a band, albeit fleetingly.

Years later, as a young adult, I pulled out my guitar, dusted it off, and decided I really wanted to learn to play, and play well. So I enrolled in classical guitar classes in the evenings at the University of New Mexico. The instructor was a renowned professor of music who was one of the five or ten top classical guitarists in the entire world. I took two semesters of instruction from him. Though I tried valiantly and practiced diligently, I didn't make much progress. As I considered enrolling for a third semester, this instructor stopped me. He simply said, "Dave, you're wasting your money and my time."

Most certainly that professor's remark was harsh but, on the other hand, he told me what I needed to hear. His was an informed and honest assessment of my ability. Although I could play the guitar well enough to informally entertain friends and family, that was the limit of my musical talent. I wasn't ever going to become a classical guitarist.

As a pastor, people frequently ask me whether honesty is always the best policy. Of course, such questions are usually framed by a larger situation which, on the surface, makes it appear that honesty will be callous, even cruel. Should I tell my mother that her cancer is incurable? Should I let my husband know that the baby I'm carrying probably isn't his? Should I keep quiet about my best friend's physical abuse of his children, or turn him into the authorities and risk breaking up a family? In our society we've become so used to the so-called "little white lie" that straightforward honesty is often made to seem wrong rather than right.

Jesus, in John 8:32, said these words: "You shall know the truth, and the truth shall set you free." Sometimes truth is hard. Many times it's difficult to speak the truth. Even more often it's tough to hear the truth. But I'm convinced that God's Word is correct -- lies, even those told with the best of intentions, entangle us. Truth and honesty set us free.

Gracefully Taking the Credit
Luke 6:31-33

It's not often that you receive credit for something you didn't do. But a lady called to thank me for visiting her sister while the sister was in the hospital. In truth, I didn't know that the sister had been hospitalized, and I therefore had not visited her. So I forthrightly told the lady who called that it wasn't me who had been there. It must have been another pastor who had visited her, and the sister had misidentified that person as me. No, she insisted, I must have forgotten. Her sister had been very specific – "Pastor Dave Ring" had visited her and offered a very uplifting prayer. Realizing that there was little point in further attempting to rebuff her offered thanks, I simply said, "I'm glad your sister was blessed by the visit," and left it at that.

That experience caused me to reflect upon the issue of getting "credit" for doing good. More often in my personal experience, the exact opposite has been the case: I've been unjustly blamed for doing something wrong – something that I actually didn't do. Maybe you've had the same experience. But being thanked for doing good -- that you didn't do? That's unique, a genuine rarity in this life.

When Jesus walked this earth, He was particularly disturbed by those who repeatedly and deliberately sought to receive public credit for their good deeds in this life. The Pharisees of Jesus' time were such people: They wanted everyone to know just how good they were, and to praise them for it. Jesus simply commented, "They have their reward." But for those whose quiet deeds of love and charity remain unknown and unrecognized in this life, Jesus also reminds us that God has eternal rewards, beyond this life, in store.

It was a bit strange, but certainly not unpleasant, to be thanked for doing something good that I really hadn't done. And I trust that God knows who really visited that lady in the hospital, and will surely reward their unrecognized good deed, if not in this life, then in the economy of eternity.

New Experience for Old Folks
Deuteronomy 34:5-7

One of the older men from one of my former congregations, a regular member of the choir, rose up in worship to sing a solo version of an old familiar hymn. It was extremely well presented, both musically errorless and spiritually moving. The congregations present at both worship services that morning broke into spontaneous applause.

Having been this man's pastor for only a little over a year, and having seen him sing in the choir throughout that period, I had assumed that solo work was routine for him. So as I thanked him after the worship service, I was surprised when he commented, "I'm sure glad I got through that. I was about scared to death." "Why's that, Bill?" I asked. "That's the first time I've ever sung a solo. It took me 80 years to work up the courage."

I can barely imagine the bravery it must have taken for this man, at the age of 80, to stand before his church for the first time and sing a solo. Most octogenarians that I've encountered are simply content to have lived to see their 80th birthday. But Bill Birrell, in his 80th year of life, dared to try something new and different -- to the glory of God.

Even those of you who know the Bible may or may not be aware that God, with interesting frequency, makes remarkable use of individuals who, by our society's standards, are already old geezers. Abraham, the exalted father of all God's people, was nearly 100 years of age when God began to express His purposes through Abraham's life. Moses, the most significant figure of the Old Testament, led the Hebrew people out of bondage in Egypt when he was 80 years of age. In the New Testament, two of the earliest witnesses to the divinity of the infant Jesus were a pair of senior citizens in the Jerusalem temple, Anna and Simeon. These are just a few examples of a consistent pattern -- God uses people of all ages, young, middle-aged, and old -- to accomplish His purposes.

Older folks in my congregations, especially those who are frail and in failing health, have often asked me, "Does God still have a purpose for my life?" My response is always an emphatic "Yes!" If God still has you breathing, then He has divine purpose for you.

Not Much of a Song Leader
Matthew 26:30

For most of my life I've considered myself "musically challenged." Yes, I've always loved music, but until I reached age 60 I honestly wasn't very good at it – though not for lack of at least occasional trying. Fortunately, I'm not tone-deaf. But I'm most definitely never going to be considered for a Grammy award. Music is one of those areas of life in which my giftedness and talent fall near the lower end of the scale. I have to really work at it to do even reasonably well.

Unfortunately for me, pastoral ministry is a field in which congregations typically expect that the preacher also be a musician. And the preacher's wife, assuming the pastor is male, ought to be a gifted pianist, or better still, a trained organist. There are probably a handful of pastoral couples out there who fit that description, but I'm not part of one of them. Most certainly I acknowledge that music is, in every time and culture, a significant element of worship to God. So I continuously struggle, always trying to expand my limited musical knowledge and ability.

In the tiny church that I served in the Big Bend town of Marathon, Texas, where 20 present for worship was a red-letter Sunday, music was a constant challenge for both myself and the congregation. That church's pianist was elderly and chronically ill, so whether or not she'd be present on any given Sunday was pure guesswork. There was virtually no one else in town who could play a note, so many Sundays we sang the hymns acapella, with myself as song leader.

The 100th Psalm in the Holy Bible says, "Make a joyful noise unto the Lord," and that's about all we could possibly accomplish in Marathon on those Sundays when I was forced to be song leader. God called me to preach, and I can do a pretty fair job at that, but song leading is definitely way out of my jurisdiction. And yet I believe God was pleased by our efforts to praise him in song in Marathon -- because we gave it all we had to give.

That's really all God ever asks of us: to give him our best. Now that I'm retired, I'm able to devote more time and effort to music, which has resulted in some personal improvement in that arena. But good or bad, I'm going to continue to offer God the best of my limited musical ability, and I trust that will always be enough.

Judge Not?
Matthew 7:1

Jim and Marge, volunteer adult leaders for the youth group of the congregation I was then serving were, to put it mildly, embarrassed. Their 15-year-old daughter, Julie, was pregnant. She really didn't even know who the father was; there were many possible candidates. They apologized to me for setting such a bad example, and asked to resign from their duties with the youth. They were planning to leave the church, move to another city, and try to start their family life over again -- where no one would know about their daughter's sin.

I counseled them not to even consider such foolish alternatives. Yes, their daughter had made a serious mistake -- one that would obviously affect her, and their entire family, for decades to come. But neither I, nor the church at large, was going heap judgment upon them. Instead I suggested ways that we could, together, make the best out of a bad situation. And besides, I told them I knew they would make terrific grandparents.

For the next seven months and beyond, that church took major steps to make this family, and especially Julie, feel very special. Before the birth, Julie was thrown two major showers by the women. When her baby arrived, the parade of gifts and supplies for the infant filled several rooms. The church had responded with huge amounts of love and not a single word of judgment.

Less than a year later, that same couple's younger daughter Jan, then 14, also turned up pregnant. When asked why she had not learned wisdom from her sister's mistake, her response was, "Julie got all that love and attention from being pregnant. I want the same."

Christians have often been accused of being intolerant of others, to the extent that many believers have backed off from ever questioning even the worst kinds of sinful behavior they observe around them. But sometimes the people of Jesus Christ need to speak a word of judgment to our contemporary society, and not merely acquiesce to wrongdoing. If we don't, we may inadvertently be encouraging additional sin.

Changing Our Values
Matthew 13:45-46

Ever since I was a child, I collected glass telephone wire insulators. Decades ago, these glass baubles were everywhere -- they lined the cross-arms of millions of telephone poles throughout the world, keeping the wires thereon from shorting out on the wood. But as telephone cable came into use, and, later, fiber optics, then, still more recently, wireless telephony, those once ubiquitous glass insulators became rarer and rarer sights. Some are still in use in rural areas, but not many. For decades, I used to search out fallen, no longer used telephone poles for the occasional unbroken glass insulator to be found thereon, and over the years had gathered quite a collection of interesting shapes, sizes, and colors thereof.

My collection was nearing 200, painstakingly discovered one by one when, in 1989, I moved to Clovis, New Mexico. In Clovis, one of the members of my church was the manager of a telephone cooperative that served a huge portion of eastern New Mexico. One day, I asked him if his company had any of those old, glass insulators stored away anywhere. He laughed. "Dave, if you'll come out to our warehouse tomorrow, you're welcome to any and all we've got."

I visited his company's warehouse the next day and there, behind the old warehouse building, were at least two hundred oil drums -- each filled with more than 500 glass insulators. There were, literally, 10,000 of them. Many were chipped and broken, but hundreds and hundreds were shiny and whole. And I could have all of them that I wanted.

For about an hour I picked through several barrels, "oohing" and "aahing" at the many beautiful insulators I was handling. But my attitude about what I was doing gradually shifted as I realized that I was no longer discovering precious, "one of a kind" collectible treasures, but simply rummaging through cans of someone else's trash.

I did carry away a few -- maybe twenty -- of the most unique among the thousands of glass baubles to be found in those cans. But having so many available somehow took the thrill out of the whole enterprise for me. Yes, I still collect insulators from time to time, but my passion for the hobby is gone. What I once thought so interesting is now merely ho-hum for me. My values were changed by that encounter -- just as an encounter with Jesus Christ, on a much more significant scale, changes our values for eternity.

Lead, Follow, or Get Out of the Way
Daniel 12:3

Every church has a Lawanda, though not often by that name. Lawanda always had something to say on any and every subject, from apple pies -- she had a better recipe -- to Zoroastrianism -- she was against it. No matter what the issue, Lawanda had to get her comments in, usually to point out something that wasn't being done right -- in her eyes -- or to suggest something that the church ought to be doing that wasn't being attempted at all.

More often than not her input was totally off the subject at hand. At a Finance Committee meeting, she made sure to point out that the church kitchen was dirtier than it ought to be. At Choir Practice, she voiced complaints that one of her old friends hadn't been visited as often as she thought they ought to be. In Sunday School, she grumbled about the worship services; at worship, she griped to those around her about the Sunday School.

Every time Lawanda began to open her mouth, most of the people around her rolled their eyes toward the ceiling. But Lawanda was oblivious. She thought she was the wisest person in the room, and everyone, especially the pastor, needed to hear her out on whatever subject she'd chosen to speak. No one took her seriously, and half the congregation made it a point to apologize to me for her. They said, "That's just the way she is. We've learned to tune her out."

I decided to try a somewhat different approach with Lawanda. After carefully explaining to the leadership selection committee my rationale for so doing, I asked Lawanda to assume a significant leadership position in that church. Somewhat as I expected, she refused. As she did so I told her pointedly, "Lawanda, if you're not willing to serve on the inside, then none of us will be willing to listen to your criticisms from the outside."

From that day forward, every time Lawanda began to expound her presumed better ways to do things in the church, I would interrupt her. "Lawanda, you don't have the right to speak about that. If you're not willing to lead, I'm not willing to listen." Dozens of others in the congregation took to saying much the same to her.

I'd like to be able to say that Lawanda finally did get the message, and join in trying to help lead, rather than simply criticize others' efforts in the church. She didn't. But the repeated experience of others interrupting her whenever she began one of her critical monologues eventually had an effect. She gradually ceased speaking out on every occasion, limiting her comments to only occasionally. It wasn't a perfect outcome, but at least it was an improvement.

Climbing to See
Genesis 28:10-12

My middle child, son Jonathan, has always been a climber. In our family we often say that Jonathan could climb before he could walk, which is literally true. His penchant for climbing has provided us with more than one interesting experience, the most memorable of which occurred on Thanksgiving Day, 1984.

At the time the Ring family was living in El Paso, Texas. We had decided to go, as a family, to view the Sun Bowl Parade down Montana Avenue through downtown El Paso. Standing there in a crowd of 40 to 50 thousand people lining the street, the four of us watched the floats go by, appropriately "oohing and aahing" at the fascinating shapes and designs.

I was totally enthralled by it all when a man standing nearby tapped me on the shoulder to get my attention. "Mister, aren't you worried about your kid?" he asked. With that, he pointed upward. There, 30 feet above the street level, Jonathan was calmly seated on the very top of a telephone pole, gleefully watching the floats go by. He'd found himself the best observation spot in the entire area.

I suppose many parents might have panicked to discover that their child had climbed a telephone pole, but from frequent experience I already knew Jonathan's climbing ability. I also knew that scaring him by yelling at him would be counterproductive. So I just calmly looked up and said, "Jonathan, come on down." By this time 1,000 folks had noticed this little boy perched high above them; nobody on that block was watching the parade anymore, all eyes were on Jonathan. When I told him to come down, he protested, "Do I have to? I can't see through all the big people down there!" "Yes, Jon, you need to come down." With that, he began climbing down, reaching the ground in just a minute or two. Everyone around breathed a sigh of relief.

In the New Testament of the Holy Bible, there's a fascinating story about a man named Zacchaeus who, although he was small of stature, wanted to see Jesus. But a crowd had gathered around Jesus, and Zacchaeus, like my son Jonathan trying to watch the Sun Bowl parade at age four, couldn't see through all those big people. So Zacchaeus climbed a nearby tree and thereby got to see Jesus. Even better, Jesus saw him, and rewarded him for his special effort by visiting his house and bringing him into the Kingdom of God.

Climbing out of the crowd, for Zacchaeus, was a very wise move. Do you also need to separate yourself from the crowd -- in order to see Jesus more clearly?

Teach the Ways of Jesus
Daniel 1:3-4

I was a very new believer in Jesus Christ and had only recently joined a church. That church, like most, was greatly in need of volunteers to work with its young people. Although I was both a novice Christian and a rather young adult -- age 22 -- I was asked to be the organizer of the church's desired young adult group. Being new to both the Christian faith and to the Church, I hadn't yet acquired the necessary wisdom to know when to say "No." So, within just a few weeks after joining, I found myself contacting a group of my contemporaries, about 30 folks ages 18 to 25, trying to start a new young adult fellowship.

By God's grace my efforts met with more or less instant success and, within just a handful of weeks, a core group of 20 young adults had formed into a combination Sunday morning class and Monday night activity group in that church. We'd been a group for a little more than three months when the church's annual ice cream social began to be planned. Someone asked, "Who'll get the watermelons?" and I eagerly responded, "The young adult group will take responsibility for getting them."

I'd volunteered because I knew exactly how and where I was going to find those watermelons. I was aware of a farmer's field nearby that contained many acres of ripening melons. So I piled three of the other young adult males in the car with me, and we proceeded to help ourselves to about a dozen of the best-looking produce from that field. The farmer would never miss them among so many thousands of others.

Later, at the church's ice-cream social, several folks complimented me on the sweetness of the melons. "Where did you get them?" I was asked. "We took them from that farmer's big field down south, just off Isleta Blvd." "What did he charge you?" was the next question. "Nothing," I replied, "We just took them." "You stole watermelons for the church's ice-cream social?" was the incredulous reply. My response was, "Sorry, but I didn't consider it stealing. Where I was raised, we often took what we needed from local fields. I just presumed it was OK."

My childhood upbringing, which was totally outside the Christian faith, hadn't included a whole lot of ethical teaching. That was the first of many times when I began to learn that Christians are expected to adhere to principles which aren't automatically understood and shared by everyone in the secular society.

From personal experience and forty-plus years later, I now realize that Christians and the churches they form often assume far too much about what people outside the church are like. Not everyone thinks, nor acts, like a Christian. Why should they -- if they've not yet been introduced to the Savior by those who claim to be His followers? And even if they've begun the journey of discipleship, it needs to be reinforced by careful and consistent Christian teaching. That doesn't happen overnight.

Wealthy – But Not Independently
Matthew 6:19-21

Back when my wife and I were both working toward graduate degrees in Atlanta, Georgia, there was a short period of time when, due to the heavy demands of our studies, neither of us was employed. We'd prepared for this by saving, in advance, to get us through financially -- albeit barely.

One afternoon during this period, Fran and I were out shopping together in a large discount department store. When we reached the checkout, the clerk tallied up our total and Fran wrote a check for the amount. The clerk looked it over, then asked Fran for her place of employment and the telephone number thereof. Fran responded by saying, "I'm not employed." "Well, then," the clerk replied, "What's your husband's place of employment and its phone number?" I spoke up, "I'm not employed either." The clerk appeared baffled. And at that moment Fran, with more than a touch of sarcasm in her voice, said, "We're independently wealthy." The clerk smiled. "Oh!" she said, then put the check in the register's till without another word.

I'm not sure what motivated my wife to make her ludicrous comment in that situation, but it certainly served the purpose of getting our check accepted. In all the span of our married life thus far, that was probably the one time we were closest to being broke -- yet Fran could dare to say, "We're independently wealthy."

Maybe not always from a worldly point of view, but it's a simple fact, from a spiritual perspective, that I've been wealthy and secure for more than 45 years now -- although by no means independently so. My Father owns the cattle on a thousand hills. When I accepted his Son as my personal Savior, I was immediately adopted into His royal family. In an otherwise uncertain world, I'm glad to know that my long-term assets are always guaranteed -- by the King of Kings and Lord of Lords.

Some of you may really be independently wealthy in this world. Others may be barely making it from day to day. Regardless, I know how you can acquire riches that will last forever. Let Jesus Christ become your Savior and your Lord. Then you, too, will be a child of the King of Heaven, secure in his love for all eternity.

Sensitivity about Giving
Luke 6:38

Who gives what in the church of Jesus Christ? Early on in my ministry as a local church pastor, I learned that many church members are sensitive about their giving to God's house. They don't want anyone to know the amount of their giving, and most certainly not the pastor.

There's a simple reason why a pastor should not be overly knowledgeable about the giving of the members of his church. Obviously, the pastor shouldn't favor those who are strong financial supporters, nor ignore those who aren't.

There is one exception I make to the above guideline: I call it the "zero exclusion." It came about this way. In the second church I served, now many years ago, everyone assumed that Paul was a top giver to the church. After all, he was chairman of the Finance Committee. In fact, he had been such, despite church bylaws to the contrary, for the past 12 years in a row. And he regularly and pointedly voiced his concerns about the ways the church was spending "his" money. Regarding church financial issues, Paul was always in tight control.

When it came time for leadership selection in the church that fall, I asked for a list, not of how much individuals had given, but simply a roster of those who had made no contribution of record during the past year. Certainly, I didn't want to select leaders who weren't also givers -- at least of some nominal amount. Paul's name was on the list of zero givers.

Wishing to offer him the benefit of the doubt, I asked Paul into my office for a short conference one afternoon. "Paul, there seems to be no record of your giving even a dollar to the church in the last several years. Surely that's in error?" He turned red, but gave me a candid reply. "When I retired seven years ago, I retired from giving to the church, too. I figure I gave enough in years past to cover me for the rest of my life."

I didn't get into an argument with Paul over his giving. I simply told him that I wasn't willing to have him control the finances of a church to which he was currently giving nothing. That church found a new finance chairman. With Paul's heavy hand off the financial reins of the church, overall giving rose 20% in a single year. And I learned to regularly employ the "zero exclusion" in selecting leadership for the churches I served.

Bridging Cultural Barriers
John 4:7-9

Harwood Church, located in the inner city of Albuquerque, had a serious vandalism problem. One of the congregation's older men, Carl, had a virtually full-time volunteer job at the church repairing broken windows. Sometimes the vandalism was more serious -- as when repeated attempts were made, thankfully unsuccessful attempts, to set fire to the chapel.

As a new, young pastor, it didn't take me long to realize that the church and the community surrounding it were very different. The congregation was primarily older Anglo persons. The community consisted of mostly young Hispanic families. The congregation drove in from the suburbs and drove back out to them, barely noticing the neighborhood around the church -- except to complain about the constant vandalism. The parsonage where the pastor was housed, however, was next door to the church -- so I was confronted by this cultural divide every single day.

It took much hard work and a lot of fund raising, most of it from sources outside the church, but I was able, 10 months after arriving, to start a summer recreation program for the community kids. An old gymnasium was part of the Harwood property. We refurbished and reopened it after its having been locked tight for more than a decade.

Most of the leaders of the Harwood congregation were unconvinced of the value of this recreation program -- until, a month after it began, Carl stood up on a Sunday morning and reported that, for the first time in years, he hadn't had to repair a single broken window during the previous week. Only then did it begin to dawn on them that investing in the community around the church could be beneficial, both to the community <u>and</u> the church.

Christian churches cannot and should not exist as cultural islands, separated from the communities which surround them. God sent Jesus into the world to show His love for it. The churches which bear His name need to do the same.

Regularly Running
Hebrews 12:1-3

As I've shared in several other of these short stories, I was for many years a diligent, daily runner. I ran one mile daily, nearly every day of my life, for 40-plus years.

Often when I would tell people that I ran every day, I'd receive odd looks because I've always been substantially overweight. So I regularly added, whenever I got those quizzical glances, "Yes, I'm fat, but I'm reasonably fit."

Shortly after moving to Big Spring, Texas, I developed a painful problem in my right foot that gradually worsened, to the extent that I finally went to a doctor for help. The doctor prescribed physical therapy, and the physical therapist told me to stop running. Frankly, I think he was more than a little surprised that I was still running every day, despite the considerable pain it caused me. So I ceased running for about a two-month period.

Within two weeks after I stopped my daily runs, I noticed that I was not breathing as freely as I normally did, that I found myself "huffing and puffing" for no reason at all. I became more restless in my sleep, and I noticed a pronounced decease in my normally high energy level.

Fortunately, the physical therapy on my foot eventually accomplished its purpose. The pain went away and I was permitted to return to my daily runs. For the first couple of weeks after I re-started running, I realized how completely out of condition I'd become -- in only two months of slacking off. But I eventually returned to my old rhythm -- my breathing improved and my energy level rose.

Far too often Christians slack off from the regular practice of the faith. They cease attending church, giving to God's work, daily prayer and Bible study. As a result, they soon become spiritually out of shape. Their attitude, their demeanor, their relationships with God and others erode. It's only when they finally realize what is happening to them, and return to active participation in the Body of Christ, that they realize how much their souls have lost.

People of God, if you are active in a church body, stay there -- and stick with it. And if you aren't, get back into a church, and soon. The health of your soul is dependent upon it.

Capable and Effective
Ecclesiastes 11:6

Miss Mattie, as my kids called her, became our next-door neighbor when we moved to Clovis, New Mexico. She was 93 years of age when we met her, although she had to tell us that in order for us to believe it. In fact, the first time we saw her, she was cutting her lawn, with a push mower no less. Mattie was hale and hearty in every way, a lady with a brilliant mind and a bright, positive Christian spirit.

In 1993, I traveled to Russia on a missionary trip and, upon returning, wanted to show my friend Mattie some of the pictures I'd taken while there. We were living in Albuquerque by then, but a month or two after my return from Russia, I made a trip to Clovis to see Mattie, and brought with me a slide projector. I began casting images from my trip on her living room wall. As the picture of St. Basil's Cathedral in Moscow's Red Square appeared, Mattie commented, "I've been there." "Mattie, you've been to Russia?" I questioned. "Yes, I went to Russia in 1959 on an agricultural exchange." With that, she found an old photo album and showed me some of her mementoes from that trip, 30-plus years previously, at the height of the Cold War. What an amazing woman!

I was living in Odessa, Texas when Mattie celebrated her 100[tth] birthday, but Fran and I made a special trip to Clovis to be a part of the festivities. Surrounded by friends and family, all the way to great-great grandchildren, Mattie proudly showed off her brand-new New Mexico driver's license, which had just been renewed for another four years. Again, what an astounding person!

The Bible speaks of quite a few men and women who, despite advanced age, remained healthy and capable, effectively serving God until, literally, the very day of their death. Moses in the Old Testament was one such, Joshua another. In the New Testament, Anna and Simeon, in Luke 2, were aged Jewish servants of God who discovered the Messiah, Jesus, long after most of their contemporaries had given up. The gospel of John was probably written by that beloved disciple of Jesus when he was 90-plus years of age. Young, old, or in-between -- if you're breathing air on this earth, you can serve God while you're here.

Discernment, Physical and Spiritual
Malachi 3:16-18

When my daughter, Joanna, was in junior high school, I helped her with a science project. It was a simple one, applying an idea that I'm quite sure wasn't new with her. She tested her classmates to see if they could tell the difference between regular and artificially sweetened soft drinks. They would be given an unlabelled cup of either Coke or Diet Coke, Pepsi or Diet Pepsi, and asked to state what they were drinking -- was it the regular, sugar-sweetened version of that soft drink, or the artificially-sweetened diet version thereof?

What Joanna discovered was that most of her classmates couldn't tell the difference between. But a few could, and those who could do so were consistently able. No matter how many times we tried to fool them, this minority of students always knew the difference. Something about their sense of taste allowed them to discern, to easily discriminate between the regular and diet versions of soft drinks. We never did discover an answer to "why" this was the case with these few, and not with the majority. Perhaps it's genetic?

One of the gifts of God's Holy Spirit, as detailed in I Corinthians 12, is that of spiritual discernment. It's a gift that I personally possess very little of, but one that my wife, Fran, exercises in much greater proportion. She can sense "good" and "bad" around her in amazing but intangible ways. There have been dozens of instances in which my wife has correctly exercised her excellent spiritual discernment.

On more than one occasion her particular spiritual gift has helped me make right decisions that I might otherwise have botched. I don't know why God has chosen to give Fran such finely discriminatory spiritual sensibilities, while I barely muddle through in that area. But I've learned to regularly seek her advice, thereby receiving the benefit of Fran's special gift from God.

In a much larger sense, the Body of Christ is like Fran and me. No single member of a church possesses all the vast array of God's marvelous spiritual gifts, but together we are able to benefit from one another's uniqueness, thereby doing God's work on a scale that no "lone ranger" Christian could ever accomplish.

Playing Dumb
Acts 6:1-4

As a local church pastor, one of the skills that I early learned was the necessity of "playing dumb" when it comes to many routine maintenance tasks in the local church. As I reveal that, I'm sure many of you are thinking, "How awful for a preacher to say such a thing." But if there happen to be any pastors reading this story, they're probably nodding in silent agreement.

Let me expand on what I mean by "playing dumb." In the first church where I was ever employed -- and there only as the part-time minister to youth -- I made the mistake, early on, of letting the congregation know that I was a former electrical engineer. Mentally, they heard "electrician" and, from that day forward, whenever an electrical problem arose in that church, it was expected that I could and should fix it. A number of members of the congregation also called me to come and fix electrical problems in their homes -- always free of charge.

In my second church, where I served as part-time associate pastor, I'd only been there a few days when a toilet was reported as malfunctioning. I looked it over, figured out what was wrong, went to the hardware store and bought a couple of parts, and fixed it. Very bad move. From that day forward, I was not only the church's plumber, but the on-call, unpaid personal plumber to at least three dozen elderly members. It literally got to the point that I had no time to do the duties I was being paid to do for that church -- plumbing was my de facto job.

Another pastor was commiserating with me about a call he'd received from the chairman of his church's Board of Trustees. Those Trustees, God bless 'em, had just voted to buy paint to repaint the entire interior of that church's sanctuary. And since all of them worked full-time jobs, they were giving that pastor the privilege of painting the sanctuary. All this came about because he'd made an idle remark about having painted houses to help put himself through college, years before.

In I Corinthians 2:2, the apostle Paul said this to the church in that city: "I resolved to know nothing while I was with you except Jesus Christ and Him crucified." Paul single-mindedly made clear to the Corinthians his purpose in being among them -- to preach the Gospel of Jesus Christ. It's a good thing he got that said early on in his relationship with the Corinthian Church. If he hadn't, they'd probably have asked Paul to make tents for all the widows in the congregation -- free of charge and in his spare time, of course.

Cold Weather in Hell
Matthew 5:22

All my life I've been a person who loves heat and abhors cold. That's why I enjoy living in hot, desert-type climates, and avoid places where winter's chill dominates the weather for more than a few days at a time. Yes, I can enjoy an occasional weekend of snow play in the mountains in wintertime, but I'm soon enough ready to return to warmer territory.

I didn't begin to realize how radically a "hot weather person" I was until after I got married. That was when my wife began insisting that I turn on the air conditioner at home in the month of July. I'm quite comfortable at 90 degrees indoors, so I rarely ever felt the need to switch on such. And later, Fran made me promise to always buy cars that were equipped with air conditioning -- an accessory I'd never thought about when I was single.

Probably the most striking evidence I have of my heat tolerance was the August day my family spent in Mexicali, Mexico. It was officially 118 degrees Fahrenheit outside that day, and I was gaily skipping down the streets, feeling totally energized by all that warmth. But my wife and three children were on the verge of passing out from the heat. I finally left them in an air conditioned store and completed exploring the town solo.

I've always been a believer in the Bible's being literally true, but have to admit I have some questions about the description of hell that's found therein. For if hell is really a hot place, to someone like me it doesn't sound all that bad. On the other hand, if there are blizzards in hell, I'd want to avoid it at all costs.

The good news is I don't have to spend a whole lot of time thinking about hell. Whether it's fiery or frosty, I'll never reside even a single minute in hell. For I've accepted Jesus Christ as my personal Savior. When I leave this earth, I'll be heading for heaven, to be with my Lord for eternity. And I'm trusting that heaven will be warm -- because, for me, it wouldn't _be_ heaven otherwise.

I invite you to accept Jesus Christ as your personal Savior, too. With Jesus, you'll experience heaven and avoid hell. And more importantly for the present, you'll begin enjoying abundant life, right here, right now, on _earth._

Change – and Adjustment
Daniel 2:21

In the spring of 2002 I organized a group of 14 persons for a short-term mission trip to El Salvador. Our planned task was to construct a concrete block medical clinic building in the capital city of San Salvador. For several months prior, I and other team members carefully organized this upcoming expedition. Despite being told that we didn't need to bring tools, a number of us begged, borrowed, and/or bought appropriate tools for working with concrete block construction. And each of us, of course, researched the place we were going, learning all we could, from a distance, about El Salvador's huge capital city, population 1.5 million.

Less than 24 hours before our departure, I received an e-mail which said that both our project and our destination had changed. We were no longer to build a medical clinic; no longer going to San Salvador. Upon arrival at El Salvador's single international airport, we would be bussed to the mountain provincial capital of Ahuachapan, a small city in the northwestern part of the country near its border with Guatemala, and there assigned a task yet to be determined.

All our months of careful advance planning went out the window. When I informed the team members of the changes, there was some initial grumbling, but to their credit, everyone was flexible enough to at least try to adjust to the altered circumstances. And frankly, it got worse before it got better. When we arrived in Ahuachapan, the only idea the people we met there had of our assignment was a crude drawing of a desired addition to their church building, something apparently conceived in haste perhaps only the day before. The local bishop, who was supposed to be our principal contact, was virtually unavailable to us, as was the pastor of the actual church on which we were to work.

Despite all these stumbling blocks, we moved ahead as willingly and cheerfully as possible. We knew that there were dozens of folks back home praying for the success of our mission -- which helped to keep us focused. We drew up better plans, made lists of what would be needed, and began acquiring tools and materials. We did our best to relate to those persons who were available to us, not fret about those who weren't. And through an amazing combination of God's grace and human effort, the job got done. By week's end, we had accomplished all we were asked to do, and more besides. My personal faith, in both God and His people, was strengthened. What the apostle Paul said twenty centuries before remains accurate today: Truly, "(we) can do all things through Christ, who strengthens (us)."

Stewardship of the Trees
Genesis 1:11-12

I did not personally know my paternal grandfather; he died when I was but 18 months of age. But I grew up, at least in part, in the house he built and the yard he landscaped. The house was solidly constructed and more than adequate, but the grounds thereof were that property's outstanding feature. Fruit and nut trees were scattered throughout the approximate two-acre tract -- apples, pears, peaches, quinces, plums, and cherries, plus walnuts and pecans, literally fell into our laps. There were grape arbors across the back of the property which bore bountifully each summer. The yard was honeycombed with rock paths, all of them lined by attractive flower gardens in an amazing geometric array and a profusion of color. For a young boy there were two especially exciting aspects to that big yard -- the rustic wooden summer house out back, and the huge swing under the big tree just a few feet beyond the back door.

That was the environment in which, during about half of my growing years, I lived. But as I moved into my teenage years, then later left home for college and returned on holidays, I gradually noticed that all was not well. The fruit trees, one by one, were dying. The flower gardens gradually disappeared; the rock paths became overgrown by grass and weeds. The summer house rotted and fell in; the tree on which the big swing had hung grew diseased and eventually had to be cut down. My parents were unconcerned with maintaining the beauty of the estate, thus it simply deteriorated from neglect.

Some years ago I inherited the remaining 40% of that property. And as soon as I did so I began trying to at least partially restore its former beauty. Most importantly, I made sure that new trees were planted in the yard. Maybe one day a boy will again swing under the canopy of a tree there. I may not ever know him, nor he me, but that's OK.

My grandfather was a good steward of what God had placed in his hands. I received and enjoyed the fruits of his labors. And I would likewise be a good steward of that which I've been given. I desire to pass on God's blessings -- for a future generation to enjoy.

A Very Personal God
John 1:47-51

The most striking "small world" incident I've ever experienced took place during the time Fran and I were serving as missionaries in the small Central American nation of Guatemala. On one particular evening we decided, after months of eating the local food, that we simply had to have some U. S.-style grub. So we headed, for the first time since we'd arrived in Guatemala City, to the one and only north American restaurant which had yet made its way to Guatemala back in 1975 – a Pizza Hut.

We'd received our pizza and were just sitting down to eat it when we noticed the older couple at the table next to us. They were Mr. and Mrs. Simpson, next-door neighbors to my home in suburban Baltimore during half of my growing-up years. They'd never before been out of the USA, but had decided to make their first foreign trip -- to Guatemala. Out of six billion souls in the world at that time, what were the odds of running into your former next-door neighbors while in an off-the-beaten-track city in the third world -- at a Pizza Hut, no less?

Is it possible for God to individually know, to personally keep track of, the teeming masses of people who fill this world today? Back in Jesus' time, the idea of having a personal relationship with God wasn't quite so incredible. The planet was thinly populated. But now, in the 21st century A. D., does God still know, still care for _me_? That's the question which, consciously or subliminally, millions of love-starved people repeatedly ask themselves today.

Fortunately, the answer hasn't changed. In Jesus Christ, God showed his love for the world -- then and now. And God showed His love for you -- whether you are the only person in the world, or one of countless billions. In fact, I often conceive it this way: If I were the one and only man on earth, Jesus Christ would have willingly died on the cross for my sins. And if you were the only person in the world, he'd have done the same for you.

Big numbers are meaningless to God; He knows and loves us, uniquely and individually, one by precious one.

Canoeing in the Swamp
Ezekiel 47:9-12

One of the most daring adventures I ever undertook in ministry was taking my then-church's youth group into the Okeefenokee Swamp in southeast Georgia for a week. There were only three adults -- myself and a young adult couple, David and Pat Hicks, who went on this expedition into the wilderness. But we were responsible for 25 youth, all the way from sixth graders through high school seniors.

Our means of transportation through the Okeefenokee was canoe, and most of these youth had never before been in one. On the day we started out, down the Suwanee Canal, it was pure bedlam as fourteen pairs of largely inexperienced canoeists tried valiantly to figure out how to paddle in tandem without tipping over nor running up on a riverbank. As the last man in the rear, and the only really experienced canoeist in the group, I watched with concern as our boats zigzagged from bank to bank up the canal. "We'll be lucky to make 500 yards this afternoon, rather than the five miles we need to cover," was my secret thought.

That week in the Okeefenokee taught me a great deal about youth and youthful behavior -- away from mom and dad as well as far removed from the familiar surroundings of modern-day civilization. It was the experience of a lifetime for many of them, most of whom had rarely been out of metropolitan Atlanta before.

One of the most rewarding memories I have of that trip was watching, again from the rearmost canoe, those youth emerge from the swamp, back down that same canal they'd barely been able to navigate going in, on the return leg of the trip. Every canoe cruised straight and true, right down the center of the waterway. A week's experience had transformed those kids into pros when it came to handling their boats. They'd become a competent lot, and I, as group leader, was justly proud of them. They couldn't wait to get back home and teach their friends the joys of canoeing.

When a person first comes to faith in Jesus Christ, initially their efforts to serve Him can be pretty erratic. An experienced Christian, observing their behavior, is likely to wonder if they'll ever really understand what following Jesus is all about. But given time and experience in the disciplines of Christian faith, eventually they become competent disciples. And then it becomes their turn to pass the faith on, to the next generation of new believers.

Carrying the Bible Around
Psalm 40:11-13

I have a friend who for more than a decade was a jet pilot in our U. S. armed services. One day he called me up and told me he would be passing through Albuquerque, where I was then living, and he wanted to show me the new plane which he'd just been assigned. I agreed to meet him at Kirtland Air Force Base, and he arranged for me to receive the necessary authorizations to meet him out on the flight line.

After he'd landed and tied down, he walked over to meet me, wearing one of those military flight jackets with extra pockets and zippers in all sorts of places. He opened the pocket on his upper right arm and took out a small book. "I thought you, being a preacher, would appreciate seeing that I carry this whenever I fly. It's my good luck charm." The book was a tiny edition of the New Testament of the Holy Bible. "That's nice," I responded, "but do you ever open it up and read it?" "Not really; I figure God will protect me when I'm flying just because I carry it," was his rejoinder.

I proceeded to look over the cockpit of the compact new fighter jet which he was flying, and noticed, stuffed into just about every one of the limited available nooks and crannies, a series of flight manuals. So I asked him, "Have you read those flight manuals you've got in the plane with you?" "Of course!" was the ready response. "I'd be a fool to try and fly this aircraft without learning all I possibly can about every one of its systems."

That gave me the perfect opening to say what I needed to say to him. I held out the little New Testament he'd handed to me. "I agree -- and you'd be equally a fool to try to fly to heaven without reading this flight manual."

As a pastor, I know quite a few people who are like my jet pilot buddy. They respect and even reverence the Bible, but they don't open it. They want to be called Christians, but they have no knowledge of what that really means -- because they've never read the basic instruction manual. They may have given their hearts to Jesus, but not their heads. Our Lord, who created all of us, wants all of us in return. Read the Bible, people of God. Learn what it says, so you can live what it requires!

Taking Care of Important Business
Isaiah 30:15

There hadn't been any warning, at least none he'd sensed. George had come home from work that evening at his usual time, 7 PM, and there it was: a note. "Found someone else. The kids are coming with me. Don't bother trying to find us. Jan."

George had then, by his own account, picked up his old Bible and dazedly leafed through it nearly all night. He knew there were supposed to be answers therein, but he really didn't know where to look. He was both stunned and confused.

And now, the morning after, George was in my office, asking me for those missing answers. He and Jan were both Christians -- at least they'd professed faith in Christ as teenagers, although they'd not gone to church much as adults -- except for showing up every Easter. And George was convinced that he'd tried to be a good husband. But the pressures of life -- running a small business, coping with financial issues, dealing with ageing parents -- all these things had combined to limit his time with his family, his time alone with Jan. Surely God couldn't hold that against him; he was doing the best he could. Yes, he realized he wasn't the best man in the world, but he really didn't deserve to have his family ripped out from under him without warning. Why had God done such a terrible thing to George?

It's always easy to scapegoat God for problems of our own making. Though I tried hard both to listen and to respond honestly, George simply couldn't see that he had allowed his marriage to deteriorate. He blocked out any possibility that he hadn't given the time and effort required to maintain a vital relationship with Jan. Further, he couldn't understand that his spiritual foundation had been eroded by long-term neglect of the things of God -- prayer, Bible study, worship. George expected that if he took care of business, everything else about his life should take care of itself. Wasn't that other stuff, after all, God's job?

A lot of folks these days, most often males, see the world much like George. If I take care of business -- if I earn a living for my family, then that's all that's required of me. It's God's responsibility to handle the rest. So there are many George's out there – who sometimes find themselves unexpectedly confronted by nasty, negative surprises.

The good news is, there's hope even for George and folks like him. No matter how long you've neglected relationships, they can usually be repaired, restored. Both relationships with God and with our families really can be salvaged. But such takes time and effort. There are no "easy fixes" to be had.

What's in a Name?
Proverbs 22:1

The official first name on my birth certificate is David. During my childhood my mother regularly employed that five letter name in a way that spelled impending danger for a growing boy. Her tone of voice when she spoke -- and sometimes shouted -- the word "David!" usually let me know that I'd better stop whatever else I was then doing and pay her my full attention. Occasionally, when the single word, "David," didn't suffice to grab me, she'd employ my middle name as well. When I heard her call, "David Zimmerman!" I knew that thunder and lightning were preparing to break forth in a matter of seconds. And on really rare occasions, when my response to her calls was delayed beyond a mother's internal limit on being ignored, she'd give me the full treatment -- my entire name shouted out in summons to dire punishment: "David Zimmerman Ring III!"

Because of those negative childhood memories, I try very hard to keep my name short and sweet with others. "Hi! I'm Dave Ring. Please call me Dave." If someone insists on repeatedly calling me "David," it produces an unconscious reaction in me that's hard to describe -- a subtle barrier is erected between me and that other person. Any time I'm in a large group situation where I'm given a name tag, if it has, "David Ring" written on it, I immediately take out a marker and change it to "Dave Ring." It's silly, I know, but I'm truly uncomfortable being called by my official, formal name.

When Jesus met, for the first time, the person who was later to become his chief disciple, he learned that this man's name was Simon Peter. Jesus apparently preferred his middle name, so Jesus called him Peter throughout most of their association. Actually, our English translations of the Bible don't give us the whole story on this: Peter means "rock" in the Greek language. But Jesus actually called Simon Peter by a more familiar, diminutive form of his official, given name: the best translation of that into English is "Rocky." I've rarely seen it expressed that way in an English Bible, but Jesus really did refer to his close friend and chief disciple, Simon Peter, as "Rocky."

Except -- after Peter had denied knowing Jesus three times over, Jesus was more than a little disappointed in his friend's cowardly conduct. When he next saw Peter after those denials, Jesus temporarily returned to treating him coldly and formally. "Simon, son of John, do you really love me?" I'll bet that hurt -- because I know how important being called by the name you enjoy really is.

Don't Sweat the Small Stuff
Luke 12:48b

Frank was a cattle rancher down in the Big Bend country of Texas. He was a member of the congregation I served in Alpine, albeit not a very active one. Shortly after I became pastor there, one of his children was killed in a tragic auto accident. I was asked to conduct the funeral, which I did. A few days after that funeral, Frank stopped by my office to thank me for conducting his son's service. He presented me a token cash honorarium -- $25 or maybe $35, I forget exactly how much. He didn't say much; he was a man of few words. But on his way out of the church, he told me this, "Preacher, if you ever have a big need, call me. Don't bother me with little stuff, but if it's a really big problem, I'm your man."

More than a year passed, during which I saw Frank occasionally in town, and on even rarer occasions in church. The church's Board of Trustees had decided to begin a remodeling project on the church buildings but, just after they got it underway, the economy of Alpine hit a slump. Cattle prices plummeted, oil busted. The church was in over its head, and the local bank wasn't happy with the prospect of loaning money to us. I talked to all the active members I could think of, and they were all already doing the utmost they could.

Finally, almost as an afterthought, I remembered Frank's offer. So I called him. He invited me out to his ranch, and we talked briefly there. I asked him, point-blank, if he could help the church out to the tune of $25,000. At the time, I was still a pretty young pastor, and this was the biggest financial request I'd ever made of anyone. I swallowed hard, awaiting his reply. He responded by saying, "Preacher, I told you not to bother me with little stuff. Are you sure $25,000 is all you need?" "Well, no, but I don't expect you to do it all. $25,000 is what we need to get us through the next month without having to send the contractors home." In response, he got out his checkbook, wrote and handed me a check for $75,000 payable to the church. As he did so, he commented, "Next time, don't ask for anything less than $50,000. I hate writing small checks."

I don't know if Frank was bragging or complaining, but I gratefully accepted his large donation. I moved from Alpine a year or so later, so I never had another occasion to test his generosity toward God's work. Frank was just one of the many colorful characters I met in the Big Bend. I suspect that, by now, he's gone on to his eternal reward in the Kingdom of Heaven.

Being Teachable
Mark 10:1

As a young man in my early 20's, I began losing hair. Every time I took a shower, it seemed I wound up with a handful of hair going down the drain. By age 23, my hairline was visibly receding. I figured I was destined to be bald at an early age.

I was 24 when my wife, Fran, and I married. Very soon afterward Fran observed that I took only a bar of soap into the shower with me. "Don't you use shampoo to wash your hair?" she asked. "No, I just use soap." Fran admonished me. "Soap is too hard on your hair. You need to start using a good shampoo. Washing with soap is probably most of the reason why you're losing so much hair."

Fran was 100% right. As soon as I began shampooing my hair, I ceased having it fall out every time I showered. Approaching fifty years later I still have an almost full head of hair. It's turned white rather than the blonde it used to be, but most of it's still there. I'm glad I listened to Fran, allowing her to teach me proper hair washing technique. It corrected a bad habit, one that was really hurting me.

As a pastor I find, sadly, that far too many of the folks I meet simply aren't teachable. They've already made up their minds as to what they want to know and don't know, what they believe and don't believe, what they're willing to do and what they aren't -- and that's just how they plan to stay. The really sad part about such is that the majority of such fixated folks that I run into aren't the elderly; rather, they're young men and women in their 20's and 30's.

When Jesus walked this earth, the greeting that those who followed Him most often used for Jesus was "rabbi." Rabbi means "teacher." The most time-consuming work for Jesus among men and women was teaching. And those who elected to follow after Him -- those who would be called His "disciples," were eminently teachable. They were willing to learn, to grow, to change -- to allow the Master to help them move away from old, negative habits and into new, transformed lives of joy, peace, love, and righteousness. A hallmark of those who first followed Jesus was their willingness to be taught. It should be no different today.

For a Friend
1 Samuel 20:42

A long-time friend of mine was going on a weekend religious retreat, a three-day venture in deepened Christian discipleship. I had encouraged him to attend such for several years before he made up his mind to go. So I was excited when I found out he was finally doing so.

At the time, I was living in Albuquerque, New Mexico -- and the retreat was being held at a campground near Durango, Colorado -- 250 miles, or 4 1/2 hours' drive away. I knew that there would be one brief opportunity on Saturday night, about 10 PM, to visit with those on the retreat -- letting them know of your personal support for their faithful commitment to Christ. I also knew that I had to preach in Albuquerque on Sunday morning at 8:15 AM.

I drove to the campground, arriving about 9:45 PM. It was summertime in the mountains; they were meeting outside. Right about 10 PM, I was able to walk over and greet my friend. As we shook hands, he stared in disbelief. "What are you doing here? Don't you have to preach in the morning?" "Yes, but I had to come. I wanted you to know I care."

A minute later, I was back in my car, headed homeward. A 500 mile round trip, nine hours of hard driving -- for about 90 seconds of Christian fellowship with a close friend. Yes, I was very tired as I stepped up to preach at 8:15 the next morning. But it was worth it. Yes, it was well worth it.

Jesus said, "Greater love has no man than this, that he give his life for a friend." Thank God, I wasn't asked to give up my life for my friend, but I did love him enough to inconvenience myself for him. And I'm glad I did.

Trust in the Lord
Proverbs 3:5-6

Bob Fielden came to El Paso, Texas to direct God's work at Houchen Community Center, an inner-city outreach to the people of the so-called "segundo barrio" of that large, two-nation metropolis. My church was one of the many supporting churches of Houchen's multi-faceted ministries, and I was a member of the governing board thereof.

Bob immediately took to his new job like a proverbial duck to water. He and I were about the same age, had children of similar ages, and we quickly became friends. I was astonished by Bob's energy level. Within only weeks after arriving, he had begun a new basketball league for teens, a program to teach older ladies how to sew, a mother-and-baby nutrition education program, just to name a few. He rapidly made the rounds, getting to know the pastors and lay leaders of the churches which supported Houchen's programs. After years of languishing at a low level of activity, Houchen Community Center was coming alive. Bob had an ambitious vision for God's work through Houchen, and dozens of others were quickly catching it.

He'd been in El Paso little more than three months when he woke up one morning with gums bleeding in several places. His wife convinced him to go to the doctor. The doctor prescribed tests. Later that same day, as a result of those tests, Bob was admitted to the hospital. The diagnosis was an acute form of leukemia, far too advanced to yield to any treatment. The doctors were amazed that he hadn't succumbed to it months before. Bob Fielden never left the hospital. Three weeks later, at age 38, he was dead.

As I conducted Bob's funeral, I wondered why. Why, God? Why take the life of this young man who was only just beginning to do so much good in a sorely-needed part of the human world? I wish I could say that I received meaningful answers, but I didn't.

To this day, I still don't know why my friend, Bob Fielden, was taken from this earth in the prime of his life. But I do know that I'm not God, and I therefore don't have to know. Rather, I simply trust that God knows what he's doing. My part, my job is to be faithful to him, leaving the rest to his providence. I'm not able to run the universe; God is.

Downplay the Wedding
Matthew 22:1-14

One of the interesting aspects of conducting weddings, as a pastor, is watching how they almost inevitably grow. For the majority of the weddings I've been asked to do, the first time I met with the couple involved and asked what kind of ceremony they're planning, the answer was something like this: "Oh, we just want a small wedding with a simple ceremony. Our guest list is very short; we only know maybe a dozen people, 20 at the outside, to invite." That's a pretty typical initial wedding plan.

About two weeks later, on average, the "first revision" call would come in. "Pastor, we've been thinking it over, and we need to invite a few more people. We'll probably have forty there, but no more than that." Two weeks after that, the second revision: "Pastor, I know we originally said we wanted a small wedding, but our families have been pressuring us to further expand our guest list. We'll have probably 120, maybe 150 there. But no more than that." And by the time the wedding actually occurs, there's been yet another upward revision -- to 200 or more.

The complexity of the ceremony likewise tends to grow. At first, there's just going to be a best man and a maid of honor in the wedding party. Then a groomsman or two is added, with equal numbers, of course, of bridesmaids. Then ushers -- to handle the increased crowd. Then a flower girl and a ring bearer. Oh -- and a friend wants to sing a solo; another friend wants to play his guitar. And we want to include a unity candle, and the grandmothers are going to light candles and read poems, and ... You get the picture, I'm sure.

I have some pastoral advice, advice that grows from having conducted well over 300 weddings. To put it bluntly, I see too many couples put too much into the wedding -- and too little into the marriage. For one thing, large weddings with fancy receptions are expensive. It's not uncommon for a newlywed couple to return from their dream honeymoon -- facing $20,000 to $30,000 worth of accumulated debt from the combined costs of wedding, reception, and honeymoon. That's a heavy burden to bring into a still-forming marriage relationship. And in a broader sense huge, fancy weddings tend to foster a sense of dreamlike unreality for newlywed couples. After the honeymoon's over, it's extremely hard to readjust to ordinary life together. My pastoral experience says that many couples would be wiser to invest less of themselves in their weddings, more in their marriages.

Lazy Fishing, Lazy Disciples
John 21:1-14

I lost my favorite fishing spot in west Texas. For a number of years, I'd been able to use a fishing cabin on Lake Nasworthy, near San Angelo, for occasional day-long fishing expeditions. This cabin was literally in the lake, on pilings, and could be reached by walking out a long dock.

Fishing there was really the lazy man's brand of angling. The cabin was well-furnished, including a big screen, cable connected TV in the living area. I could open a trapdoor in the floor area, sit down in a reclining, overstuffed armchair, turn on a favorite movie, drop a line down and fish with an absolute minimum of effort. One afternoon, I pulled in four nice ones while enjoying an HBO movie in air conditioned comfort. It doesn't get any easier than that.

Unfortunately, my friends who owned that cabin decided to sell it, so I had to return to the prospect of fishing in the outdoors, subjected to the elements of sun, wind, and water. It was a tough adjustment, but I managed somehow!

It's amazing to me how many folks today come into a church expecting the lazy man's brand of Christianity. The pews need to be cushioned, the temperature a constant 72 degrees Fahrenheit, the ushers friendly, and the sermons short. There'd also better be a spacious nursery with a qualified professional staff for my kids, a reserved handicapped parking spot in front of the main door for my mother, and a pastor who sympathetically listens to my every problem whenever I choose to show up, unannounced, and plop down in his office for two hours. Oh, and furthermore, never, never ask me for money, or I'll be gone faster than you can say "Jesus!"

While there certainly is one verse in the Bible which affirms that Jesus' yoke is easy and his burden is light, there are also other verses which indicate that Christian faith may not always be smiles and sugar candy. One of my favorites, which the laid-back cadre of Christians hate to hear, is this: "Deny yourself, take up your cross, and follow me." But I guess that's probably in the same category as asking for money to today's lazy-boy Christians.

Effective Service Behind the Scenes
Exodus 4:10

There was a particular lady in one of my former churches who, every week, prepared a dozen or more sets of supplies and materials for what were called "busy bags." These "busy bags" were handed out to the children who attended worship there. While mom and dad were listening to the sermon, four-year-old daughter could be coloring a picture of Jesus, the good shepherd. Seven-year-old son could be solving a Bible puzzle, finding the word "Bethlehem" hidden among an alphabet soup of letters on a page.

These busy bags were an invaluable aid to both the preacher and the congregation; adults could focus their attention on the worship of God in ways that children aren't yet mature enough to grasp. And the children could enjoy exploring the things of God at a level appropriate to them. Thus this lady's ministry was a wonderful, behind the scenes labor of love that benefitted hundreds of people each Sunday.

At one point I needed a number of lay persons to speak before the congregation at worship. Knowing this lady's proven dedication to her church, I asked her if she would be one such. She initially said, "OK," but later called me up to say, "I'm sorry. I just can't do that. I'm not able to talk in front of a group of people. Please find someone else."

It was at that point that I realized the mistake was mine, not hers. Out of respect for me she'd automatically assented to something that was outside the realm of her giftedness. I should have approached her differently, first asking if she was comfortable with speaking in front of people. There are those who are, and those who aren't.

Both in 1 Corinthians 12 and in Romans 12 of the Holy Bible, the apostle Paul talks at length about the various spiritual gifts given by God to be exercised within the Body of Christ, which is the church. Some have been given gifts which are public and up-front, like preachers and teachers. And others have been gifted with talents and abilities which serve the church behind the scenes -- like intercessory prayer, and liberal giving and, although the Bible doesn't say it in these words -- preparing busy bags for the children to enjoy in worship. All believers in Christ have been gifted, and all need to exercise their particular gifts in the church which bears his name.

Staying Awake
Proverbs 20:12-13

Saint Paul tells an interesting story, found in the 20th chapter of the Biblical book of Acts, concerning a young man -- probably just a boy -- with the odd name of Eutychus. Eutychus bears a unique distinction in Christian history: He's the first person known to have fallen asleep during a sermon. According to the Biblical narrative, Paul preached long into the night, and Eutychus, seated on a window ledge listening, eventually fell asleep. As he relaxed, he tumbled out the window, suffering a fall that almost killed him.

I would never be so presumptuous as to suggest that falling asleep during one of my sermons is all that dangerous. And I freely admit that I've lulled more than one person into dreamland with my messages. The most interesting sermon sleeper that I ever had, oddly enough, was on a morning in Alpine, Texas when I was actually telling the story of Eutychus in the sermon. The child who had been the candle lighter for that worship service was seated on the very front pew and, as I preached about Eutychus and his nap, this boy punctuated every phrase with his snoring. The entire congregation got some hearty laughs. The snoring young man woke up just in time to extinguish the candles at the end of the worship service. I'm sure he wondered why everyone gave him such odd looks as he did so.

As a preacher I long ago learned not to take myself too seriously. My messages, my admonitions, my advice aren't particularly weighty. If folks forget most of what I said 10 minutes after they leave a church service, well, that's just human nature. On the other hand, I always remind people to take what Jesus said with the utmost of seriousness. You can ignore Dave Ring -- that's no big deal. But you ignore Jesus Christ at the peril of your soul. Pay attention to Jesus -- stay awake; keep alert. Listen carefully to all that Jesus says -- and put it into practice in your daily life.

God's Interest in Genealogy
Matthew 1:1-17

One of my church members was telling me about a family reunion that she'd just attended. Unfortunately, while she was there her voice gave out, and she was reduced to whispering. An older lady herself, she commented, "None of those old folks could hear me after that, so I just came on home."

Family reunions really do bring out the old folks, plus the middle-aged and the young. Not long ago I read an article which indicated that family reunions have become an "explosive growth" phenomenon throughout this nation. As more and more families spread to the four winds, coast to coast and beyond in our highly mobile society, the desire to at least occasionally come together and know one's kin is heightened.

Although such is ultimately not the case, I was raised to believe I was the only son of an only son of an only son. So on my father's side of my family, there wasn't much opportunity for a reunion. My mother's side was more numerous, but no one ever proposed that we get together. However, in 1990 I did attend the one and only family reunion I've yet had the opportunity to enjoy -- for my wife's family. It was held in Spartanburg, South Carolina, with about 100 folks attending. It was a memorable weekend, and my now-adult children still talk about the many cousins and other members of their family tree they met there.

The Bible is full of family trees, the technical name for which is "genealogies." "Abraham begat Isaac and Isaac begat Jacob, and Jacob begat Joseph and Joseph begat Manasseh...." and so forth. I used to think such long lists of names were boring, but I've gradually learned that they serve a wonderful purpose. They are God's way of proudly displaying his family tree – the chosen human family of God on earth.

The Bible also tells us that the listing of the family tree of God is still in process of being written. It's called the Lamb's Book of Life. It will eventually contain the full complement of the chosen people of God across all time and over the entire earth. If you don't already belong to this most wonderful family, there's a simple way to be adopted into it. When you accept Jesus Christ as personal Savior, you become one of the specially chosen, adopted children – of Almighty God – forever.

Adult Versus Childish Knowledge
Deuteronomy 11:18-19

One day while talking with my then-young adult daughter I got something of a surprise. She was planning a trip to Albuquerque, the town which I, for lack of any other, consider to be our family's hometown. I've lived there four different times over the course of my life thus far, so from the perspective of an itinerant preacher it's the closest I come to having a place to call "home."

My daughter had spent six of her growing years in Albuquerque, so I assumed she knew the town as well as I. But when I started explaining to her the various places she should visit and the particular streets she would need to travel on, she said, "Dad, you've lost me completely. I don't know my way around Albuquerque at all."

When she said that I was at first totally shocked. I mean, I know that city backwards and forwards, so I assumed that my daughter, having lived there for six years, also knew it well. But when I began to more carefully consider her lack of knowledge, I realized that the time she spent there was from ages 6 to 12 for her. It's really quite obvious why she doesn't remember places and streets and how to get around in Albuquerque. She was only a child while living there.

My daughter's lack of knowledge of Albuquerque reminded me of the lack of Biblical knowledge that I often encounter in adults who claim to be Christians, sometimes even those who are faithful church attendees. What I regularly discover is that such folks have only childhood memories of Bible study – in Sunday School or Vacation Bible School or while on youth retreats. Since becoming adults, they've chosen not to become involved in further Biblical exploration, neither on their own nor with others. They may clearly remember the story of David and Goliath, but ask them to open their Bibles to Paul's letter to the Romans, and they're clueless.

2 Timothy 3:16-17 from the Bible says this: "All Scripture is inspired by God and is useful for teaching, for reproof, for correction, and for training in righteousness, so that everyone who belongs to God may be proficient, equipped for every good work." People of God – Bible learning isn't just for kids. Whether you're 8 or 80, for your entire lifetime you need to regularly study God's Holy Word.

God Offers Good Counsel
Job 12:13-14

I am not a good counselor. It's simply not one of my gifts. Whenever folks approached me to say, "Pastor, I need to see you for some counseling," I regularly responded with, "Let me be brutally honest with you. If I had a problem and needed counsel, I definitely wouldn't go to me." That's how poor a counselor I am. It's really not that I was trying to avoid pastoral counseling. I simply know, from experience, that I'm no good at it. I admire those pastors who <u>are</u> good counselors, and I never hesitated to refer folks in need of counsel to them.

Once, however, I ran into the exception that proves the rule. A lady insisted on coming to me for counsel, even after hearing my disclaimer regarding how rotten a counselor I am. I listened to her story for about 20 minutes, and the whole time she was telling it, a particular scripture verse kept running through my head.

When she finally paused to breathe, I told her what was happening in my mind. I said, "I believe you need to hear this scripture verse," then proceeded to quote it to her. As I related the single verse, it was as though I'd hit this lady on the head with a 2-by-4. She grew absolutely quiet for an uncomfortably long time. I'd begun to think I'd really offended her when she finally spoke again. "I never thought of that," she said. "Now I know what I need to do. Thank you." After we shared a brief prayer, she rapidly departed, satisfied that her need for counsel had been met.

Hebrews 4:12 in the Holy Bible says this: "Indeed, the Word of God is living and active, sharper than any two-edged sword, piercing until it divides soul from spirit, joints from marrow. It is able to judge the thoughts and intentions of the heart."

I still believe that in most instances I'm a lousy counselor. But sometimes the Holy Spirit of God works wonders, even with cracked pots. It really wasn't me who said anything significant to that lady; rather, it was the Word of God which reached her heart.

The Same Man in Two Different Circumstances
Matthew 5:47-48

I recall a member of one of my former churches who was a chronic nit-picker. For purposes of this story I'll call him Charlie. He perennially complained about anything and everything at church, mostly insignificant stuff that, to me, was barely worth concern. A stickler for detail, if even a single typographical error appeared in a Sunday church bulletin, he felt it was time to fire the church secretary. Because of his constant whining about its errors and shortcomings, I saw Charlie as a problem person for that church, and I confess to more than once wishing that God might see fit to move him to another city or another church.

One spring when I was recruiting a Volunteers in Mission team to travel to a foreign nation and do some church construction, Charlie signed up. I was totally surprised. Although I really needed team members, I wondered if having Charlie on the team was going to be worth the aggravation. So I carefully warned him of the many inconveniences he would face in traveling on a mission outside the U. S. – hard beds, no air conditioning, no hot water, unreliable plumbing, strange food, etc. He insisted he could handle it, and I eventually ran out of objections.

From the moment we departed on the mission to the moment of our return, Charlie was a totally different person. He was everything he needed to be – flexible, tolerant, helpful, hard-working, a real team player. I couldn't believe it was the same person. While we were there I told him, "Charlie, I didn't know you could be such a wonderful person. I'm really glad you came on this mission."

The strangest part about Charlie's behavior was that, when we returned home, he immediately went back to being the negative nit-picker that he'd been before. When I pointed out his falling back into his old behavior pattern, he simply said, "Preacher, I don't expect much elsewhere. But here in my church, I expect everything to be perfect. Jesus told us to be perfect, so I believe my church should measure up to Jesus' standard."

I was never able to convince Charlie that his expectation was unrealistic, but from then onward I at least understood <u>why</u> he was the way he was. I've never yet found nor been part of that perfect church Charlie was seeking, but I sincerely tried to make every church I served a little better – and a bit closer to the perfection that our Lord ultimately expects of us.

Long-Distance Relations
Acts 15:3-4

Virtually every church has members who are active and involved in the life of that congregation – and members who aren't. So it was that, when I became pastor of the Marathon United Methodist Church in the Big Bend country of Texas, I was given a list of 45 members – about 30 of whom were actually resident in that town, but the remaining 15 who lived, literally, all over the country.

A few months after I became pastor there, my family and I decided to take a vacation trip to San Diego, California. As we prepared for the trip, I remembered that one of the non-resident members of the Marathon Church had a San Diego address. Thus when we got to San Diego, I decided to look him up.

With some simple researching of an old-fashioned telephone directory I discovered that this gentleman, Arnold by first name, was a neighborhood barber with a shop near San Diego State University. So I and my family headed over to his shop one afternoon while we were staying in San Diego. I walked in and introduced myself. "Arnold, I'm Dave Ring. I'm your pastor from Marathon, Texas – and I've come by to visit you."

After he got past the initial "You're kidding" response, Arnold proved to be a very likeable fellow. He was truly impressed that I had taken the time and effort to look him up – halfway across the country. That initial visit turned into thirty years of friendship. Although I long since ceased to be a pastor in Marathon, I and my family visited Arnold in San Diego on a number of occasions, and I had the privilege of hosting him in my Texas home – actually in a couple of my Texas homes as I moved from place to place. And ultimately I had the sad but significant duty of conducting Arnold's funeral – burying him in his family's plot in the tiny cemetery in Marathon, Texas.

One of the exciting things about being part of the Body of Christ on earth – the Church – is that Christians have relatives all over the world. Once you're adopted into the family of God, you've immediately got millions of brothers and sisters spread throughout the planet. And sometimes, all it takes is a simple introduction to make a lifelong friend within the wonderful, worldwide fellowship of believers in Christ. I invite you to try it the next time you're on an out-of-town trip – visit a church and make a new Christian friend or two while there.

Karma for the Elderly
Leviticus 19:32

As a pastor I found myself visiting often in eldercare facilities. Years ago, such used to be routinely termed "nursing homes," but the various kinds and levels of care that are available today make that an outdated term. Over the years I've probably made several thousand such visits thus far, and although now officially retired I will probably make many more in future years as long as I'm able. Visiting in eldercare facilities has brought me some interesting wisdom.

One of the insights that I've garnered from all this visiting of the elderly is the following -- as the Bible says in Galatians 6:7, "Whatever a man sows, that he will also reap." That's quintessentially true in eldercare facilities. While there are some obvious exceptions – when, for example, a man or woman has outlived all their close relatives and friends – I find this to be the rule: The elderly who were reasonably positive people when they were younger are visited when they get old. And the elderly who were hard to get along with in earlier years are forgotten.

As I say that, I realize it sounds harsh – but it's merely observable truth. If you spend your time loving your family and making friends while you're young and active, you'll most likely be loved and cared for by your family and friends in old age. But if you are self-centered and harsh with others in your earlier years, you'll probably wind up alone and ignored when you grow old.

There's a widely-accepted concept in our popular culture today that the elderly in general are lonely and neglected. In truth, some are. But many aren't. And the difference between the two groups is usually well-established -- long before they grow old.

"Whatever a man sows, that he will also reap." That's godly truth for us all, young and old.

Lying for the Lord
Psalm 14:1

In the spring of 2003 I had the first of two opportunities to visit the island nation of Cuba, one of the world's last strongholds of the political philosophy called "communism." During much of the 20th century communism was the global archenemy of democracy. Fortunately, communism's international influence sharply waned with its rejection by Russia and its allies in the early 1990's. But the 11 million citizens of Cuba, under the long-term leadership of Fidel Castro and his successors, have continued to live under communistic rule.

A basic tenet of the communist philosophy of life is atheism – the belief that there is no God. Although I, as a Christian pastor, attempt to remain politically neutral in many circumstances, the atheistic philosophy of communism puts it in direct conflict with the core principles of my life.

One of the items which the Methodist Bishop of Cuba asked me to bring on my first trip to Havana was Spanish-language Bibles. So I and my traveling companion both loaded our suitcases with Spanish Bibles. When we arrived in Havana he was fortunate – his luggage was passed over without inspection. But mine was flagged, and I had to try to explain to a Cuban government official why I was carrying a hundred or more Bibles – when my official visitor's permit to Cuba was to be only a tourist.

I could have simply told the truth – but to do so would have meant that the Bibles I carried would have been confiscated and destroyed. So I had already prepared myself for the possibility of being questioned, and had some elaborately crafted answers ready – and successfully employed them. I didn't exactly lie to the Cuban government, but I didn't tell the whole truth either. By so doing I was able to get the Bibles into Cuba – for use in spreading the gospel of Jesus Christ to the precious people there.

Even under such clear-cut circumstances it made me uncomfortable to lie. But as Peter and other followers of Jesus did in Acts 5:29, when there is no other alternative, "we must obey God rather than men. "

Yes, I visited Cuba twice as a Christian pastor – and I believe it was God's will that I went there and took illegal Bibles to the Cuban people. But I'm very glad I live in the U. S. A., a democratic nation wherein I can freely and openly share my faith, and don't have to lie to maintain my allegiance to Jesus Christ.

The Cost of Divorce
Matthew 19:4-6

They were one of the most active, supportive, well-rounded families in the congregation I was then serving. Both adults had excellent professional jobs; their children, a pre-teen boy and a teenage girl, were top-notch students, involved in a variety of sports and community activities. They were, to my thinking, an "all-American" Christian family.

When someone told me that they were divorcing, I at first thought they were mistaken. But when I talked directly to her, then him, I discovered it was sadly true. I tried to interest them in counseling – neither would come. I asked what the issues were that were driving them apart, and received only vague answers. There was nothing concrete -- no abuse, no drug or alcohol habits, no major financial problems. They'd just discovered that neither was perfect, and so they each had decided to look for someone else -- that ideal person they were afraid they'd missed.

It proved to be a messy divorce – legal fighting over custody of the kids and joint property issues wiped out a huge portion of their financial resources. Both immediately dropped out of church and within a few weeks their kids disappeared from youth fellowship, too. For some months I did the best I could to maintain contact with them. He wound up losing his job and turning to alcohol for solace. She moved in with a man who sexually abused their daughter. When I last heard of them, the lives of all four were woefully conflicted.

Divorce is unquestionably a leading cause of both social and economic woes among American adults today. And the children of divorce fare even worse. Yet ½ of all couples who marry in this country divorce – and those statistics are virtually the same among Christians as non-believers. Couples split from what they consider to be a bad marriage – and most of the time, both parties wind up in even worse circumstances. Divorce rarely solves problems – it simply creates newer, bigger ones.

Solomon, the wisest king of ancient Israel, once wrote this Proverb: "May you rejoice in the wife of your youth, may she satisfy you always, may you ever be captivated by her love." That was very good advice 3,000 years ago. It remains the same today.

Alcohol's – and God's – Power
Proverbs 20:1

Joe had fallen off the wagon. A year before, we'd hired Joe as our church's custodian, knowing that he had a severe, chronic alcohol problem. He was both in AA and taking a drug called "antabuse" to keep his alcoholism at bay. And for quite a long time, all had gone well. He lived at the church in a couple of rooms that we'd converted into a small apartment. He kept himself neat and clean. Although it wasn't required of him, he started attending one of the church's evening Bible studies. Later, he began showing up at Sunday worship. And one Sunday, three months before, he'd walked forward and publicly committed his life to Jesus Christ. There wasn't a dry eye in the sanctuary that Sunday morning, for virtually everyone in the congregation knew Joe's checkered history. For thirty years he'd battled alcoholism, and not often with success.

When Joe didn't show up for work for the second day in a row, I sensed something was wrong. So I knocked repeatedly on his apartment door. Eventually he answered – and I immediately knew he'd gone back to the bottle. He looked terrible and smelled worse. He'd actually managed to drink while taking antabuse, which is designed to make you very sick if you try to do such a foolish thing. Joe was an absolute mess.

I helped clean him up to the extent possible. He wasn't in any shape to talk at that point, so I told him just to get some sleep and come to see me in my office the next day.

The next day he showed up as requested, clean and sober once again. "Are you going to fire me?" was his first remark. "No, Joe," I responded. "I'm not going to fire you. You're fighting a tough disease, and you just lost a battle. I want to help you win the next one. I don't believe Jesus would fire you after one mistake, so neither will I." Joe was amazed. He'd been fired so many times in the past that he just came to expect such whenever he stumbled.

Joe stayed with us for about six more months. When he finally decided to quit, of his own volition, it was to reconcile with his wife – from whom he'd been separated for more than three years. I don't know what happened to Joe after that; I lost track of him. But I trust that the grace of Jesus Christ, which Joe found in a church I served 25-plus years ago, is still with him to this day. Alcohol's a tough foe. But Jesus is a powerful Savior.

In-Womb Baptisms?!
I Corinthians 18:7-8

She worked in the office of the town's sole gynecologist, an office which was located directly across the street from the house where I was then living. Because she was the doctor's employee, he kept close watch on her first pregnancy. At seven months, problems began to arise. Two weeks later, he was convinced that the baby would not survive another 24 hours – it would be born dead.

That M. D. was a member of my congregation. The young lady who worked for him had only nominal exposure to the Christian faith, but just enough so that, even in her grief at the prospect of delivering a dead baby, she was worried about her baby's soul. He called me to come and talk with her.

So it was that I baptized that baby while still in its mother's womb. There's no exact Biblical precedent for this sort of situation, but I do know that God once told the prophet Jeremiah, "Before I formed you in the womb I knew you, before you were born I set you apart." So I don't consider it impossible that God's grace could reach even an unborn child. The mother was aided in her grief by this rite of divine attention to her dying baby.

Stranger still, years later and in a different city, I was asked to do much the same thing again. This one was a high-risk premature delivery, and the likelihood of survival of the infant after delivery was remote. So I baptized that child in the womb as well. After delivery, it – actually a tiny little girl -- survived for just four days. But the parents were greatly comforted by the knowledge that their daughter had been specially marked by the grace of God through Christian baptism.

Some Christian traditions require that one "understand" baptism in order to receive it. I'm a pastor with an earned doctor's degree in Christian ministry, and I don't even pretend to fully understand Christian baptism. It's one of God's mysterious gifts of grace, a gift that I'm pleased to share with any and all, regardless of their ability to understand it. I don't have to "understand" a gift in order to receive it. If baptizing a dying baby can provide comfort to grieving parents, I'll gladly do such whenever asked.

Sticking to What You're Called to Do
Deuteronomy 22:8

As a younger preacher I did a lot more things that are outside the job description of a pastor than I did later on. Quite often, when I saw something that needed doing around a church I was serving and I couldn't enlist a layperson to do it quickly enough to suit me, I'd just do it myself. But on more than one occasion this sort of "working outside my calling" by God got me into trouble.

One year, it was time for the changeover from heating to cooling at my church in El Paso, Texas and the particular lay members who were supposed to take care of this chore kept dragging their feet. I tired of hearing complaints from worshippers of being too hot in the sanctuary on several successive Sundays, so I simply climbed up on the church roof and accomplished the necessary changeover work myself. Unfortunately, while up there I crawled under a duct that had a wasps' nest on its underside – and received 17 stings as a result.

Just a few months later, at that same church, after repeated entreaties to others had yielded no result, I climbed up into the attic crawl space over the church's nursery to replace a broken ceiling panel. Somehow or other I inadvertently stepped off the rafters. I crashed through the ceiling and wound up, literally, in the middle of one of the topmost of a two-tiered set of baby cribs in that nursery. I didn't hurt myself, but the major hole I left in the ceiling was pretty hard to explain to that church's Board of Trustees.

In the early Christian church, the apostles had to complain in order to get the laypeople to stop asking them to do all manner of tasks unrelated to their callings by God. Acts 6:2 records their complaint: "It would not be right for us to neglect the ministry of the word of God in order to wait on tables." I've actually felt that way on more than one occasion -- when I was asked to do something that bore no relation whatever to my calling as a pastor. But sometimes, I myself was guilty of taking on chores that weren't asked of me.

With time and age, I learned the wisdom of allowing the Church, also known as the Body of Christ, to solve many of its own dilemmas. When each member thereof fulfills his or her assigned role, the Church – like a human body – functions smoothly. Together, in unity, the people of God can accomplish much, to his glory! If you are a member of a church, I trust you're doing your rightful part therein.

Disaster Recovery
Luke 6:47-49

In 1969 Hurricane Camille, with winds in excess of 200 miles per hour when it made landfall, devastated the Gulf Coast of Mississippi. My parents' home there, located about ½ mile inland from the beach, suffered extensive damage. I was away at college at the time. Months later, the next time I was able to get back to Mississippi, most of the damage had already been repaired. But one of the pecan trees in the front yard had been damaged so badly that its trunk literally looked like a corkscrew. It leaned precariously over the front sidewalk, with multiple branches hanging so low that we seriously considered cutting the entire tree down. But instead, my parents ultimately decided to re-route the sidewalk around it, waiting to see if it would live or die on its own.

Over the next thirty-five years, that pecan tree gradually undid the damage done to it by that 1969 hurricane. Upon their deaths, I inherited my parents' assets, including that Mississippi house. When I finally, with great reluctance, sold that property in 2004, I took a long, last look at that tree. It was healthy and strong. Just a few degrees of "lean" remained to remind me of the major damage it had suffered three and a half decades before.

As a pastor I often deal with people whose lives have been devastated by personal calamities. A mother's quiet existence shattered by the suicide of a teenage son. A veteran suffering from post-traumatic shock after months on the battlefield. A high-flying financier bankrupted by the burst of a "stock market bubble." The list could go on and on.

Some folks, like that tree in my Mississippi Gulf Coast front yard, gradually regain their strength and health after such a crisis. Others never do. A significant number of such become the "homeless" who meander the downtown streets of every city in our land.

I don't have a smart answer that will bring restoration to all of the shattered lives I've seen, but I do know how to avoid being completely blown away by the storms of life. Faith in Jesus Christ provides an anchor that will hold even against the strongest "life-hurricane" that can ever confront a human being. Personal crises and calamities will inevitably confront us all, but Jesus will see you through the worst of such – and help you to heal afterward.

Clearly Letting Others Know
Joshua 24:15

For its 50th anniversary celebration, the church I was then serving decided to hold one big worship service together on a Sunday, instead of the usual multiple separate worships, followed by a major church-wide dinner. At the dinner, I noticed Mike, who always attended the early worship, staring oddly at Steve, who was a regular at late worship. I walked over to the two of them and said, "Mike, do you know Steve?" To which Mike replied, "Of course I know Steve. We work together in the same office. But I never knew he was a member of this church. I really didn't even know he was a Christian."

That's not the first time that ever happened in my ministry, nor will it likely be the last. Today's Christians have strayed so far from the commission of the Lord Jesus Christ to "go into all the world and preach the gospel" that most believers are unrecognizable from the world at large. Two members of the same church can work in the same office for years on end – and know nothing about each other's faith.

Many Christians whom I know, when challenged on their lack of overt witness for the Lord Jesus, counter by saying, "Oh, I don't witness with my mouth; I witness with my life." This contemporary concept is called "lifestyle witnessing." Supposedly it's equally or more effective than speaking words about Jesus.

From the Bible, I recall that Jesus lived a perfect life for nearly three decades in the town of Nazareth. But when he finally rose up to preach the Word of God, his neighbors and friends were completely surprised: "Who does He think He is? He's nobody special; we all know Him, He's just the local carpenter's son." If the most perfect life ever lived didn't get anyone's attention, the whole idea of lifestyle witnessing is suspect. When Christians aren't speaking up for Jesus, there's not much witnessing going on. When members of the same church can rub shoulders with each other daily – with neither realizing the other is a believer – there's certainly nothing happening to attract the attention of non-believers.

If you're a Christian, it's time to open your mouth for Jesus. Tell others that you believe in Him – and tell them why. They just might be interested in listening. But you'll likely never know – unless you try.

Not <u>My</u> Sins!
John 2:1-11

I was raised in a secular home; I became a Christian at age 20. My wife, Fran, was raised in a Roman Catholic Christian home. Neither of us, therefore, grew up around the American Protestant attitude toward the consumption of alcohol. That attitude, as I've experienced it, seems to be a largely double-standard which says, "Don't drink alcohol – in front of other church members."

Shortly after Fran and I married, we attended a meeting at my home church in Albuquerque in which there was discussion of what to sell from that church's booth at the New Mexico State Fair. They wanted to find a "high profit" item that would help the church financially. Fran, brand-new in the church, piped up with "Let's have a liquor wheel – you know, raffle off bottles of liquor. We could make a lot of money for the church that way."

The stunned looks on everyone's faces were plain for her to see. Having been a member of that church for a couple of years already, I knew that Fran had just suggested not one, but two, of what that church considered to be the gravest of sins: drinking and gambling. I did my best to help her out of the hole she'd dug: "Honey, they don't do those sorts of things here." Forty-plus years later, some of the oldest women in that church still remember that incident – and still consider my wife a hardcore sinner because of it.

As a pastor, I'm always fascinated by what particular folks consider to be the "worst" of sins, and how they often tend to ignore other wrongdoing. Some decry drug abuse, but ignore starvation. Others are incensed by widespread sexual immorality, but overlook cheating on one's taxes. As you might expect, most folks tend to highlight the sins of others, but to downplay their own.

The Bible says this: "All have sinned and come short of the glory of God." And the Word of God also says this of Jesus Christ: "If we confess our sins, He is faithful and just and will forgive our sins and cleanse us from all unrighteousness."

I'm a preacher, yes. But I'm far from perfect; in the purity of God's sight I'm a serious sinner. But praise God, Jesus has forgiven me. And He'll do the same for you – all you need to do is ask Him.

Public Prayer
I Timothy 2:1-4

Why do folks always ask the preacher present to offer the blessing for food, or the prayer of invocation for the meeting that's about to begin? No matter where I go, how well-known or unknown I may be, as soon as folks find out that I'm a Christian minister, if there's a prayer called for, I'm chosen the one to deliver it. "Oh, Pastor Ring, of course you'll want to do the invocation for our Firemen's Fund Raiser dinner." "Pastor Ring, will you please offer the blessing for our food tonight?" And I usually say, "Yes," and do so, for to refuse would cause an unnecessary scene.

Honestly, though, I really don't feel comfortable praying publicly in many situations. When I don't know 95% of the people in the room, I'm uncomfortable with being asked to pray on their behalf. Since I don't know their needs, how can I possibly pray appropriately for them? But I also realize that most folks aren't actually looking for <u>real</u> prayer in a public situation. They simply want "window-dressing," "filling a square" of sorts. "Our program says we're supposed to have a prayer of invocation, so let's find a preacher to do that."

I'm also uncomfortable when asked to offer the prayer of blessing at family meals in other people's homes. Especially if the father or grandfather of that household is present, he really should be the one to offer such. God's Word says that he's the spiritual head of his household. I'm merely a guest. Once in a great while I'm both pleased and relieved when, at someone else's family dinner, the man of the house spontaneously offers prayer – without ever asking me. Frankly, that's the way it's supposed to be.

On the other hand, in most of the worship services I conduct, I offer a public prayer that's called the "pastoral prayer." In that situation, since I'm the person in charge, it's appropriate that I either do pray or choose someone to do so on my behalf. Occasionally someone will comment to me thus: "I didn't like what you said in your pastoral prayer today." My response is always, "That's OK, because I wasn't praying to you."

Public prayer is a strange issue. In our contemporary culture, lots of folks are incensed that a so-called "separation of church and state" in our nation limits public expressions of prayer. But ask many of those same folks to pray publicly, and they'll be the first to say, "I'd be uncomfortable doing that." So I guess preachers like me will always be asked to do a lot of public praying, whether we like it or not.

Prayer as Conversation
I King 19:11-13

What is prayer? A long time ago, I learned this simple definition: Prayer is conversation with God.

If I'm to actually converse with another human being, that conversation needs to be two-way. I speak while the other person listens. Then they speak and I listen. It's a dialogue, involving us both as sometime talker, sometime hearer. If only one person talks 100% of the time, that's not a conversation – it's a monologue, a lecture.

I'm a pastor -- a preacher. Preachers love to talk. When preachers get together, there's an abundance of talk. In several cities where I've pastored there have been "pastors' prayer groups" that have formed. Since I'm a great believer in prayer, and likewise a strong proponent of Christian unity, I've tried valiantly to take part in such groups. But I usually fall by the wayside after only a few sessions, for these "pastors' prayer groups" don't really get involved in much prayer. Rather, they're times for multiple monologues in which the preachers present take turns addressing God for five to ten minutes each. As soon as one preacher finishes, another jumps in. If there should ever be a pause of more than three seconds, it seems that someone always gets uncomfortable and starts singing a praise chorus to fill the gap. If God should ever want to answer, he'd have absolutely no opportunity. Every available second is filled by eager preachers talking to him.

We preachers are all fallible human beings, myself most certainly included. If even groups of preachers can't get conversational prayer right, we probably shouldn't be critical of ordinary folks who have trouble finding time to pray or knowing how to pray when they do find the time. I don't pretend to have the "last word" or any "ultimate wisdom" on the subject of prayer, but I do offer this small guidance: When you pray, be sure to take adequate time to listen for God's answer.

It's Christ's Church!
I Corinthians 1:11-13

Every time I began a new ministry at a particular church, there were folks who, on the way out of church, told me, "We're really glad you're here. We didn't like the last preacher, so we stopped going to church. This is our first Sunday in this church in three years." I suppose they thought they were flattering me with such accolades.

On the other hand, after I'd been at a church for a couple of years, there were always folks who came up to me to say, "This will be the last time you see us. We don't like your preaching, so we're dropping out of this church." I suppose such folks thought they were hurting my feelings with their criticism.

The upshot of this matter is that both kinds of responses to me, or to any given preacher, are wrong – wrong according to the Word of God. Any church, if it's worthy of the name, is the Church of Jesus Christ. It's never "Pastor Dave Ring's church" or "Preacher Paul Bradley's church" or "Elder Jane Cooper's church." And therefore, becoming active in a church because of one's liking of a given pastor, or leaving a church because of disliking a pastor, is simply wrong. The Spirit of the Lord doesn't move in and out of churches based upon who is, or isn't, currently the pastor thereof. And neither should the people of God.

In the church that I served in Odessa, Texas, one of the elderly ladies with whom I repeatedly clashed once told me this: "Preacher, I don't like you. But this is my church. So I'm not about to let you, nor any other preacher, run me off." Frankly, that lady and I saw eye to eye on at least that one issue. I didn't particularly like her either. But my respect for her was increased because of her uncompromising loyalty to her church.

Jesus often referred to believers in him as sheep, but never as grasshoppers. A lot of today's Christians need to keep that in mind – and stick with the churches they're already in, rather than periodically jumping from one flock to another based upon personal whims.

Showing Hospitality
I Chronicles 12:39-40

There was a wonderful woman in the church I served in Big Spring, Texas who regularly brought treats to the staff of the church. Once monthly, unasked and unbidden, she provided home-made cake sometime during a regular business day. She'd been doing this for decades – since long before I came to be the pastor there. We never knew exactly when she was going to show up with cake, but she always did – about once a month. She didn't say anything as she left it, and we who worked in the church may or may not have actually seen her bring it in. When we did, we of course said "thank you" to her. Her cakes were delicious, and a wonderful morale builder for both staff and pastor. If we were having a tough day, it made it go a little smoother, a little sweeter from then on.

This lady wasn't otherwise in the forefront of things at that church. She wasn't a leader of any ministry or group. She was simply a quiet, faithful, supportive person. She had a talent for baking tasty cakes – and she regularly blessed her church's staff with that talent.

The Bible doesn't specifically mention "cake baking," but there's an assumed background to such found throughout the Scriptures. God's people are supposed to consistently demonstrate the gift of hospitality, both to one another as well as to strangers. Some of the harshest of God's rebukes to be found, both in the Old and New Testaments, are given to those who failed to show hospitality to others, especially those in real need.

Failure to show hospitality is a sin of omission, just as adultery and murder are sins of commission. You might think it strange to place lack of hospitality on a par with adultery and murder, but the Bible really does just that. The Parable of the Good Samaritan, told by Jesus in response to the question, "Who is my neighbor?" is an example of the importance God places upon hospitality – even when it's an imposition to have to show such. Remember, too, that the Bible negatively highlights the lack of hospitality shown by the Bethlehem innkeeper -- who refused entry to Mary and Joseph when Jesus was about to be born.

I'm quite sure the "cake lady" at my Big Spring church wasn't trying to win points with God by bringing cakes to her church's staff. Rather, she was regularly and consistently demonstrating the gift of hospitality to others, and I'm equally sure that God was pleased by her actions. Christians, in an era of rampant suspicion of those next door and "neighborhood watches" against strangers, we each and all need to be more hospitable people.

Enjoying One's Work
Ecclesiastes 3:22

Now that I'm officially retired, it seems I'm frequently talking with other folks who are nearing retirement. Once in a great while I hear in such conversations that workers are going to miss their jobs once they retire. But mostly what I hear said is more like this: "I'm counting the days till I'm done, once and for all, with my 'blankity-blank' job."

It's hard for me to understand those widespread negative sentiments toward one's work, for I honestly never experienced such. I began my working life as a young adult engineer at one of the United States' premier scientific institutions, Sandia Laboratories. There my mind was continually stimulated and challenged by my colleagues and the projects we pursued. I genuinely looked forward to arriving at work virtually every day.

A few years later God called me into Christian ministry. I left engineering reluctantly – and only because it was God who was doing the asking. After a couple of years of re-education I began serving God in various ministerial roles -- first as a missionary in Guatemala, then as a pastor of local churches in several different states.

By the time I reached retirement I had served eight "appointments," as United Methodists call them, for a total of ten local churches. Lest you think I'm some sort of "Pollyanna," I thoroughly enjoyed just nine of ten of them. One – for a single year – was a complete bust. But 90% of my pastoral experiences were good and positive. I tried, and mostly succeeded, to leave the churches placed in my care better off than when I received them. And I met a lot of wonderful people along the way.

I'm genuinely sorry when I hear folks on the verge of retirement express disappointment and even anger over their many years of working life. I pray that God will grant them rest and relief in their latter years. But as for me, I'm filled and satisfied with what's behind me – and looking forward to whatever God may have ahead for me.

Flowers and Worship
I Kings 6:14-18

In every one of the churches I was privileged to serve, there was at least one "flower lady." This was the woman or women – I'm not being sexist; it really was invariably females – who made it her personal ministry to see that fresh flowers were set forth at each and every worship service in the church. In some churches there were several more than a single woman involved – three or more of my congregations had flower calendars and flower committees.

I was very glad to have such women in my churches, for flowers were one "frill" that simply didn't register on my radar screen. I appreciated the flowers provided and arranged, and tried to regularly thank the ladies involved in seeing to their provision. Having flowers in worship certainly enhances the appearance of the sanctuary. But they're obviously not essential to focusing one's attention upon God.

On the negative side, in one congregation I had the misfortune of having two "competing" flower ladies. They were supposed to alternate in their duties – one every other week. But far too often they clashed over the nature of the flowers provided. If the color of the arrangement one of these ladies set forth was primarily blue, the other complained that it should have been red. If the one set out lilies, the other maintained that it should have been tulips that week. And of course, each tried to involve me in their floral mini-war. Staying out of their rivalry wasn't easy, but I somehow managed to do so.

There are dozens of "little things" that go into maximizing the opportunity for the worship of God in today's churches. The seating, the heating, the lighting, the sound….the list could go on. For some people, one or two such items are of greater import than others. Hence the "flower ladies" in every congregation.

Not being one such, I'm genuinely impressed that the Lord raises up these "detail" people. Whatever it takes to better focus more of us upon the praise and worship of God, I'm for it.

Helping the Poor
Leviticus 25:35-36

A friend of mine was recently talking with me about having delivered food boxes to a number of needy families in one of the poorer sections of the city in which we both currently live. Apparently this was my friend's first experience with seeing, up close and personal, the places and faces of poverty. He was both amazed and dismayed. He exclaimed, and I quote, "I had no idea things were so bad for people right here in our own city."

Because I'm a minister he went on to ask me one of the big "why" questions: Why does God permit such poverty to exist? So I started to explain that, at least in the 21st century USA, much of what he had seen was the result of repeated bad choices on the part of those found therein: drug abuse, domestic violence, sexual depravity, etc. But then he responded with the easily expected further query: "OK, that may explain the plight of the adults, but what about the children? Surely they don't deserve what they're experiencing." To which I could only reply, "You're right. Unfortunately, there's always a ripple effect. Whatever we do, for good or ill, inevitably affects those around us."

Being a "Wesleyan" Christian, I believe in free will. God doesn't, in my opinion, pre-destine nor determine the details of our lives. His overall plan is to draw, via the love of Jesus Christ, as many as possible to Him. But within that outline, we each are granted a tremendous amount of maneuvering room. Every day we make choices – choices that count. Some make good choices that lead to better choices and outcomes. Some make bad choices which lead to worse choices and outcomes.

Notwithstanding, the good news is that we always have opportunity to repair and undo the consequences of bad choices – both our own and those of others. My friend was doing exactly that as he delivered those food boxes to our neighbors in need.

Jesus, while on earth, said these words as recorded in the seventh chapter of Matthew's gospel: "The poor you will always have with you, and you can help them any time you want." Yes, there's a huge amount of poverty and need in our world, both near and far. And no, I don't have a magical, pat answer that neatly explains all of why that is. But I do know that I can roll up my sleeves and do my part to alleviate some of that need. And so can you.

What Should I Call Him?
John 18:35-37

King of Kings and Lord of Lords. That's one of the many "royal" titles often accorded to Jesus. As God's Son, he's superlatively royal, the greatest such ever.

The problem with employing royal nomenclature to describe Jesus is that fewer and fewer people in the world today have a frame of reference for such. Democracy is our contemporary world's most predominant form of government. And democracy's remaining major competitors, socialism and communism, share this with it: None of them require royalty. Kings and queens, princes and princesses, lords and countesses are fast fading from importance.

I'm often puzzled by the American fascination with British royalty. When the reigning English queen has a health issue, it's major news in the USA. When a new baby is born into the family of British royals, Americans "ooh" and "aah" at photos thereof. And most of all, whenever there's a "royal wedding" time stops while tens of millions of Americans spend an entire day watching, over and over again, video of the event.

Perhaps I'm a curmudgeon in this regard. To me, this nation was founded in the rejection of British – or any other – royalty. The English King George III was a villain who inspired the American revolution. When the rebellion succeeded the commander of the colonial army, George Washington, was offered kingship by those around him. He firmly and unequivocally rejected it, and American democracy was subsequently born.

Notwithstanding, the question of what to appropriately call Jesus remains. He's certainly not a "president," because he was not elected and he can't be impeached. He's not a "prime minister" for the same reasons. And he's obviously not a dictator, for he doesn't forcibly impose his will upon anyone.

I'm still struggling some with this one. Since Jesus' Kingdom is, by his own admission, not of this world, I suppose that the changing fashion of titles for earthly rulers doesn't really apply. If Jesus was King of Kings and Lord of Lords when the universe began, then I suppose that should be good enough for me. Even though I obviously don't fully understand the meaning thereof I say, "Yes, Lord, you are exactly that!"

Christmas Fanatics
Luke 2:4-14

My wife and I are "Christmas people." We have more Christmas decorations than any other earthly possession. Over the decades we've lived on the earth we've thus far moved 17 times. And whenever we move, those who help us pack and load our "stuff" are amazed at how much of it is Christmas. In terms of weight, I would venture to guess that 1/3 of our total worldly goods is Christmas.

The Christmas season at our house begins around November 1st each year. If she doesn't start then, my wife won't be able to put out all of the indoor Christmas décor that needs to be in place in time for December 25th. I, on the other hand, don't have to begin my portion of the work, annually, until the day after Thanksgiving. The outdoor decorations are my responsibility. It typically takes about two weeks to get them all in place and cheerfully lighted. In that regard global warming is actually my friend, for I increasingly don't have to face as harsh of weather as in decades past.

Of course I'm well aware that Christmas is a "Johnny come lately" among Christian celebrations. It wasn't observed at all for the first 1,000 years after Christ's birth. And I'm further knowledgeable that December 25th is a very unlikely date for the actual birth of Jesus. Based upon the gospel accounts a spring date is much more probable.

I also acknowledge that Jesus' birth, while certainly important – since it's the starting point of his earthly life – pales in theological significance to both his death on the cross for human sin and his Resurrection from the dead for our eternal salvation. That's all true – but I'm still unabashedly a Christmas person. I love everything about Christmas, both the sacred and the secular.

As a pastor I used to annually celebrate "Christmas in July" in my churches. To me, one Christmas celebration annually isn't enough. Jesus' birth is important enough for two – or maybe more – observances. My congregations used to think I was crazy for inviting them to sing "Hark the Herald Angels" and "Silent Night" in 100-degree weather, but I did it anyway. And you know, afterward a significant number of them confided to me that they actually liked doing so!

Chronic Speeding
Acts 5:27-29

For three years of my early ministry I was a modern-day "circuit rider," serving two churches in the Big Bend country of Texas located thirty-one miles apart. The way their Sunday morning worship services were scheduled, if everything went like clockwork, I had exactly 30 minutes to drive between them. At fifty-five miles per hour, which was the nationally-imposed legal speed limit on Texas highways back then, it couldn't be done. And when the early worship service at the first church ran over by a few minutes, I was in a real time bind.

The people of these two churches were otherwise pretty good folks, but they were doggedly stubborn regarding the starting times of their worship services. Although I repeatedly pleaded for more time to travel between them, I got absolutely nowhere. Neither church was willing to budge. Neither would alter the opening of its worship by even five minutes.

As a result, not surprisingly, I accumulated four speeding tickets in a very short time while attempting to hurriedly travel my circuit on Sunday mornings. They all came from the same Department of Public Safety officer, the one who regularly patrolled that section of U. S. Hwy 90 which I had to travel. Although I repeatedly explained to him my time dilemma, he was very unsympathetic to my plight. "Tell it to the judge" was his only response.

One particular Sunday morning, at my second church, there was an infant baptism scheduled. And who should stand up to serve as godfather to the child, in full uniform, but the DPS officer who'd given me those four tickets! When the father of the child started to introduce him to me, I told him it wasn't necessary. "We've already met," I said.

Although nothing was voiced by either of us, after that baptism I was never again ticketed by that officer. And I'm sure he had ample opportunity to do so. I guess he decided that my work for God was really important enough to overlook a little extra speed by a circuit-riding preacher on an otherwise empty stretch of U. S. 90 on Sunday mornings. A couple of years after I left that circuit, the speed limit on Highway 90 was raised back up to 70 miles per hour. Now, praise the Lord, the pastor who serves that circuit can both serve God's people and obey man's rules without an every-Sunday struggle.

Talking About the Weather
Ecclesiastes 11:4

Climate change due to global warming is a fact of life in the 21st century A. D. Weather extremes – dangerously hot, dry summers and/or bone-chillingly cold, snowy winters are becoming the norm rather than the exception for earthly life today, especially in what used to be termed "temperate" latitudes, which are where most of our planet's population resides.

Weather, which is the short-term, immediate expression of climate, has long been a common topic of conversation among people. It's an ice-breaker, a starter for many dialogues, particularly when you're meeting someone for the first time. With weather and climate now being genuinely newsworthy many days annually, I'd venture to guess that such conversations are more common than ever before.

But even two millennia ago Jesus the Messiah was well-aware of our human penchant for discussing the weather. He once commented thereon in Matthew's gospel, chapter 16, as follows: "When evening comes, you say, 'It will be fair weather, for the sky is red,' and in the morning, 'Today it will be stormy, for the sky is red and overcast.'"

Sometimes, however, "talking about the weather" is a method of avoiding more significant interaction with another person. When there's an important issue to be resolved between two parties, "Let's talk about the weather" can be a metaphor for evasion. Jesus was also well-aware of this, as he continued in Matthew 16 to note, "You know how to interpret the appearance of the sky, but you cannot interpret the signs of the times."

There's lots of "weather talk" out there today. Some of it is appropriate – just simple, light-hearted conversation. But some of it is avoidance. Many times Christians incessantly "talk about the weather" with their non-believing friends, when they should be moving on to the discussion of more significant issues: life, death, and the meaning thereof. Sometimes we actually need to steer our conversations away from trivia – weather, football, vacations, etc. – and onto weightier subjects such as God, Jesus, and salvation. I'm not saying we should all major in 24/7 evangelism. However, maybe we ought to consider our faith worthy of at least occasional mention with and among our friends and neighbors.

Crowd Estimation
Matthew 16:9-10

One of the semi-special talents that I possess is the ability to accurately estimate the size of crowds. My wife and others who know me well have tested me many times over several decades on this. Whenever we go into a baseball or football stadium, she will routinely ask me, "How many people are here today?" I'll scan the view and, after a few seconds' pause, say "About 18,000." Later, when the attendance is announced over the loudspeaker, we'll hear, "Today's attendance is 18,142." On a smaller scale, when we walk into a church service, she'll sometimes say, "What's today's church attendance?" I'll look the sanctuary over and respond, "Two hundred and forty-five." On the way out, to check myself, I ask the chief usher, "What's today's attendance?" And he'll respond, "We counted 251." My estimates aren't spot-on, but they're close enough to be reliably more than mere guesses.

Now before you think this is some sort of weird voodoo, I'm by no means the only one who can do this. Quite a few engineers – which is what my first career was – can produce similar results. Our brains are wired in such a way that we unconsciously observe areas and volumes and densities and the like, then calculate and spit out numbers when asked. I can tell you the square footage of your living room after just a momentary glance. I can rapidly calculate, just by looking, then predict whether the sixteen boxes you are planning to put in your pickup truck's bed will fit or not. And I can estimate the crowd present at the circus performance within plus or minus two percent. It's an "engineer thing."

One of the few events of Jesus' earthly ministry that is included in all four of the gospels – Matthew, Mark, Luke and John – is what is commonly called "the feeding of the five thousand." According to the gospels Jesus provided a meal of bread and fish by the lakeside to an audience of "five thousand men" – plus an unspecified number of women and children – who had gathered to hear him speak. This was, of course, a great miracle. And it was later duplicated with a different crowd of "four thousand men."

I may be one of the few to consider this, but I've always wondered: Who counted the men that were present? Did Jesus perhaps send out his 12 disciples with this charge: "I want you to count this crowd, so I'll know how many I need to feed?" No, I don't really think it happened that way.

We know, of course, that four or five of Jesus' closest followers were fishermen. But those two feeding miracles required a different sort of background. I'm convinced that at least one of Jesus' disciples was an early-day engineer. So when Jesus proposed to feed the crowd, that disciple likely said to him, "Master, I can tell you that are about 5,000 men out there. Plus there are 4,500 women and 12,500 children. So you'll need to prepare enough for 22,000 to eat." Crowd estimation: It's a useful talent, both in Jesus' time and now.

Is It Really in the Bible?
II Timothy 3:16-17

With Biblical illiteracy on the rise as fewer and fewer people actually read the Scriptures, it's truly amazing to me what folks believe to be of Biblical origin, but which actually isn't. I don't know how many dozens of times I've had someone say to me, "You know, preacher, the Bible says that God helps those who help themselves." That may be a modern American truism, but it's definitely not found in the Bible. In fact, there's an actual verse in the Bible, Romans 5:6, which says the exact opposite: "While we were helpless, Christ died for us."

One of our nation's founding fathers, Benjamin Franklin, was unwittingly responsible for a number of the non-Biblical quotes that somehow or other are thought by many to be found in Holy Scriptures. "God helps those who help themselves" is one such. Another that I've heard quoted as coming from Jesus' mouth is this: "A penny saved is a penny earned." Jesus definitely didn't say this; pennies hadn't even been invented during Jesus' earthly lifetime. Franklin did say it – but he was only quoting an already popular saying that had been floating around for several decades prior to him. The latest non-Biblical "Bible verse" I keep hearing is this: "Beer is proof that God loves us." This one, too, is derived from Franklin – but it's a misquote even of him. What he actually said was "Wine is proof that God loves us."

In case you really are curious as to what the Bible says – and doesn't say – the most obvious way to find out is to actually pick up a Bible and read it. Even in an increasingly secular society, there are enough Bibles in print, in English, to provide two to every man, woman, and child in the USA. And if you are afraid you might have difficulty comprehending the Bible, there are now nearly 100 English versions, ranging from the scholarly to those that are deliberately translated to be understood at a 3rd grade reading level.

The Bible is the Holy Word of God. Read it, study it, learn it. You'll be the better for it, now and for eternity.

A Very Long Church Service
Joshua 8:33-35

I was in what the United Nations labels the world's poorest nation, the Democratic Republic of the Congo in Central Africa. The Congo is the "bottom of the barrel" in economic terms. Ninety-nine percent of the people in Congo endure hard-scrabble, subsistence agricultural lives. Every waking moment merely surviving is at the forefront of their existence. I and six others – from the US and from Denmark – were there to work on a project to provide clean, running water to the 45,000 residents of the Congolese village of Musumba.

While in this village of Musumba I went to church on a Sunday morning. The church building – a structure provided by Christians of other nations – was old and tattered but serviceable. The worship began at 9:30 AM. And at 12:30 PM it was still going strong. The faithful sang and danced, listened to scripture and messages, and sang and danced yet more. Worship, for them, was truly a celebration – the high point of an otherwise arduous week of simply living.

When the worship service finally drew to a close at 1 PM, after 3 ½ hours, I found myself saying, "How do they endure that every week?" And almost immediately I realized how wrong I was. They weren't enduring an overlong worship service. Rather, they were excited to generously offer something back to God, something of value -- to both them and us. Materially they don't have much of anything in the Congo. They certainly don't have money to give. But their time, like ours, has high value. For a Congolese villager, any waking hour taken away from farming is a risk to their very survival. Despite that, they gladly and generously give a huge block of time, weekly, to God's glory.

How many Americans would enjoy a weekly worship service in excess of three hours in length? We might endure it, as I did, but enjoying would not readily come to mind. Nonetheless, I learned something from the Congolese style of worship. And I've stopped looking at my watch while I'm in church on Sundays – or at least a lot less so.

Remembering Sonya
James 1:27

Sonya was a four-year old resident of Patronato Contra La Mendicidad, the "Orphanage Against Begging," in Guatemala City. While in Guatemala and as part of our mission work in Guatemala City, my wife Fran and I regularly helped secure food and clothing for the many children in this woeful facility. They had been brought to this orphanage by local city authorities who wished to keep the tourist-friendly areas of Guatemala City clear of any hint of poverty. Hence the obvious name: "Orphanage Against Begging."

In the midst of well over 100 institutionalized children, from babies to teenagers, Sonya stood out. Most of the children there were sullen and resentful, arguably for legitimate reasons. In addition, many of them were at least minimally brain-damaged from chronically poor nutrition. Sonya, obviously of Mayan heritage, always seemed bright and cheerful despite the miserably drab surroundings in which she existed.

Fran and I were attracted to Sonya from our first visit to the orphanage onward, and after a few months asked if we might take her home with us for a day. The authorities in charge were indifferent; as long as we didn't let her loose on the streets, we could do whatever we wanted with the little girl. If we brought her back the next day, fine. If we didn't, she wouldn't be missed.

We put Sonya in the church's van and drove her to where we lived, a two-room apartment on the second floor of the Union Church of Guatemala which housed us. As soon as we entered the apartment, Sonya looked around, screamed, and curled up in a fetal ball. She stayed that way all night and the next morning. Fran tried hard to hold her, trying to get her to relax and "open up"-- but she simply wouldn't.

One of that church's members was a medical doctor, so we telephoned and begged him to come and see Sonya. He came, and after examining her told us a strange but plausible tale. Sonya was used to living in a gray, bland, largely featureless world – the orphanage. Our apartment, with its many colors and objects, was assaulting her senses. It would take time for her to process all that she was seeing for the first time. He assured us she would likely return to normalcy in a day or two.

As the doctor predicted, Sonya did return to being a normal four-year-old within a couple of days. We returned her to the orphanage with the intention of eventually legally adopting her. Unfortunately, a few weeks later a major earthquake hit Guatemala City while we were back in the USA. All of Guatemala was chaotic. It took us months to discover that the "Orphanage Against Begging" had been hard hit. Sonya and many of the other children there were never accounted for. But we trust that, whether still on earth or already in the Kingdom of Heaven, Sonya is safe in God's strong arms of love.

Accepting God's Will
Romans 9:11-17

Two friends of mine, both fellow-members with me in a barbershop singing chorus, were diagnosed with serious forms of cancer. After local treatment options proved too limited, both were sent for state-of-the-art care at the famed Mayo Clinic in Rochester, Minnesota. After two months there, both men returned home. One came back on the road to full recovery. He was cancer-free, cured. The other came home to hospice care and death only a couple of months later.

When Jesus walked this earth, two of the three closest of all his followers were a pair of brothers – James and John. Along with Peter, they were Jesus' most cherished disciples. Shortly after Jesus ascended into Heaven, Acts 12:2 reports that one of these two brothers, James, was summarily killed upon King Herod's orders. John, on the other hand, went on to live a long, full, and productive life as an apostle. John wrote the gospel which bears his name, plus as many as four other books of the New Testament. Christian tradition informs us that, alone among the original 12 disciples, John died of old age after ninety-plus years on the earth.

The obvious question such disparate outcomes raises for all of us is why. Why did one of my friends survive cancer and thrive while the other passed quickly away? Why did Jesus allow one of the two of his favorite brother-disciples to disappear with barely a mention, while the other went on to do great things for the spread of first-century Christianity? Why, God, why?

There's no simple, formulaic answer to this and other weighty theological "why" questions. The Bible devotes an entire long book, the story of Job in the Old Testament, to reviewing these sorts of issues from a variety of viewpoints. Ultimately Job was reminded by God of his limited human perspective on such huge, universal matters and admonished to accept the will of his Creator.

Even Jesus, when faced with the enormity of suffering and the horror of the cruel method of death he could see ahead of him, was not beyond posing a major "why" query to God. But Jesus also had the wisdom to qualify his questioning with knowing acceptance. "Father, if it be possible, let this cup pass from me. Nevertheless, thy will be done."

Ultimately, that's the best answer I can offer to some of the tough questions life presents to us in this world. "Lord, even though I don't understand why, your will be done."

Are There Pets in Heaven?
Genesis 1:24-25

A little girl of about six whose cat had recently died presented me with the kind of question that a preacher often gets asked, "Is my kitty in Heaven now?" I told her this, "God made your kitty, and God loves all the creatures that He makes. So of course God will take care of your kitty." That wasn't quite specific enough for her. So she asked again, "But is my kitty in Heaven now?" And I had to say, honestly, "Since I haven't been there yet, I don't know enough about Heaven to say for sure. But I don't think you need to worry about your kitty. Just trust her to God's love." That's the best I could offer her, and this second time she seemed to be satisfied with my answer.

Americans, of all peoples on earth, have developed the greatest amount of sentimentality around their pets. Elsewhere pets are appreciated, but held in relatively low esteem. When a pet dies, folks just get another – if they care to. But in our culture, many pet owners actually consider cats and dogs to be members of their family and grieve for their loss as much or more than for a close relative. I've never been asked to conduct a pet funeral as yet, but I know quite a few other ministers who have.

There's really no evidence in the Bible regarding the ultimate fate of animals beyond earthly life. The Scriptures were inspired to show humans the way to God, not pets. However, we do know that there is plant life in Heaven – the Bible references green fields and flowers being seen there – so it's not much of a logical leap to assume that animal life could be found in the Kingdom's afterworld as well.

We do know that when Christ returns and the "new heavens and new earth" are revealed – essentially the restoration of "Garden of Eden" conditions – there will be all sorts of plants and animals found therein. In the sixth chapter of his writings, the prophet Isaiah describes the very different conditions that post-apocalyptic animal life will experience: "The wolf will live with the lamb, the leopard will lie down with the goat, the calf and the lion and the yearling together; and a little child will lead them. The cow will feed with the bear, their young will lie down together, and the lion will eat straw like the ox."

I don't know for sure what happens to beloved pets after they die. But I do know the way to Heaven for precious men and women, boys and girls. Follow Jesus, and he will be for you the way, the truth, and the life – now and forever.

Storage Issues
Matthew 6:19-21

My wife and I were heading for a fairly new and almost immediately very successful contemporary business: a container store. Basically, this is a fancy way of selling a variety of boxes, tubs, trunks, shelves, closets, and other items that help folks organize and hang on to our much "stuff" in today's American society.

Of course, I couldn't help but call to mind the Biblical image of the "parable of the rich fool" which Jesus told in Luke's gospel, chapter 12. A particular farmer had a surplus of grain, so he decided to build extra barns to hold such, then gloat over his bounty. But God admonished him of his mortality, reminding him that his life could be over tomorrow, so what he had stored might never actually benefit him, but only his heirs.

A few years back I was one of those heirs. Upon the deaths of my parents I inherited two packed houses. Both of them were long-term ancestral homes from several prior generations of my family. In Mississippi, I acquired my mother's family's home, dating back some sixty years and three generations. In Maryland, it was my father's family's property, going back five generations and a full century. And in both cases, it seemed that my family predecessors had decided to keep and store just about everything. It took me months to sort and decide what to throw away, sell, and/or actually keep from the Mississippi house. And the Maryland house ultimately required that Fran and I move back therein and spend three years sorting, discarding, preserving, selling, and otherwise dealing with a century of family belongings located on four levels of garage, cellar, attic, and actual living space. We held so many estate sales and auctions that I lost track of the actual number. And the multiple truckloads of "junk" given to the local Goodwill store led to us being recognized by name to many of the personnel there.

I certainly don't think my parents, grandparents, and the generations prior thereto were "fools" for keeping and storing belongings that ultimately came into my possession. Their decisions to keep so much led to a number of what I consider to be heirlooms, "treasures" that came out of that experience of sorting through much past possessions, items which my wife and I will someday pass on to our children. Whether they accord them the same value or not will be their decisions.

But as we headed to the container store to buy a couple of "tubs" in which to store artificial trees until next Christmas season, I was thereby made newly aware of the transitory nature of earthly life. I'm very glad that I have the Heavenly treasure of life eternal through Jesus Christ awaiting me beyond this earth, and not simply a houseful of earthly treasures. I hope you have the same!

A Self-Driving Donkey
Jude 11

After more than a century of automobiles being driven in the US and much of the world by people, we are presently experiencing a relatively rapid transition from human-controlled to computer-controlled personal transportation. In all likelihood my generation's great-grandchildren will grow up accepting "self-driving" cars as the norm, and consider vehicles with steering wheels to be old-fashioned chariots ultimately destined to be enshrined in museums.

A major issue for those of us who are used to doing our own driving is trust. Can we really trust machines to make life-and-death decisions for us as we hurtle down the roadways and highways? Even more, can we entertain the possibility that they might actually be better drivers than we are?

All of which leads me to recall an ancient story from the Old Testament, shortly after the Exodus of God's people from Egypt. This particular story comprises the entirety of the 22nd chapter of the Book of Numbers, an oft-avoided and rarely-read portion of God's Holy Word. According to this account, there was a prophet named Balaam who was on his way to visit an official of Moab, a rival nation which often clashed, back then, with God's chosen people, the Hebrews. Balaam was riding on his donkey when the animal, three times, refused to proceed down the trail Balaam wished to traverse. Each time Balaam beat his animal for refusing to obey him. The third time, the donkey simply laid down and refused to move despite being beaten. At that point God miraculously allowed the donkey to speak. Basically Balaam's donkey said, "I've been reliably carrying you for years. Why don't you trust that I know what I'm doing?" At that moment God allowed Balaam to see a previously invisible angel with a drawn sword blocking the path. Had the donkey obeyed his master, Balaam would have been killed.

Sometimes even a "dumb" animal can sense things that we humans cannot. We use trained dogs to sniff out survivors of earthquakes buried under rubble, acknowledging that their ability to smell far exceeds our own. Perhaps someday we'll also be able to acknowledge that a sensor-equipped computer's ability to drive cars exceeds our own as well.

Trust. It's something we humans have a hard time giving. We prefer to do it "my way." Can we trust that Jesus, God's Son, knows the way to the Father far better than we do? Or do we have to continue futilely trying to earn God's attention and favor by our own actions? I hope, for your soul's sake, it's the former.

Jesus is Gonna Win!
Matthew 16:18-19

It was one of those oddities in sports that helps keep folks interested and excited. Between the two teams that were competing one was clearly superior, the other was the obvious underdog. The sportscasters had pre-analyzed the outcome and were unanimous in their predictions. Team A would win; team B would be defeated. And so the game went, pretty much according to plan. Halfway through the allotted time, Team A was so far ahead that fans began leaving. A third of those watching on television became bored and switched to another program. But shortly before the end, Team B inexplicably rallied. They caught up. And just as time was expiring, they won. Wow!

Ever since the Christian faith began, its early and sure demise has been forecast. After the earthly death of Jesus, no way could a ragtag band of uneducated young men from the sticks of Galilee keep it going. Not quite a century later, when Rome got wind of its growth, the great emperor would easily snuff it out. Six hundred years later the aggressive rise of the Muslim faith would send Christianity to its grave. It would die of its own weight during Europe's Dark Ages. In the 1500's no way could Christianity possibly survive its schism between Catholicism and Protestantism. The foolishness of belief in a Resurrected Christ would never stand up to the humanist wisdom of the Enlightenment. More recently, science and technology would put a quick end to Christianity and all other religions. And so on and so forth.

Two millennia since the time of its founder, Christianity has somehow outperformed and outlasted its many predicted extinctions. More than once it's taken a "Hail Mary" last-second miracle to do so, but somehow faith in Jesus is yet around – and still winning new converts.

As I hear almost daily of the downsizing and closure of churches, as I read "polls" which indicate steady loss of interest in the practice of the Christian faith, as I listen to friends and even family members who admonish me that I'm on board a sinking ship, I simply shake my head, smile, and continue to press on with the Gospel of Christ.

For me and for a lot of other believers Christian faith isn't a game, it's life itself. I and they have confidence that just before all time expires, Jesus is going to win. Wow!

When Ancestry Doesn't Count
Jeremiah 31:29-30

At least two, maybe three hundred times in my years as a pastor, after introducing myself as a Methodist preacher to someone I was meeting for the first time, I've been told some variation of the following: "Let me tell you, my great-grandfather was a Methodist circuit-rider." They don't know it, but that assertion just revealed to me something significant – not about their ancestor, but about them.

Certainly, I have every respect for the circuit-riding preachers of old -- Methodist, Baptist, or other – who carried the Gospel message throughout this land during the nineteenth and early twentieth centuries. I myself can actually claim to have been a circuit-rider for three years, albeit not on horseback, but by automobile. I served two churches located 31 miles apart, with only 30 minutes' travel time between them. But that's another story.

The circuit riders of old were so numerous, especially in certain regions of the country, that almost any family whose history goes back a century or more includes at least one such. So I'm not at all surprised that so many folks have told me that they have circuit riders in their family tree. But what the person who, first thing out of the box, is really telling me by such a statement is basically this: "I don't have much faith myself, but my ancestors did." I've come to realize that, almost without exception, someone who makes that sort of statement to me on our first meeting isn't an active member of any church.

While having a "circuit rider" in one's ancestry is definitely something to be proud of, it won't get you into Heaven. The Bible is very clear on this: God has no grandchildren. As far back as the time of the Old Testament prophets, God made that plain – see Ezekiel 18 if you require a proof text.

Certainly it's a blessing to have persons of outstanding faith and Christian character in one's family tree. But neither your grandmother's nor your mother's faith will save you. God has only children, never grandchildren. We each need to form a personal relationship with God through his Son, Jesus Christ. Then, and only then, will we become part of the greatest family of all time – the family of God in the Kingdom of Heaven.

Getting to the Core
Mark 12:28-31

What's essential and what's trivial? For Christianity, what's the indispensable core of the faith, and what's simply a matter of choice or custom? As a pastor I've discovered that the answers to those questions vary widely from church to church, believer to believer.

In one of my churches there was major controversy over the color of new carpet to be run down the center aisle of the sanctuary. Ultimately three families left that church because their color choice did not prevail with the majority of members. But in that same church there was a Sunday School class debating the importance of the virgin birth of Jesus Christ from his mother Mary. When they asked me to weigh in on the issue, I candidly stated that I personally believed in the virgin birth. For that day forward, I was considered a hidebound conservative to that congregation.

In another of my churches there was ongoing conflict as to on which side of the sanctuary to place the US flag. Some maintained that the place of highest honor for the flag was on the left side of the podium and some that it was on the right. When asked, I said I really didn't care. As a citizen I have high respect outside the church for the US flag. But inside the church, which I consider an outpost of the Kingdom of God on earth, I'm much more concerned for the place of the Bible than the location of a national flag. In that congregation, I was branded a flaming liberal.

What's essential and at the core of Christian faith? And what's peripheral and of lesser import? Too often I've discovered that peripheral issues generate much controversy and division, while essentials are rarely discussed and affirmed.

Fortunately, while living among us Jesus, the founder of Christian faith, was asked to weigh in on this very subject. The dialogue, as recorded in Luke 10:25-28, went thus: On one occasion an expert in the law stood up to test Jesus. "Teacher," he asked, "what must I do to inherit eternal life?" "What is written in the Law?" he replied. "How do you read it?" He answered, "'Love the Lord your God with all your heart and with all your soul and with all your strength and with all your mind'; and, 'Love your neighbor as yourself.'" "You have answered correctly," Jesus replied.

There you have it, folks. Not my wisdom, but Jesus'. Love God and love your neighbor. Those are the true essentials of Christianity.

Faithfully Showing Up
Psalm 26:2-3

Some decades back, my father received a "perfect attendance award" from the shipyard company he was then working for in Pascagoula, Mississippi. During the previous year, among the 400-plus employees of that company, he had been the only one who had clocked in for work for every one of his scheduled shifts. When asked at a company banquet why he had done so, he simply replied, "I thought you were supposed to come to work."

I'm not sure of the source of this maxim, but it's one I've heard often: "Eighty percent of success in life is showing up." Over the years I've supervised enough employees to understand the veracity of that statement. I've heard hundreds of excuses for not showing up. Some are valid: "I was sick." Some are less so: "I forgot to set my alarm." But valid or invalid, they're a substitute for actual performance. The person who shows up and actually does what he or she said they would do moves ahead of the absentee and the sporadic attendee. Multiply that sort of solid, steady performance over many days, weeks, and months – and you've got a recipe for some success.

As a pastor who has worked primarily with volunteers over many years, I'm particularly impressed by those who show up to do work that isn't required of them. Every church, every charitable organization, every "cause" has regular, committed supporters who aren't there only "once in a while" and who make a point to willingly do what isn't asked. Rather, they do it because they want to. To me, that's success with a capital "S."

In the realm of Christian faith regularly showing up is termed "faithfulness." It's considered a fruit of the Spirit of God, one of nine such listed in Galatians 5:22. And moving yet deeper into God's Word, faithfulness is not simply a gift from our Creator to humans, it's a mark of the character of God Himself. Lamentations 3:23 says of God, "Great is your faithfulness." We can count on God; he's always there for us. He shows up; He's got perfect attendance to the works of his hands ever since the Creation itself.

Coincidence -- or Divine Appointment?
John 14:15-17

I needed to have my eyes examined and it had been five years since my last such exam. I was living in a different location, but positively remembered my eye doctor from previously. So even though it required me to drive 100 miles each way to see her, I scheduled an appointment – a month ahead – with that ophthalmologist.

The night before my eye appointment I received an e-mail from a friend from whom I hadn't heard in more than a year. He'd just experienced a very sudden, tragic, unexpected death in his close family – and asked for my prayers. And he lived in the city to which I was to travel the next day for my eye exam. So of course I called him up and invited him to lunch there. We wound up having a meaningful time of sharing. I was able to comfort and pray for him in person, a spiritual uplift for both of us.

What are the odds that I would already have been traveling to that man's hometown on the particular day that he most needed my personal ministry to him? Four, five, six or more factors had to line up in order for that to happen. Coincidence? Perhaps, but I personally think not.

After serving God for most of my life, I've experienced far too many such "coincidences" to ignore the possibility that God's Spirit actively guides my path in life. While I certainly don't believe in rigid determinism, there have been countless subtle, and occasionally not so subtle, "nudges" from God in my journey through this world.

There's a familiar passage of Scripture in the Old Testament where Elijah the prophet is hiding in a cave to escape the pursuit of the evil King Ahab. He needs guidance from God. Here's what Elijah experienced, as recorded in I Kings 19: "Then a great and powerful wind tore the mountains apart and shattered the rocks before the Lord, but the Lord was not in the wind. After the wind there was an earthquake, but the Lord was not in the earthquake. After the earthquake came a fire, but the Lord was not in the fire. And after the fire came a gentle whisper." And God, with the guidance Elijah needed, was in the whisper, not the cataclysms which preceded.

Perhaps God hits you upside of the head with a 2" by 4" to get your attention. That may be your personal experience. But that's rarely been mine. Instead, God's Spirit regularly directs me through subtle coincidences – gentle guidance which lets me know that while I'm responsible for my life choices, I'm not out there alone.

More Than Suggestions
Deuteronomy 5:1

I issued a challenge to the congregation present in one of my churches on a particular Sunday morning, unabashedly offering a financial reward. First, I asked those present to raise their hands if they believed in the great Ten Commandments as found in the Old Testament of the Holy Bible. Every hand in the sanctuary immediately went up. Then, I held up and offered a ten-dollar bill to anyone who could – without opening a Bible -- actually state the Ten Commandments in order. It quickly grew very quiet in that sanctuary.

After an uncomfortable fifty seconds or so of the silence, one woman tentatively raised her hand. "I think I can name them all," she said. I invited her to do so – and she proceeded to tick off all ten. However, she didn't get them in order, placing the eighth such, forbidding theft, ahead of the seventh, forbidding adultery. Nonetheless, I was duly impressed and offered her the $10 reward, which she declined.

What I did that morning wasn't new to me; I had seen another preacher do just the same thing with a congregation twenty years before – and with a very similar result. Church people typically claim to believe in the Ten Commandments, without actually knowing what they're declaring they believe in.

In the larger culture outside the church, in recent decades there have been periodic flare-ups affecting American society at large concerning the Ten Commandments and their appropriate role, or the lack thereof, in the public consciousness. Some folks want to see them prominently displayed in or on public buildings, others say such is contrary to the United States' prohibition against the establishment of religion. Heated arguments inevitably ensue. And each time that happens I think to myself, "Does either side really know what they're talking about?"

The Ten Commandments are set forth in two places in the Old Testament – Exodus 20:1-17 and Deuteronomy 5:7-21. They're very much worth believing in. And, better still, they're worth living. However, it's very hard to live what you don't know. So instead of vaguely "believing in" the "big ten," learn them. Then you'll actually know, and be able to live, God's great Ten Commandments.

The Big One That Got Away
John 21:1-7

I'm a lifelong fisherman. As a boy, my father taught me both fishing and hunting. The fishing stuck; the hunting didn't. I like to fish wherever there's water – streams, ponds, bayous, lakes, rivers, inlets, bays, oceans. And I'm definitely not a fishing "snob;" rather, I'm happy to catch whatever finds its way onto my hook or into my net. Any species, large or small, freshwater or salt; I simply enjoy fishing.

I was deep sea fishing off the coast of Honduras in Central America. While the boat I was in was trolling less than a mile offshore, the water was genuinely deep – over 700 feet. After two hours of catching nothing, my rod bent as something took the bait. Line began to rapidly spin off the reel. I grabbed the pole and pulled back. There was definitely a fish on the other end, a large fish.

For the next half hour, I struggled to catch that big fish. I would gain a little line, then lose some as the fish pulled harder. The captain of the boat employed the motor of the vessel to help tire the fish. Finally, it seemed the creature was wearing out. I could sense victory near and was looking forward to actually seeing this – perhaps the biggest fish I'd ever caught.

And then it happened. All of a sudden the line went slack, and I immediately knew the fish was gone. I reeled in the remaining line. The fish had broken 60-pound test line. So although I never really saw it, I knew for sure the fish was big. For the rest of my life I'll remember it as the big one that got away. Maybe some other fisherman will have the pleasure of catching it; I certainly hope so.

Jesus chose at least five of the closest dozen of his earliest disciples from among the ranks of fishermen. And most every Christian knows that he told them they would no longer be fishing for fish, but for human beings. The specific quote, found as Matthew 4:19 in the Holy Bible, is this: "Come, follow me," Jesus said, "and I will send you out to fish for people."

Over the decades I've served as a minister in Jesus' name, I've had the privilege of carrying out his commission to fish for people. After sharing the Gospel with them in a variety of ways, I've had the satisfying experience of seeing and hearing many dozens of men and women, boys and girls profess their faith in Jesus.

But there have also been some who, like the big fish who broke my line off the coast of Honduras, have gotten away despite my best efforts. Nonetheless I trust that God will, by His grace, send out other fishers to complete the catch, so that those too may be included in the wonderful Kingdom of God. Perhaps you will be one of those fishers. I most certainly hope so.

A Joking Fool for Jesus
Proverbs 17:22

I love to tell jokes. I've done so all my life. I'm not exactly sure how nor why I got started with joke telling, but I really do enjoy thereby giving folks a smile, a chuckle, or maybe even a laugh. I even appreciate the "groans" from those who respond to one of my puns or deliberately "dumb" jokes.

It's interesting to me that church people are usually the toughest audience for my jokes. When I first began to pursue ministry as a career I was often admonished, "Lose the jokes." Dozens of church leaders have sat me down to counsel me thus, "Being a Christian is serious business. There's no legitimate place for humor in the church, especially from a pastor." To which I usually reply with some variant of this response, "I don't ask you to take me seriously. By all means take Jesus seriously, but not me."

The church in America today is having a hard time remaining relevant to society. In a secular culture which says "yes" to virtually anything and everything, the church is regarded as a bastion of "no:" No dancing, no drinking, no sex, no fun, no joy – and most certainly no jokes. The church's secret, or maybe not so secret, motto seems to be: Remember that hell is out there just waiting for all who don't devoutly follow Jesus.

On the night in which the birth of Jesus Christ was announced to the world at ancient Bethlehem, I recall that an angel of the Lord said, "Don't be afraid. I bring you good news that will cause great joy for all people." I further recall that the apostle Paul, in his letter to the early church at Galatia, wrote that those who followed Jesus would exhibit the following qualities: love, joy, peace, patience, kindness, goodness, faithfulness, gentleness and self-control." These are nine "fruits" that the Holy Spirit of God will enable Christians to show before the world. Note that "joy" is number two thereof, second only to love alone.

While I'm very aware that "joy" is far broader and deeper than being a teller of jokes, I would dare to point out the obvious: "joy" and "joke" have the same verbal root. So while acknowledging that we live in a difficult world, I unapologetically continue not to focus upon sorrow and sadness, but upon joy – interspersed with more than a few jokes.

Lighten up, church people. To God be the glory!

Riding with the Police
Matthew 5:14-16

For three years I served as a volunteer member of the Police Oversight Board of Albuquerque, New Mexico. One of the regular duties of serving as such was to take part in "ride-alongs" with police officers. This meant that I spent eight to twelve hours, depending on the length of the particular shift, in the front passenger seat next to a uniformed, on-duty policeman on patrol. (I was never paired with a policewoman, so my personal experience was only with policemen.)

Every one of those police ride-alongs began somewhat cautiously for both me and the officer. Frankly, I was a little uneasy being in close quarters, for an entire day, with a policeman. Although, aside from a handful of traffic tickets over a lifetime of driving, I don't personally have negative experiences with police, I've heard dozens of stories of bad interactions with the police from friends, congregants, and family members. And, for his part, the officer was duly worried about being paired with a clergyman. Only one of the dozen or so officers with whom I rode was an actual churchgoer.

By the end of the shift, however, in every case I and the officer had bonded. I proved my worth to them by helping handle the several crisis situations, minor or major, with which they had to deal. And they, each and all, proved to me their worth as competent and effective law enforcement officers.

It was interesting to see these officers gradually "loosen up" during our time together. I wasn't with them to evangelize, so I deliberately tried to avoid any religious conversation. But once they had decided I was a reasonable fellow human, they were inevitably curious. What does a minister do, and why do they do it? What's the church, and what's its purpose? And eventually the conversation typically turned to personal needs. Could I offer advice to help a failing marriage? A teenage daughter was running off the rails – was there any hope for restoring her equilibrium? And so it went. You can share a lot with a person continuously sitting next to you for the better part of an entire day, especially when you have to jointly confront an amazing array of crises spread throughout that shared day.

Somewhere along the line I've heard this said, "You may be the only Bible another person ever reads." Christians are continuously being observed by the secular world; our conduct shapes others' perception of Jesus. I certainly hope that my ride-along experiences with police officers reflected positively on my Lord and Savior. And I further hope that all who read this are effective witnesses for Jesus to their non-Christian friends.

What It Takes to Be a Winner
Romans 10:9-11

We'd just completed another two-and-a-half week series of sporting competitions called the Olympics. In this particular case it was the Winter Olympics, which aren't my personal favorite. Nonetheless it was exciting to watch the fantastic feats of the skiers, snowboarders, ice skaters and dancers, and so many other winter Olympians from all over the world.

Just being invited to be an athlete at an Olympics is a testimony to one's prowess in his or her chosen sport. And for every Olympian present to represent their country, there are hundreds more whose performance, while good or even excellent, was not up to Olympic quality. They are sitting at home, watching these ultra-outstanding competitors excel at what they also love to do.

And of course, we all know that when their particular event is over, there's only one gold medalist chosen. Oh yes, there are silver and bronze awarded to the runners-up. But there are also all the other competitors who don't win anything and who must return home and, for the rest of their lives, fantasize about what might have been, but wasn't.

The frustration and heartbreak of these non-medalists is a large part of each after-event sports coverage by the many media who broadcast the Olympics. Often it seems to me that sports reporters deliberately highlight the shattered life-dreams of those who didn't win more than the victory celebrations of those who did.

Even though I honestly do enjoy watching the Olympics, there's something inside me that finds an event which produces far more losers than winners less than completely satisfying. Sure, I realize not everyone can be a world champion. But to focus your whole life, for years on end, striving toward something that ultimately eludes you -- well, that just doesn't seem right to me.

Fortunately, the Christian faith isn't at all like the Olympics. Jesus Christ has proclaimed that, in God's sight, even the worst loser in this world can be a winner. Eternal life is the "gold medal," and God offers it freely to any and all, through Jesus. By his grace, I invite you to claim that prize!

Power Outage
Luke 8:23-25

A major winter storm moved through the State of Maryland. We were, at the time, living in my former childhood home in Baltimore, preparing it for eventual sale. The electric power went off – and stayed off for what at the time seemed like an eternity.

Very soon, in just a few hours, the house grew cold. For even though we had a fuel-oil furnace, it required electricity to switch it on, and there was none. On the other end of the temperature issue, our freezer and refrigerator were no longer cooling, so the frozen food items therein began to slowly but surely thaw. And worst of all, the sump pump in the basement was no longer operating, causing our basement to fill up with water – eventually to about six inches deep.

My wife Fran and I put on several additional layers of clothing and coats and wrapped up in blankets. The outside temperature, which soon became the inside temperature as well, stayed just barely above freezing. We weren't in grave danger of hypothermia, but we were definitely cold. And we had flashlights and candles, so we weren't in total darkness, but it was gloomy even in the daytime.

We played cards, read books, and generally commiserated with each other. We had a battery-operated portable radio; thus we could listen to what was happening in the world around. But we had no spare batteries for it, so we had to carefully ration our use thereof. Our cell phones also still worked, but with no way to recharge them we had to sparingly manage how we used them, too.

Several times we almost decided to get in the car and drive through the lingering storm to find a motel which still had its power on. And Fran had relatives about 50 miles away who had power; we would be welcome with them – if we could get there. But on the other hand, we didn't want to leave our house when power might be restored at any moment – and we'd need to then immediately begin the work of restoring things to normal, especially in the flooded basement.

After 39 hours the electric power came back on. We knew it immediately as lights turned on. Within a few hours the house was back to toasty warmth. And within a few days our basement was again dry, although it took considerable work on our part to help make it so.

What's the spiritual point of this story? Simply this: Suppose the power of God suddenly went out. God's Holy Word, the Bible, tells us that the very fabric of the universe is sustained by his constant attention. If God looked away from us for even an instant, we would cease to exist. "In him we live and move, and have our being."

Living without electricity in the 21st century is both inconvenient and uncomfortable. But we can survive. Living without the power of God is both unthinkable and impossible. Praise God; may we never experience a divine power outage!

Honoring Your Parents
Matthew 15:3-6

One morning I was asked to visit with an older lady whose adult son had unexpectedly died during the night before. I went and listened, for a considerably long time, to her story. While she was obviously distraught from the loss of her son, she had additional concerns, significant fears which overrode her immediate grief.

This elderly woman had very recently moved from a distant state to live with that son, her only surviving child of an original three. Although she herself was still reasonably hale and hearty, the idea behind the move was convenience -- so the son could be present to care for her as she further aged.

But that's not how it played out. Now, suddenly, she was alone in a strange community to which she was very much a newcomer. She had no friends, no other family, no clubs, no faith community, no regular activity groups. And she wasn't really the outgoing type – especially at her advanced age she didn't know how to make new friends, create new associations.

I suggested the obvious. She should seriously consider moving back to her former location, where she had established roots and at least a potential support system. But this recent move had pretty much exhausted her financial resources, at least for the immediate time frame. Maybe she could save up from her Social Security for a couple of years. For the present, she was stuck.

Unfortunately, over my decades as a pastor I've seen variations of this same scenario play out dozens of times. Adult children convince aging mom and/or dad to move near to, or in with, them in a town far distant from the parents' familiar locale. In some families this proves to be beneficial for all concerned. But in too many others the results are more negative than positive. The adult children wind up moving elsewhere due to job changes, leaving their parent(s) alone in unfamiliar circumstances. There's a falling out within the family, or a divorce, so that living near to or, worse yet, living in the same house becomes oppressively uncomfortable for all concerned. The old folks feel isolated, pining for their lost associations and familiar contacts. Or, as happened in this case, the child predeceases the parent.

The Bible tells us clearly that we are to "honor" our parents. It's one of God's great 10 commandments. But is it "honoring" for parents to be uprooted by their children and placed in unfamiliar circumstances in old age? Every family situation is different, but experience teaches me that great care needs to be exercised on the part of both parents and children before relocating mom or dad for convenience sake.

Firing a Church Member
James 2:8-11

In one of the towns where I used to pastor, a prominent woman in the community, the one and only female vice-president of the largest local bank, was a member of my congregation. From my pastoral viewpoint she was a "middle of the road" church member – fairly regularly attending worship but not otherwise involved in the life of the church body. Early on in my ministry there, I tried several times to enlist her into involvement beyond mere worship attendance, but each time she said she was far too busy. So after a while I simply accepted her as an attendee interested in nothing more – like many other church members I've known.

One day she showed up at the church office and asked to see me. I gladly received her and, as soon as she sat down, she said, "I'm a busy person, so I'll get right to the point. We recently discovered that our bank's employee Gladys Smith (not her real name) is a...." Her voice trailed off at that moment. So I responded, "I'm sorry; what is it you want to say?" She stammered, hesitated, then finally stated what she had planned to say. "Gladys Smith is a lesbian. As soon as we found this out we fired her from her job at the bank. I want you to know this, because you'll obviously want to fire her from the church too."

All this happened quite a few years ago, before "sexual orientation" became a non-discrimination category in employment. But what really threw me in this woman's disclosure to me was neither Gladys' supposed homosexuality nor her losing her job at the bank. Rather, Gladys was simply another member of the church, exactly like the woman speaking to me. She wasn't an employee. So from a church point of view the idea of "firing" her was completely ludicrous.

Churches don't "hire" and "fire" members. The church is a voluntary association. Members come and go as they please, not as the pastor pleases. Yes, I realize there are some churches which can, in theory at least, involuntarily "dis-fellowship" or "excommunicate" a lay member, but such is very rare. And it's nonexistent in my brand of church.

Since this bank VP was so completely out-of-touch with reality on this subject, I purposely avoided getting involved in an argument with her. I simply thanked her for the information she'd shared, told her I realized how busy she was, then sent her on her way. And I very deliberately "forgot" what she wanted me to do.

Three or four years later, after I had moved on to another church assignment, I discovered that this prominent bank official had been indicted for fraud by the U. S. government. After a plea deal, she wound up sentenced to six years in a federal prison and paid over a million dollars in fines and restitution. I guess she wasn't a perfect person herself.

Secrets
Luke 8:9-10

I grew up in a family which had a lot of "secrets." For example, one of my aunts birthed a child out of wedlock. That was supposed to be a secret, not to be shared with anyone outside the family. Frankly, it wasn't much of a secret. I think half the community knew the situation, and the other half didn't particularly care to know or not know.

Two family secrets which impacted me personally were the fact that my "uncle" Bob, who lived next door to us while I was a child, was actually my half-brother. I was deliberately misled about this relationship until I was in my 20's and discovered the truth. And even stranger was the fact that I had yet another half-brother, Ron, whose existence was deliberately hidden from me until I was 60 years of age. After I found out, I asked several cousins if they knew about Ron, and they said, "Yes, but your parents instructed us not to tell you, so we never did." That family secret prevented Ron and me from enjoying each other's brotherly friendship for six decades.

In the Christian Gospels, especially the book of Mark, there is a recurrent "secret." On more than one occasion when Jesus miraculously healed someone from a disease and the person healed therefore recognized that he was God incarnate, he instructed them not to say anything to anyone about his identity. Several times while Jesus was teaching his disciples the truths of God and they thereby understood him to be the Messiah, they wanted to immediately share that glorious knowledge with the world. But Jesus said, in effect, "No, keep it a secret, at least for now." More than once, Jesus even instructed demons which he had cast out not to share that he was God's Son. Theologians have termed this the "Messianic secret."

Why did Jesus want His true identity kept secret? Why didn't he want the world to know that he really was the Son of God? If you read the Gospels carefully enough, you'll see that early on in his three-year ministry, Jesus always asked for secrecy about himself. But as his time on earth drew toward what he knew to be its God-ordained end, he gradually ceased requesting silence and secrecy. Perhaps if the truth about who Jesus was had been circulated prematurely, he might have been arrested and killed too soon, before he had fully accomplished his purposes while on earth.

Christians today aren't required to keep Jesus' identity a secret. Instead, we are instructed, by Jesus himself, to tell the world. There's no need to hide the truth: Jesus really is the Son of God!

A Wandering Aramean
I John 2:15-17

Over our lifetimes thus far, including the four decades that we served in itinerant ministry, my wife and I have lived in a total of 17 different locations and in 21 different houses. Thus one of the odd categories of expertise we've developed is the ability to rapidly evaluate the "livability" of a given house. We can quickly tell, for example, whether or not a bathroom – be it fancy or plain – is laid out in such a way as to actually allow someone to get clean therein. Just a glance gives Fran a sense of whether or not a particular kitchen lends itself to easy meal preparation. Will a bedroom closet allow enough clothing to be hung therein? We can immediately tell. And so forth.

Other than perhaps assisting prospective home buyers in their evaluation of possible purchases, I'm not sure that our acquired ability in this arena has practical value. I suspect that overzealous real estate agents would hate to deal with us, as we could quickly deflate their claims concerning any given property's attractiveness.

Most everyone has heard the proverb, "a house is not a home." It's something we've tried to live by as we've moved from town to town and house to house throughout our lives. Home is wherever we are – for whatever length of time. While I understand the reluctance to move on the part of folks who have stayed in a particular house for several decades, I don't share it. When it's time to move, I say take the memories with you – and go.

One of the things I admire about the distinctively Jewish portion of Judeo-Christian tradition is the understanding of one's self as part of a "pilgrim people." In the recitations of standard Jewish prayers this phrase from Deuteronomy 26:5 is featured, "My father was a wandering Aramean…" The reference is to Abraham, the first man of notable faith in God. Abraham trusted that God would provide for him whenever and wherever he was sent by the Almighty. And God repeatedly uprooted Abraham's household, even during his old age.

Remember, people of God – nowhere in this world is ultimately our home. We must live in the world, yes. And we must ever strive to love this world's people, yes. But don't get too comfortable in whatever circumstances you may find yourself. Sooner or later, God is going to move you.

False Alarms
Matthew 24:5-6

The Trustees in charge of caring for the buildings of St. Mark's Church which I pastored in El Paso, Texas signed up with a security company. Company personnel came and installed alarms on all the doors and windows of that church's several buildings. If someone entered a building, they had just 90 seconds in which to enter a code on the keypad located nearest the door, or the alarm would go off. Likewise, they had to enter the code when exiting, lest the alarm be tripped. In addition to making a loud racket in the building itself, the security company monitoring the system would be notified, they in turn would immediately notify the police, who would then dispatch officers to check on the situation.

Unfortunately, although we made sure all of the church's staff as well as many of the lay leadership were provided with the proper code, quite a few of them failed to properly use it when entering and/or exiting one of the buildings. Thus we experienced a large number of false alarms in the initial several months after we acquired the alarm system.

Five months into our having this security system, I and the chair of the church's Trustees were summoned to the office of the Assistant Chief of Police of El Paso. His officers, he reported, had already been dispatched a total of 31 times to the church in response to alarms. Every one of them had proven false. If this kind of situation persisted, the El Paso Police were preparing to bill our church $150 per future false alarm call to which they were forced to respond.

With that financial penalty hanging over their heads, St. Mark's Trustees quickly met and, although the alarm company was owned by a church member who was actually providing the service to us for free, decided to shut it off. The frequent false alarms were too much of a worry to be worthwhile.

As a Christian pastor, I've regularly, indeed almost constantly, had to deal with another kind of "false alarm" throughout my four decades of service to Christ and his church. There are always fresh rumors that the "end times" foretold in the Bible are upon us and God's "final judgment" is but days away. Inevitably, a handful of members of the churches I've served buy into the latest such scenario, and try to convince me and the rest of the church to scurry around and "get ready" for Christ's imminent return.

My response to these alarmists is always the same. "I am already ready," I say, "for our Lord anytime he chooses to wrap things up." The best, indeed the only, preparation necessary is to believe in Jesus. You don't have to do anything differently. Simply trust Christ, and let him bring you through the end, whenever it may come – for you or for our entire world.

Too Much of Good Things
Mark 6:30-35

My wife and I were invited to three-in-a-row charity auctions. Friday night's was for a worthy children's charity. Saturday night's was for another worthy children's charity. And Sunday afternoon's was for – you guessed it – yet another worthy children's charity.

We went to the Friday evening event, and it was a lot of both fun and excitement for us. We attended the Saturday evening event, and found it enjoyable but tiring. But by the time Sunday afternoon came around we said to one another, "Let's pass on this one. We need some rest."

In the medium-sized city in which we currently live, Albuquerque, New Mexico, there are some 400 locally-based charities. And there are thousands more national and international charities with local affiliates. Most, if not all, of these seek to meaningfully address legitimate human needs.

People who are open to helping others are, and probably always have been, in short supply. So it is that the few who are willing are repeatedly solicited for their aid. And eventually, their enthusiasm and energy drained, they simply have to say "no" to the next request, no matter how legitimate it may be.

Jesus, when He lived as a man among humans, experienced this very dilemma. As soon as folks became aware of his remarkable abilities to help and heal others, plus his obvious willingness to do so, he was besieged. After only a few weeks in ministry, his disciples reported that he couldn't even approach a town without virtually everyone therein seeking his aid. And give aid he did, until he was both physically and emotionally drained.

For a while Jesus was able to extricate himself from the crowds of aid-seekers by withdrawing to the countryside – the "wilderness" as the Bible terms it – for rest and recuperation, both physical and spiritual. But eventually the thousands seeking his help began following him even into the open country. That's how we got the Sermon on the Mount and the several accounts of the miraculous feeding of 4,000 and even 5,000 people recorded in the New Testament.

As I run low on energy from being solicited too often by too many needs and good causes, I simply have to "ration" my involvements. I wind up picking and choosing, sometimes ignoring precious persons and important issues I really care about – but lack the time and stamina to pursue.

As the Son of God, Jesus probably had deeper energy reserves than anyone else – certainly far greater than mine. Frankly, I don't know how Jesus managed to never turn away a needy human being. But I'm very glad he didn't.

How about you? Are you open to helping those in need – at least to the extent of your reasonable human ability? Helpers are in short supply. Please try to be one.

A Jokester Preacher?
Proverbs 17:22

I was born on April 1st. That makes me an "April fool." As a child I was often the butt of jokes, usually around the time of my birthday. For one example of this, when I was in the ninth grade my birthday fell on a weekday during the school term. A friend of mine who had a pool table in his basement invited me to come home with him after school that day. At his house we started down the steps into the basement, someone flipped on the lights, and there were forty or fifty of my friends and classmates gathered below. They all yelled "Surprise!" and then immediately left. That's the sort of thing which regularly happens when you're an April fool.

Once I grew up I decided to turn things around. Instead of always being the butt of jokes, I became the quintessential teller of jokes. At this point in my life I have jokes for every theme and every occasion. Folks are regularly amazed that I can recall so many jokes. I don't know how many jokes I actually know, but it's definitely, without embellishment, in the thousands. Every once in a while, someone suggests that I switch to "stand-up comedy" for a career. I always respond, "Thanks, but I think I'd best keep my day job."

My "day job," which is also my calling by God, is as a minister of the Gospel of Jesus Christ. That naturally involves regular preaching. Not every sermon I preach has a joke therein, but most of them do. Many of my messages are "bookended" by jokes – one at the beginning and one at the close.

Some people appreciate my regular use of humor in sermons, some don't. But one of the most interesting aspects of that is, now that I'm retired, when I occasionally go back to churches I've served and regularly hear, "I didn't appreciate your jokes when you were our pastor, but now that you're gone, I miss them."

There are yet some folks out there who continue to challenge me thus: "How can you be both a jokester and a preacher? Preachers are supposed to be serious, but I can't take you seriously." My regular response is this: "I don't ask that you take me seriously. But please take Jesus very seriously."

Uncle Ralph
Acts 16:14-15

My wife's Uncle Ralph was an interesting figure throughout much of my married life. He was a man of many sides, having spent his early life in the Atlantic City area of New Jersey during the era of alcohol prohibition and the resultant "bootlegging" industry that it spawned. During the Second World War he worked in the shipyards of Baltimore. Still later he moved to Emmitsburg, Maryland where he raised his family, owned several businesses, and even became the town's mayor.

Although his family around him were nearly all faithful Christians, Uncle Ralph somehow missed out on that part of life. He wasn't anti-religion; he just managed to sidestep it. When everyone else in the household was getting ready to head out for church on Sundays, he'd wish them well. If someone specifically invited him along, he'd typically say, "Thanks, but not today." Once in a great while he'd actually go, but only to satisfy others.

Although he was more than a generation older, Uncle Ralph and I developed something of a special friendship over the years. I enjoyed hearing his many colorful stories. And he was quite open to my lightly sharing a bit of the gospel with him, although he wouldn't allow the discussion to proceed very far.

Uncle Ralph had one minor "vice" that I helped indulge. He smoked cigars – but just one and only one per day, which I didn't consider a significant health hazard. Since I traveled to a number of other countries on mission journeys, Uncle Ralph would ask me to bring him souvenir cigars from wherever I had been. Twice I went to Cuba, which is considered the pinnacle of cigar production quality among those who care about such. When I brought him Cuban cigars after those two trips, he was ecstatic.

As Uncle Ralph neared 95 years of age, both he and I sensed that his time on earth was drawing to a close. So I began regularly pressing him just a little harder about accepting Christ as personal Savior. Eventually he said, "OK, I'm ready. Let's do it."

Thus one Easter afternoon I baptized Uncle Ralph, with his family gathered around, in his son's home. He publicly professed his faith in Jesus Christ. Everyone was pleased and excited for him. And I'm quite sure there was rejoicing in Heaven as well.

Less than a year later I conducted Uncle Ralph's funeral. It was an especially joyous occasion for me, for I knew for certain that he had moved on to be with Jesus in God's Kingdom. So far at least, Uncle Ralph – at 95 – is the oldest person I've had the privilege and pleasure of helping lead to Jesus Christ.

It's never too late, folks. If you haven't yet accepted Christ, today could be your day of beginning a life of faith in him. Please seriously consider it; it's the most important decision you'll ever make.

An Unusual Easter Worship
Psalm 28:6-8

It was Easter Sunday morning. The 11 AM worship service was packed. All the various elements of Christian worship unfolded flawlessly – especially the music. While searching for a new paid staff person, our volunteer fill-in choir director, a long-time member of the congregation, had taken his job very seriously, practicing the chancel choir long and hard on several magnificent numbers which they then performed flawlessly. Their last of three anthems drew a long and heartfelt round of applause.

As I stepped up to the pulpit to preach I glanced at my watch. 11:58 AM. Really? Yes, all the other elements of worship had taken up virtually the entire hour allocated. I was confronted by a dilemma which, in thirty-plus years of pastoring, I'd not faced before.

I'm a preacher. It's what God called me to do. While holding the title of "pastor" I was called upon to teach, counsel, administer, and a myriad of other tasks and duties involved in directing the life of a Christian church. But my basic gift – my calling by God – was and is to preach the Gospel of Jesus Christ.

For Easter Sunday I'd done my very best to fully prepare for the most excellent annual opportunity to do just that. My sermon was ready and waiting, a carefully polished silver bullet honed by a fresh infusion of the wonderful Resurrection of Jesus. But at 11:58 that morning, as I stepped up to preach, I felt one of those nudges from God which even a preacher champing at the bit to let loose couldn't ignore: "Don't. Save it for another time and opportunity."

So I simply said to the gathered, full sanctuary: "Folks, it's 11:58 AM. You've heard the Resurrection gospel beautifully sung. The Word of God has been read. We've prayed together with 'Alleluias' and 'Amens' galore on this glorious Easter morning. I believe that's sufficient. And now let's receive the benediction." With that, I dismissed the congregation.

On the way out perhaps a total of five people complained to me about the lack of preaching. Two said, "You should have preached, even if it meant running over half an hour." But the vast majority commended me for the wisdom of foregoing the sermon. Most agreed that they had already clearly heard the Gospel through the other elements of worship that morning.

That was a once-in-a-career preaching experience, or the absence thereof, for me. I don't ask that it ever be repeated, for I still believe that preaching the Gospel of Jesus Christ is my primary life-calling. But said or sung or preached, I hope that you clearly hear the Gospel – and respond by making Jesus your personal Savior and Lord.

God of Many Second Chances
Isaiah 38:1-6

Back when I lived in Baltimore, Maryland, there was a local business that sold building materials salvaged from other structures which had been torn down. This business had several acres of old warehouses containing a vast treasure trove of such. (I'm not trying to promote this particular firm; I honestly don't know if it still exists or not.) The name of the business was "Second Chance."

This wasn't a unique enterprise, of course. "Habitat for Humanity" has dozens of "Habitat ReStore" locations spread across our nation which offer the same sort of merchandise. What intrigued me with this particular business was its personnel. Everyone who worked there, and there were dozens, was a convicted felon who had served their time for a crime or crimes, and was now working to earn a living and thereby help get their life back on track. Hence the "Second Chance" nomenclature, appropriate not only for the building materials it sold, but for the men and women who labored there.

It's virtually unquestionable that our society does not treat those who have committed a crime with even a grain of compassion nor forgiveness. Rather, it's all about punishment. Once convicted they are marked for life. Their actual prison term may encompass a year or a decade or more, but they are never really released. Post-incarceration jobs are almost impossible to find. Employers shy away as though their past mistakes were a catchable plague.

Suppose the Apostles Peter, John and Paul, or even our Lord and Savior Jesus – were to include their arrest history on an employment application today? They wouldn't stand a chance of being hired. And if they didn't list it up front, a standard criminal background check would quickly winnow them out.

Fortunately, our God is very unlike the American criminal justice system. God offers a second chance – and a third, and a fourth – and many more beyond. Jesus was once asked about the limits of forgiveness: How many times should a sinner be forgiven? His reply – literally 490 times – was intended not to set a high numeric limit, but to imply that forgiveness be limitless.

I'm very glad God offers second chances – and more besides. Because I often need them. And whether you think so or not, you do too. We all do. And thank God, they're readily available!

Darkness and Light
Psalm 18:28

One of the two houses in which I remember spending a substantial portion of my childhood was located on the Gulf Coast of Mississippi. Naturally, being located in a warm, wet climate, that house was plagued by bugs – insects of various kinds. We had screens to keep out most of the pesky mosquitoes. But we had little or no defense against the ubiquitous "creepy-crawlies" of that area – the most numerous of which were cockroaches.

All my life I've gotten up once or twice each night to make a quick visit to the bathroom. And when I did that in our Mississippi house, I often heard a crunching sound under my bare feet as they crushed roaches which failed to get out of the way.

Obviously, I really didn't want to look at what was happening on the floor beneath me. But once in a while I would bravely flip on the light switch and observe dozens of those roaches scurry for the walls. Somehow or other they would always find tiny spaces between the boards through which to disappear. In only a moment the floor was clear. Roaches hate light; darkness is their preferred environment.

Genesis 1, verses 3 and 4, says this: "God said, 'Let there be light,' and there was light. God saw that the light was good, and he separated the light from the darkness." In referring to Jesus, John 1, verses 4 and 5, reads, "In him was life, and that life was the light of all mankind. The light shines in the darkness, and the darkness has not overcome it."

The engineer/scientist in me understands that neither physical light nor darkness are intrinsically good or bad. But the theologian/pastor also recognizes that from a spiritual standpoint light is good, while darkness is not. Much like the cockroaches which infested my childhood home in Mississippi, evil thrives in darkness. But when the light of God, most clearly represented in Jesus Christ, shines forth, evil scurries away – disappearing into the cracks and crevices, the shadows of this world.

At this point in my life I'm glad to be living in a house where cockroaches aren't an issue. And I'm very glad to have the light of Jesus Christ in my life, overcoming the spiritual darkness of this world. I wish the same for you on both counts.

Strange – and Strained – Relationships
Mark 14:66-72

Over the course of a lifetime I've had several relatives with whom contact is, to say it the clearest way I know how, episodic. One cousin in particular, who is near to my own age and was a close friend during our mutual childhood, is a classic example of this. Throughout our adult lives she has come and gone, come and gone, into and out of my life probably a total of six times thus far.

I won't hear from her at all for five, six, maybe as long as seven years. She doesn't respond to cards, e-mails, telephone calls, nor texts. I begin to wonder if she's still alive. Then all of a sudden, out of the blue, she reinitiates contact. She glosses over her years of silence by saying, "I've been busy." Then she calls, writes, etc. almost every week. She wants to know everything about me and to share everything with me about her. So I respond, valiantly trying to keep up with her frequent communications and queries.

This typically lasts for a year, maybe two. Then one day it summarily stops. No reason, no explanation. Totally unresponsive silence. I naturally wonder if I've said or done something to upset her. The communications blackout continues for years. And then one day she unexpectedly opens up again. So it continues in almost cyclical fashion.

This odd pattern of behavior is similar, but not identical, to the rocky, uneven relationship between two brothers of Old Testament Biblical import, Esau and Jacob. Throughout their lives these twins vacillated between closeness and distance with one another – between love and hate, respect and disdain, intimacy and aloofness. The story of their strange relationship, found in Genesis chapters 25 through 33, is one of ups and downs, ins and outs, alliance and enmity.

Jacob became the ancestor of the Israelite people, the Jews. And Esau was the progenitor of at least one segment of the Arab population. Considering their sources, it's no small wonder that Jews and Arabs are caught up in difficult, ever-shifting relationships of friendship and strife to this very day. Read the story of Jacob and Esau in the Bible; it may provide you fresh insight into contemporary geopolitical realities.

Not Taking 'No' for an Answer
Romans 2:7

A severe hailstorm swept over the neighborhood where I live. My house didn't experience any obvious and immediate consequences, like broken windows or torn-off roof shingles. But a visual survey of the roof made it clear that its post-storm condition wasn't as it had been before. There were "pock marks," some pretty deep, all over the roof surfaces. So I called my insurance company, to which I was paying for hail-damage coverage, and asked that they send someone to inspect my roof.

As it turned out, my entire neighborhood had been impacted by this storm, so everyone around me was likewise calling their insurances. Many, many roofs for blocks in all directions around were repaired or replaced. Local roofing companies did a brisk business for months afterward near my location.

After my requests had been ignored and delayed for months on end, I finally convinced my insurance company to actually send out an adjuster. He climbed up on my roof and, ten minutes later, came back down to tell me it had experienced no real damage and, therefore, I had no basis for an insurance claim.

I might have left it at that, but my adult son, who is an attorney, wasn't satisfied. He explained to me that, in his professional experience, it was more or less "standard operating procedure" for an insurance company to say "no" to a claim the first time. Those claims which were pursued a second, or perhaps even a third, time were more likely to be approved.

He even knew a different adjuster who would come out and inspect the roof. She did so, spending more than an hour up there. She took quite a few pictures which clearly documented the damage. We filed those with the insurance company and, within weeks, received a fair settlement for the claim. The roof was repaired, and all was well.

Jesus told two interesting stories, the first found in Luke 8 and the second in Luke 11, about the value and importance of persistence. The first concerned a woman who demanded justice from a judge who ignored her until she eventually wore him down. The second was of a man who went to a friend's house, late at night, asking for a loaf of bread to help feed his unexpected guests. The request was initially denied, but the man kept on knocking – until his friend finally got up from bed and provided what he was asking for.

Don't give up too easily, people of God. Sometimes, in this fallen world, persistence is necessary. "No" can be changed to "yes" -- if you continue to try.

Don't Go Alone!
Romans 10:14-15

While planning for one upcoming year's mission trip that I was to lead, one of the men who was planning to accompany me, and who lives in El Paso, Texas, sent me an e-mail asking a couple of questions. As a postscript to that e-letter, he said, "By the way, Ryan Smith says to say hello to you. He's an active leader in our congregation here."

I've changed his name in this story, but 20-plus years previously Ryan Smith was a member of the youth group of the church I was then serving in El Paso. He was an intelligent and inquisitive young man, always asking those "tough" questions that can't possibly be addressed with simple, one-sentence answers. Many were the times when Ryan sat in my office for over an hour plying me with queries that caused me to do both a lot of research and much personal soul-searching.

About a year after I first got to know him, Ryan decided that he was ready to profess personal faith in Jesus Christ and join the Church. I was pleased to have had a role in helping to lead him toward that all-important decision, a decision with wonderful, eternal consequences.

Frankly, I'd forgotten about Ryan during the intervening years, but it was a renewed pleasure to learn that he was still involved in a church of Jesus Christ. He's in a different congregation than the one I used to serve in El Paso, but that's unimportant. He's still an active Christian – and that's a blessing indeed.

I believe it was the Rev. Billy Graham who said these words, "For a Christian, the next worst thing to not going to heaven at all is to go to heaven alone." What he meant by that remark is that every believer in Jesus Christ bears the responsibility of leading others to belief in Jesus. Sadly, the vast majority of Christians never help win anyone else to faith in Christ. This is true primarily because they don't even try.

When I get to heaven, it will be exciting to meet those I've helped to lead to faith in Christ, both the ones I remember and the ones I don't. Christians, how about you? Who will accompany you through those pearly gates? Surely you don't want to enter heaven alone!

Stars – Earthly and Cosmic
Psalm 8

When I was a child the United States of America consisted of 48 states. There had been that many parts and portions to the country for more than two generations, going all the way back to 1912 when Arizona was the final prior addition.

That changed in 1959. In that year Alaska and Hawaii were added to the nation, making a total of fifty states – a number which continues into the present day. Few people recall this detail, however: There was a brief period, from January to August 1959, when the USA consisted of 49 states. Alaska became a state early that year, then Hawaii in the late summer of the same year.

Because it was known in advance that both of these then-territories were slated to become states in rapid succession, relatively few United States flags were produced which had 49 stars in their display field. I don't clearly recall who gave it to me – I think it was one of my great-aunts – but I happened, as a pre-teen, to acquire one of those short-lived flags with 49 stars.

For two decades I owned that somewhat unusual flag, but while living in Atlanta, Georgia I lost it to a break-in and burglary. I'm sorry that I no longer have this odd piece of US history as a keepsake. Forty-nine star flags have become minor collectibles by now, and they're available – not too expensively – on the internet. Notwithstanding, I miss mine.

In the 21st century AD, we realize that the stars in a US flag, representing states in an earthly nation, are merely infinitesimal specks in the vastness of God's creation. We're now aware that the universe is limitless, and the number of stars therein uncountable. Several millennia ago, however, when humans still mistakenly thought that their land, their nation, their world was the center of everything, God revealed Himself to a man of his own choosing named Abraham. He then invited Abraham to venture outside and gaze at the night sky in its vastness.

While Abraham was thus focused upon the "big picture" of the creation, God told him this: "I will make your descendants as numerous as the stars in the sky and will give them all these lands, and through your offspring all nations on earth will be blessed." Even though humanity, with its territories and states and inflated self-importance, isn't much in the natural scheme of things, God has chosen us for special attention. That's why Jesus came to earth. And that's why we need to worship him.

Calluses on Our Ears
2 Samuel 6:20

While I was a teenager I was given an inexpensive guitar which I gradually learned to play. I never advanced very far, but eventually could manage to strum three or four chords in a couple of keys. I also learned the value of a "capo" for switching keys, which rendered me a bit lazy toward learning additional new chords. (Later, as a young adult, I tried taking classical guitar lessons – but that's a different story.)

One of the obvious things every guitar player realizes, early on, is that you have to develop calluses on your fingers and thumb. Guitar strings are sharp metal; picking and strumming them hurts soft skin. So you have to play frequently and practice playing enough that your fingers develop hard spots where they meet the strings. Those are calluses, and they're very necessary to keep guitar playing from being overly painful. You can lessen the stress on your fingers by switching to nylon strings, but some callusing is still needed.

Also as a teenager I learned the street vocabulary of the inner city of Baltimore, which included a ton of swearing, vulgarities and obscenities. My parents employed much the same coarse language in our home, so I wasn't directed away from this crude vocabulary.

When I became a Christian as a young adult I gradually learned that the trashy words of the streets weren't acceptable in the Church of Jesus Christ. Thankfully I had several mentors and caring companions who helped me to clean up my language over a period of several years. By the time God called me into the ministry, I had a less offensive vocabulary – which is rather necessary for a pastor. I still backslide verbally once in a while, but not often.

Unfortunately, I'm discovering that my teenage language of the streets is gradually permeating the whole of our society today – including the church. The so-called "adult language" of television and movies is becoming standard fare everywhere. And frankly, I find myself becoming desensitized to it. It's as though my hearing is developing calluses. It no longer causes me to wince to hear a string of cursing and vulgarities. I know that shouldn't be happening, but it's hard to withstand the continuous onslaught of linguistic nastiness that regularly grates on my eardrums.

Ephesians 5:4 says that obscenity and coarse joking are "out of place" among Christians. I agree, but also realize that I'm swimming against a huge cultural tide. Christians, we not only need to clean up our actions, but our words as well -- so we don't develop calluses on our ears.

Morality Without God?
Matthew 23:23

As the veneer of Christianity increasingly disappears from contemporary society, I see leaders of the secular world valiantly attempting to establish a basis for morality that doesn't require God. In other words, since everyone automatically knows that murder is wrong, we don't need God to tell us, "Thou shalt not kill." Rather, we can figure that out for ourselves. Taking someone else's possessions is obviously bad behavior, so there's no need to be told, "Thou shalt not steal." On the other hand, helping the poor and disenfranchised is universally recognized as good, so we shouldn't require Jesus to tell us so. "Non-theistic ethics" are a purported wave of the future.

Unfortunately, not everyone in this world agrees. Some folks lack any moral compass whatever. So if someone else gets in their way, they simply kill them. From their viewpoint it's no big deal. You have a car and I don't. So I take yours. What's wrong with that? On a mass scale, there are actually global movements in our world which purport that hate, rather than love, is the ultimate "good." Thus without an absolute standard – God – everything else is relativized. And our world becomes increasingly lawless and chaotic.

Actually, all of the above is not a new phenomenon. It was tried – and found wanting – more than three millennia ago. The Bible records a 400-year span of Middle-Eastern history during which people tried to set their own moral standards without reference to God. It's recorded in the Book of Judges, which sums itself up by repeatedly saying, "in those days every man did what was right in his own eyes." You can look this up in Judges 17, 18, 19, 21 and other places in that book.

Assuming we don't want this world turned both inside out and upside down in moral terms, we need to reinstate God in his rightful place – as the absolute "gold standard" for such. Only when we measure our conduct against God's norms, and not our own, will we truly understand genuine right and wrong.

Blessings
Acts 15:32-33

For most of my life, going back at least four decades, I've employed the term "Blessings!" in saying "farewell" or "goodbye" to someone else. Most often it's accepted as simply that – a way of ending time together with someone else. But occasionally someone will ask me, "Why do you always say 'Blessings!' when finishing up a visit?"

Much of the time I simply respond with, "It's just my way of saying, 'I wish you a good day.'" However, some folks aren't satisfied with that explanation and ask further about the meaning of "blessings." More than a few non-religious people are concerned that I'm somehow inserting God into an otherwise worldly conversation. And even a handful of Christians have questioned me as to whether I, a human being, should be attempting to offer "blessings" to anyone else. They believe that "blessings" are exclusively God's province.

To fellow-believers who question the appropriateness of a human being offering "blessings" to another, I can respond thus: While it's certainly true that the ultimate source of blessings and goodness is God from the time of Creation itself, it's also true that God's people have long offered blessings to both one another as well as to those in the world at large. Biblically, the first time that blessings were offered by men and women to one another appears to be when Rebekah was leaving her family to become the wife of Abraham's son Isaac way back in Genesis 24. After that first notation, there are dozens more examples in the Bible of people offering blessings to other people throughout the Bible, both in the Old and New Testaments. So it's definitely Bible-approved.

As for those few secular people who don't like me extending "blessings" to them, I usually respond by saying, "Would you prefer that I leave you by saying, 'curses' instead? I mean, if my offering you 'blessings' is silly and meaningless, so is 'curses,' right?" That usually ends the discussion – and maybe even leaves them with something to think about.

Long ago I was told by a Jewish rabbi friend, now deceased, that I should offer my blessings to others at least nine times daily. That was probably the start of my regular use of "blessings" as a farewell word. I don't know if this was just that particular rabbi's personal custom or something more pervasive in Hebrew tradition. But either way it's a good thing. Blessings to you all – and I invite you to pass them on!

You Can Go Home Again
James 1:16-18

Change, of course, is a given in the world today. With the pace of change inexorably accelerating, if you leave a particular place and come back as soon as six months later, it may neither look nor feel like the same place. Hence the oft-applied truism: "You can't go home again."

Immediately following our wedding in 1971, my wife and I left a suburb of Baltimore, Maryland where we had both spent a number of our childhood years, relocating 2/3 of the way across the North American continent to Albuquerque, New Mexico. Much later, upon the deaths of my parents, I inherited my family home of five generations back in that old locale. Still later, when I retired in 2011 with a total of forty years having passed, we moved back into my childhood home in suburban Baltimore in order to ready the property for eventual sale.

After four decades of absence we didn't expect to find much that was familiar. Amazingly, we were surprised to discover that wasn't the case. In that particular neighborhood it often seemed that time had stopped. Friends and neighbors had aged, of course, but many of them were yet in their old familiar places. Businesses we had patronized as teenagers were open and operating. One particular incident that seemed almost surreal was when we were eating dinner in an old, family-owned restaurant and were greeted by the owner, who was in his 90's. Decades before he had regularly walked around the place nightly to greet customers – and he was still doing exactly that.

At my wife's behest we began regularly attending the church in which our wedding had taken place. Many of the names and faces were new and different, but a significant percentage of them were the same – or at least the next generation of familiar families. The sanctuary looked and felt unchanged, as did the downstairs fellowship hall. They were recognizable and almost instantly comfortable for us. We were "home again."

I'm not one who prefers to resist change by majoring in nostalgia. But once in a while it's nice to experience sameness and familiarity, or at the very least to have a solid anchor for our lives in the midst of prevailing winds of change. For Christians, Hebrews 13:8 promises this: "Jesus Christ is the same yesterday, and today, and forever." With Christ, you really can go home again, and again, and again.

Behemoths and Leviathans – and God
Isaiah 41:10

Each year the movie industry can be counted upon to present new and different monsters, all of them bigger, nastier, and scarier than the year before. They may be monsters arriving from other parts of the galaxy, monsters emerging from under the earth's surface, monsters created by scientists' experiments gone bad – their possible sources and origins are part of the creative process for cinematic authors and producers.

From childhood onward it seems that many people actually enjoy being frightened by monsters, especially when they know in advance there's no actual danger involved. Something in our human nature says, "Come on – try to scare me!"

Interestingly, the Old Testament of the Bible contains two categories of monsters, one of them land-based and the other aquatic. The land-dwelling monsters were called "behemoths." They're not described in much detail, beyond the simple attribute of being big and scary. Although they were considered vegetarians – see Job 40 – you certainly didn't want to get in their way. Perhaps they're actually rhinoceroses or maybe hippopotamuses; the ancient Hebrew people had only limited knowledge of these large African animals.

In the water were even scarier creatures, which the Bible calls "leviathan." It's not clear whether there were multiple such monsters or just a single particularly nasty one. But the Jews back then, most of whom had little experience with the sea, were very afraid of these creatures. They were classic sea serpents -- giant snakes, as described in Isaiah 27:1. Many who dared to sail the seas claimed to have seen them, some even believed their shipwrecks had been caused by such.

Personally, while I can appreciate a scary story or even an occasional monster movie, I most certainly don't desire to live a life of constant fear. And the very good news, found throughout God's Word but most clearly expressed in the overwhelming love of Jesus for humanity, is that God doesn't desire us to live in fear, either. While an occasional reminder of the Old Testament "fear of God" may be useful, that's not the primary way by which God wants to relate to us.

I John 4:18 says it better than I possibly could: "There is no fear in love. But perfect love drives out fear, because fear has to do with punishment. The one who fears is not made perfect in love." Don't be afraid, people of God. There really aren't any big, scary monsters out there. Rather, the love of God, made perfect in Jesus Christ, is ever ready to embrace you.

Two Kinds of Tithes
Malachi 3:8-10

I regularly receive a monthly statement from my bank. With a minimum of effort, I can use it to re-construct where most of my financial resources went over the past month. That in turn tells me where I place financial value in my life. For example, the largest monthly outflow from my account goes to pay the mortgage on the house. Keeping a roof over my head is obviously a high personal priority.

Another interesting record of my life, also organized in monthly fashion, is the calendar I maintain. For many years this was a paper document, but more than a decade ago I entered the modern era. Now my calendar is resident, along with a lot of other personal information, on my "smart" phone. When I choose to look back at the prior month, it's quite easy to review where I've spent my time and with whom.

This is not a new thought with me, but it's one that is definitely worthy of serious consideration: For contemporary people in "western" society the bank statement and the calendar, considered together, say a great deal about our personal values. Together they reveal how we expend two of our most precious resources: time and money.

God's Word, the Bible, admonishes us to return to God, as "rent" for life itself, a tenth of whatever we've received. It's called the "tithe," and it's been around for at least three millennia. Abraham, the first notable man of faith in God, rendered a tithe of his substance – back then crops and livestock – to God's representative, a priest named Melchizedek, way back in Genesis 14.

Ever since then, there's been argument among those who follow God about what really constitutes a tithe. Jesus got involved in this ongoing debate while disputing with a group of the religious leaders of his day, called Pharisees. Tithing controversy still rages today.

Interestingly to me, however, is that the major portion of "tithe" arguments concern the substantive side – for us, that's money. But I seldom hear mention, and very rarely equal emphasis, upon the temporal side of tithing. In other words, how much of the time we've been given do we actually return to God?

There are 168 hours in every week. A tithe of those would be about 17 hours. Let's see – I go to church on Sundays. That's an hour, maybe two. I read the Bible daily – for maybe 30 minutes. I pray several times daily – perhaps another 30 minutes' total. Sometimes I help sort food for the hungry at the local food bank – that's another two hours. What else? 17 hours every week? Wow, that's a lot!

How about you? Does God regularly receive a tithe of the resources placed in your care, both money and time?

Superlative God
Revelation 4:8

We live in a world of superlatives, both positive and negative. Here are a few examples: A generation ago, if a sports team defeated another in competition, they won and the other team lost. But that's not enough today. Winners "annihilate" the opposition; losers are "sent packing." In the world of politics, it's much the same. If one candidate receives 55% of the vote while the other gets just 45% -- a net 5% difference -- the greater vote-getter achieved a "landslide" victory, while the lesser was "humiliated." Should a flood sweep through a neighborhood, the resultant damage is predictably described by this statement: "It looks like a war zone!" Should a man consume 500 hot dogs in an hour in an eating contest, it's a "new world's record." And so on.

We've become so used to superlatives that "normalcy" is no longer normal. If someone asks, "How are you feeling today?" the simple response of "OK" is almost never heard. It's either, "Excellent!" or "Today is the worst day of my life!" Any less of a response, on either side of the scale, raises eyebrows.

In the time of the Old Testament Hebrew people in the Bible, language had not yet progressed to the point of expressing superlatives. There was no way in Biblical Hebrew to say, "That's the best ever." But if the Hebrews back then wanted to emphasize something, they simply said it multiple times. For example, Job was an extremely rich man. So the Bible says that, back-to- back, twice over. In the Psalms, if something was very beautiful, it says so twice via back-to-back verses – slightly changing the order of the words. Likewise, in the Proverbs.

There was one exception to this. God was so completely superlative as to be in a class by God's own self. God got a three times repeat. That's why we hear God repeatedly described as "holy, holy, holy." This Hebrew method of expressing a true superlative via thrice repetition was reserved to God alone.

Today's a good day for me. But it's probably not the "best day of my life." On the other hand, God is superlative yesterday, today, and forever. Isaiah 6:3 says, "Holy, holy, holy is the Lord God Almighty; the whole earth is full of his glory." Amen!

Accepting Our Dumb Dog
Romans 8:31

While living in El Paso, Texas we bought a dog for our growing family. He was a young sheltie whom we named Benji. Unfortunately, Benji was the absolutely dumbest dog we've ever known. He simply could not learn even the simplest commands, such as "sit" or "be quiet." Various behavioral reinforcements, both positive and negative, were repeatedly tried and failed. At first we thought he was being stubborn, but eventually we arrived at the conclusion that Benji wasn't trying to resist us; rather, he simply didn't understand.

After sharing our frustration concerning Benji with friends, we got a recommendation from several for a dog "obedience school" nearby. We spoke with a lady there who had been in the dog obedience business for several years and had trained hundreds of animals, and she confidently boasted, "I've never yet had a failure." So we enrolled Benji in her obedience school for a month. At the end of that month, she sheepishly returned Benji to us with the statement, "I've just had my first failure." Our money was refunded with no argument.

Benji lived with us for eleven years in three different locations. I realize how harsh it sounds to say this about him, but Benji remained stupid throughout his life. Both we and our children gradually learned to lower our expectations of Benji, although our kids often noticed other families' pet dogs and wondered why our dog, by comparison, was so "dumb." But Benji was loveable, at least within the parameters of his many limitations, and every time either Fran or I suggested getting rid of him, our kids were horrified. When he finally died of natural causes, we each and all experienced an odd mix of both grief and relief.

During Benji's tenure with us, I learned to appreciate the famous "serenity" prayer of the American theologian Reinhold Niebuhr. You've probably heard it: "God, grant me the serenity to accept the things I cannot change, courage to change the things I can, and wisdom to know the difference." Its Biblical bases are several, but the clearest is Philippians 4:7, "And the peace of God, which transcends all understanding, will guard your hearts and your minds in Christ Jesus." I never understood Benji, nor did Benji understand us. But I believe God placed him in our home to help us learn some lessons in simple acceptance.

Has God placed someone or some circumstances in your life which are helping to better teach you acceptance?

Avoiding Worldly Politics
Luke 22:28-30

I have two long-term friends who are each deeply committed to their respective political persuasions. The one is a dyed-in-the-wool right-wing conservative, the other a left-leaning liberal – or "progressive," to employ contemporary terminology. As a result, I receive, daily, a large number of "forwarded" political e-mailings from each of these two divergent camps. Years ago I mastered the art of hitting the "delete" button on my computer and phone, which helps me maintain some measure of sanity given their constant onslaught of all-politics all-the-time.

Both these friends are frustrated with me for the same two reasons. First, I refuse to take their particular side in political debate. And second, I maintain that worldly politics is not my primary concern.

Certainly, I understand that I currently live in the "real" world. I'm not a head-in-the-sand ostrich. Political issues and the outcomes thereof affect me and those I care about. I try to stay reasonably well-informed about such, and I regularly vote. But I don't believe that God sides with either the right or the left. And further, I don't believe that worldly politics is of critical importance. Certainly it's less important than the Kingdom of God.

When Jesus walked this earth, virtually everyone around him repeatedly tried to involve him in political issues. Basically, his followers wanted him to lead a political rebellion against the major worldly power of that day – the Roman Empire. But Jesus steadfastly refused. Even when his life was at stake and he might have avoided crucifixion with carefully crafted political responses to the Roman governor, Pontius Pilate, he maintained his distance from such. In response to Pilate, in John 18:36 he simply stated, "My kingdom is not of this world." That answer, of course, frustrated Pilate – who was a thoroughly political creature.

No, I'm not Jesus. And I'm not totally disengaged from the affairs of this present world. But like Jesus, I try to maintain ultimate loyalty to God's Kingdom. That regularly frustrates my political friends.

I don't know if you're "political" or not. But regardless of your political persuasions or the lack thereof, I hope you know Jesus and, like him, know that your ultimate allegiance is to God's eternal realm.

Valuing Volunteers
1 Chronicles 29:14-18

My wife was repeatedly asked to "volunteer" to teach her adult Sunday School class. Ultimately she agreed, and spent several hours during the week prior preparing for the session she would teach – reading, taking notes, praying, outlining – all the necessary disciplines to offer a well-thought-out presentation to her fellow students. I wasn't there personally to hear her, but afterward I did hear from several of the class members saying she had done a good job, presenting a lesson they found both thought-provoking and faith-forming.

A few days later we were sharing a meal with several friends from our church. One of them, a man who is a recently retired high-school teacher and a fellow-member of Fran's Sunday School class, used the meal conversation as an opportunity to repeatedly fault her as to what she had done wrong in her class presentation. From his perspective as a professional educator, there were numerous things she had done which she shouldn't have done and yet more things she hadn't done which she should have. She took it all good-naturedly, but it was pretty hard to swallow for a volunteer largely untrained in formal educational techniques.

From its outset both the Christian faith and the Church which promotes and sustains it have been largely composed of volunteers. Jesus' original disciples were all volunteers; not a single one of them was compelled to follow him. Fast-forwarding to the present, the army of the faithful contains no draftees; the Church continues to exist through the voluntary contributions and efforts of millions of willing laity.

As a pastor and one of the few paid workers in the churches I served, over the years I received my share of criticisms. I considered those an expected part of the job. But what I found odd was the huge volume of criticisms levied by laity against other laity. These were all volunteers – far too often harshly evaluating their fellow volunteers.

All people are precious in God's sight. Volunteers are especially so. The Lord considers those willing to be volunteers in God's service as royalty – the Bible even says so in Judges 5:9. And we, as God's servants – volunteers one and all – should affirm, not criticize, one another's service to God and God's Church on earth today. Thank a volunteer every time you have opportunity!

Credit Scores
Romans 10:9

In recent years Americans have increasingly become aware of the existence and importance of "credit scores." For decades now, banks and other financial institutions have kept track of the history of how we have, each and all, used money. Some of us have been more responsible with our finances, some less so. All of that has been tabulated and, in the electronic era of "big data," carefully distilled.

Whenever you pay off a large bill responsibly over time, your credit score goes up. And conversely, whenever you fail to pay in a timely fashion, or not at all, your credit score goes down. And horror of horrors from the financial point of view, if you declare bankruptcy your credit score goes in the toilet. Even if you start over again and begin to rebuild your reputation for bill paying, you will be considered a poor credit risk for a very long time to come – up to a decade.

Because this credit score system has become a fact of our lives, many people have similarly extended the concept to their relationship with God. If you go to church regularly and live a good life, God is pleased and your "heaven score" increases. On the other hand, if you rarely pray and maybe cheat on your spouse, God is upset and your "heaven score" plummets. So be good, go to church and smile a lot – and you'll surely be on the road to heaven.

Most Americans, including even many who call themselves Christians, simply do not understand the plain fact that God maintains no such scoring system. We cannot please God by our piety and good deeds. Over and over again the Bible says that God loves us because of who God is, not because of what we do or don't do. He loves us so much he sent Jesus to die for our sins and reconcile us to himself. God's favor is never earned; rather it's given. That's called "grace."

Potentially, every person can be a recipient of God's grace. You can't do anything good enough to earn it, nor bad enough to lose it. Grace is a free gift from God through His Son Jesus Christ. Acts 16:31 says, "Believe in the Lord Jesus and you will be saved." That's the long and short of it.

Throw away the scorecard, people of God. Instead, rely completely on the grace of God found in his Son, Jesus.

The Right Size
John 21:20-23

As we were sorting through some old "stuff" to decide what to discard, give away, or keep, I came upon my high school letter jacket from decades ago. It was in pretty good shape considering all the years which had passed since I'd last worn it. As I looked it over and briefly considered trying it on for old time's sake, there was one obvious problem – it was much too small. The me "then" and the me "now" weren't even close to the same size.

There's an interesting aspect, not often noted when the story is read, to the well-known Old Testament Bible tale of David and Goliath. When David volunteers to fight against this giant Philistine, King Saul offers to loan David his own suit of armor to protect him in the coming conflict. In I Samuel 17:38-39, David actually tries on Saul's armor, but can't even walk around in it. The reason is obvious – Saul is a very tall person; I Samuel 9:2 says he was a head taller than anyone else in Israel. David, on the other hand, is of ordinary height. So Saul's armor doesn't fit. David takes it off and, in effect, responds to Saul with, "Thanks but no thanks." Then he goes on, armor-less except for God's protection, to easily defeat Goliath.

When it comes to the clothing we wear, we all understand that wearing something the right size is significant. But often in the Christian faith we fail to extend this simple idea. Instead, if I believe that John 3:16 is the single most important scripture verse in all the Bible, then you should too. If Sam thinks that volunteering at the local food bank is the appropriate way of carrying out God's will, then everyone who dares to call themselves Christian should also be so doing. Anything else isn't real dedication to the Lord. Sally feels that singing the "old hymns" draws her closer to Christ, so contemporary music shouldn't be used in the church. And so on.

One of the issues that is making Christianity less attractive than it might otherwise be in our present-day world of multiple options and choices is this "one size fits all" approach to the faith that many believers and, indeed, many entire church bodies, take toward being included therein. But when we read the Gospels, it's clear that Jesus treated and valued each of his disciples as unique individuals. He didn't ask the same of Peter as he did, for example, of John. Following Jesus wasn't, for him, a matter of placing everyone in a standard-sized box.

People of God, it's our job to invite others to follow Jesus. But let's allow him to choose the individual "right size" for each of their particular discipleship "garments."

Hidden Second Talents
Matthew 5:14-16

A fellow pastor and personal friend of mine was about to leave his church after a long and fruitful ministry there. I knew him to be a powerful preacher of the Word of God. His messages were regularly used by God both to draw people closer to Christ as well as to impel them to serve their fellow human beings in Christ's Name. By God's Spirit he often helped make Christian disciples for the transformation of our world.

A couple of weeks before the end of his tenure, he made a special request – to be allowed to sing a song in worship. Of course the music director said yes. And sing he did – with a powerful bass voice that rang the rafters of the sanctuary. His timing and tonality were perfect. His interpretation of the song he'd chosen to sing was emotionally engaging. It was one of the best solos I've ever heard in any church – and I've heard a lot of church solos.

I and many of the other folks who heard him sing were amazed. Of course we had already realized that he could, to state the obvious, "carry a tune." But we had no idea of his previously hidden reserve of talent in the area of music. To us, he was a preacher – and a good one. But an equally good musician? Wow! What a surprise!

Certainly I've known multi-talented, singing preachers before. To be honest, and this is simply my personal observation, all of those I've experienced were "OK, but not exciting" in either category. This excellent pastor's reserve of musical ability was an unexpected second blessing from an already successful preacher. He really was a "two-talent" man.

That surprising experience got me to thinking more broadly about previously hidden talents later discovered among those already highlighted in Holy Scripture. For example, Moses was a great prophet of God who, of necessity, later proved also to be a savvy administrator. David was a highly competent shepherd within whom beat the heart of a great warrior. Paul was a smart Bible scholar whom God employed as a fruitful evangelist. There are many others.

I further wonder how many "hidden second talents" are out there among God's people today. I'm sure many of us have, like my singing preacher friend, one or two or even three unrevealed competencies that could be well used by our Lord in the building of his Kingdom. Are you willing to let him employ your talents – all of them -- in his service?

An Abrupt End, But Life Goes On
2 Timothy 4:7

I've mentioned more than once in these devotionals that I used to be a runner. More truthfully, later in life I became more of a jogger than a runner, but overall I regularly headed outside each morning and attempted to run – at least one mile – virtually every day, rain or shine, cold or hot, for 40 years from my early 20's to my early 60's.

All those years of running came to an abrupt end on February 1, 2009. It was a Sunday morning. I'd gotten up very early in order to get my run completed, then shower and be ready to preach the 8:15 AM worship service at my assigned church. A dusting of snow had fallen during the night before, but it wasn't enough to slow me down. I had almost completed a mile loop and was within a block of my house when I slipped on a hidden patch of ice, covered over by the fresh snow. As I went down I heard a nasty snap, which hurt a lot. My right ankle had shattered in several places.

At the hospital an orthopedic surgeon immediately operated on that ankle, repairing three fractures using seven screws and a four-inch steel plate. He employed a spinal anesthetic which allowed me to remain awake and watch the entire procedure. And he told me that, once healed, I would be able to walk normally, but probably never again run.

That doctor was quite correct. After several months of healing followed by lengthy physical therapy, I was again able to walk normally and painlessly. However, standing on that foot without moving for more than a minute or two always causes that ankle to begin hurting. And running is simply out of the question – the ankle won't bend quickly enough to allow such.

And just how does God fit into all this? Within five minutes after I arrived in the hospital's emergency room, a friend was there to comfort and support me. He was the Jewish husband of one of my church's members. He came, he said, because he realized that on a Sunday morning Christians needed to be in church. And speaking of which, my wife had immediately notified the lay leader of our congregation who, I was later told, seamlessly picked up the mantle of leadership and conducted the two Sunday morning worship services at the church. Many prayers were offered for my healing – during the very time the surgeon was repairing my ankle just two blocks away.

By that same afternoon I was home from the hospital – along with lots of pain medication – and spread out in my easy chair while the youth group from the church enjoyed a "Super Bowl Party," as previously planned, at our house. All I could do was watch, wave, and smile. My running days had abruptly ended, but by God's grace life went on.

A Creative Solution to Cohabitation
John 4:16-18

Like most preachers today I'm disturbed – maybe that's too mild a word – by the "living together without benefit of marriage" that is rampant among couples in our contemporary society. It's wrong; it's sin – it's clearly contrary to the laws of God. I fully realize that in so saying I'm swimming against a powerful cultural tide, but I can't bend on this without breaking. On the other hand, I'm not about to outwardly judge any particular unmarried, cohabiting couple – I leave all such to God.

Decades ago, while I was serving a church in El Paso, a man who had been a leading layman in one of my prior churches in a different city called me to share his concern for his mother. That lady, a widow in her late 60's, was living in El Paso with a man to whom she was not married. Her son was deeply concerned. Would I please call her and talk to her about her sinful lifestyle? This was a bit of a twist from what I usually hear – normally it's parents worried about their kids doing this sort of thing – but I agreed to contact her.

This lady and her live-in "boyfriend," a man likewise in his late 60's, proved to be quite a challenge to my Christian faith. As I got to know them, I soon discovered why they insisted on living together without marrying. She was the recipient of a few hundred dollars monthly of survivor's Social Security benefits from her late husband. He, likewise, received minimal Social Security benefits. Such was the sole income for each of them. Pooled together, those two income streams allowed them to live a Spartan but tolerable existence. If they married, her benefits would cease and they would be plunged into real poverty. It was a dilemma I'd not previously considered.

Fortunately, when one lives in El Paso, Texas there are creative possibilities not available to those living farther from the US-Mexico border. I suggested we cross that border and there I would marry them in the sight of God. No secular license would be necessary. So it was that she and her man invited all their immediate families to a small Christian wedding in another jurisdiction. It wasn't a perfect solution, but it brought them into compliance with the laws of God. I'd rather please Him than anyone else.

Today's Not-So-Exhaustive Concordances
Hebrews 4:12

Like many pastors, I know a lot of Bible. Not surprisingly, the Bible is very much part and parcel of both me and my occupation. But I honestly don't know the entire Bible; it's a very long book. In fact, it's sixty-six books rolled into one. Despite its overall length, I suspect there are a few pastors in our world who have memorized the entire Bible from cover to cover, but I'm not one of them. So when I'm trying to look up a specific verse or research a particular theme from the Bible, I often need help.

For much of my pastoral career, I found that help in the form of Bible concordances – reference books which sort and categorize the thoughts and messages to be found in God's Word. My personal favorite was "Strong's Exhaustive Concordance." A Bible reference tool which has been around for at least a century, "Strong's Exhaustive Concordance" contains, in large part, a dictionary of each and every word found in the Bible. I used to joke that it was rightly called "exhaustive" and that you had to be "strong" to use it, since it's an oversized volume which weighs about 10 pounds. I still have a copy of it on my home office bookshelves. I probably used my "Strong's" for Biblical reference help more than a thousand times over the first three decades of my ministry.

But after the inception of the internet and the associated programmatic applications (termed "apps" for short) which allow us to efficiently mine its worldwide trove of data, Bible apps began to appear. At first they were merely online versions of the Bible itself. But as they further developed, they took over – and surpassed -- the role of Bible concordances. Today they are amazing reference tools which allow anyone to quickly read Scripture in any of dozens of versions and languages and, further, to do in mere minutes the kind of Bible research which used to take me hours to accomplish.

I still run into folks these days who say to me, "I don't have time to read the Bible and, besides, it's too hard to understand." In answer, I simply pull out my smart phone, hit one of the Bible apps I've got on it, and show them a modern-language version of the Bible. And I further tell them, just in case they can't understand something, to highlight the word or phrase in question and ask the app for further explanation.

Reading the Bible today is simpler and easier than ever before. Learning and understanding the Word of God is no longer "exhaustive." In this regard, modern technology is a true blessing.

Is God Calling?
Matthew 9:35-38

Almost anyone who has even passing exposure to the Bible and either the Jewish or the Christian faith has heard the story of God's call of the prophet Isaiah. It's found in Isaiah, chapter six. To recount it in summary form, Isaiah has a vision of God on His heavenly throne. God calls out, "Whom shall I send?" And Isaiah responds, "Here am I, Lord. Send me." Isaiah's call by God is clear, immediate, and decisive.

A friend of mine was attempting to discern God's call on his life. He was in late middle age and had spent most of his earthly years in a very different field of endeavor, a scientific occupation. But of late he had a nagging, repeated feeling that God wanted him to pursue some sort of ministry service. He asked me for advice because he knew my similar background – I was an engineer/scientist prior to becoming a pastor/preacher. The difference was that God's call had come to me while I was yet a young adult.

I responded that, in my personal experience, God had been a "relentless gentleman." I first became aware of God's call on my life perhaps five or six years before I fully responded thereto. Initially I tried ignoring the sense that God wanted to radically change my life's direction. But the conviction that God wanted me to surrender my life to Him steadily grew. So I then tried delaying and bargaining. "Lord, if you'll just leave me alone for a while, I'll eventually try to see things your way." Again, the feeling that God wanted me to change direction kept growing. Then I attempted "partial answers." I did a lot of part-time ministry work – weekend missions, fill-in preaching, serving as a summer Christian camp counselor, etc. These weren't enough to ease God's quiet but growing inner pressure on me. Finally, I yielded: "OK, Lord, I'm yours – all the way." Only then did the pressure abate, replaced by a sense of "sunshine on my back." And that's how I've continued to feel God's presence ever since.

I shared this personal "call" experience with my friend, at the same time telling him I also knew many others in various fields of ministry, both full and part time, whose call experiences were quite different. God works in as many different ways as there are different people he's called.

At present as I write this, I don't know how my friend's answer to God's call will take shape – it's still in process. And I also know that God is calling many more folks to serve him. Could you be one of them?

Pick Your Battles
Daniel 11:33

This seems almost like ancient history to me today, but only about three decades back a friend and fellow pastor was being interviewed by local television media concerning his position on a proposal to legalize "bingo" playing in the state where he lived. At the time, that particular issue was highly controversial and prominent leaders were lining up on both sides to register either their backing or opposition thereto. When the reporter asked my pastor friend where he stood on this, he replied, "I think we've got bigger fish to fry." That response didn't satisfy the interviewer. "You don't have a position on bingo?" she continued. To which he further replied, "We've got poverty, homelessness, drug abuse, and gun violence to deal with. Once all those are resolved, I might have time to consider where I stand on bingo."

I was teaching a four-session "new member orientation" class for adults who had either recently joined or were considering joining my congregation. One young man therein had lots of questions, each asked with great fervency. Some of his queries were significant; for example, where does this church stand on the divinity of Jesus? Some were less so; for example, does this church allow instrumental music in worship, or just acapella singing? Question after question tumbled from him. Eventually some of the other members of the class complained. "We want to hear what Pastor Dave has to say. This isn't just your private class. We're here, too!" The young man walked out and, sadly, never returned to that church.

Jesus told two short stories, or parables, which are recorded back-to-back in Luke's Gospel, chapter 24. The first one concerned the issue of building a tower – Jesus said make sure you have enough funds to complete the project, or don't start it in the first place. The other featured a king who was considering war against another – Jesus said make sure you have sufficient troops or don't enter the fight at all. Both these parables are referred to as "count the cost" examples.

In an era of controversy and polarization over virtually anything and everything, I believe it makes good sense that Christians more carefully choose our involvements therein. While we may be tempted to "rise up" at any and all possible provocations, every seeming challenge to our faith and its principles, continuous conflict is not God's plan for his church nor his chosen people. Pick your battles, children of God.

Good Trustees
1 Corinthians 12:4-11

The Church is not a building. Rather, the Church is the people of God. I've taught this simple principle so many times that it seems obvious and almost trite to me, but most people never really understand it. To them the tangible, physical plant which has a sign on it saying "church" is just that – the Church. To some extent, I'm glad some of the "new generation" churches are rejecting the ownership of buildings, choosing rather to rent space for their gatherings. That underlines this basic truth: The Church is people rather than structures.

That being said, most church bodies do have buildings associated therewith. And buildings don't take care of themselves. One of the "surprise" duties which come with the territory of being a pastor is responsibility for managing and maintaining a church's buildings. Fortunately, however, this is one task I've never had to face alone. In every church I've served there were persons – mostly men – who were drawn to the tasks associated with property management and maintenance. In my particular experience, these persons were called "trustees."

In the Old Testament of the Bible there were priests of the temple of God. Biblical priests were descended from Levi, one of the twelve sons of Jacob, through Aaron the brother of Moses. They were responsible for the conduct of sacrifice and worship by the ancient Hebrew people, positions similar – but not identical -- to pastors today. And there were also a cadre of other men who did not conduct worship, but were responsible for keeping the temple of God open, clean and in good repair. They were likewise descendants of Levi through a different ancestor named Korah. The Korahites, often referred to as "gatekeepers" of the temple, were the trustees of ancient Israel.

Good trustees are, for a church body, worth their weight in gold. When the heating system fails in the dead of winter, they're speedily on the job seeing to its repair so the congregation can focus on worshipping God rather than shivering on a Sunday morning. When someone comes up to the pastor in the middle of a service to whisper in his or her ear that the women's toilet is overflowing, he or she can quickly beckon a trustee to see to the resolution of that mini-crisis while the rest of God's people continue to sing Christ's praise.

Good trustees can be just as important, in their own right, as pastors and preachers in keeping the church of God moving forward. They aren't specifically enumerated in any of the New Testament's "gifts of the Spirit" lists, but in my experience they probably ought to be.

Why I Like Peter
John 21:15-19

One of the earliest followers of Jesus was a man whose original name was Simon, but whom Jesus called "Peter." Peter was one of Jesus' closest inner circle of just three disciples – Peter, James, and John – thus he receives a great amount of attention in the four gospels of the New Testament in the Bible. Plus he is considered the author of two short letters which are also included in the New Testament.

I was asked to don a costume and play Peter for a week of Vacation Bible School at my church. Wanting to do a good job for the approximately 130 children who would see me as Peter, I re-read all of the scriptural passages in which Peter has a role, as well as researching some of the extra-Biblical traditions which have grown up around him.

Peter first appears in the gospels as a fisherman. Since fishing is one of my personal favorite sports, I immediately felt a kinship with him. However, Peter didn't fish for fun as I do. Fishing was Peter's means of livelihood. And Jesus, soon after he met Peter, lured him away from fishing with the promise, "Follow me, and I will make you a fisher of people." I found that interesting, as Jesus likewise took me away from my original vocation, engineering, to serve as a minister for him.

Peter is both the first of Jesus' disciples to clearly recognize who he really is – the Son of God – and the first of his disciples to blatantly deny him. Throughout his approximate three years of travelling with Jesus, Peter's faith was strong one minute and weak the next. He was very human – and so am I.

After Jesus' crucifixion, resurrection, and ascension into Heaven, Peter became the de-facto head of the fast-growing Christian church movement. Roman Catholics consider him the first "pope." Peter did wonderful and even miraculous deeds on behalf of his Lord Jesus. But he also remained subject to missteps and errors, such as when he foolishly came into conflict with the early church's chief evangelist, Paul, as recorded in Galatians 2. Certainly I've never been a pope, but I definitely have made my share of mistakes while attempting to serve Jesus.

It was an honor for me to play Peter. I can identify with him in several significant ways. And I look forward to actually meeting Peter in the Kingdom of God.

Brainy Town
Proverbs 1:7

My last five years of active, full-time employed ministry were spent as pastor of the First United Methodist Church of Los Alamos, New Mexico. Los Alamos is a relatively small city – 12,000 inhabitants – known worldwide for having been the birthplace, in the 1940's, of the atomic bomb. Three generations later, in the 21st century, Los Alamos continues as home to one of this world's premier scientific laboratories. Nuclear science remains a strong focus of Los Alamos' research, but their endeavors currently span almost any subject you can imagine. For example, the full-body scanners through which millions of airline passengers worldwide must presently pass for security purposes are a result of Los Alamos' scientific labors.

Almost everyone in Los Alamos is intelligent. High IQ's and lists of advanced college degrees are par for the course in Los Alamos. In that regard, I recall the first time I met with my then-new church's administrative body. The chairman thereof introduced me around the table to the dozen or so gathered thus, "Dr. Ring, this is Dr. Jones. And this is Dr. Miller. And this is Dr. Gonzales…." As he went all the way around the group, I quickly noticed that every single one of them, male and female, held the title of "doctor" – as do I. So when he finished I said, "Since we're all 'doctors' of one sort or another, let's just go by first names. I'm Dave." The group visibly relaxed. "We hoped you'd say that," one of them commented.

Preaching and teaching the word of God in Los Alamos was a constant intellectual challenge. No "lazy" sermons nor "simple" answers were allowed. No assertion was permitted to pass without thorough critique. Many of the lay members knew as much scripture as I; thus I was regularly called upon to back up my statements with solid Biblical references. Yes, I was repeatedly intellectually challenged – and my faith grew as a result.

To me, the best news about brainy Los Alamos is that hundreds of precious persons there believe in Jesus. Some of this world's brightest individuals are smart enough to realize they yet need God in their lives for today, and they further need a Savior for eternity. Unfortunately, there are some atheists in Los Alamos, but science hasn't displaced God for many of the most brilliant scientists I've ever known.

What If We Live a Very Long Time in This World?
James 1:27

In relation to contemporary young adults, one of the root dilemmas of the Church and the Christian faith it purports to represent is the belief, which is becoming increasingly common among the young, that they will never die. Thus, they have no need for "religion."

When I first heard this I thought, "How silly!" But as time goes on I'm hearing it more and more. It's even been surveyed – about 1/3 of the "millennial" generation believes they will be immortal here and now, in this world.

When you give this idea some careful scrutiny, it's not hard to see how it arises. From the time of Jesus until the dawn of the 20th century, lifespan in the world at large was truncated by high rates of infant mortality. If you lived past your fifth birthday you had a reasonable shot at making it to 70 or even 80 years, but more than half of infants didn't. Once modern medicine began conquering childhood diseases, lifespan worldwide increased rather quickly. Throughout the past century-plus it's been on the upswing. Percentage-wise the fastest-growing category of lifespan, worldwide, is now persons aged 110 or more. They're termed "supercentenarians."

Against this background of seeming inexorable lifespan increase it's relatively easy to see why today's young adults imagine they can be immortal in this world. Quite a few sincerely believe that science will "solve" death before they grow old enough to have to face it.

Unfortunately for that assertion, it's mistaken. The Bible, God's Holy Word, clearly says so in Hebrews 9:27: "...it is appointed for men to die once..." And for those who don't believe the Bible, scientists are also discovering that multiple elements inherent in human biology point toward a 120 to 125-year upper limit to lifespan. As medical science continues to advance, more people than ever before may approach this limit, but that's as long as human life can get.

Even so, contemporary young adults are rightly expecting to live a very long time in this world. And so the old evangelistic query, "Do you know what will happen to you when you die?" has largely lost its imperative. A more significant question for them is "What do you want your long life to count for in this world?"

Interestingly, somewhere between three-fourths and eighty percent of Jesus' teachings are concerned with the second query. Based upon the Gospels, Jesus really was more of a "here and now" rabbi than an "after you die" Savior. And that means the Church, if it is to remain relevant and, indeed, survive in the 21st century, must re-orient itself. "Back to the Bible" could mean giving up an oversell of "pie in the sky" and focusing upon the present needs of precious people in this world. Consider such seriously, people of God!

Somewhere In-Between
Matthew 22:36-40

Leviticus 19:27 says, "Do not cut the hair at the sides of your head or clip off the edges of your beard." This is one of many laws which men of early Israel were taught to strictly observe. It was clearly assumed that every adult Israelite male be bearded and rarely if ever trim that beard. They took "beardedness" very seriously; in fact, even the enemies of Israel knew this so well that they sometimes shamed Israelite captives by shaving one side of their faces, cutting off half their beards, then releasing them. Thus visibly marked, these men were not permitted to re-enter the Israelite community until their beards had sufficiently re-grown to fully obscure the missing parts – which could take months.

"How silly!" may well be what you think. It's certainly what I think. Bearded or clean shaven, or somewhere in-between, are all equally acceptable for men in our society. And the length of one's facial hair obviously has little or nothing to do with someone's devotion to God. But for God's special people 3,000 years ago, it was a very serious matter. It made its way into the Holy Word of God – and it's still there.

There are several thousand "laws" in the Old Testament of the Holy Bible which remain within what we hold to be the sacred Word of God. Yet we have gradually moved away from most of these, considering them to be "ceremonial" regulations rather than actual "moral" law of God. A thousand years after it was originally given through Moses, the early rabbis among the Hebrews codified "the law" via some 613 commands. But that's obviously still a pretty large number.

Christians, for our part, tend to say we recognize just the Ten Commandments from the Hebrew law as being of real significance. But does that mean we should ignore, for example, the several prohibitions in Leviticus and other portions of the Torah against incestuous sexual relations, prohibitions which are not covered in the great Ten? Of course not. On the other hand, regulations concerning the washing of pots and bowls, despite their repeated mention in the Torah, are probably not of great concern.

Jesus weighed in on this issue, albeit deliberately not in great detail. His two memorable "Great Commandments" – love the Lord and love your neighbor – are widely known and widely quoted. And most certainly, if regularly and fully followed, they would make for a much better world.

Should men shave regularly? Should women wear hats while in church? Love the Lord and love your neighbor – and make those sorts of decisions for yourself.

The One in the Middle
Acts 10:34-35

Jesus told an interesting story, traditionally called the "Parable of the Talents," concerning the wise use of resources placed in our care. As related in Matthew 25, three servants of a king were given various amounts of money to work with – respectively five, two, and one bags of gold (or "talents" in older Bible versions) – while the king went away for a long time. When he returned to settle up accounts with his servants, the servant with five bags had earned five more; likewise, the servant with two had doubled what he had been given. But the single-bag (or talent) man had done nothing. The first two were rewarded for their faithfulness, the last punished for his lack thereof.

Over the years I've heard a number of sermons on this story, each of them underscoring Jesus' already obvious point – the five talent man was prudent and the one talent man foolish. But the interesting thing, to me, is that I've rarely heard mention of the "two talent" man. He's the overlooked, forgotten "man in the middle."

For his part, the one in the middle was just as wise and equally as successful as the widely-extolled five talent servant. There's an oft-quoted maxim in the realm of economics: "It takes money to make money." Under that rubric, the two talent man likely had to work harder than the ten talent guy to achieve equal results, as he was starting from a smaller base.

Whether it be economic resources or God-given personality traits, most of us consider ourselves to be more like unto the one in the middle. We probably don't view ourselves as rich, smart, and/or athletically gifted. On the other hand, we're likely neither economic nor mental nor physical fools, complacently sitting upon and squandering what has been entrusted to us.

The good news of the Gospel is that those of us in the middle can succeed, in God's sight, as fully as those much more gifted and talented. All disciples of Christ are "saints" in his sight. And the reward offered for faithfulness is the same for all: "Well done, good and faithful servant. Enter into the joy of your Lord."

Remote Control
2 Kings 5:1-15

My home in New Mexico has, of late, added some fancy 21st century technology. Because Albuquerque is located in a semi-desert climate region, if one is to have any sort of lawn or greenery a sprinkler system is pretty-much required. And that system has to work faithfully and regularly in order to be considered of genuine value. My yard now has a sprinkler system consisting of five "zones," any and all of which I can control from my smart phone. This past February, things got out of whack and my lawn was in danger of drying up. The sprinkler "app" on my phone warned me about this, and I was able to remotely reset the system from where I was – which happened to be several thousand miles away, while on a mission trip to Honduras. Amazing!

Inside my house, even more recently, we've added nine new "state of the art" smoke detectors. These are unobtrusively attached to our ceilings, silently monitoring the air around for traces of smoke from a potential fire as well as doing double-duty as carbon-monoxide sensors. Should one or more of these experience an alarm, I'll be instantly notified via my phone. But as long as they're operating normally, I have peace of mind knowing that my home is safe from fire danger. Like the sprinklers, they can be checked and adjusted from virtually anywhere on this planet. Awesome!

In Matthew 8:15-13 in the New Testament, a Roman centurion – an officer in charge of 100 soldiers – asked Jesus for help. One of his servants was suffering painfully from a serious illness which had paralyzed him. Jesus offered to go to this man's house and heal the servant. But the centurion said, in effect, "No. You don't need to come. I believe you have the authority to heal him from right here." Jesus was highly impressed by this man's faith in him, and said so. And he further went ahead and did what the centurion had asked. The story concludes by saying, "And his servant was healed at that moment." Wonderful!

Jesus didn't have the benefit of modern remote control technology. Notwithstanding, by the miraculous power of God Jesus was able to heal – even at a distance. And Jesus is yet in the business of healing and working many kinds of miracles, even though he's no longer physically present with us. Just like the Roman centurion, faithfully ask -- and allow the Lord to amaze and surprise you.

A Fishing Story about Children
John 21:1-6

In my Los Alamos pastorate the congregation contained, as is very common these days, a number of single mothers attempting to raise children on their own with little or no male influence present. One of those young women, who had heard about my love of fishing, commented to me that she wished her son, about 10 years of age, had someone to take him fishing. On my next outing with my "fishing buddy" James, I made him aware of this. He had an idea – "Let's get our Men's Club to set up a Saturday 'teach kids to fish' day."

The idea caught on with the church's men, so a late spring date was set and advertised. Half a dozen parents signed their kids up. Some came along with us, some just sent their children. We travelled to a reasonably nearby fish hatchery in the Jemez Mountains where there was already a "children's pond" liberally stocked with rainbow trout. Each man paired up with a child, provided bait and tackle, and attempted to teach them how to fish.

Before that day was over, every boy and girl in the group had experienced the delight of bringing in at least one trout. Some caught several. It was all "catch and release," which made for even more fun for the children as they watched their catch swim away after having briefly held the wriggling creature. Combined with a picnic lunch, the experience was a fun-filled, memorable day for all concerned. And a number of meaningful relationships between children and adult men were thus begun.

It was a foregone conclusion that, perhaps ¾ of a year later, the question began to be asked in that church, "When will our next annual 'teach kids to fish' day be held?" Already, after only one attempt, this had become an "annual tradition" for that congregation. To my knowledge, this event still happens each spring in Los Alamos.

It's widely-known that Jesus selected five or more of his twelve original disciples from among the ranks of fishermen he found along the shores of the Sea of Galilee in Israel. Being a fisherman myself, I have some thoughts as to why that was the case. Most fisher-folk I've met, men and women alike, are "can do" people. Many of them are also not solitary fishers; they're also "people" persons who enjoy being with and sharing significant experiences with others. So I further understand why Jesus invited these men not to fish for aquatic species alone, but also, with him, to be fishers of people for the Kingdom of God.

Cutting Corners
Proverbs 12:15

St. Mark's, the church I once served in El Paso, Texas, built a new educational building while I was there. It was a large, two-story structure that evolved from a simple design I'd actually first drawn on a napkin at a restaurant while sharing lunch with several of the church's leaders. Of course, that basic design went through many iterations with the architect, builder, etc.; the finished product was far more elaborate than my simple initial sketch. Once built, this building opened to better accommodate the needs of that growing congregation. And when it opened, everyone was well-pleased with it.

Later I moved on to another church, then another. Almost a decade after I'd left St. Mark's, I received a call from one of that church's leaders. They were experiencing major leak problems with the roof on that educational building. They'd tried several rounds of repairs, but the problems persisted. And so they went back to the original design drawings and found that the drawings showed four roof drains, but only two had actually been built. The Trustees from that time had mostly moved on to other locations, just as had I, so they couldn't easily be queried. Could I possibly recall anything about this inconsistency?

I replied that, yes, I knew exactly what had happened. While the building was still under construction but near to completion, I and the then-chairman of the church's Trustees had gone up on the roof and observed the discrepancy between the design drawings and what was actually being built. We'd called the contractor and complained to him. All three of us had then gotten up on the roof together and we two listened while the contractor tried to convince us that two large drains were actually better than four smaller ones. It was a "hard sell" and, while I didn't buy it, the Trustees' chair ultimately did – and he had the authority to approve it. I protested, but in this regard he outranked me. So the contractor got to shave a little off of his costs, and the church wound up with what I personally considered a substandard roof design.

A decade later, that decision had come back to bite them. St. Mark's had to completely re-roof their educational building – redesigning the roof so that the originally planned four drains were actually incorporated. A minor saving – perhaps $2,000 -- for the contractor wound up later costing that church nearly $100,000.

There's an interesting discussion in Paul's first letter to the church at Corinth concerning "cutting corners" in the moral realm rather than merely the physical. In chapter five of that letter, Paul makes the members of that church aware that they are, without objection, silently acquiescing to sins which simply should not be found among Christian believers. Paul employs a metaphor of "leaven," which the ancient Jews often associated with sin, and warns them that this relatively minor deviation from Christ's expectations could eventually grow to permeate and ruin their entire lives.

People of God, avoid cutting corners -- both in your relations with others here on earth and in your devotion to your Savior.

A Long and Ultimately Successful Search
Ecclesiastes 11:1

I was asked to visit a woman in one of our local hospitals. Someone at church, as I was greeting folks departing Sunday morning worship, handed me a piece of paper on which was written her name and the name of the hospital and room number. I asked who she was and the person handing me the note said, "I really don't know. A visitor handed this paper to me and asked if I would pass it on to the pastor and request him to visit the lady. And that person has already gone out the door."

OK. Such was an odd way to be asked to make a hospital call, but it wasn't anywhere near the strangest request I'd ever received. So later that afternoon I headed to the hospital and room therein to which I'd been asked to go. Right away I realized something was amiss, as there was a man occupying the sole hospital bed in that room.

I then went to the nurse's station, showed the lady there the piece of paper I'd received, and asked if this woman had been moved to another room or, perhaps, released from the hospital. She put the name into the hospital's computer system and, very quickly, said "I'm sorry, but this person isn't in our data base." "So that means she's been released?" I asked. "No, it means she's never been here at all," was the reply.

All right. I suppose it would have been reasonable to give up at that point, but I had a "gut feeling" I should keep trying. So I thought a moment. The hospital room number was on the seventh floor. There was only one other hospital in the city which had seven or more floors. Maybe they'd gotten the hospital's name wrong. Unfortunately, with today's patient privacy regulations, I couldn't simply call and ask the other hospital if this woman was there and expect an answer. I would need to actually go there.

I drove to the other hospital, went up to the seventh floor, and walked into the numbered room. Déjà vu. There was a man in the bed. So again, I went to the nurse's station and asked about the woman whose name I had. This time I hit pay dirt. She was in that hospital, and had that very afternoon been moved to a room on the fifth floor.

Finally, I found her. An older lady, she was delighted to be visited by a pastor, and immediately asked if I could serve her Holy Communion. I told her I didn't have my portable communion set with me, but I could come back with it the next day. We enjoyed a fairly lengthy conversation, mostly about her illnesses and her family situation. I prayed with her, and yes, I went back the next day and served Holy Communion to her.

That's it. That's the whole story. I saw this lady but twice, and that's all. She didn't contact me later, although I'd left her a card with my phone number and e-mail address. She didn't ever visit my church. I don't know what ultimately happened to her.

But to me, this limited encounter wasn't a waste of time. As a pastor, I frequently care for people who aren't "officially" members of my church flock. And as a Christian, all persons are precious and worthy of my concern. I trust the same is true for you.

Spiritual Gifts
Hebrews 2:3-4

Back when my wife and I were just getting started in Christian ministry, the church we served in Nashville, Tennessee had a choir member who was a delightful lady and who invited us to accompany her to a major "revival" event held by a then-famous musical evangelist. It was housed in the largest venue available at that time in Nashville, the city's civic auditorium. The evening we went it was packed to the full; we wound up seated in the second-tier balcony.

The evangelist came out, sat down at his piano, and began a two-hours-plus non-stop gospel presentation employing equally intertwined singing and preaching. Both I and the lady who had invited us were captivated by his high-octane style of Christian "infotainment." But my wife Fran was uncomfortable throughout. More than once she leaned over to me and quietly whispered, "There's something wrong about all this." When the time of invitation was finally offered, Fran quickly said, "Let's get out of here!" I'd never seen her react so negatively to a Christian gathering.

Less than a year later, this evangelist was humiliated in a very public, major sex scandal which completely destroyed his ministry "empire." When this news broke, while Fran didn't bring it up with me, I did so with her. "How did you know?" I asked. "I'm not sure. I just had a creepy feeling about him from the first moment he came onto the platform," she replied.

That was the first time, but by no means the last, that I learned my wife has a gift of "spiritual discernment," which is listed among those gifts of the God's Holy Spirit to Christian disciples in 1 Corinthians 12. God often allows her to see both the "good" and the "bad" in people and situations to which I am completely blind. I'm a preacher and a teacher – those are more tangible spiritual gifts. But Fran's gift of discernment has proven of value to me and our joint labors for Christ on more than one occasion.

Throughout the New Testament there are numerous references to "spiritual gifts" which God imparts to the followers of Christ. No one individual is given all of these diverse gifts. And therefore, as the early Christians quickly discovered, we must work together to fully utilize the vast array of gifts and talents which God offers. That's why we have congregations and churches. And that's why "solo" Christianity is rarely effective or successful.

What are your spiritual gifts? How are you using them to build up the Body of Christ, to the glory of God?

Missed Opportunity
John 9:4

Highland Church in Odessa, Texas was a slowly but steadily declining medium-large congregation of primarily white families who early-on recognized that their "glory days" were already behind them. I, as their current pastor, led them through several rounds of self-assessment and goal-setting workshops. The results thereof were quite clear: Highland was located in the very middle of what had gradually become an almost completely Hispanic neighborhood. The church needed to deliberately begin transforming itself from an Anglo, English-speaking congregation to a multi-cultural, bilingual (English and Spanish) church body. Most of the congregation understood and agreed with that assessment, and were excited by the prospect of such transformation.

Unfortunately, several of the church's most affluent families did not share that vision. This handful of wealthy folks, while not directly opposing the prospect of such transition, offered an appealing "delaying tactic." If their church was going to attract and welcome new and different folks, it first needed to make the physical plant more pleasing. Extensive remodeling, both outside and in, was called for. And they would generously supply the lion's share of the funding required for such. It was an offer that couldn't easily be refused.

I continued at Highland throughout the external phase of this physical revamp. The church's several brick buildings were subjected to a construction renewal process called "tuckpointing" which made the walls themselves appear brand-new. The windows and their frames were replaced. The church's ageing exterior signage was replaced with new billboards. All this took a couple of years to complete. And when it was completed, I certainly had to admit the buildings were more eye-appealing.

Before the interior remodel began, I moved on to another pastoral assignment. But the process continued as planned. I was actually invited back to see the results, some four years later, and had to admit they were impressive. Everything looked wonderfully new.

Nearly six years had elapsed, however, during all of this "preparation" phase. During those six years Highland's existing congregation had continued to decline both in numbers and energy. The will to follow through on outreach to the surrounding community had diminished considerably. Highland now had beautiful, spiffed-up buildings with relatively few and mostly older people to fill them. Their window of opportunity for transformation had passed.

In Luke 9:59-62, Jesus invited two different men to follow him. Both said they would, but asked to first be allowed to take care of other needs and priorities. To both, Jesus said in effect, "No, now is your time." Now is always the best time to follow God's leading.

Forbidden Fruit
James 1:13-15

The story of mankind's "fall" away from God's grace in the Garden of Eden, as found in Genesis 3 in the Bible, is one of the most widely known of all Biblical narratives. God had said not to eat fruit from the "tree of the knowledge of good and evil." But the serpent in the garden talked Eve into trying it, and she in turn gave some to Adam, and the deed of disobedience was done. As a result, God banished them -- and from that time onward, human life has no longer been "a walk in the garden."

There's a tremendous amount of complex theology which has arisen from this Biblical short story, but one widely taught and quite simple aspect thereof is usually wrong. Ask 100 people who know the story, "What was the forbidden fruit?" and almost all of them will respond, "an apple."

While it's not impossible that the fruit eaten by Adam and Eve in the Garden was an apple, it's very unlikely that it was. The Hebrew text simply says it was "fruit." There are dozens of fruit candidates from ancient times in the Mideast which fit that generic description. However, wild apples in those days were hard little marbles which, even when fully ripe, tasted extremely both bitter and sour. (Think of a crab apple.) Had Eve taken a bite of one of them, she most likely would have quickly spit it out and definitely not have passed the remainder on to Adam. It was not until about the 12th century B. C. that apple cultivation eventually resulted in the size and sweetness among apples we've come to expect today.

The identification of the "forbidden fruit" as an apple arose from a linguistic error made when the Bible was translated from Hebrew into Latin. The Latin words for "apple" and for "evil" are very similar. So, somewhat like unto a modern-day pun, the forbidden fruit was mistakenly identified as an "evil apple." And the terminology stuck.

It's much more likely that the forbidden fruit was the one of the Old Testament's more frequently mentioned fruits, the pomegranate. Or it might have been a grape, or a cluster of grapes.

Regardless of what it was, Adam and Eve disobeyed God by eating it. Then they compounded their disobedience by lying to God about what they had done, then further tried to blame each other and/or the snake for the deed. That's how sin works – it compounds until we are totally hamstrung by it.

How can we get out of the web of human sin? How do we return to harmony and fellowship with God such as Adam and Eve knew before the "fall?" Actually, there's nothing we can do. But Jesus Christ can, and has, done it for us. His grace is sufficient to restore us to God's original intent for humanity. Let Christ return you to original righteousness. (And eat all the apples you want!)

Dreams
Daniel 2:1-3

Unlike the vast majority of human beings, I don't dream. Actually, I've been corrected numerous times when I make that assertion, especially by health professionals. "Everyone dreams," they say. "You just don't remember your dreams." OK, I suppose I can accept that. Assuming I do dream, I don't ever recall anything therefrom. For me, sleep is simply a blank slate.

Certainly, while awake I have plenty of "daydreams" of situations and possibilities which may or may not ever come to fruition. To some extent I envy those who do dream in their sleep – and can recall enough of those dreams to later describe them in the daytime.

The Holy Bible is full of dreamers and their dreams. A simple Biblical word search for "dreams" yields nearly 100 results, scattered all the way from Genesis in the Old Testament to Jude in the New. Dreams, in pre-Christian times, were one of God's common ways of revealing Himself and His will to humanity.

Joseph in the Old Testament was the greatest of all "God-dreamers." The Bible, starting in Genesis 37 and continuing for a dozen chapters thereafter, dubs Joseph a "master of dreams." Joseph's dreams from the Almighty got him into life-threatening situations, but also ultimately redeemed Joseph and, through him, all of God's chosen people from the brink of extinction.

Interestingly enough, the only God-dreamer specifically named in the New Testament is also a Joseph. The earthly "foster father" of Jesus, Matthew's Gospel records five different times Joseph's having dreams revealing God's direction to him, both before Jesus' birth and during Jesus's infancy.

Dreams as God's way of revealing His will to sleeping humans appear to have ended once the Holy Spirit was poured out upon Jesus' followers at Pentecost. The last specific God-dream noted in the Bible was that of Pilate's wife just prior to the Crucifixion. Visions, on the other hand, which are granted by God's Spirit to awake persons, have continued and perhaps even multiplied since Pentecost. But that's a different subject.

Sleep well tonight, people of God. May the Lord grant you peaceful dreams – refreshing you for his work in the days ahead.

Therapy Pools
John 9:1-12

My wife Fran is a survivor of a once-common childhood disease which has now been almost eliminated from our world called "polio." A crippling and often fatal ailment, it damages both nerves and muscles. And for those who have survived its initial onslaught during childhood, it often manifests itself anew in middle-aged adults with fresh neuromuscular problems termed "post-polio syndrome."

Since the age of 45, Fran has been fighting post-polio syndrome. For her, one of the more effective treatments to combat its effects is warm-water exercise, typically in a physical therapy swimming pool. In all of the most recent five places we've lived, we've had to find a suitable therapy pool for Fran to exercise in, pretty much every other day of her life.

Her ailment, especially the pain therefrom, responds well to warm-water therapy. But it has to be "warm" water, neither too cold nor too hot. The water temperature maintained in most regular swimming pools, even the indoor variety, is too cold for her – typically only about 80 degrees Fahrenheit. And the temperature of most Jacuzzis and other hot water pools is too hot – usually 100 degrees plus. The "sweet spot" for Fran is warm water at 90 to 92 degrees. Such warm water therapy pools are rare, but fortunately they do exist.

There's a story related by John's Gospel, chapter five, of a "therapy pool" located in Jerusalem in Jesus' time. It was called the Pool of Bethesda (or Bethsaida) and the Jews of that day used to bring dozens of the disabled there on a regular basis.

While just being in, or even near, the water of this pool was obviously considered beneficial – which explains why so many in need were brought there, there was one particular characteristic of this particular pool which was unique. Tradition held that occasionally an "angel" from God would appear and stir the pool's water. The first invalid to enter the pool immediately thereafter would be miraculously healed.

As Jesus was passing this pool one day, he noticed a crippled man who had been lying there a very long time – the Bible says 38 years – waiting to be healed. But because of his condition, he had never been able to be the first one to get into the water during one of those "special" healing times.

Jesus healed him, simultaneously saying "Get up! Pick up your mat and walk." The man did so, and soon was in trouble with the Jewish authorities because he was thereby violating a Sabbath rule. But that's another story.

It's interesting to me that therapy pools have been around for so many centuries. I'm not surprised, however, that Jesus visited one during his time on earth. Healings, both spiritual and physical, have always been one of his specialties. Ask Jesus to heal you – in whatever ways you may need.

An Odd Offer
Acts 17:22-34

I met John while serving as a "resident assistant" for a dormitory floor of young men at Michigan State University. John was "connected" in what was then called the Mafia or "La Cosa Nostra." He was a son of one of the powerful "five families" thereof. Because he had shown himself, as a teen, to be intelligent, his family had decided to educate him to eventually take over some of the "business" side of their endeavors rather than to be more directly involved in criminal activities.

To me, John was a really nice guy. As we got to know each other he often ruminated over whether or not, once he earned his degree, he would actually return to involvement in his family's "business." We became friends, keeping up occasional correspondence for some years after I left MSU.

I became an engineer, married, then eventually answered God's call to full-time Christian ministry. In 1973 I let all my friends know I would be heading off to seminary. Many told me I was a fool for leaving a lucrative career for what they imagined to be the poverty of ministry.

John had a different sort of response. He called me and said, "Dave, I know that ministers don't make much. So I'd like to help. One of my shops prints millions of dollars' worth of counterfeit food stamps each month. Let me send you $1,000 a month worth of those to assist you and your wife."

As a good friend, John's heart was obviously concerned for my welfare. But as a non-Christian he had no clue that what he was offering was not only illegal, but also morally wrong. Slowly and lovingly I tried to explain to John that, while I much appreciated his concern, there was no way I, in my soon-to-be role as a Christian minister, could accept his offer.

Frankly, I guess I didn't do a very good job with my explanation, as from that day forward John and I steadily drifted apart. I don't know what he's doing now, nor if he's even still on this earth. But I certainly hope he found Jesus somewhere along his path of life.

This world and the Kingdom of God have very different values. It's our job, Christians, to first introduce worldly people to Jesus -- and then to begin to teach them the principles of God's Kingdom. They can't be expected to act like Christians -- until they are.

Where to Start?
Acts 8:26-38

Reading the Bible is one of the basics of Judeo-Christian faith. While, strictly speaking, Bible reading is not absolutely necessary for eternal salvation, it's most certainly a very direct way to learn about God and how to sustain a relationship with God.

As a pastor I've been asked hundreds of times by persons just beginning to have interest in reading the Bible, "Where do I start?" It's an obvious question. As a book, the Bible is big and thick. In most English versions it's nearly a thousand pages – more if the font it's printed in is large. And some of the versions it's found in can be pretty difficult for the average modern-day reader.

The first part of my response to this question is, "Try a modern translation." On the one hand, not an "old English" version which presents it in a linguistic style contemporary people must struggle to comprehend, but on the other not one of the "paraphrase" or "storyteller" versions which unabashedly deviate from the actual Biblical text. My personal favorite is the New International Version, but there are at least half a dozen other good possibilities – among which the New American Standard Version and the New Revised Standard Version readily come to mind.

The second response I offer is, start in the New Testament. Don't try the obvious method by which most books are read, from first to last page. While Genesis and Exodus are relatively enjoyable reading, many first-time Bible readers bog down in the "details" of Leviticus and Numbers and ultimately give up.

And now, where to begin in the New Testament? At that point my advice depends, in part, upon who is asking the question. Most of the time I recommend one of the gospels. For adult men, I typically choose Mark. For adult women, Luke. For teenagers of both sexes, John. Occasionally, if the person, of either sex, is somewhat "intellectual," I'll suggest reading Matthew first.

After reading one or two of the Gospels, I usually recommend that folks try the Book of Romans. Romans is a clear "road map" of God's "plan of salvation" for his people. Without over simplifying, Romans can become a "key" for many readers to subsequently understand many other books of the Bible.

The Bible is actually a collection of originally separate books, 66 in all, so "jumping around" is OK. It's not like a novel, where there's a singular storyline that requires following a narrative from start to finish. Yes, the Bible does contain consistent themes, but they are often discovered "over, under, around and through" what is read, rather than from following a prescribed reading formula.

Once you've gotten a good start, cut loose and read wherever and however you feel led. Old or New Testament, it's all good and all useful toward forming your faith.

Who Can We Trust?
Proverbs 3:5-6

Is there anything in life today which is trustworthy? There are so many competing opinions on every subject that the very idea of "facts" is now questionable. I may have a set of facts to back up my way of thinking, but you may have "alternate facts" which, to you, are of greater importance.

And what about people? Who can be trusted? Of course, we all know that used car salesmen and politicians perennially fall at the proverbial bottom of the barrel when it comes to trustworthiness. But unfortunately my profession, that of clergy, no longer commands much, if any, respect. Too many scandals, too many moral failures, too many well-publicized violations of trust by ministers and priests have taken place in recent decades. The high ground of trust has eroded away, undermined by our own failings. About the only remaining professions in which a majority of people still express confidence are doctors and judges, and that majority grows slimmer with each passing year.

And what about God? Is God trustworthy? Yes, a significant majority of people still say they "believe" in God, but what does that really mean? Can you count on God for understanding, and maybe even help, in time of need? Is your faith as yet solid, or has it become a bit shaky these days?

Like many other issues, this "crisis of trust" in life isn't really a new phenomenon. Way back in the Old Testament there was a prophet named Elijah who dared to actually test, in full public view, the trustworthiness of God. He gathered thousands of God's people around a huge altar piled high with both sacrificial bulls and the timber with which to burn them, then had that altar drenched with water so many times over that it couldn't possibly be ignited. Only then did he call upon God to receive this offering. And fire came down from the sky and completely consumed Elijah's sacrifice, then and there removing all doubt that God was really in charge. You can read this story in its entirety in 1 Kings 18.

It's a tough world in which to find anything or anyone to trust. Virtually everything – and everyone -- has been relativized. Everyone, that is, except God. God is, ever and always, completely worthy of my trust – and yours.

High-Value Intangibles
Isaiah 44:6-23

At least two of the largest companies in the world today, Apple and Microsoft, basically sell "thin air." Yes, Apple does produce lots of cellular telephones, but that company's most important commodities are items you can't hold in your hand: information and communications -- and the virtually instantaneous access thereto. The same for Microsoft, and Google, and Facebook, and dozens of other 21st century giants. Their primary products, considered to be worth hundreds of billions of dollars, are intangibles.

Compare that to the last century when the worldwide "biggies" among companies sold easily identifiable products: oil, automobiles, steel, household appliances, airplane engines, etc. All those were things you could see, feel, touch, hear, perhaps even taste. But that's now "old school." It really is a brand-new world where intangibles triumph.

Contrary to a lot of the grumbling that I hear among Christians about having to adjust to a "post-Christian" world, this should be seen as a positive by people of faith. For two millennia we've been promoting an intangible God whose Son, while once flesh and blood, is now represented on earth by an ethereal "Holy Spirit." You can neither touch nor apprehend God with any of the other four common human senses.

Decades ago, I used to often encounter these sorts of questions from confirmation class youth: "Why can't I see God? Why can't I touch Him?" As an ex-engineer, I would respond by immediately turning on a nearby portable radio. "Where is that sound coming from?" I would ask in response. And then I would explain that there are invisible radio waves all around us which that radio can detect – but we can't. Radios are built for that purpose. And the human soul is built, by its Creator, to be a God-detector.

In a world where the value of intangibles is soaring, the reality of an intangible God should be becoming easier to promote than ever before. Indeed, many people today already consider themselves to be vaguely "spiritual but not religious." While I personally dislike that terminology, I understand that it's our job, as Christians, to help them employ their intangible souls to "laser focus" that amorphous "spirituality" upon the ultimate source of all value: an omnipresent, loving God.

People of faith, tell others about Jesus. Help make the intangible God real for them!

I Really Needed Help!
Exodus 18:13-26

He called just before midnight, waking me from a sound sleep. How or why he picked me, I don't really know. He simply said he knew I was a pastor. Then he said he was planning to commit suicide. That fully woke me and certainly got my attention.

What followed was a rambling tirade of scattered thoughts and complaints which, frankly, made little if any sense. I'm neither gifted nor well-trained in the area of counsel, so I didn't have a clue as to what was really going on. After about fifteen minutes of listening, I decided to take a risk. So I interrupted his monologue with this: "It's the middle of the night and I'm obviously not at my best. Can you come into my office and see me tomorrow at 10 AM? I'll be much better able to listen to you then." He responded with, "No, I'll be dead by then." To which I replied, "If you're going to kill yourself anyway, it's no big deal to let it wait a few hours. You want me to hear you, and I'm willing to listen. But now's not the best time for me." Grudgingly, he said, "OK. I'll be there at 10. But I'm still planning to kill myself right afterward." I said, "I'll see you at 10," and hung up.

At that point, I knew the crisis had passed. As agreed, at 10 AM the next morning he showed up at my church office. By that time, I had enlisted the help of one of my colleagues in Christian ministry who was a skilled counselor. Together we met this young man. He was a lot more rational in the light of day than he'd been the night before. Drug abuse was the root of his problems, and my colleague knew of a treatment program to which he could immediately be taken. To my knowledge, he's still alive today.

The Book of Ecclesiastes in the Old Testament is a difficult one to understand. The writer thereof self-identifies as "The Teacher," and Biblical tradition holds that he was Solomon, the proverbial wisest king of ancient Israel. There's a lot of esoteric philosophy in Ecclesiastes, as well as much concern with "meaninglessness." But there's one verse of Ecclesiastes which has stuck with me for decades: chapter 4, verse 9. It says, "Two are better than one, because they have a good return for their labor." It's been helpful to me on many an occasion. I know I don't have to try to accomplish the many tasks of God's work alone. In fact, it's almost always better to seek help. Just a little farther along in Ecclesiastes, chapter 4 and verse 12, God's Word says "a threefold cord is not easily broken." In other words, enlisting more than one helper can be better still.

I know a lot of people who try very hard to be faithful to God and to accomplish His work – alone. Long ago, I learned there's a better way. Effective Christianity has never been a solo enterprise. Jesus didn't try to go it alone; he gathered disciples to help with His mission. Two or three working together don't simply add strength, they multiply it. 21st century people of God, heed the still-accurate wisdom of "The Teacher" of ancient times.

Right-Sizing
Psalm 131:1

The largest of the ten churches I served while in active ministry was the First United Methodist Church of Big Spring, Texas. At the time I became senior pastor there it encompassed nearly 1,000 members on roll, three separate campuses, and 31 total employees on the church's staff.

Certainly, not every staff member at that church was my direct responsibility, but all of them required my personal attention from time to time. And overall administration was a huge portion of the pastor's responsibilities in that church: managing half-a-dozen buildings, raising over a million dollars annually to fund the church's many ministries, maintaining relations with other area pastors and community leaders, etcetera and etcetera. Yes, I do know how to delegate duties, but in this particular situation the senior pastor's personal involvement was strongly expected in almost everything.

Three years into my tenure there, I had an "epiphany" of sorts on a particular Sunday morning. I was, as pastors typically do, shaking hands with congregational members on the way out of one of the worship services. And as I was doing that, I realized I didn't know the names of most of the people I was greeting. I'd been their shepherd for three full years, but this pastor did not yet know his flock.

Shortly thereafter I spoke with my "boss" in the United Methodist connection, the District Superintendent. I told him I wished to be assigned to a church about half the size of the one I was currently serving. I wanted to be able to actually know the precious persons who had been entrusted to my pastoral care. He was surprised. Such a request is almost never made; it's an unspoken but widely held belief among pastors that "bigger is better" in regard to church assignments. He tried to talk me out of my idiocy, insisting I was doing a fine job where I was.

It took two more years and a change of District Superintendents for my expressed desire to be taken seriously. I repeatedly had to carefully explain that I was not trying to say anything negative about this large church I was serving. Rather, it was my conviction that, for me personally, the assignment was uncomfortably too large.

Eventually I got my wish. My next church was almost exactly half the size of Big Spring First. And for me, it quickly became my most successful pastorate. Not too big, not too small, but – praise God – just right.

As a disciple of Christ, does God have a "right size" assignment for you?

Hospitality
Hebrews 13:1-3

While I was part of a construction mission team to the Democratic Republic of the Congo, it was highly important that we visit with, and receive the blessing of, the local tribal chief. Were we to have attempted significant work on the water system we had gone there to repair without the chief's full knowledge and assent would have been unwise, as the local people would have refused to interact and work with us.

Several days passed until we were finally invited to a formal audience with this tribal chief, whose official title, translated into English, was "Mwanti Yav." Unlike the vast majority of the people of his village who lived in tiny adobe huts with thatched roofs, he had a semi-spacious home which almost resembled a U. S. residence.

Once properly introduced and seated, we were offered a variety of snacks and beverages, most of which were items unfamiliar to us. Notwithstanding, to have refused such would have been an affront to the chief, so we eagerly partook. The chief actually spoke some limited English, and with the further help of a local pastor who could translate, we communicated fairly well. We spent an hour or more describing our project plans to him. Ultimately we received not only his blessing to proceed, but an offer of significant help with both labor and building materials.

As we were leaving, the chief indicated that he wanted to further provide us a gift we could later eat – a live goat. Of course we couldn't say no. We took our leave of the Mwanti Yav after many rounds of handshakes and thanks.

In the pre-dawn twilight early the next morning, just as we were waking up, a young man showed up at the house where we were sleeping, leading a goat on a leash. He tied it to a tree in front of the house and left. We weren't quite sure what to do with the animal, but the local man we had hired to cook for us during our stay expressed no hesitation. Within hours the animal was slaughtered and by evening we were enjoying goat steak. During the following week we further enjoyed goat soup, goat meat sandwiches, and goat just-about-everything. Frankly, I enjoyed eating goat a lot more than the caterpillar stew I'd been offered to eat the night before the goat arrived.

Hospitality, both given and received, is a major theme of the Bible. The lives of Abraham, Moses, and David in the Old Testament are replete with hospitality lessons. Jesus' first miracle was one of hospitality – providing wine at a wedding feast in Cana of Galilee. Probably the most significant Biblical hospitality encounter of Jesus was with a Samaritan woman as chronicled in John 4. The simple exchange of a drink of water became the basis of major life-changes for both the woman and her entire village.

People of God, regularly and liberally give and receive hospitality with those around you. Such positive behavior can and often does lead to significant advances for the Kingdom of God.

When You Just Can't Please
Matthew 11:16-19

This particular story, with only slight variations, happened to me in three different churches. Many churches have their share of older ladies (in my personal experience there weren't similar older men) who, for a variety of reasons, say they aren't able to attend their church – but wish they could. And of course, they spread this narrative to their friends and neighbors, so that their unmet need is widely communicated to the church's leadership.

In the first such situation, the church had a van. Thus I enlisted a volunteer van driver who was willing to make a round of the neighborhoods and pick these ladies up. There were six such women involved. At first, the driver was able to average picking up five of the six each Sunday morning. But just a couple of months later, one lady decided she no longer wanted to "get made up" on Sundays, so she dropped out. Another protested that entering into the church's van was too difficult, although we provided a step-stool. A third just lost interest. And so on. Within a year, the driver was regularly picking up only one lady. So we found a member-neighbor who would pick up this woman and ceased the van service.

In the second, since I'd already been through the first church's experience, I began by individually enlisting member-neighbors who didn't mind stopping on their way to church to pick up an extra woman. Pretty much the same pattern ensued. We started with willing neighbors bringing in half-a-dozen older ladies each Sunday. Within six months it was down to three. And within a year, the number making themselves regularly available to be brought to church had dropped to zero. The third church was another van situation and almost a carbon-copy of the first. As soon as regular transportation was made available, the desire to actually come to church gradually dissipated on the women's parts.

The oddity about all this was that, in each and all of those three churches, soon after regular Sunday morning transport to church was no longer made available, we started receiving the same complaints from virtually the same cadre of women. They wanted to come to church but had no way to get there. They expected the church to provide a special service for them – which they could then choose not to use. Or more likely they just wanted an excuse to gripe about the church.

Jesus ran into this same "impossible to please" mentality with some of the Hebrew people whom he encountered. They complained that John the Baptist was too strict. So they came to Jesus – and then grumbled that he was too loose. You can read this particular story in Luke 7:31-35. Jesus simply shrugged them off, and continued his ministry among those who were willing to actually hear what he had to say.

Sometimes, you just have to ignore the complainers. Stay positive and forge ahead with the Gospel!

The Same Core Belief
Mark 9:38-40

The Abaza's (I've changed their name) were active leaders in one of the churches I served in Texas. I considered them and their three teenage children among the ten or so most supportive families in that congregation.

Interestingly, the Abaza's weren't formally members of that church. They were Egyptian Christians who had left their home city of Alexandria as Muslim persecution of the Christian minority there intensified. He was a physician who had to begin again from scratch in the US, but by the time I knew him had established a thriving local practice.

I learned a great deal from the Abaza's about their particular branch of the Christian faith, termed Coptic Christianity. I'd never really known much about it before I met them. Coptic Christianity is one of the oldest forms of the Christian faith; the congregation in Alexandria, Egypt is actually mentioned in the New Testament as one of the first such established outside ancient Israel. Neither Catholic nor Protestant, and not exactly Orthodox but similar thereto, Coptic Christianity has survived, largely unchanged, since the time of the first apostles. Obviously, there aren't many Coptic Christians in America, and in the contemporary world there are relatively few Copts to be found anywhere.

The Abaza family attended my church not because it was doctrinally similar to theirs, but because we allowed them to receive the Sacrament of the Lord's Supper, or Holy Communion, without requiring them to relinquish their Coptic roots and become Methodists. To them, regularly receiving the Lord's Supper was extremely important. And not many churches in that Texas city practiced "open" communion, permitting non-members to participate therein. Ours did, so they felt welcomed and reasonably comfortable. And since they were receiving their spiritual nurture in our church, they gladly both served in and gave to it.

There were many differences between Coptic beliefs and my own, but there was one indispensable commonality: our shared faith in Jesus Christ as Lord and Savior. So I didn't try to "convert" them to my particular church, and they didn't try to convert me to theirs. Rather, we set aside our differences and enjoyed the fellowship of shared belief in God's Son.

People of God, the world will pay a lot more attention to our faith if and when we unite around one Lord Jesus Christ, rather than continually divide over trivial matters.

First and Second Priorities
Matthew 22:36-40

One particular Sunday morning in the church I was then serving in Los Alamos, New Mexico, there were five different "good causes" being promoted in the church's entry area. The Boy Scouts were selling popcorn to support their troop activities. Not to be outdone, the Girl Scouts were selling cookies to support theirs. Several of the church's youth were attempting to enlist sponsors to help underwrite their upcoming mission trip to the Four Corners Navajo Reservation. The church's women's group was selling items left over from their bake sale the day before. And the church's missions work area was attempting to sign up folks willing to travel to Nicaragua for a water-well drilling project.

Frankly, I hadn't really thought about this unplanned confluence of solicitations. Each of the projects represented seemed to me a worthy enterprise. And each had come to me at different times during the prior week to ask permission to solicit. But for individuals arriving at the church on that particular Sunday, the practical effect was a "run the gauntlet" experience to be endured as they attempted to enter God's house for morning worship.

Thus I was not really surprised when, a few days later at a Church Council meeting, one of the congregation's most respected leaders suggested that a "policy" was needed to limit the number of appeals that could be made in the church's entryway on any given Sunday. After some debate, it was decided that a maximum of three such solicitations could be allowed, only when approved by the pastor and on a first-come, first-served basis.

I certainly had no objection to this new policy. It saved me from having to "pick and choose" who could, and who could not, approach the members of our congregation on Sunday mornings. I was glad that the church was involved in so many worthy charitable endeavors. But sometimes "good" can become the enemy of excellent. Worship time is reserved for God, the greatest of all human concerns. Other endeavors, even including charity, are secondary.

Jesus was once asked to sum up God's expectations for His highest creation: humanity. He did so in two Great Commandments. First, love God. And second, love your neighbor – your fellow human. Since Jesus ordered God's expectations in that manner, so should we.

Inadvertently Starting Something New
Mark 10:13-16

In 1987 I was invited to Australia to preach at a number of locations throughout that single-nation continent. Then well-known international evangelist Sir Alan Walker was the source of my invitation and the Uniting Church of Australia was my host. I spent 35 days crisscrossing Australia and learned a great deal about that vast but thinly populated land, so similar to my home country, the U. S., in many ways but so different in others.

At my first stop, a Uniting Church in suburban Brisbane, I was asked if I had any special requests before worship began. I replied that, in addition to offering the main sermon message, I would also like to do the children's sermon for the kids present. That request was met with blank stares. "What's a children's sermon?" the local pastor asked. "It's when you invite the kids up front and present a short gospel message on their level of understanding," I explained. "Never heard of such a thing. But you're welcome to try, if that's what you want," was the response.

Halfway through the service I invited the children present up, and proceeded to offer a three-minute message just for them, about twelve in number. Then I sent them back to sit with their parents. Having a children's sermon wasn't anything special to meI don't recall what I preached about in the main message, and neither did anyone else. All discussion following the close of worship centered on my having offered a message for the children. Those Australian Christians had never seen anything like that before. They loved it, and immediately began to solicit their pastor to add such to regular Sunday morning worship services.

In the eight different locations where in preached in Australia that month, from Brisbane to Perth and from Darwin to Hobart, I offered a short, separate gospel message for the children. In all eight churches it was a brand-new idea. And in all eight it was very well-received.

For several years after my visit there, I corresponded with three or four pastors of the Uniting Church in Australia, and from their perspective it appeared I may have inadvertently started a "movement" in that Christian denomination. The idea of having a children's sermon as a regular part of worship spread far and wide. I'm glad I was a catalyst for such.

In Jesus' day children were not well-regarded. Much of that likely had to do with the prevalent sky-high rate of infant mortality. Parents were simply afraid to become "attached" to their children, for one of every two wouldn't survive to see their fifth birthday; two of every three likely wouldn't attain the age of 10. So when Jesus invited children to approach him and actually spent time talking with them, it was a social revolution. And when he further dared to say children might be closer to the Kingdom of God than adults, it was a religious bombshell.

Today's Christians highly value children. We want them to know Jesus -- who already loves them. And that's a very good thing!

Global Experiences
Mark 16:15

My adult son Jonathan recently inspired me to buy a world map with metal backing. Framed and hung on a wall in our living room, I am able to place small magnetic pins on this map wherever I've traveled throughout planet earth.

After creating this map display, I newly realized how truly fortunate I have been – how privileged to have experienced such a variety of locations and cultures. I've got pins emplaced on my map throughout the Western Hemisphere, from Alaska in the north to Chile in the south – and virtually every other nation in-between. I've visited some very important countries such as Russia and China and Israel, as well as some out-of-the-way islands such as Roatan, Dominican Republic, and Fiji. I've been to places very similar to my homeland – New Zealand is one such example. And I've been to locations where I felt myself "a stranger in a strange land" – the Democratic Republic of the Congo immediately springs to mind.

A handful of my 40 or so global destinations have been for personal vacations. Another handful occurred early in my life as business travels while an engineer. But the clear majority of my global treks have been for Christian mission purposes. I've preached revival in Cuba, helped build churches in Paraguay, taken medicines to children in Siberia (in winter, no less). I've provided hot water heating for senior citizens in Ecuador, given glasses to teens in Honduras, taught and encouraged other pastors in Australia.

It's been an always exciting and sometimes wild ride to go where the Lord's work has taken me thus far; I even got caught up in a South American governmental coup on one occasion. I still try to embark on one or more such new adventures, usually as part of a mission team, annually. Serving Christ is, for me, very much a worldwide endeavor. Precious people everywhere need to hear the Gospel and to experience both its spiritual and tangible benefits in their lives today. And I'm excited to be a part of God's plan to accomplish those purposes.

Just before he ascended from the earth, Jesus left this commission to his followers as recorded in Acts 1:8 – "…you will receive power when the Holy Spirit comes on you; and you will be my witnesses in Jerusalem, and in all Judea and Samaria, and to the ends of the earth." I consider myself unusually blessed to have been enabled by God to help carry out that global calling on the Lord's behalf.

Where and to whom might God be calling you?

Languages: Spoken and Unspoken
Genesis 11:1-9

I've lived in a variety of locations from coast-to-coast in the USA and, for a time, in Latin America. But despite such a "cosmopolitan" life history, I retain a definably Southern USA accent. My mother was a Mississippian and a substantial portion of my childhood years were spent there. Those two influences combined to make me, language-wise, a "Southerner" forever. The simplest illustration of this is when I try to say "you all." Unless I really concentrate on slowly and distinctly enunciating these two words, it inevitably comes out "y'all."

While my wife and I were preparing to travel to China to teach English in the summer of 2011, I tried to learn the rudiments of Mandarin, the dominant language of more than a billion Chinese. In the past, languages had come easily to me; I'm fluent in three and passable in two more. But all of my prior linguistic experience had been "Western." Oriental languages, especially Mandarin, are very different in nature. They are primarily tonal rather than grammatical. The same written term, depending on how it is voiced, can mean five completely different things. It's possible for "Westerners" to become passably fluent in Mandarin, but rarely perfect. In order to fully embrace Mandarin, you must grow up hearing it from infancy. Otherwise, your inflections will stick out like a Mississippi Southerner trying to mimic a Bostonian Yankee, and your words thus sound garbled.

There's a significant narrative in the Bible concerning language and its importance. In the era of the Judges in ancient Israel, the inhabitants of the territory of Gilead were warring against their near neighbors, the descendants of Ephraim. However, because these two peoples were nearly identical, they couldn't easily tell one another apart. Who was friend and who was foe? The Gileadites developed a unique method to determine such. When they encountered a man of unknown origin, they would say, "Speak the word 'shibboleth.'" The Ephraimites had grown up saying it slightly differently. They would reply, "sibboleth." Their accent would thus betray them. As recorded in Judges chapter twelve, this slight difference in pronunciation could mean life or death.

Fortunately, there's a language available to all of us that doesn't rely upon grammar nor intonation. It's not a spoken language at all. Rather it's a language of action: the language of love. Jesus employed it on many occasions. As examples, he visited (and healed) the sick, fed the hungry, cared for children, comforted the lonely and the grieving. None of those actions required actual speech on his part. We can do the same. Jesus specifically called upon his followers to visit the sick, feed the hungry, take care of those in prison. You can fill in dozens of other loving opportunities.

Even without words, God's people can do a world of good. And when we're fortunate enough to share a common language with those we love and serve, that opens even more wonderful possibilities.

It's Christ's Church!
I Corinthians 1:11-13

Every time I began a new ministry at a particular church, there were folks who, on the way out of church, told me, "We're really glad you're here. We didn't like the last preacher, so we stopped going to church. This is our first Sunday in this church in three years." I suppose they thought they were flattering me with such accolades.

On the other hand, after I'd been at a church for a couple of years, there were always folks who came up to me to say, "This will be the last time you see us. We don't like your preaching, so we're dropping out of this church." I suppose such folks thought they were hurting my feelings with their criticism.

The upshot of this matter is that both kinds of responses to me, or to any given preacher, are wrong – wrong according to the Word of God. Any church, if it's worthy of the name, is the Church of Jesus Christ. It's never "Pastor Dave Ring's church" or "Preacher Paul Bradley's church" or "Elder Jane Cooper's church." And therefore, becoming active in a church because of one's liking of a given pastor, or leaving a church because of disliking a pastor, is simply wrong. The Spirit of the Lord doesn't move in and out of churches based upon who is, or isn't, currently the pastor thereof. And neither should the people of God.

In the church that I served in Odessa, Texas, one of the elderly ladies with whom I repeatedly clashed once told me this: "Preacher, I don't like you. But this is my church. So I'm not about to let you, nor any other preacher, run me off." Frankly, that lady and I saw eye to eye on at least that one issue. I didn't particularly like her either. But my respect for her was increased because of her uncompromising loyalty to her church.

Jesus often referred to believers in him as sheep, but never as grasshoppers. A lot of today's Christians need to keep that in mind – and stick with the churches they're already in, rather than periodically jumping from one flock to another based upon personal whims.

Life Insurance
John 3:15

Back when I was approximately 40 years of age and our three children were about 9, 6, and 3 respectively, my wife came to me with what I considered an unusual request. "I want you to buy more life insurance," was her appeal. "Why?" I responded. "Because you keep going on mission trips to dangerous places. If you're killed on one of those ventures, I'll need considerable financial support to fall back on while I figure out how to support and continue to raise our kids."

While I'd never actually considered that possibility, she was quite correct in her concern. Only a few months before I'd been in the South American nation of Paraguay while a governmental "coup" was being put down. It didn't actually affect me nor our team's mission efforts directly, but it made international news. From my wife's perspective, reading about fighting in Paraguay's capital city of Asuncion while I was near there in that small nation, it was worth worrying about. Of course she had faith in Christ and strongly believed in the power of prayer. But she also understood that sometimes bad things do happen even to good people. So my taking the practical step of buying extra life insurance wasn't an unreasonable idea.

This now three decades later memory popped up anew for me when I received notice from my insurance company that the double-indemnity "accidental death benefit" rider on my life insurance policy had been discontinued because of my advancing age. And that's now OK – the kids are long ago raised, so that extra financial cushion is no longer needed by my wife.

In having my memory thus jogged, I was also reminded that I have another life insurance policy which doesn't expire and whose benefits will never be reduced. It's issued by the Lord Jesus Christ, and the premiums are prepaid, by him, for all eternity. Jesus signed this policy on my behalf with his own precious blood, shed on the cross for my redemption from sin and death.

Of course I'm going to die sooner or later. And when I do, all the promises of that "policy" will immediately come into effect. The only cost to me was accepting Jesus as my Savior. Abundant, eternal life in the Kingdom of God will be mine. Wow – what benefits!

Those very same benefits which I expect to enjoy are available to any and all who may be reading this short personal story of mine. The "terms" of the policy are exactly the same – accept Jesus as your Savior, and let him take care of all the details. Amazing – but true!

Reading Scripture -- Again and Again
Joshua 1:8

For several decades now I've been methodically reading the Bible. Every day I read two chapters – one each in the Old Testament and the New Testament. In most English translations the Old Testament contains 929 chapters. The New has 260 chapters. That means I can complete a reading of the New Testament about once each nine months and of the Old about once each 2 ½ years. Whenever I finish a testament's reading, I merely begin that testament over again.

This is one of my self-chosen disciplines as a Christian. God doesn't require it of me, and my standing with him isn't improved by Bible reading. My Biblical knowledge, however, has been gradually enhanced. I don't claim to be a Bible "scholar," but on the other hand I'm somewhat proud to be firmly grounded in the holy word of God and reasonably knowledgeable thereof.

There's a wonderful amount of really good news to be found throughout the Bible. Some sections of scripture are genuinely a joy to read. The book of Ruth in the Old Testament and the Gospel of John in the New immediately spring to mind for me. Some parts of the Bible are primarily informative – 1 and 2 Samuel in the Old Testament and Acts in the New fit that category. And some portions of the Bible are, being honest, rough going for me as a reader. I find Numbers and Jeremiah in the Old Testament to be real slogs. Likewise, Hebrews in the New.

Regardless of whether I personally consider a particular passage of God's Word exciting or boring, I realize it's all there for a purpose. And I've long ago discovered that the scriptures I find most significant and life-changing aren't the same as those which others may deem deeply important. The meaning and impact of scriptures are individual and personal – as they should be.

One of the many promises of God to be found in the Bible is a blessing simply for reading it. Revelation 1:3 is the location of that particular promise. There are hundreds, perhaps even thousands, more promises and blessings from God spread throughout his holy word to us. I invite you to read the Bible, regularly and diligently. It's always a worthwhile endeavor and, at times, an exciting adventure.

Taking Up the Cross
Matthew 10:38

Crosses -- I like crosses. I have a substantial collection thereof, including a "cross wall" displaying several dozens in my house's hallway. However, this came back to "bite" me somewhat when the director of an Easter pageant for the church I was then serving said, "Pastor Dave, since you've often told us how much you like crosses, how would you like to play Simon of Cyrene in our Good Friday enactment and carry the cross for Jesus?"

Admittedly, I hadn't ever paid much attention to the role of Simon of Cyrene in the Biblical accounts of the Crucifixion of Jesus. To me he was a minor character, just a face in the crowd who happened to be standing in the wrong place at the wrong time. A Roman soldier spotted him and demanded, as soldiers could in those days, "Carry this criminal's cross." Simon was thus abruptly thrust into the drama of the Lord's last human day on earth. Did Simon know anything about Jesus before that moment? The Bible doesn't say.

That church I was then serving had a "life-size" cross, about twelve feet in length and six across. Thankfully, although it appeared on the outside to be wooden, it wasn't made of wood. Rather, it was Styrofoam, painted brown to give it a wooden appearance. Despite being a light-weight "fake" for the real thing, it was both bulky and heavy enough for me to have to handle.

That brief, simulated experience of Christ's actual journey along the "Via Dolorosa" stimulated my thinking about Simon of Cyrene. What little the Bible actually does say about him implies, but does not say explicitly, that he was a Jew of Greek heritage, probably in Jerusalem for the Passover festival. Suddenly he was introduced to Jesus in a horrifying way at the worst possible time in Jesus' earthly life. He had to struggle under the weight of Jesus' cross for half-a-mile or more, a weight likely in excess of 100 pounds. Even by dragging, rather that actually carrying, it would have been a significant burden.

In Luke 9:23 Jesus said to those who dared listen to him, "Whoever wants to be my disciple must deny themselves and take up their cross daily and follow me." We immediately think of that in spiritual terms. But for Simon of Cyrene it was a literal, physical experience. And we don't even know whether or not he wished to actually be one of Christ's disciples.

What we do know is that this strange encounter with Jesus must have had a lasting impact on Simon. Mark's gospel, specifically chapter 15 and verse 21, identifies Simon of Cyrene as "the father of Alexander and Rufus." In so mentioning them, Mark obviously knows these men as, like him, early followers of Jesus. Thus it's not much of a logical stretch to suggest they first heard about Jesus from their father Simon, who had actually taken up Jesus' cross – and continued to follow him thereafter.

Crosses. I like them because Jesus transformed the cross from an instrument of torture into a marvelous symbol of abundant life. Take up the cross, people of God, and show the world its transforming power.

Turning Negativity Upside Down
Romans 10:15

Starting early in my ministry, as many pastors do, I regularly stood at the door of my church's sanctuary while the Sunday morning worshippers were departing in order to share greetings and blessings with them. And of course, many of them offered brief comments, in passing, to me regarding the Gospel message I'd just presented: "Good sermon, preacher." "Something to think about." "Thanks for your message." "I really thought your sermon was stupid!"

When I got home later that day, guess which of the parishioners' comments I remembered most clearly? If 50 people had said something positive to me and only one had voiced a negative, it was inevitably the negative upon which my afterthoughts focused. It took me the better part of a decade to overcome that automatic focus on the negative, and to adopt a "balanced" approach to hearing my congregations. Once I finally came to that point, I began to appreciate that far more of my members were supportive than I'd previously considered.

Years before, while in graduate school, I'd taken a management course which included a unit on group dynamics. When an idea is proposed to a group and six persons comment favorably about it, on average one negative comment will be sufficient to shoot it down. Psychologically, negativity is six times more powerful than positivity. That's why political ads are so often negative about the opposition. They work; people believe negativity quickly and unthinkingly.

All modern media know that negative stories sell ads and thereby generate revenue for them. "If it bleeds it leads," thus we are fed a daily diet of carnage, crime, destruction and death. Positive accounts, if presented at all, are considered "feel-good fluff."

The Gospel of Jesus Christ, at its core, is supremely positive. As expressed by an angel to startled Bethlehem shepherds in Luke 2:10, the coming of Jesus Christ into this world is intended to bring "good news that will cause great joy for all people."

Regardless of what the secular world would supply us, and regardless of whatever psychological predispositions may be in the human brain to embrace negativity, Jesus Christ has come to turn this world and its human proclivities upside down. By Kingdom standards, right is more powerful than might. Truth is more believable than lies. Life is triumphant over death. Satan is an already defeated foe; God is in charge -- now and for eternity. Faith, hope and love – all mega-positives – govern. Hallelujah!

Nativities – and the Nativity
John 1:14

In another of these devotionals I've already admitted that I'm a Christmas fanatic. One specific aspect of that is the collecting of "nativities."

My wife and I avidly collect nativities. We've acquired somewhere between 100 and 200 thus far, and every year it seems we add one or two more. Just when we think we've got enough such, we spot another with a unique design and say, "We need to add that one to our collection."

Over the centuries of celebrating the birth of Jesus, Christians have developed many traditions around the brief Biblical narratives which Luke's and, to a lesser extent, Matthew's gospel writings provide regarding this, one of the most significant events in all of earthly history. One of the more common of these traditions is the display of what is called a "nativity," or a "manger" scene. In Spanish they're called "belen" for Bethlehem, an attempt to show what was taking place in Bethlehem when Jesus was born. Nativities are no more and no less than sincere human efforts to depict the miracle of the birth into our world of the One whom Christians believe to be God's Son. Some are large and complex, with many figures from both the Bible and Christian tradition included; others are small and simple, including only the minimal characters directly mentioned in the Bible itself.

In several of the towns where we've served there have been churches which annually sponsor nativity displays. Word gets around, and pretty soon we're invited to display one or more of our nativities in such. We enjoy that, especially because we thereby get to see some other really interesting nativities that others have acquired or, in some cases, designed themselves.

It's important, however, to make a clear distinction between a "nativity scene" and the actual nativity of our Lord and Savior Jesus Christ. A nativity scene is merely useful to point us toward a great spiritual truth. God became flesh and dwelt among us. Our Creator became our brother human. And that is truly, incomparably amazing!

Does Prayer Really Make a Difference?
Isaiah 38:5

There are increasing numbers of folks today who minimize the value of prayer. When there's a major disaster, or a senseless killing, or some other tragedy, it's a normal reaction, certainly among many Christians, to say, "I'll put that situation/those persons in my thoughts and prayers." But instead of responding by saying "thanks," those of our increasingly secular world are saying, "We don't want thoughts and prayers; we want real help." In their minds "I'll pray for you" has no meaning. It's just religious mumbo-jumbo.

Way back in Old Testament times there was a king of ancient Judah whose name was Hezekiah. Following after the incomparable King David, none of the kings of God's people of old, either of Judah or Israel, was particularly pious, but Hezekiah was one of the better such. He strongly encouraged the Jews under his rule to worship God and avoid the idols of the many nations which surrounded them.

Unfortunately for Hezekiah, while he was still a young man he came down with a serious illness. God sent the prophet Isaiah to him to say, "Set your house in order, Hezekiah, for you are surely going to die. You will not recover." But in the face of this pronouncement of impending personal doom for him by one of God's chosen spokesmen, Hezekiah refused to accept his fate. Instead, scripture (2 Kings 20:2-3) says that he turned his face to the wall and prayed.

Hezekiah knew that God had already made up his mind. Hezekiah was a goner. Notwithstanding, he dared to pray. And – amazingly – God changed his mind because of Hezekiah's prayer. God instructed Isaiah thus: "Go back and tell Hezekiah, the ruler of my people, 'This is what the Lord, the God of your father David, says: I have heard your prayer and seen your tears; I will heal you. On the third day from now you will go up to the temple of the Lord.'" -- 2 Kings 20:5.

Even when the future had already been revealed to him, Hezekiah prayed. And his prayers actually changed the will of God. A man, an ordinary man, altering the plans of God. Amazing – truly amazing!

Does prayer really make a difference, or is it just a spouting of empty words? Certainly, I believe in taking action where action is appropriate. Prayer, for me, isn't an automatic "go to" response. But prayer and action together – now that's a powerful combination. I can't guarantee that prayer will always yield a desired result, but prayer definitely carries significant weight with God. Don't ever idly dismiss prayer's value.

What's The Worst Sin?
1 John 1:9

What is the worst sin of all? Most reasonably well-informed Christians should be able to answer that question. It's the blasphemy of the Holy Spirit." Such is the one and only "unforgiveable" sin, as stated by Jesus in Matthew 12:32. The exact quote is this: "Anyone who speaks a word against the Son of Man will be forgiven, but anyone who speaks against the Holy Spirit will not be forgiven, either in this age or in the age to come."

The problem with this particularly flagrant sin is that no one really knows what it is. Study a dozen Biblical scholars regarding the above-quoted verse, and you'll likely find just as many different interpretations. Frankly, I've given up on worrying about that one; if I really don't know what "blasphemy of the Holy Spirit" is as a sin, I doubt I could commit it.

Aside from that enigma, what's the worst sin? Many folks would point to the breaking of one of God's great Ten Commandments. Murder ranks very high on the "bad" scale. Adultery almost equally so, although a lot of us tend to expand the definition thereof to erroneously include any and all sexual sins. And covetousness, which has become a catch-all to accuse someone of when you can't think of anything else. Interestingly enough, we don't seem to get particularly concerned about idolatry in the present day, although it's listed before these others. We're too sophisticated to worship idols today – except perhaps for money, success, or fame.

As a pastor, I believe I've discovered what most of my parishioners consider the worst of all sins: It's the sin their neighbors commit. It's never their particular personal sin – that's trivial. No, it's what someone else, whom they know, is doing that's really sinful. I may regularly cheat on my income tax, but that's a far less significant sin than my cousin's six-month affair with his wife's sister. I may beat my kids to the point that they have to be taken to the hospital, but that pales in importance to my across the street neighbor's addictions to drugs and alcohol. And so on....

The true answer to "what's the worst sin" is this: There's isn't one. All sins are equal – equally missing of the mark of God's intended holiness for his people. No one's sin is "worst" and no one's sin is "lesser." Romans 3:23 says it this way: "...all have sinned and fall short of the glory of God."

The good news is that even the "worst" sin – as well as all other sins – are forgiven by the grace of our Lord. All you have to do is ask, and your sins will be blotted out, covered by the blood of Jesus. And that's really good news even for the worst of sinners, including you and me.

Other Sheep?
Hebrews 11:3

As a child, I was fascinated by science-fiction. I read all the classic SF authors and thereby, in my mind, traveled to the moon, the planets, the stars. The most amazing part of all this was, while what I read was obviously fiction, the advance of real science almost kept pace with those writers' fantasies. By the time I was a teenager, men were poised to land on the moon – and were seriously preparing to go beyond, visiting the planets and even stars.

Later, as a young man, I had the good fortune to be loosely associated, through my early career as an engineer, with some aspects of the U. S. space program. I helped design instruments that later flew on satellites orbiting the earth. I analyzed data received from outer space. I "lived the dream" for a boy who had grown up reading science-fiction.

One of the realizations that has stuck with me from those early decades of my life is how small humanity is in relation to the vastness of the universe. Modern science has corrected our earlier mistaken belief that we were somehow the center of everything. That misconception was never actually taught in the Bible; rather, it was a false extrapolation beyond scripture. Indeed, the writer of Psalms was correct and on target when he wrote, in Psalm 8, "When I consider your heavens, the work of your fingers, the moon and the stars, which you have set in place, what is mankind that you are mindful of them, human beings that you care for them?"

That "smallness" being acknowledged, however, it is undeniable that God has a special spot in his heart for humanity. He sent himself, as Jesus, to prove his limitless care for us. Ultimately I don't know why – but I'm very glad he did.

One of the many unusual things Jesus said while among us humans was, "I have other sheep which are not of this fold." That statement of our Lord, recorded in the New Testament as John 10:16, is open to speculation and extrapolation. It may simply imply that Jesus foresaw the expansion of the Gospel beyond the Jews to the entire human world. Or it might even suggest that there are other populations of sentient creatures, like humanity, in need of salvation on other worlds. Yes, that's science-fiction thinking, but today's science-fiction, in my personal experience, can become tomorrow's science fact.

It's a big universe, people of God. And an even bigger God who made it all. Praise him for his limitless creativity!

A Second Impression
Acts 9:26-28

Preparing for the funeral of a beloved elderly "saint" from my congregation, I encountered some heavy going while attempting to deal with her closest next-of-kin, a sister who lived 700 miles away but who wanted to specify every detail of the service. Up-front, she admitted to me that she wasn't a church-goer. Notwithstanding, she had strong opinions about all aspects of her deceased sister's departure liturgy, even down to which verses of which hymns should be sung. And she had plenty of "guidance" for me as to what I should, and should not, say in the funeral message.

This sister wouldn't be flying into town until just a few hours before the actual funeral time, so virtually everything had to be negotiated in advance with her via telephone and/or e-mail. Three frustrating days of exchanges between us had left me hoping, frankly, that her plane might be delayed past the time of the service. But such wasn't the case. She arrived on schedule and showed up at the church an hour before the start time.

As soon as I saw her come in, I steeled myself for meeting this "tough old bird" in person. But I was in error. She sweetly introduced herself, thanked me profusely for bearing with her during all the preparations, and told me how grateful she was for my conducting her sister's service. I kept waiting for the "other shoe to drop," but it never did. By the time I said farewell to her a couple of hours later, I had revised my opinion. The lady wasn't a "bad" woman, not at all. She was actually pretty nice.

It's ingrained in human nature to evaluate people based on first impressions. Social scientists have even studied this phenomenon and found that, in most cases, first impressions become lasting impressions. The first sixty seconds of our interactions with someone new determine much concerning our long-term future relationship with that person. But sometimes, first impressions have to be re-evaluated.

In the first chapter of John's gospel in the New Testament, there's an interesting "first encounter" between Jesus and one of his future core disciples, a man named Nathaniel. Nathaniel's friend Philip wants to introduce him to Jesus, but Nathaniel isn't interested. He's already heard that Jesus is from Nazareth, and to Nathaniel that's bad news. Without even seeing Jesus in person, Nathaniel has a negative first impression: "Can anything good come from Nazareth?" Philip simply replies, "Come and see."

When Jesus later actually meets Nathaniel, he is amazed by Jesus' foreknowledge of him. His first impression of Jesus is completely turned around and he excitedly embarks on the road to discipleship.

People of God, keep an open mind to others. Sometimes first impressions are accurate. But sometimes they are wrong. Let's give precious people a second, and maybe even a third, or more, chance to become our friends. We may thereby open up additional opportunities to make disciples for our Lord.

Strange Tongues
1 Corinthians 14:9-11

In church on a Sunday morning, a young woman I'd not previously met came up to me and said, "Buenos dias." I replied, "Buenos dias," which is the common greeting for "Good morning" in Spanish. From years of Christian service in Guatemala long ago, I retain passable Spanish fluency. The young lady smiled and began engaging me in conversation – in Spanish. She explained that she spoke no English, and was delighted that she had found a fellow worshipper who could speak her language. Ten minutes later, as I glanced at my watch, I realized that it was just five minutes before the beginning of worship. I told her, still in Spanish of course, that I needed to quickly move into the sanctuary to begin worship. She continued talking until I finally, with apology, simply had to walk away from her.

That experience put me in mind of the several occasions when I have been in situations where I could not speak the local language. In Fiji, in China, in Congo, in half-a-dozen other countries, there were times when I was desperately searching for someone – anyone -- who could speak even a few words of English. And when I found such a person, I would try to stick with them as long as possible. I suspect those were occasions when I seemed like that woman who wouldn't stop talking to me until I had to actually walk away from her.

There's an interesting story, very early in the Old Testament of the Bible, concerning the possible origin of different languages among the peoples of our planet. Genesis 11:1-9 relates the account of Babel, where humans attempted to build a tower up to heaven itself. To prevent this, God "confused" the languages of the builders, so that they could not understand one another. The prideful project was thus stymied. From this story we get the term "babbling," which refers to people speaking to one another without any comprehension. For several centuries now, dedicated Christian missionaries have labored long and hard to translate the Bible into one of the several thousand languages in which it had not previously been written. In more than a few cases, the translators had to first help create a written language for peoples whose only method of communication was oral. Their many life stories are truly fascinating.

It appears that modern technology is on the cusp of developing "universal translation" software which will effectively undo the confusion of languages that has plagued humanity for millennia. We may soon be able to speak into our "smartphones" in our native language and have the instrument speak out for us in a different tongue. Perhaps I could thus have meaningful one-on-one conversation with an Arabic speaker without that person having to learn English, nor me to learn Arabic. What an advantage that would be for spreading the Gospel of Jesus Christ! Lest you think this a questionable idea, be aware that in Acts 2:5-12, during the giving of the Holy Spirit to the early disciples, God temporarily suspended the confusion of languages among all present, so that each one heard and understood everyone else's speech. Praise God for new possibilities to speak the good news of the Gospel to all those in need of its saving power, the world over!

Wishing for More Daylight
Revelation 21:23-25

I'm always bemused by the time shifting which takes place in most of this nation each spring and fall. In the spring of each year we set our clocks forward an hour, and in the fall we set them back. This annual practice creates a half-year of what is called "Daylight Saving Time" or "DST" for short. To me, it's like cutting the top end off of a sheet and sewing it back at the bottom. Ultimately the sheet is still the same length.

"Daylight Saving Time" is an idea first proposed in 1895 and adopted by as many as 70 countries at one time or another. The US has observed DST more or less continuously since 1918, shortly after the nation entered into World War I. The original rationale was that it would conserve industrial energy for better focus on the country's war effort.

Today DST is falling out of favor. Its energy-saving benefits are no longer significant, and its disruptive effects on human health from the twice-yearly confusion of daily routines are raising serious questions concerning its usefulness. I expect to see it quietly disappear within another decade or so.

There was a singular occasion in the early history of God's people in Israel when the desire for a longer period of daylight was actually granted by God. Joshua, Moses' successor as leader of God's people, asked God to hold the sun back from going down so that he could complete the defeat of Israel's enemies in a battle. And, according to scripture, God did exactly that. The sun remained high in the sky for almost an entire extra day. This was a notable, one-time miracle. God's word records it in Joshua 10:13-14, "The sun stopped in the middle of the sky and delayed going down about a full day. There has never been a day like it before or since, a day when the Lord listened to a human being."

Unfortunately, Daylight Saving Time has never created any additional daylight. I wish it could do so. Like most people, I prefer light to darkness. While there's obviously nothing inherently "wrong" nor "evil" about natural nighttime, daylight simply feels better to me. I love being in the light – both physically and spiritually. And I look forward to the Kingdom of God, where the light of God's glory shines 24/7 – through eternity. I hope you do, too!

Too Much of the Same Old Thing
Revelation 21:5

Recently I met a man who is devoted to entrepreneurship. He's well under 40 years of age but has already founded three companies in three very different fields of endeavor, taken each of them to global prominence, then cut them loose, personally cashing out and moving on to something new. Now he's on his fourth such endeavor. And he confidently expects there will be a fifth, a sixth, and so forth.

On a smaller scale, many of the current generation of young adults in the US have no intention of pursuing a single career path for the entirety of their working years. Rather, they deliberately plan to change jobs about every five years of their lives. Those job changes may require learning a set of skills and experiences totally unrelated to the previous. But they're not at all afraid of such innovation.

How completely different this is from the generation in which I grew up! For my contemporaries, setting out on a single career path and gradually moving upward therein was the expectation. A job with one company for a lifetime was the norm. I was a notable exception thereto – after being educated and beginning a career as an engineer I changed, at God's leading, into Christian ministry after a decade. And virtually all my friends and relatives, at least initially, considered me a fool for so doing.

Decades ago, folks would marvel when I told that personal story. Today, it's no big deal. Young adults do similar things all the time.

One of the major problems for the Christian Church, as it attempts to minister to today's young adults, is that we don't yet "get it." We're still highlighting the unchanging nature of God to a generation for whom that concept is outdated and boring.

Is God powerful enough to make a boulder so big he can't move it? Thankfully, God is smart enough not to be entrapped by such a paradox. And the unchanging God is, at one and the same time, a God of spontaneous creativity. God's amazing creativity is what today's people need to at least occasionally hear from the Church of Jesus Christ, not just the past constancy of the "rock of ages."

Long ago the prophet Isaiah (43:18-19) warned God's people against too often looking behind them. "Do not dwell on the past. See, I am doing a new thing! Now it springs up; do you not perceive it?" If the Church is to meaningfully impact the future, forward is the direction God's people need to face.

Staying Hydrated
Genesis 21:25-31

Living in a semi-desert climate as I presently do, water is unquestionably the most important resource to sustain human life in this area. Without fresh, potable water no one could live here. In many other places where I've lived, water wasn't an issue – its easy availability was simply taken for granted. Water in Albuquerque, New Mexico is hard to find and, therefore, expensive. But it's very necessary, thus worth it regardless of cost.

I've had the privilege of traveling to the Holy Land twice in my life. And I've discovered that the climate in and around Jerusalem is very similar to that of New Mexico. Thus the availability of fresh water is likewise, for God's original chosen people, a major concern.

There are just two open sources of fresh water in the Holy Land: the Jordan River and the Sea of Galilee. Both figure prominently in a number of Biblical narratives. Otherwise, the land is dry. There are no brooks, streams, nor lakes. Thus there are also dozens of Biblical references to "wells" that modern-day readers may pass over without a second thought. Wells were the "go to" option for securing water in the Holy Land. Wells had to be dug. Wells must be maintained in order to continue yielding water. Some of those wells were established thousands of years before by the famous patriarchs of God's people – Abraham, Isaac, and Jacob.

Jesus had a notable encounter in the territory north of Jerusalem, near a Samaritan village called Sychar, with a woman who was approaching a well, originally dug by Jacob long before, to draw water. It's recorded in the fourth chapter of John's gospel in the New Testament. Jesus was thirsty and asked the woman for a drink. They then entered into a discussion which moved quickly from "drinking" water to "living" water. Jesus thereby was offering to fill her with the Spirit of the Living God.

Interestingly, the Biblical narrative doesn't say whether or not Jesus actually received a drink of water from the woman. I certainly hope he did. But from the woman's reaction, it's obvious that she received much more from Jesus than the simple exchange of a cup of water. She even invited all her friends and neighbors to come and see if He might, in fact, be God's promised Messiah.

Drinking water is necessary to maintain human bodily health. And living water, from God, is necessary to maintain the human soul. Stay hydrated, people of God, with both kinds.

The Value of a Mentor
Matthew 10:1

When I was hired, while still completing my education for Christian ministry, as the associate pastor of East End United Methodist Church in Nashville, Tennessee, the senior pastor was at the other end of his ministry career -- within less than a handful of years of retirement. So from the outset of our relationship, he told me that our roles would be reversed from the normal expectation: I could pastor the church while he stood ready as my backup. He wanted me to thereby have maximum opportunity to learn and experience the full range of expectations and demands of pastoral ministry.

There were plenty of "ups" and "downs" to my time at East End, but the fact that I had an experienced senior minister with whom to consult at every turn was uniquely affirming. It provided me a sense of confidence which carried well beyond, to future times when I was truly on my own in ministry. My two years at East End with Pastor Ted were foundational for many of my later successes.

When Jesus walked this earth, he very deliberately gathered around him a core group of followers. He carefully instructed them in matters pertaining to the Kingdom of God for a period of about two years. And then, as recorded by Luke in the tenth chapter of his gospel, Jesus sent them forth on their own. They would be empowered as his representatives wherever they traveled. "Whoever listens to you listens to me; whoever rejects you rejects me," said Jesus. And when they returned to Jesus with joyous reports of success, Jesus was likewise joyful. He had successfully passed on to them the good news of God's salvation and they, in turn, were now passing it on to others.

From personal experience I can testify that it's a blessing indeed to have a mentor in the Christian faith. To actually have Jesus as one's mentor – that's truly wonderful. And the amazing fact is, we all have that possibility. As Jesus promised his early disciples as he prepared to leave this earth, "I will ask the Father, and He will give you another Helper, that He may be with you forever; that is the Spirit of truth...." (John 14:16-17).

That promise is still in very much in effect. The Holy Spirit, God's presence in the world today, is available to all followers of Jesus for guidance, comfort, and strength. And since God is One, that Spirit is actually Jesus Himself. There's no better mentor.

Just as I did, I hope that each and every follower of Jesus has at least one earthly mentor to help them in their formation as disciples of Christ. And even more importantly, I hope that each of God's people regularly looks to the Holy Spirit of Jesus for mentoring as we attempt to spread the good news of the Kingdom to a world in dire need of the redemption offered by the Gospel.

Weather and Sports Prayers
Matthew 6:9-10

Back when I was pastoring in an area of west Texas where cotton farming was one of the sources of livelihood for several of the families in my church, I was often asked to offer prayers for rain. "Please pray for rain for our crop, pastor. It really needs it." Once in a while I was asked by the same folks to pray that rain stop. "Please pray for the rain to stop, pastor. Any more rain this week and our cotton will rot in the field."

The other side of this "weather" prayer issue was the west Texas oil field owners and workers who were also well-represented in that congregation. They were constantly soliciting me to pray for dry weather. They almost never wanted rain; they couldn't work when it was raining. Rain endangered their means of support.

In a different category I also received hundreds of requests for "sports" prayers. The town of Odessa had two high schools. Both were fiercely competitive in the arena of sport. Especially regarding the sport of football, which was (and still is) a secular religion in west Texas, I was hounded weekly by parents and youth who asked that I pray that Permian High would win. Or, conversely, pray that Odessa High would win. Those requests became insanely ridiculous when Permian and Odessa met for their annual football rivalry. You might think I'm joking, but I was several times offered cash money to pray for victory by one or the other school. Of course, I turned it down.

This is one of the obvious reasons why I'm very glad that I'm not God. Can you imagine the number and intensity of prayers that are offered to God, many by sincere believers, for contradictory outcomes? "O Lord, let me win the lottery so I can pay for my sister's cancer treatments." "O Lord, let me win the lottery so I can feed all the homeless in this city." "O Lord, let me win the lottery so I can give the money to my church." Multiply those three simple prayer requests by 100,000 regarding the same lottery prize, and you can easily grasp my point.

I believe in the power of prayer. I've personally witnessed the effectiveness of prayer hundreds of times. Sick people have been cured, impossible causes miraculously funded, horribly broken relationships mended. But some prayers – like "weather" and "sports" prayers – are best left unprayed. Rather, simply allow God's sovereign will to be exercised, trusting that His outcome will be the best for the most. God is God; we are not.

Making It Harder Than It is
Matthew 11:28-30

One of the interesting aspects, to me, of the Biblical account in Genesis 2 and 3 of the creation and subsequent "fall" of Adam and Eve concerns Eve's recollection of God's singular restriction on what she and Adam may and may not do while living in the Garden of Eden. In Genesis 2:17 God tells Adam and Eve, "You must not eat from the tree of the knowledge of good and evil." But when Eve recalls this prohibition in Genesis 3:3, she quotes God thus: "You must not eat fruit from the tree that is in the middle of the garden, and you must not touch it."

Did you notice Eve's significant addition to God's admonition? Not only does she remember what God actually said, she adds to it. Beyond the prohibition on eating its fruit, she puts the tree itself out of bounds – "you must not touch it." Eve has added an additional layer of complexity to the restriction, thereby making God's command more stringent than it originally was.

The ancient Hebrews were well-known for repeatedly doing the same. God gave 10 original commandments to His people. Moses brought these down from Mt. Sinai and read them to God's people. Ten commandments – simple and basic – defining God's expectations. But by the time the leaders and priests of God's people had finished their embellishment of these, compiled in the Biblical book known as Leviticus, there were 613 "laws" which had to be followed. Being a follower of God had become considerably more complicated than obedience to ten simple commands.

By the time Jesus came to earth, a cadre of rabbis called "Pharisees" had further added to even these 613, with thousands upon thousands of scrolls of legal jargon – the Talmud and the Mishnah -- which even they could not always understand. They had carefully built layers of fencing around God's law so that the law itself would never be transgressed. And from a practical standpoint, sincerely following God had become impossible.

Fortunately, Jesus took the opposite tack. Returning to the original Ten Commandments, he dared to simplify even these. To be a disciple of Jesus, a God-follower from his perspective, you need follow only two Great Commandments: Love God and love your neighbor. Basic, simple – easy to understand, easy to follow.

Love God and love your neighbor. People of God, there's no need to make it harder than it is.

Fishbowl Living
1 Samuel 16:7

Early on while following God's leading into full-time Christian ministry, my wife and I began to experience the "fishbowl" nature thereof. At every assignment, some of our parishioners watched us like hawks, continuously checking for any possible chinks in our armor. This may be hard to fathom for some, but in one particular church we even had a member who, on more than one occasion, rummaged through our household trash which we had placed outside for pickup, searching for anything which might be "incriminating." In another church, there was an older lady who lived near us who actually kept a log of our comings and goings. She sometimes knew better than I exactly when I left home and when I returned to the parsonage on any given day. She kept a separate log of my wife's departures and arrivals. And she proudly made others aware of her treasure trove of information, bragging about how carefully she "kept tabs on" her pastor's, and his wife's, conduct.

Frankly, while some folks might have been "creeped out" by this kind of close scrutiny, we simply accepted it as part of our calling. We were doing nothing that we needed be ashamed of, so we had nothing to hide.

When this fishbowl existence became more difficult to accept, however, was as our children grew into teenagers. Just like us, they were carefully scrutinized by our church members and, at times, by the community at large. I can recall half-a-dozen occasions when one of their public school teachers called to report some minor misdeed by one of them. Those calls would always be prefaced by, "This is such a small thing that I wouldn't say anything to most parents, but I know that your son/daughter is a preacher's kid, so you should hear this." My children eventually became resentful at being held to impossibly high standards. Decades later their relationships with the Church continue to be strained as a result.

Both the Old Testament prophet Jeremiah (chapter 31) and the prophet Ezekiel (chapter 18) made it clear that lumping children's conduct in with that of their parents -- and vice-versa -- is simply wrong. Every man or woman will be evaluated by God for their own conduct, not for who or what their parents are and do. Make sure, people of God, that your own life is above reproach – and thereby be less concerned about that of your neighbors -- or your pastors.

Good Out of Bad
Job 13:15

I was comforted by one of the simplest personal examples I've seen of God's bringing good out of bad. A close, long-term friend of mine died suddenly and unexpectedly. There was absolutely no warning; he came home from work one evening, watched TV until bedtime, went into the bathroom – and collapsed. He was instantly gone.

As his close friend, I was asked by the family to conduct the funeral. It felt very strange; I had never expected to attend his final rites, much less conduct them, since he was younger than me. But as a pastor you sometimes have to put your own grief aside in order to ease the stresses on others.

At the funeral two men who were formerly very close to one another, but who had been estranged for a considerable period of time, were both in attendance. They hadn't spoken to each other for more than a year. They were also both very close to my deceased buddy. And I was also personally involved with both of them and, despite repeated efforts, had been unsuccessful in my attempts to repair the breach between them.

I'm not exactly sure what happened, but somehow the experience of shared loss drew them back toward one another. By the end of the day, they were talking – at length. Losing a mutual loved one had bridged the gap and begun to restore their former friendship. Seeing them back in communication eased my own grief at the loss of my now-departed pal.

Way back in the Old Testament, in the Book of Genesis, there's a classic example of how God can bring great long-term good out of transient bad. Joseph, the youngest of 12 sons of the patriarch Jacob, was sold into slavery by his brothers who both envied and hated his closeness to their father. Decades later, after a roller-coaster ride of life for Joseph, he was able to rescue his entire family from starvation. When Joseph's brothers feared that he would retaliate against them for what they had done to him, Joseph simply said, "Do not be distressed and do not be angry with yourselves for selling me here, because it was to save lives that God sent me ahead of you." (Genesis 45:5)

Romans 8:28 in the New Testament is often quoted by Christians: "And we know that in all things God works for the good of those who love him, who have been called according to his purpose." Sometimes it's not easy to see the truth in that verse of scripture, particularly when struggling with life-and-death issues. But rest assured, people of God, our Lord really does know what's He's doing -- always.

My Namesake
Psalm 51:1

David. David is the second-most-frequently named person in all the Bible, mentioned over 1,000 times throughout both the Old and New Testaments. The repeated occurrence of his name in Scripture is second only to that of Jacob, whose name benefits from the fact of being identified with Israel, the term used to refer to all of God's original chosen people. And the name David actually occurs slightly more often in Scripture than that of God's son Jesus, obviously because Jesus is found only in the New Testament.

David was a complex character whose long life is chronicled throughout many chapters of the Bible. He began as a shepherd boy and wound up as the greatest king of ancient Israel. He was a man of deep and fervent devotion to God – for example, the 23rd Psalm – and a man of raging passions and unbridled lust, even to the point of adultery and murder – consider his treatment of Bathsheba and her husband Uriah. David was a poet and a warrior, a statesman and a mercenary, a fount of wisdom and a fool on the brink of insanity. His life is a case study in convolution and contradiction.

Through all of David's twists and turns, there was one still-point in his life: God. And God, for his part, was so impressed by David's unfailing devotion to him that God often termed David "a man after God's own heart." In the Hebrew language the name David means "beloved," and David was much beloved of God. Before David's death, God promised him a never-ending line of succession to the kingship of Israel. That promise was fulfilled in Jesus, who is referred to several times in the New Testament as the son of David.

For three millennia now, the name David has continued to be a popular one. I bear that name and am proud to enjoy it. It's a blessing indeed to carry the moniker of such a great and noteworthy man.

That being said, however, the name David does not, in and of itself, render me either "beloved of God" nor "a man after God's own heart." God has no grandchildren. I must stand or fall before God based on my personal dedication to Him, not on my name.

As you read this, I obviously have no idea what your name is. I hope it's one you bear proudly. Regardless, God doesn't particularly care what your name is. Rather, he cares where your heart is, where your devotion lies.

Put your trust in God, and in God's Son Jesus Christ. Jesus is the name above every other name, including that of David.